FILM AND STEREOTYPE

D1096951

FILM AND CULTURE SERIES

FILM  AND
STEREOTYPE

A Challenge for Cinema and Theory

JÖRG SCHWEINITZ

Translated by Laura Schleussner

COLUMBIA

UNIVERSITY

PRESS

NEW YORK

Columbia University Press
Publishers Since 1893
New York   Chichester, West Sussex

Originally published by Jörg Schweinitz as *Film und Stereotyp.*
Eine Herausforderung für das Kino und die Filmtheorie.
Zur Geschichte eines Mediendiskurses, copyright © 2006
Akademie Verlag GmbH, Berlin.

Translation copyright © 2011 Columbia University Press
All rights reserved

Library of Congress Cataloging-in-Publication Data
Schweinitz, Jörg
    [Film und Stereotyp. English]
    Film and stereotype : a challenge for cinema and theory /
Jörg Schweinitz ; translated by Laura Schleussner.
        p. cm. — (Film and culture)
    Includes bibliographical references and index.
    Includes filmography.
    ISBN 978-0-231-15148-1 (cloth : alk. paper) —
    ISBN 978-0-231-15149-8 (pbk. : alk. paper) —
    ISBN 978-0-231-52521-3 (e-book)
    1. Stereotypes (Social psychology) in motion pictures. I. Title.
    PN1995.9.S6956S3413   2011
    791.43'6552—dc22   2010044342

Columbia University Press books are printed on permanent
    and durable acid-free paper.

Designed by Lisa Hamm

This book is printed on paper with recycled content.
Printed in the United States of America

c 10 9 8 7 6 5 4 3 2 1
p 10 9 8 7 6 5 4 3 2 1

CONTENTS

ILLUSTRATIONS

INTRODUCTION

Isn't a stereotype a still image? Do we not have a dual relationship with platitudes: both narcissistic and maternal?

—ROLAND BARTHES, "UPON LEAVING THE MOVIE THEATER"

The stereotype can be evaluated in terms of fatigue. The stereotype is what begins to fatigue me.

—ROLAND BARTHES, *ROLAND BARTHES*

In his film *Die Koffer des Herrn O. F.* (*The Suitcases of Mr. O. F.*, Germany, 1931), Alexander Granowski presents an ironic fairy tale about the modern capitalism of the era and reflexively touches on the world of cinema. The director of a fictive film company explains his business strategy: "Problems make you go broke. Comedies bring dividends. . . . Why are we a world-class company? Because we produce comedies! I beg of you!" A song follows, sung from off-screen, as a coloratura in the style of an operetta aria referring to the popular film genres of the period. "Sound film comedies" and "sound film operettas" (*Tonfilm-komödien* und *Tonfilmoperetten*, the German counterparts to the American film musical) always depicted the complications of a love story, and they did so with frequently recurring narrative and visual motifs. This is alluded to in the lyrics from Granowski's film:

He loves,
she loves,
we love,
they love,
they all, all, all, all love.

While the song is sung, a series of six fictive film posters with extremely similar compositions appears on screen. All show an embracing couple from the waist up, the woman always holding a guitar. The motifs differ only in superficial detail, mostly in a different hat or pair of glasses.

The effect is immediately repeated, whereby the song, now sung to a marching rhythm, refers to the military comedies (*Militärschwänke*) popular in Germany at the time.

> Barracks air,
> Barracks smell,
> Barracks magic.
> Marching is such fun.

Another series of posters appears, each depicting an officer and a woman with a horse. These images too are almost identically composed and vary only in a few minor details, most obviously in the form of the helmets.

The current of filmic self-examination running through this sequence widely epitomized the contemporary discourses on cinema of German film critics and theorists around 1930. In this example, a motion picture from the period addresses a characteristic trend of its own medium. Only peripherally does it concern a satirical take on the cinematic glorification of military ritual, which was also ridiculed by the progressive film criticism of the time. First and foremost, the sequence from Granowski's film caricaturizes the *stereotypization of film*. This is perhaps the first time in the history of film that a motion picture explicitly conducts a brief reflexive discourse on this theme, which constitutes the main topic of this book.

Incidentally, in its satirical display of stereotypes the film employs the device of synchronic, intratextual serialization, a standard technique used for visual and self-referential representations of the phenomenon. This will be described in more detail further on.

Not even a decade prior to Granowski's persiflage of the film business's repetitive and reductive compulsions, in the first half of the 1920s intellectual aficionados of cinema such as Béla Balázs had associated the medium with very different hopes and utopias. Euphoric ideas about the future of film as art were based on the idea that cinema was destined to cultivate a *new visual culture*: the long-deplored conventionality and abstraction (arising therefrom) of the culture of language and writing—asserted under the banner of language skepticism (*Sprachskepsis*)—could be overcome by the visual and concrete medium of film.

Toward the end of the decade, such euphoria had given way to disenchantment, including among film critics. Intellectual observers now became aware of the medium as an *all the more powerful agent of the conventional*. They now realized that conventionalization of cinema did not fail to affect the sphere of

FIGURE 1 Series of fictional film posters from the motion picture *Die Koffer des Herrn O. F.* (*The Suitcases of Mr. O. F.*, Alexander Granowski, Germany, 1931).

gestural and visual expression. Through the constant repetition of patterns reduced in complexity it standardized the imaginary of large masses of people, even on an international scope. Cinema tended to create globally widespread visual imaginations and forms of expression.

Fixed schemata were now observed everywhere in the worlds of narrative and in their visual composition. They reoccurred in extended series of films and were progressively automatized and conventionalized, thus becoming intersubjectively established. This concerned patterns of plot structure (including the macro- and microstructures of narrative) and character construction as well as patterns of acting, visual style, the combination of image and music, and so on. Around 1930, the great majority of German commenters massively criticized this trend, either from the standpoint of ideological critique or, predominantly, in terms of aesthetics and style.

A major cause for these serial tendencies was soon found: film's industrial mode of production, which was associated with the reigning capitalistic conditions of commodification and distribution. The second half of the 1920s was pervasively marked by rationalization and full industrial mechanization, and the New Objectivity blossomed in Germany. Against this backdrop, metaphors from the spheres of industrialization and mechanization were popular in cultural discourses and ultimately entered into thinking on cinema. Long before Horkheimer and Adorno criticized the "culture industry" (particularly Hollywood) and its tendency toward the intertextually and culturally conventionalized schema—the stereotype—critical observers around 1930 described cinema as a "dream factory" (Ilya Ehrenburg) and "fantasy machine" (René Fülöp-Miller) or talked about the "standardization" (Siegfried Kracauer, for example) and "Taylorism" (Willy Haas) of film, or even the "ready-made film" (Rudolf Arnheim).[1]

Some theorists recognized even then that the much-repeated schemata that had developed into stereotypes were not only based on the routine of cyclical production but also were repeated because they functioned so well. In other words, they were evidently (reciprocally) coordinated with the dispositions, expectations, and desires of a wide audience. With film, entertainment had finally become standardized "manufacturable goods"[2] that could be traded worldwide, and "spiritual needs" could be satisfied "with a *standardized article* which would not only be manufacturable but which would also offer each customer something that suited him,"[3] as René Fülöp-Miller concluded in 1931. In this conception, stereotypes function as audience-coordinated product standards with obvious parallels to the satirical statement of Granowski's fictional film mogul.

During the period around 1930 when the topic of the stereotype was "discovered" by film theorists and critics, the assessment was overwhelmingly clear—

and negative. The stereotype, usually described as "standard," was considered the absolute opposite of positive critical terms such as "artistic," "creative," "nuanced," "true," "individual," or "original." Today, such a Manichaean view seems overly simplified, at the very least. A limited perspective, it has meanwhile become practically unacceptable.

In the media world of the early twenty-first century, the trends toward filmic—or more generally speaking, audiovisual—stereotypization and conventionalized patterns of (visually or narratively) reduced complexity have assumed such quality, quantity, momentum, and ubiquity, with corresponding schemata having taken over our imaginary worlds to such an extent, that the idea of creating films untouched by such factors seems truly anachronistic. Whereas even before film, popular storytelling was considered to great extent an art of repeating and reduced forms and also had the function of promoting popularity, in our contemporary world of media there is no form, no image, no narrative idea, and no structure that, once it has "caught on," remains without an extended series of successors. Digital imaging pushes these trends to the extreme. Once conceived and developed at high cost, digital design schemata that produce a certain effect (for example, a dissolving figure or other transformations through "morphing") are repeatedly employed—undergoing only superficial changes in appearance—through the use of the same software. Indeed, an aesthetic schema can even be patented and legally copyrighted via the usually extremely costly software used to generate it. Countless television channels, videos, DVDs, and multimedia applications additionally ensure the constant presence and availability of already similarly structured or even identical productions shown repeatedly.

Even singular, actual events—media images of catastrophes, terrorist attacks, royal weddings, funerals, and so on—are today, once they have initially attracted mass interest, followed by an endless succession of medial replays of all kinds, from direct recapitulations to all possible sorts of paraphrases and even fictionalized reenactments such as docudramas or major motion pictures. Usually this practice is pursued to the point of completely wearing out any original emotion. This mechanism also characterizes the stereotypization of fictional structures (especially in their late phase). Previously stirring images are transformed into mere semiotic signals, which, like hieroglyphs, now refer only symbolically and in a strangely abstracted manner to an original event, which now may be recalled by the mere quotation of fragments. With respect to the omnipresent serialization of narrative media products Umberto Eco emphasizes the sense of being transported into an "era of repetition,"[4] and Roland Barthes describes the media as "repeating machines."[5]

In the cinema, the audience mostly inhabits imaginary worlds whose regularity, coherence, and reductive simplicity are produced by repetitive forms that have become conventional and are used in a more or less automatized manner. Spectators of genre film or TV series are familiar with the repeating and similarly constructed figural types and stereotypical plot elements attached to them; they know the conventional type of music that is employed, when, for example, danger looms in a thriller or horror film. The audience is aware of the customary visual staging of chase scenes. It knows how a saloon is supposed to look in a Western, how aliens appear in a science-fiction world, and what kinds of rituals unfold in these locations. It also knows that it does not bode well if during an embrace one partner demonstratively stares straight ahead (in the direction of the camera) over the other's shoulder. The audience has learned all this not through experience in their everyday lives outside the media (insofar as such an existence is still possible) but over the course of many years of spectatorship in the intertextual space of filmic imagination. The latent knowledge gained here constitutes what is generally described as "media competence." The underlying stereotypes form and structure the intersubjective imaginary world of our time. The stereotypes of popular film therefore simultaneously become *cultural* signs.

Anyone making fiction films must do so in relation to current stereotypes. Those aspiring to emancipate themselves from such stereotypes and demonstratively formulate difference cannot forgo at least taking these patterns into account. Stereotypes are powerful because they are based on well-functioning structures coordinated with recipient dispositions, with previous experiences, wishes, and expectations, and these structures themselves have shaped viewer dispositions on a mass scale. Today, far more common than the attempt to demonstrate difference, however, is the ambition to use, not merely reproduce, the world of stereotypes and thus to achieve some measure of confident mastery over them. Often this amounts to simultaneously using the patterns as symbolic forms while playing with them creatively on another level. The interplay of stereotype and difference is as much of an issue in this case as emblematic or allegorical composition. The latter seems appropriate to the stereotype, but repetition successively leads to such emotional wear that, in the sense already indicated, an "abstract" perception of the given form as a symbolic entity is consolidated.

Another potential creative approach to stereotypes that strengthens their symbolic employment lies in their filmic reflection, or *reflexive* use of stereotypes. In this case, the film conducts more or less pronounced discourses—sometimes critical or satirical, sometimes mildly ironic or even transfiguring—about the world of stereotypes it now inverts. Originally comic or carnivalesque, this approach was later adopted by the avant-garde and is now widely established in mainstream

cinema and fictional forms of television such as soaps. This particularly characterizes productions identified as *postmodern*. This treatment of stereotypes is part
and parcel of the post-1980s TV style that John Caldwell terms "televisuality."[6]

All in all, the stereotype seems to have particular significance for the age of
audiovisual mass media. The latter produce their programs in historically unprecedented quantity and seriality, thus maintaining their virtually constant presence;
they thereby address formerly inconceivably large and often global audiences. Processes of stereotypization are thus precipitated in large number and concentration,
with a dynamic that is highly accelerated in comparison with previous societies.
Furthermore, they gain an incredibly broad intersubjective base among recipients.
In sum, all these aspects have inspired the idea of undertaking a nuanced, comprehensive, and detailed study of the stereotype from the point of view of film studies.

But why from the perspective of cinema? As the first audiovisual mass medium
in history, film set the pace of this development, which was *reflected upon* by film
theorists, practitioners, and critics—already before the widespread use of television and other media—in accompanying discourses. As a cultural and aesthetic
institution having evolved over the course of over a century, cinema today is still
affected by the various phases of intellectual response to the stereotype phenomenon, to which it presents the most diverse range of practical approaches. Thus,
the general idea of this study readily presented itself: to investigate the connections among the development of the medium, stereotypes, and the mechanisms
of their formation with a focus on film. This approach makes it possible to outline
a paradigm of audiovisual media culture in the twentieth century.

This study will examine different aspects of *stereotype and film*, as reflected in
the organization of the book. The initial focus of part 1 (in chapter 1) is to specify
the key concept of the "stereotype" in theoretical terms. Here, one confronts the
problem that the term is used in various academic discourses and thus refers to
quite a diverse range of subject matter, research interests, and theoretical concepts. In psychology, the concept of the stereotype is predominantly associated
with conventional images of people who belong to certain groups or classes. Situating the concept within the study of the idiom, one branch of linguistics regards
stereotypes as recurrent utterances that have become conventional. In the study of
literature, when the term is not primarily used in referring to the literary presentation of images of the Other (in the sociopsychological sense), it often denotes
conventional patterns, for instance of style. And in art history one finds "stereotype" defined as a highly reduced, conventionalized schema (sustained in part by
the imaginary) of visual representation.

Within a theory of the stereotype not strictly adhering to any of these given
lines of questioning it is necessary to explore structural similarities among all of

the individual concepts and circumstances while remaining acutely aware of the differences among them. One must look for similarities and links that would explain why in each case the use of the term "stereotype" is valid to a certain extent. Here important facets will be established in grouping such similarities together.

Stereotype formation is understood as a *special conventionalized form* of schematization. A fundamental objective of this inquiry is to comprehend stereotypization in line with *pragmatics and constructivism* as a *process indispensable* to cognition, communication, and behavior and as one that intervenes in many different levels and areas of these activities—as a "mechanism," however, whose tendency toward stabilization always has a "downside" as well as critical issues that require a creative, self-critical, and reflected approach. Once repertoires of similarities among discourses on the stereotype have been outlined, then on this basis it will be possible within the scope of the discussion on the stereotype *and cinema* to widen the examination to discourses operating with other terms, including "standard," "pattern," "schema," "formula," "the formulaic," "the ready-made film," "cliché," and so on, while remaining closely tied to the classical issues and concepts of stereotypes. This latter step will be essential, for one, because in contrast to theoretical discourses on film and aesthetics carried out in French, and to a certain extent also in English, in German the term "stereotype" long remained associated with the more restricted sociopsychological usage, with the above-mentioned terms often employed instead, especially regarding stylistic devices and related aspects. In sum, the aim of the approach pursued here is to free the theory of the stereotype from disciplinary constraints without leading to arbitrariness.

Chapters 2 and 3 of part 1 deal with the specific significance of the topic for film and illuminate the forms and functions of stereotypization within cinema. These sections concern a number of questions such as: How are tendencies toward stereotypization manifested in film, and in what way is this reflected on the different structural levels of the medium? How can one explain the specific origins and functions of the affinity of popular films to conspicuous stereotypes? How are film genres, including hybrid genres, to be understood on this basis? And to what extent does the concept of the stereotype provide a helpful perspective on cinematic genre theory? Also, why was the fundamental response to the stereotype among critics so vehemently negative, especially in the early German discourses on the topic?

Which brings us to another aspect, namely, the intellectual or film-theoretical discourse on the stereotypes of popular film. The present survey gives particular consideration to this topic, largely by tracing its theoretical and historical development. Part 2 provides a close examination of different historical phases of film theory's discourse on the stereotype and its prevailing paradigms. These not only include the fundamentally critical position of classical German film theory, which emerged against the backdrop of an aesthetic rejection of all things conventional, as a legacy of both the romantic aesthetic tradition and language skepticism (*Sprachskepsis*). They also encompass the later appreciation for stereotypes—precisely as *conventional forms with a tendency toward abstraction*—within the incipient semiotic thought of the filmologists Cohen-Séat and Morin. Finally, this history also includes the postmodern, reflexive celebration of stereotypes as free-floating semantic material readily available for hybrid (re)construction.

Media-theory discourses always maintain multiple relationships to the practical media developments of their periods. It is not necessary to subscribe to all of New Film History's lofty demands when assuming that the historical study of film theory may transcend a purely theoretical framework. Cross-references between the film-theoretical discourse on the stereotype and different filmic uses or the practical treatment thereof, and the exploration of interactions between them, are programmatic for this study, regardless of their theoretical or theoretical-historical focus.

The final segment of the book, part 3, contributes two case studies on three films that conduct discourses on the stereotypes of film—as examined up to this point from the perspective of film theory. The first analysis comprises two films from the 1970s by Robert Altman that *critically* address the stereotypes of the Western genre. The second deals with the acting technique of Jennifer Jason Leigh in the Coen brothers' film *The Hudsucker Proxy* (1994), which reflexively presents and celebrates stereotypes in a "postmodern" sense by adhering to a strategy of reflexive transfiguration.

Illustrating two basic variations of the reflexive approach to stereotypes, these two film analyses conclude the survey and, by way of *pars pro toto*, also represent its guiding principle. Although the historical and theoretical analysis of this final section was developed by following multiple stages or paradigms of the theoretical "approach" to the stereotype, it too, like the book as a whole, is not obsessed with completeness or the ambition to create a closed system, an endeavor that would be questionable from the start. More important than any pretensions to exhaustiveness or definitiveness are the inspiration and threads that this book may provide for further reflection and additional analysis.

EDITORIAL NOTE

This book was prepared in the second half of the 1990s and written just before and after the year 2000, although its inception and early research dates further back. The study was presented in 2002 as the author's second thesis (*Habilitation*) at the University of Konstanz and was published in slightly revised form in 2006 by Akademie Verlag Berlin. The translation largely corresponds to the German edition (at the time of going to press in 2005). With respect to the American readership, some text passages have undergone minor modification, and additional selective reference is made to more recent secondary literature in English, without any claim, however, to being exhaustive.

ACKNOWLEDGMENTS

I would like to express my gratitude to the Deutsche Forschungsgemeinschaft (DFG) for generously funding the study with a research grant. Special thanks go to Wolfgang Beilenhoff, Heinz B. Heller, Knut Hickethier, Tom Gunning, Thomas Koebner, Thomas Y. Levin, Karl Prümm, Irmela Schneider, Hans Jürgen Wulff, and Peter Wuss, who graciously supported my work during the phases of conception, research, and writing with research facilities and provided me with numerous opportunities for developing and testing some of the book's core ideas in classes and in exchange with students, namely as visiting professor or research fellow at the Universities of Freie Universität Berlin, Chicago, Klagenfurt, Marburg, Potsdam, and Princeton.

Without the many talks and discussions with friends and colleagues, their suggestions, encouragement, and assistance, the long haul of the project would have been hardly manageable. On this count, I am especially indebted to Margrit Tröhler, Anne Paech, and my fellow editorial board members of *Montage AV*, above all Britta Hartmann and Frank Kessler. Special thanks go to Eberhard Lämmert and Joachim Paech for their continuous support during the second-thesis procedure at the University of Konstanz.

Peter Heyl and Sabine Cofalla of Akademie Verlag Berlin expertly saw the manuscript through to its German publication. In 2008, the book won the Geisteswissenschaften International Award, a prize for the promotion of translating German works in the humanities, donated by the Thyssen Foundation, the Börsenverein des deutschen Buchhandels, and the German Foreign Office.

I am indebted to Christine Noll Brinckmann for her suggestion of the series of images on the cover of this book, which show the visual stereotype of women behind the window.

I would further like to thank Henry M. Taylor for our joint discussions concerning appropriate English professional terminology and for his useful suggestions of specialist terms while intently accompanying the translation process; Mona Salari for her bibliographical research; and, above all, Laura Schleussner for her dedication and precise translation work, her intensive search for hard-to-find sources of English quotations, and her abiding patience with the author's requests.

PART I

STEREOTYPE THEORY

Concepts, Perspectives, and Controversies

ONE

THE STEREOTYPE IN PSYCHOLOGY
AND THE HUMANITIES

The systems of stereotypes may be . . . the defenses of our position in society. . . . No wonder, then, that any disturbance of the stereotypes seems like an attack upon the foundations of the universe.

—WALTER LIPPMANN, *PUBLIC OPINION* (1922)

The word "stereotype" is used in various theoretical disciplines. Upon closer examination, one finds that the term refers to quite heterogeneous phenomena in each respective field. In one, it signifies prejudiced and socially widespread ideas about foreigners. In another, stereotypes are associated with linguistic formulas that take the form of standardized expressions, and in still others they are considered standardized images and even naturalized recurrent patterns of narration. These kinds of semantic oscillations do not only occur along the dividing lines between disciplines. In many cases, they cut straight across specific discourses. In light of this and the tendency of "stereotype" to convey multifaceted meanings, the theoretical significance of the term and its historical development are worthy of some attention. This not only makes it possible to clarify different concepts of the stereotype, but it also simultaneously delineates a horizon of questions and positions that directly or indirectly shape the discourse on stereotypes in film. Films, after all, are complex phenomena, and as such they can be examined from the perspective of various disciplines. As a result, stereotype concepts from almost all fields have been applied to film and related audiovisual media. One can certainly study films as documents that reflect socially current conceptions about people (*Menschenbilder*), but one may also—more in the sense of film aesthetics or narratology—analyze stock formulas of images and sound design, or character and plot construction, and so on. The term "stereotype" may be applied in all of these different cases, in each instance with a shift in theoretical perspective, which is not always noticed. An examination of the different theoretical orientations of stereotype concepts promotes an awareness of these shifts and prevents the concepts from simply being lumped together—as the use of one and the same term might suggest. At the same time, this approach also offers the opportunity of a more generalized theoretical and conceptual reflection of "stereotypes," which may also be of conceptual use for a theoretical approach to film.

CONCEPTS OF THE STEREOTYPE
IN SOCIOPSYCHOLOGICAL DISCOURSE

Social psychology stood out in its ability to claim and circulate the term beyond a narrow circle of experts. Social-psychology studies—or, more generally speaking, those in the social sciences—dealing with the topic of the stereotype number in the thousands. However, a close look reveals that there is no clearly circumscribed, consistent, and generally shared concept even within this field. Given that different conceptual approaches offer quite disparate constructs of what is considered a stereotype, even within social psychology a lack of certainty predominates about the discursive object.

Sociological theories on the stereotype were inspired and strongly influenced by a book on public opinion by the American journalist Walter Lippmann, which was initially published in 1922.[1] The term features prominently in the book. Even today there is hardly a relevant work that successfully avoids mentioning this book when proposing a specific use of the expression. Lippmann merely developed *very broad* ideas and generally investigated the nature of the stereotype in terms of the "pictures in our heads"[2] that is, our thoughts as contributing to "an ordered, more or less consistent picture of the world."[3] However, the concept was soon more narrowly defined: normative ideas, attitudes, or expectations *concerning people* and used to make judgments about them. This more limited definition still persists in the social sciences today. Studies published in the early 1930s by the American scholars Daniel Katz and Kenneth Braly[4] on racial stereotypes proved to be very influential in terms of promoting this more restricted meaning of the term. For their studies, the two psychologists developed their famous attribute-list procedure.

To simplify and without going into the many conceptual differences among adherents to Katz and Braly's line of research,[5] stereotypes are standardized conceptions of people, primarily based on an individual's belonging to a category (usually race, nation, professional role, social class, or gender) or the possession of characteristic traits symbolizing one of these categories. This concept focuses on belief patterns and emphasizes their guiding influence on attitudes and perceptions.

The different approaches within the social sciences attribute to these belief patterns an entire battery of optional characteristics weighing in differently on individual definitions. Stereotypes are thought to be (1) the relatively permanent mental fixtures of an individual (*stability*); (2) intersubjectively distributed within certain social formations, for which they assume the functions of consensus building and standardization (*conformity*); therefore, (3) they do not, or only seldom, rely on personal experience but are primarily socially communicated (*second-hand nature*); in addition, (4) they are limited to the simple combination of a few characteristics (*reduction*) and (5) accompanied by strong feelings (*affective coloration*). Finally, (6) functioning automatically, stereotypes are considered to substantially interfere with the processes of perception and judgment, which they influence and even determine (*cliché effect*). Regarding the function of stereotypes, the term is therefore generally associated with making judgments, and (7) stereotypes are often ascribed the status of inappropriate judgments (*inadequacy*).

Katz and Braly also laid the groundwork for this final point—merely by the nature of their experimental setup, which was clearly focused on judgments about people based on individual characteristics. Another contributing factor was their choice of subject matter, that is, their primary interest in negative attitudes toward other races. For the two psychologists a stereotype was therefore a firmly rooted impression of another person, "which conforms very little to the fact it pretends to represent, and results from our defining first and observing second."[6] The theoretical construct thus derived from Katz and Braly was targeted at investigating warped, malicious, and, to an extent, even pathological[7] aspects of perceptions and judgments about people. It soon became an established reference for progressive concepts. Stereotypes were largely understood in the manner suggested by the title of a later study: "stereotypes as a substitute for thought."[8]

"The masses" were considered particularly susceptible to stereotyping. According to theorists influenced by mass psychology, such as Adam Schaff, the masses seemed to consist of people who spontaneously "do not account for the role of prejudice in behavior. Given that these are the so-called masses, this phenomenon assumes special and often socially threatening significance."[9]

It was thought that one could exert a positive influence on the social climate by didactically creating an awareness of the fallacy and irrationality of stereotypes. However, there was a conceptual turnaround in the 1950s, and the work of a number of theorists took on a pragmatic orientation.[10] There was a greater inclination to raise questions about the possible benefits of stereotypes—still considered to be stabilized conceptions about people—and to consider their causation. A number of theorists now also emphasized the productive, regulatory functions of stereotypes for cognition, social orientation, and intersubjective behavior—functions that were only to be gained at the expense of deficient representations of reality.

Apart from the continuing thematic focus on the stereotype as conceptions about people, this conceptual shift was more in line with Lippmann's original intentions. Close in this regard to the philosophy of pragmatism, Lippmann considered the existence of stereotypes, for all intents and purposes, an *ambivalent* phenomenon. He simultaneously emphasized both the deficient and the functional nature of stereotypes—and argued that they were contingent upon each other. In order to account for this ambivalence he made a number of now classic arguments, which are restated here in some detail, because Lippmann's extraordinarily influential position is often presented in an oversimplified and sometimes biased manner.

Lippmann's point of departure and first argument was the functionalism of stereotypes as stabilized cognitive systems of individuals. Citing John Dewey, Lippmann saw the world as "one great, blooming, buzzing confusion"[11] that was too complex and dynamic for human perception and cognition. In order for things to take on meaning, he further quotes John Dewey, it is necessary to introduce "(1) definiteness and distinction and (2) consistency or stability of meaning into what is otherwise vague and wavering."[12] Stereotypes thus make a substantial contribution to introducing this kind of definiteness and consistency into the world of perception.

What cognitive psychologists would later address with terms like "cognitive structure" or "cognitive schema" is basically already implicit in Lippmann's concept. He established the idea of stereotypes as structured mental concepts with a simplifying function, which, as deeply ingrained impressions, are particularly persistent and which guide and even enable perceptive, cognitive, and judgmental processes. On the one hand, they function like *symbolic mechanisms*. When a trait is recognized and perceived as a core attribute, this data is quickly allocated to a certain preexisting complex of ideas. Thus, "we pick recognizable signs out of the environment. The signs stand for ideas, and these ideas we fill out with our stock of images."[13] Afterward, we see "what our mind is already full of"[14] in the thing just categorized. On the other hand, from this perspective stereotypes appear to be a kind of *screening filter* that provides cognitive relief. They organize one's necessarily selective gaze, which tends to emphasize everything that repeats itself in similar form and satisfies the stereotype, while other things that do not correspond to the stereotype tend to be played down or even overlooked: "For when a system of stereotypes is well fixed, our attention is called to those facts which support it, and diverted from those which contradict."[15]

One can certainly observe the complementary effect, in which discrepancies with firmly entrenched expectation patterns may heighten a sense of difference. Nevertheless, later theorists, for whom the word "stereotype" was synonymous with "prejudice," primarily referred to the mechanism of blocking out differences.

Although in Lippmann's work the idea ultimately predominated that stereotypes were to be understood as pragmatic reductions made from a selection of real invariants in the outside world,[16] in his thinking about the principles of this kind of reduction he often likened the idea of stereotypes to *actively formed subjective constructs*, which were always dependent on the disposition and interests of the subject. This becomes particularly apparent when he links his concept—if only in passing—with ideas about objects that are not part of an individual's immediate realm of experience and that cannot be observed with one's "own eyes."[17] He considered stereotypical ideas about such phenomena to be constructs based on social projections. In light of actual experience, these constructs always proved to be a kind of pseudoknowledge or at least hazy knowledge.

This is where his second fundamental line of argument comes into play. For Lippmann, stereotypes function as *intersubjective systems of integration*. Despite their deficits, he believed them to be patterns of cognition coordinated with cognitive or behavioral expectations that society or a group places on the individual. As social "codes,"[18] stereotypes are thus subject to cultural "standardization,"[19] which they in turn support. As a result, "at the center of each [moral code] there is a pattern of stereotypes about psychology, sociology, and history."[20] As a consequence, stereotypes always also represent *instances of intersubjective consensus and social orientation*. For Lippmann this was essential to functioning interactions: "In the great blooming, buzzing confusion of the outer world we pick out what our culture has already defined for us, and we tend to perceive that which we have picked out in the form stereotyped for us by our culture."[21]

Nonetheless, in his view stereotypes are not simply rubber stamps applied from without, but rather they adapt themselves to an individual's inner disposition, upon which they also exert an influence. They are "loaded with preference, suffused with affection or dislike, attached to fears, lusts, strong wishes, pride, hope."[22]

In this context Lippmann ultimately regarded the function of stereotypes as systems for creating and maintaining identity—thus he formulated his third, now classic argument on the value of stereotypes. The degree to which stereotypes are appropriated and habitualized by the individual parallels the extent to which they shape the latter's personality. Stereotypes thus ultimately become part of an individual's "defenses":[23] "A pattern of stereotypes . . . is the guarantee of our self-respect; it is the projection upon the world of our own sense of our own value, our own position and our own rights."[24] Lippmann adds: "There we find the charm of the familiar, the normal, the dependable. . . . No wonder, then, that any disturbance of the stereotypes seems like an attack upon the foundations of the universe."[25] For this reason, stereotypes are also deeply rooted in the emotions, and their confirmation is experienced as positive.

When one steps back to survey Lippmann's overall concept, it becomes clear that he did not represent the stereotype as a clearly defined "object." It is no coincidence that his basic formulations, such as "the pictures in our heads," operate on the level of metaphor. Hence, at first glance there seem to be valid objections to the hazy and noncoherent aspects of his stereotype concept, which integrates psychosocial functions or processes that are by no means synonymous. These objections, however, miss the point. On the one hand, Lippmann's outline, with its vividness and diversity, proved de facto to be extremely influential (not only) in psychological research. On the other, it was obviously not his intention to articulate an unambiguous category.

What resulted instead is an open construct—a kind of fuzzy concept—about a complex of interdependent psychic mechanisms. A construct that is *ultimately* intended to represent a comprehensive epistemological problem: the discrepancy between the "outside world" and the world of perception, thought, and communication—broken down into relatively stable cognitive structures—the very world of the "pictures in our heads" and "our repertory of fixed impressions."[26] Lippmann's entire theory strives to raise awareness of the highly diverse nature of perception and thought as always culturally or socially constructed—and for the associated discrepancies between mental representation and reality. Figuratively speaking, he funnels the mental fallout from quite heterogeneous processes into a container called the "stereotype."

Despite its rather diffuse character, Lippmann's concept is implicitly structured around two inseparably linked motifs of thought, which provide coherency. One is the *typological-schematic motif*, which initially enables a selective and, in his wording, economic processing of information. The second is the motif of a special *stability (habituality and conventionality)*, through which the results of adaptation processes—quasi-automatic in congealed form—can be reused to produce the already mentioned effects of identity and consensus.

Although he always described stereotypes in terms of cognitive *losses or distortions*, Lippmann considered stereotypes to be of an ambivalent nature and thus did not just emphasize their deficits in order to lament them. Instead, he sought to give this core dimension of loss and distortion a quite positive accent: it is the necessary price for the capacity of orientation. He basically did not consider perceptions of the outside world and ideas about reality to be conceivable in complete or absolute terms, nor to be void of subjective or cultural predispositions and interests, but always to be context-bound outcomes. Hence, the tendency of distortions or losses did not appear to be a problem, at least as long as the stable "pictures in our heads" functioned sufficiently in a given practical context. Here, Lippmann approximates the basic tenets of modern behavior-oriented cognitive science[27] as well as those of John Dewey and William James's pragmatism, to which he explicitly referred. In principle, Lippmann wanted his stereotypes to be understood as *productive* variables helping individuals come to terms with their surroundings and stabilizing social behavior. He felt confident that "the abandonment of all stereotypes for a wholly innocent approach to experience would impoverish human life."[28]

At the same time, he indicated the problem of the latent tension between the stereotype (as a fixed, context-based form) and shifting contexts, which could lead to errors in judgment. He therefore considered it desirable to have a reflected and flexible relationship to one's own stock of stereotypes. Flexibility and reflection ensure that the latter are not confused with absolute knowledge. For as soon as we become aware of the relativity of our knowledge as a "loosely woven mesh of ideas," then "when we use our stereotypes, we tend to know that they are only stereotypes, to hold them lightly, to modify them gladly."[29]

While the revision of social psychology's discourse on stereotypes in the 1950s resulted in a return to Lippmann's more pragmatic point of view, the semantic scope of the term "stereotype" usually remained limited to the topic of conceptions about people. Since then, there have been ongoing attempts by individual authors to redefine the term and make it consistent or compatible with their predominant theoretical concerns and terminology. This has led in a number of quite different directions. Usually one coherent idea is plucked from Lippmann's repertoire of arguments, placed in the spotlight, and interpreted or developed on the basis of new theoretical approaches. Precisely because he described more of a syndrome than a category, Lippmann has, in this regard, inspired a complex discourse, which has been continuously updated—and to some extent expanded upon in concentric directions—by *the complex of themes, arguments, and intellectual ideas* that he largely helped shape.

Below I will discuss two such trends in current social-psychological research on stereotypes—a field today so vast that it is almost impossible to survey.

In Germany around 1960, it was mainly Peter Hofstätter who reemphasized the value of stereotypes in terms of Lippmann's functionalism. Building on Lippmann's repertoire, his concept mainly developed the *intersubjective integration system* and linked it to the traditional focus of the term on conceptions about people. He thus treated stereotypes as notions that remain relatively uniform over time and that are held and communicated by a group about its own members or those belonging to a different group (auto- and heterostereotypes). These ideas appear to be preconceptions,[30] since they codetermine individual processes of perception and judgment as preexisting patterns. Like Lippmann, Hofstätter emphasized instances of loss or distortion, which he also justified as the cost of functionality; he was mainly concerned with the functioning of social interactions. The presentation of this argument takes up a remarkably large amount of space, in which he particularly stresses the problem of fictive, "second-hand" notions.

Stereotypes are considered by Hofstätter to be "ideas for which the statistic validity has not been tested, although which we nevertheless nurture with a good degree of certainty."[31] As a rule, they rely on formulaic fictions, which is why the "knowledge that is manifested in a stereotype . . . deserves little respect in and of itself."[32] As institutions of social consensus and as models for the identity consciousness of a group, stereotypes are nonetheless indispensable, because they do not have "a descriptive but [in a social sense] regulatory function."[33] However, Hofstätter also adds a qualification: "stereotypes of a invidious nature"[34] must be combated.

While a main branch of social-psychology research and its stereotype concepts continued (and still continue) to foreground such intersubjective functions, group dynamics, and mechanisms of sociocultural adaptation, another line of research gained influence in the 1980s, which placed more emphasis on intrasubjective topics, namely the cognitive nature of the mental apparatus. Thus, authors such as Tajfel[35] or Lilli[36] based their concepts on Lippmann's argument, according to which stereotypes, as cognitive patterns, are considered the *necessary* result of the human psyche's limited ability to accommodate the dynamic multiplicity of information.

Lilli in particular sought to explain the process of stereotyping—and its accompanying distortions—as having a single basic psychic cause. The need to create cognitive transparency through the classification of stimuli is inevitably coupled with distortions. These distortions result from the human psyche's affinity for accentuations: "Facts that contain the same orientational characteristic (label) and that therefore fall into the same class are considered to be more similar than they are (*generalization*)."[37] And: "Facts that contain different "labels" and thus fall into different classes are considered to be more different than they are (*dichotimization*)."[38] The "distortional effects" of generalization and dichotomization are thus systematically manifested in stereotypes or stereotyped perceptions.

Thus, understanding stereotyping primarily as a cognitive function in itself and therefore approaching stereotype theory primarily from the perspective of cognitive psychology—and not, or at least only secondarily, from that of social pragmatism—is an ongoing trend. This is illustrated, for example, by the studies edited by Daniel Bar-Tal et al.[39] and particularly those written by the American psychologist Walter Stephan. Whereas Stephan does situate his concept within the traditional social-psychological topic of the image of the other and considers stereotypes to be "cognitions concerning groups,"[40] he is nevertheless most interested in how expectations shaped by stereotypes affect cognitive processes. Within the framework of a model he develops—"the model of cognitive information processing"[41]—stereotypes appear as sets of characteristics associated with defining base categories. Stereotypes can thus be conceived as hierarchically organized mental schemata.

On the one hand, Stephan's work evinces a proximity to cognitivist approaches based on the problematic premise that significant aspects of human intelligence resemble the operation of a computer.[42] On the other, Lippmann's issue of distortion once again takes center stage: information conforming to stereotypes is emphasized versus the partial suppression of nonconforming data.

This brief overview of these two trends suffices to offer an impression of the range and conceptual diversity of social psychology's discourse on stereotypes— and also an impression of partial regularities and similarities that constitute this discourse, which shall be addressed again at a later point.

This kind of insight also proves helpful when examining more closely which "stereotype" concepts are pertinent to the analysis of linguistic statements and media texts, including film, because the analysis of media-text content is frequently determined by social psychology's (or related ethnological) research interests and correspondingly based notions of the stereotype.[43]

This approach from a disciplinary context suggests itself, given that media reflect the knowledge of the world, ideas, attitudes, and expectations of the individuals that they address. Conversely, the media also plays a substantial role in communicating and distributing corresponding ideas and attitudes—including those which can be understood as "stereotypes" in the sense already described. The latter are concretized by the media in narrative and visual form. Lippmann already pointed this out in regard to film.[44] And stereotypes are generally reshaped and modified by media and thereupon serve as the basis for further text production.[45] Media texts consequently are interesting documents for social research of a social-psychology bent, which frequently takes the form of a content analysis of film, television, literature, and other media, including language.

A journalistic study by Franz Dröge from the 1960s could be considered a prototype of an approach regarding texts as being primarily documents of the social psyche.[46] Dröge clearly sees the concept of the stereotype as logically situated in attitude research. To a great extent his ideas are in line with Hofstätter's. For Dröge, stereotypes are conceptions about people, groups, nations, and so on—beliefs standardized according to the specific group membership of the individual holding the given notion (autostereotypes and heterostereotypes). He then sought to use content analysis to objectify stereotypes understood in this manner as "coagulated elementary particles"[47] within the communicative content of journalistic texts.

To cite a film-related example, a quite similar concept and analytical aim characterizes the study produced at roughly the same time by Peter Pleyer on the reproduction of national stereotypes in popular German feature films.[48] Ten years later, the British film scholar Steve Neale also used the term "stereotype" (in pointing out a larger field of similar discourses in his own country) in reference to conceptions about people, which are rooted in everyday consciousness as prejudice.[49]

Published in the early 1990s, Irmela Schneider's[50] studies on American television series shown on German TV displayed an interest in texts not merely as a reflection and document of prefabricated patterns but emphasized the active role of the media in forming stereotypes. The research that still continues to dominate, however, is concerned with an interest in conceptions about people, which enter the realm of everyday beliefs. Traditional social-psychology themes and content analysis clearly prevail. One the one hand, Schneider's conceptualization of stereotypes as multipart "hierarchically structured mental schemata"[51] is explicitly informed by the cognitive-psychology interpretations of Tajfel and Stephan. On the other, however, articulating stereotypes as "cognitive processes with social consequences,"[52] Schneider nevertheless focuses on the capacity of these patterns to foster *intersubjective integration*. She thus views *one* of the functions of stereotypes in the reception of television series as semantic: "stereotypes are transindividual constructs of meaning."[53] The recourse to "schemata enabling a stable and invariant attribution of meaning"[54] (because largely consensual) limits the receptive semantic variability otherwise characteristic of art. This means a sustained reduction of polysemy.

Schneider explains the main difference between her work and the traditional approach of social psychology in that the latter hardly addresses the medial means through which stereotypes are acquired. Her goal is therefore to analyze the bulk of series on German TV as such an instance of socialization. Specifically she aims to

> investigate which recurrent combinations of characteristics can be determined for character types by means of a content analysis of the series, in order to be able to draw conclusions about what kinds of stereotypes may be cultivated by watching these shows. On this basis it is then possible to formulate a hypothesis about what potential consequences this could pose for social behavior.[55]

Here stereotypes appear as consensual nodes within "common world knowledge."[56]

W. J. T. Mitchell also refers to the term "stereotype" in his studies on the emotional appeal of images and pictures in everyday life. He thereby clearly adheres to a sociopsychological understanding in describing the stereotype "as a medium for the classification of other subjects,"[57] particularly of "those classes of people who have been the objects of discrimination, victimized by prejudicial images."[58] That means that he is also primarily interested in stereotypes as "bad, false images that prevent us from truly seeing other people."[59] But he is far more realistic than the stereotype critics of the 1970s in emphasizing that "stereotypes are, at a minimum level, a *necessary* evil, that we could not make sense of or recognize objects or other people without the capacity to form images that allow us to distinguish one thing from another, one person from another, one class of things from another."[60] Not only in this context is he skeptical of the idea of naive enlightenment: "If stereotypes were just powerful, deadly, mistaken images, we could simply ban them, and replace them with benign, politically correct, positive images. . . . However, this sort of straightforward strategy of critical iconoclasm generally succeeds only in pumping more life and power into the despised image."[61]

As the theorist of the "pictorial turn," Mitchell is naturally also interested in visual concretizations, for example, when Spike Lee "stages the stereotypes quite literally as freestanding, living images—animated puppets, windup toys, dancing dolls."[62] Indicators are not recurring visual patterns but cognitive patterns; that is, he ultimately understands the stereotype as a sociopsychological category: "Stereotypes are not special or exceptional figures but invisible (or semivisible) and ordinary, insinuating themselves into everyday life. . . . They circulate across sensory registers from the visible to the audible, and they typically conceal themselves as transparent, hyperlegible, inaudible, and invisible cognitive templates of prejudice."[63]

Literary studies have also been influenced by social psychology. This is illustrated by works such as *Studien zu Klischee, Stereotyp und Vorurteil in englischsprachiger Literatur* (Studies on the Cliché, Stereotype, and Prejudice in English Literature) published by Günther Blaicher in the volume *Erstarrtes Denken* (Frozen Thought).[64] Blaicher was interested in "literary stereotyping" as an expression of an author's prejudices: "a reality formed by prejudices," the prejudices of the "intended readers," and the prejudices of the actual readership, which surface in the process of reading.[65]

Similar objectives—also borrowed from sociology—were pursued in the studies of twentieth-century authors of literature and narrative television formats assembled by Elliot, Pelzer, and Poore in their volume *Stereotyp und Vorurteil in der Literatur* (Stereotype and Prejudice in Literature).[66] There is an interesting semiotic difference made here between the way that fixed, recurrent patterns can function on two distinct levels to inform a text. One is the immediate level, drawing on the discourse of social psychology, of "highly simplistic and therefore implausible characterization(s) of individuals and groups."[67] The second, however, is the (somewhat vaguely outlined) level of noticeable, repetitive language-style patterns that have achieved intertextual/conventional stability. An explanation of the link between these two levels, the "linguistic and stylistic stereotype and socially conditioned prejudice," is the editors' stated objective.[68]

Although here too the concept of the stereotype appears to be associated with patterns on the level of linguistic expression, its roots in social psychology and content analysis still predominate. Given the intention of proving a connection between these two levels, only those recurrent linguistic or, respectively, narrative patterns are deemed "literary stereotypes" that can be interpreted as a "pictorial, linguistic concretization of prejudice."[69] Even if Elliot, Pelzer, and Poore maintained the effectiveness of stereotypes in the spirit of Lippmann's pragmatic functionalism, their focus on the link between patterns of content/cognition and language/style patterns presented them with a problem similar to that of the linguist Uta Quasthoff. She approached stereotypes from the perspective of linguistic utterances and arrived at the following definition:

> A stereotype is the verbal expression of a belief which is directed towards social groups or single persons as members of these groups. This belief is characterized by a high degree of sharedness among a speech community or subgroup of a speech community. The stereotype has the logical form of a judgment, which ascribes or denies certain properties (traits or forms of behavior) to a set of persons in an (logically) unwarrantably simplifying and generalizing way, with an emotionally evaluative tendency. The grammatical unit at the basis of the linguistic description is a sentence.[70]

In Quasthoff's work, stereotypes are no longer treated as the actual formulaic notions or judgments applied to groups but as *verbal expressions* of these socially standardized notions. However, for her this does not affect the obvious grounding of the term in social psychology. In any case, the *stable coupling* of formulaic language content (convictions about people) and formulaic linguistic form, which Quasthoff more or less takes for granted, cannot be considered valid.

Among the insights provided by semiotics is that one semantic value can be represented by a multiplicity of symbolic forms. In her critique of Quasthoff, Angelika Wenzel determined that "the formulaic nature of stereotypes is only in part applicable to stereotypes,"[71] although except for a few varying ideas she largely shares Quasthoff's ideas about stereotypes.[72] Wenzel does, however, make it clear that indicators of stereotypes—that is, stable "formulas"—should be sought not on the level of linguistic expression but in meaning. She considers it necessary to perform "a critical *content* analysis in order to uncover these stereotypes,"[73] because it is not possible "to achieve an operationalization of the concept of the 'stereotype' "[74] primarily through linguistic indicators. Even more unequivocally than Quasthoff and others,[75] Wenzel thus dispenses with a *more narrowly defined linguistic stereotype concept* in favor of an investigation into the heterogeneous linguistic representation of stereotypes, which are logically situated in attitude research combined with content analysis.

THE CONCEPT OF THE STEREOTYPE IN LINGUISTICS, LITERATURE, AND ART HISTORY

Based largely on social conceptions about people and corresponding thought patterns expressed in the content of speech and texts, the concepts discussed thus far essentially apply topical issues in social psychology to the fields of film and other media. In addition, there are other concepts of the stereotype primarily focused on standardizations in the form of speech and text, on standardizations of expression. They situate the stereotype indicator on this level and thus clearly break with the logic used in social psychology. Such concepts can be found in theories relating to almost all media, from linguistics to literary theory and art history.

Within the field of linguistics, this different understanding of the stereotype is "naturally" allied with the study of the idiom. This research is not primarily concerned with the question of how the formulas discussed in social psychology are represented linguistically but instead with the way that the medium of language functions within the scope of its own usage. Reusable phrases tend to be flagged as stereotypes. Florian Coulmas discusses stabilized lexeme connections, which are "conventionally used [by a community of speakers] to say certain things and [which] have been learned by the speakers independently of the grammatical rules of the language."[76]

Coulmas' study *Routine im Gespräch* (Routine in Conversation) discusses this concept as well as related pragmalinguistic research traditions in detail—and works from the idea of a context- and function-based standardization of linguistic expressions: "The similarity of the functional tasks that verbalization must perform in comparable situations renders the invention of new expressions superfluous, and often one can rely on the reserve of one's communicative experiences, employing one's memory instead of the imagination."[77]

This is how stereotypes develop. What the author means here are fixed collocations, which seem to appear at the very juncture of language usage and the language system. The gradual stabilization of a phrase within language use to the point at which it actually takes on the characteristics of a stereotype, that is, when it has become conventional, can be studied by examples of "when and how events of language use become established on the level of the language system."[78]

Proceeding from here, Coulmas emphasizes that stereotypes, integral to the language practices characteristic of a particular group and lifestyle, are dependent on context and situation.[79] The analysis of such specific usage requires a "theory of speech situations."[80] In particular, routine formulas—the kinds of verbal stereotypes that Coulmas discusses in depth while only touching on figures of speech, adages, and platitudes—are the result of "situational standardization."[81] "Consolidated in speech, they are organized reactions to social situations,"[82] and the exchange of such reactions belongs to the "rituals of everyday life" that "regulate many aspects of everyday interaction."[83] Therefore, such stereotypes do not only operate as functionally adapted fixed forms, but over the course of time they also undergo the linguistic change that accompanies social change. And they also act as reference to the given situational context at the moment of their occurrence. According to Coulmas, the referential nature of stereotypes is much more significant than that of mere lexical items.[84]

Consequently he argues for a functional theory of meaning, since the semantic content of verbal stereotypes cannot be sufficiently analyzed on the basis of lexical decomposition alone. For Coulmas, this results in specific "problems of connotation, which in this context become prominent as 'social meaning' to the same degree that propositional meaning recedes into the background."[85]

Coulmas is not alone in his understanding of stereotypes—which is a more narrowly defined linguistic approach than that of Quasthoff and Wenzel.[86] French theorists, such as Michael Riffaterre,[87] Gérard Genette,[88] and Roland Barthes,[89] particularly tend to use "stereotype" to denote recurring standardized lexeme connections, without, however, investigating this issue nearly as systematically as Coulmas.

Stereotypes come into play in the writings of Riffaterre when he investigates the function of clichés in literary prose. As a theorist of style, he considers the cliché a special form[90] of verbal stereotype (fixed lexeme connections)—and it is a special form that entails a "style factor," that is, a metaphor that has become conventional. In a pragmatic sense he also interprets the cliché as a functional factor, which carries a crystallized effect. "An effect is therefore, if I may say so, canned."[91]

Riffaterre, whose stylistic investigation deliberately introduces the horizon of aesthetic values, generally suspects the stereotype, or cliché, of having undergone a latent loss of meaning. This suspected impoverishment, however, clearly differs from the deficits assumed by social psychologists. It is characteristic of aesthetic-stylistic concerns, and in this context it often dominates thinking about stereo-types. As formulaic, readymade units, stereotypes have naturally been criticized as banal and unoriginal. These aesthetic objections will be elaborated further on. Such reservations were expressed most forcefully by Roland Barthes: "Nausea occurs whenever the liaison of two important words *follows of itself*."[92]

Riffaterre, however, takes pains to present a more nuanced view. He insists: "Even if the cliché is always a stereotype, it is not always banal; one perceives it as such, merely when originality is currently in fashion as an aesthetic criteria; at other times it is categorized as the *Gradus ad Parnassum* and recommended as 'pleasant phrase,' 'a natural adjective,' etc."[93]

In addition, he also believes—in this regard a functionalist through and through—that even the aesthetic judgment of "banality" does not affect the practical functionality of a cliché; that is, it cannot be truly equated with an inhibited function of the formula, as one ought not "confuse banality with wear."[94] In addition, a differentiation—of consequence for stylistic critique or aesthetic judgments—must be made between two distinct functions of stereo-typed phrases in literary texts. Ultimately it makes a difference whether the phrase is presented as (1) "a constitutive element of the author's writing" or (2) "as an object of expression . . . as a reality exterior to the author's writing,"[95] for example, in a character's speech.

While Riffaterre, like Coulmas, places great emphasis on the role of conven-tion in his concept of the stereotype or cliché, for Genette the frequent occur-rence of a lexeme connection in the work of an author is apparently sufficient to constitute a stereotype. In his analyses of pastiche and parody he thus uses the term to discuss the multiple appearances of "recurrent phrases"[96] such as "rosy-fin-gered dawn" or "swift-footed Achilles" in Homer's *Iliad*, which he considers "self-quotations"[97] due to their frequent repetition. Like Coulmas, he also emphasizes how a stereotype functions as a kind of connotative reference to the context in which it appears, in his case the work of an author. Here, the stereotype becomes a "Homerism": "Each Homeric formula . . . already forms a class of multiple occur-rences whose use by another author, whether epic or not, is no longer a quotation from Homer, or a borrowing from Homer, but rather a true Homerism—the defi-nition of a formulaic style being precisely that nearly all its idioms are iterative."[98] From the point of view of stylistic criticism, Genette does admit that such verbal stereotypes (even in an author's writing) are potentially appropriate to specific contexts, inasmuch as this pertains to certain types of historical text types like the epic, which introduce a corresponding horizon of values.

* * *

When the discussion turns to the analysis and composition of entire texts, the referred-to object of the term "stereotype" once more shifts markedly away from the described linguistic-idiomatic association with conventionally fixed and recurrent word groupings and toward larger structural or stylistic phenomena of literary texts or those in other media.

Here—as in the work of Yuri Lotman—the term primarily surfaces in discussions of the "model-clichés"[99] in texts and is used more or less synonymously. However, unlike in linguistics, in this context the term cannot be situated within a specific level or unit. Lotman's recourse to the word "structure" already indicates that he means constructs tending to exhibit a similar variation in scope and relationship to a textual level as that of "structures." Admittedly, he is concerned with particular structures, that is, those so deep-seated and familiar to the audience that—as expected patterns within the organization of a text—they can be classified as "cultural codes."[100]

Without specifically going into the process, degree, and scope of such codification (one may assume that he means a process of conventionalization), Lotman points out the result: "a frozen system of characters, plots and other structural elements."[101] His examples and frequently used terms like "cliché" also indicate that he is thinking about relatively compact and incisive patterns. In other words, he essentially envisions structures similar to those described by John Cawelti,[102] for example, who talks about narrative "formulas" with reference to popular storytelling (in literature as well as other media), or those of Umberto Eco, who reflects on "the iterative schema"[103] in mass culture, with which the audience is very familiar.

Given that the pragmalinguist Florian Coulmas examines verbal formulas "conventionally used to say certain things"[104] because they fulfill similar functional requirements of verbalization in comparable situations, it would be feasible to develop something analogous to this on the level of conventional textual formulas: a kind of pragma*semiotic* concept. This would mean analytically placing stereotypes organizing a text within the context of the functional requirements that gave rise to the context that originally fostered the formation of these stereotypes. For example, stereotypes could be examined as a "canned" response to the widespread desire for emotional involvement (for example, in experiencing suspense) and for identificatory participation, or as a reflection of ideological and mythological needs.

To take this analogy one step further, a functional theory of meaning for stereotypes of textual organization is possible on this basis. Such a concept accentuates the ritual and context-based nature of such patterns and explains phenomena such as the diminishment of propositional meaning and the emergence of referential functions (pointing to original functional contexts). A range of such aspects has in fact been studied in literature and film studies (to be discussed in depth further on) but often without explicit association with the term "stereotype."

Although Lotman does specifically mention the term, he is not interested—in contrast to a functional, pragmatic position—in the causes and contexts of the functionally determined emergence of stereotypes as textual organization or in the reasons why stereotypes are often readily received. Neither does he address otherwise much-discussed questions concerning the qualities of the formulas, for example, to what extent they are ideological or adequately reflect reality. The possible loss or distortion of *content* is not an issue for him. Of sole importance to Lotman is the fact that structural clichés exist and, most importantly, that they are preserved as stereotypes in the consciousness of those producing and receiving a text: "Stereotypes (clichés) of consciousness play a great part in the process of cognition and, in a broader sense, in the process of information transfer."[105] Consequently, they function as codes.

In this case, the issue is less the "normal" or simple reproduction of stereotypes and more the manner in which they are referred to when it comes to determining difference. For Lotman, the "intrusion of disorder, entropy or disorganization into the sphere of structure and information"[106] is ultimately a process fundamental to the production of specific artistic information and aesthetic quality. The play with the tension between expectations shaped by stereotypes and various actualizations of stereotypes in text is what actually interests him about the question as a whole:

> The perception of an artistic text is always a struggle between audience and author. . . . The audience takes in part of the text and then "finishes" or "constructs" the rest. The author's next "move" may confirm the guess and make further reading pointless (at least from the perspective of modern aesthetic norms) or it may disprove the guess and require a new construction from the reader.[107]

Stereotypes are of central importance in this process. However, this is not their primary significance, which instead entails the very *establishment* of order, consistency, and predictability. Within Lotman's structural aesthetics, due to the conventionality of these patterns they consequently serve as a common foil for what is ultimately a formal game between the text and the reader, the basis for "artistic systems of this type."[108] Expectations are roused in the reader in reference to stereotypes, and corresponding differences are systematically organized within the text.

But Lotman does not envision absolute difference. In addition to an aesthetics of opposition he postulates an aesthetics of identity. While the aesthetics of opposition evokes the stereotype in the consciousness of the reader by means of the text, only to then destroy it, the aesthetics of identity very much focuses on the deliberate reproduction of salient repetitive patterns at one pole of the text. At the other, however, a wide range of lively material comes into play, which constantly varies the stereotype and combinations thereof. Lotman describes this using the commedia dell'arte as an example: "It is revealing in this sense that *commedia dell'arte* has, at one pole, a strict set of images and clichés with certain possibilities and certain prohibitions, while at the other pole, it is constructed as the freest sort of improvisation to be found in the history of European theatre."[109]

In France, Ruth Amossy developed a literary semiology of the stereotype (with reference also to audiovisual media), which she outlines in her 1991 book *Les idées reçues*.[110] Apart from a number of differences, her semiotic-aesthetic approach has many similarities to that of Lotman. This is already apparent in an early essay from 1984,[111] which shall be discussed first.

In this essay, Amossy also emphasizes that all possible structural levels of a text, from the thematic level to that of the characters and narrative macrostructure, can be subject to stereotyping, and she links this issue with a reference to particularly conspicuous stereotyping in mass literature and popular culture overall. In addition, Amossy is also less interested in a pragmatic analysis that attempts to functionally interpret stereotypes as an answer to certain sets of conditions and needs. Like Lotman, she is concerned with the fact, in and of itself, that "recurrent and frozen"[112] patterns occur and have therefore become conventional models. Building on this idea, her argument also points toward a tension in the relationship between author/text and recipient: "the stereotype stands at the junction of text and reading. It is necessarily reliant on an aesthetics of reception."[113]

Amossy's aesthetics of reception not only assumes that stereotypes are entrenched "in the reader's cultural memory"[114] and thus can become cognitive factors for reception—and also for the perception of difference—that is, factors that an author must anticipate. Moreover, she envisions an extreme reading strategy that summons the power of the deep-rooted stereotypes as already described by Lippmann: emphasizing stereotype-compliant information and partially repressing noncompliant information. She calls this "stereotyped reading":[115]

Reading picks out all the constituents of the description which correspond to the preexisting pattern. In doing this, it trims, prunes, and erases. All nuances which are not immediately relevant are rubbed out. All variants are reduced and reintegrated willy-nilly into the initial isotopism.[116]

Reading thus recuperates the maximum number of variants and differences while working to reduce them to the Same and Known. Everything that perversely disturbs this harmony of fixed traits reunited in a stable pattern is relegated to the level of "remnants." For the reader forming the stereotype, these remnants are hardly a problem. Whenever reading does not purely and simply skip them, it . . . neutralizes the remnants without difficulty.[117]

Producing distortion and loss, stereotyped reading for Amossy is a process that strives to conform to stabilized stores of belief and knowledge, to tried and true ideas; it is based on excessive pleasure in encountering repetition: "Stereotyped reading allows us to stay on this familiar terrain, where everything has the reassuring form of déjà vu. We have nothing more to learn; we must simply recognize the same in novelty and difference."[118]

A text can thus deliberately serve such a reading strategy by confirming the stereotypes it incorporates. However, a text can also resist stereotypes through the creation of difference, that is, by contrasting stock formulas with a "reworking of models and problematization of commonplace visions."[119]

Amossy's essay from 1984 clearly reflects her critical distance to the stereotype and her emphasis on the loss of meaning it incurs (within the context of a clearly representation-oriented position on literature). "For us the stereotype is the point at which repetition becomes routinization, and complexity becomes the most outrageous schematization."[120] Here Amossy indicates that the pleasure found in repetition is solely an aesthetic point of friction—in contrast to her later study from 1991.[121] Nevertheless, an argument for a functional approach follows, which in 1984 she understands primarily as the necessity for considering the individual treatment of a stereotype when making an aesthetic judgment about its textual performance. Such judgments must differentiate between the pure confirmation of a stereotype and a contrasting creation of difference. At that earlier point, for Amossy the only appropriate aesthetic use of the cultural patterns was to deconstruct, contrast, and neutralize them and to destroy automatisms. This is obviously analogous to Lotman's category of the aesthetics of opposition; she favored the logic of this concept.

Within the scope of specific text-based concepts of the stereotype, "text" can be understood in a broad, semiological sense, as art historians such as Ernst Gombrich and Arnold Hauser also use the term "stereotype." They do so with intentions similar to those of Lotman and Amossy, namely to describe conventionally fixed and recurrent structural patterns of representation. Naturally they are concerned with *pictorial representation*. Given the visual nature of film, a look at their ideas will conclude this overview.

In the field of linguistic and textual analysis, the stereotype is often coupled with the term "formula," and Hauser also uses the word "stereotype" to identify formulas—"formal principles"[122] (*stehende Formeln*) of visualization that have developed in the context of the fine arts (though not in isolation from other cultural discourses). Hauser primarily views stereotypes from the standpoint of how communication functions: he considers them as operating within a specific art-historical formation as succinct and conventional schemata of visual composition and thus also as rules for the creation and reception of images. As conventionalized representational patterns shared and accepted by artists and viewers within a given period, stereotypes come close to being cultural codes. Hauser himself uses the metaphor of the "language of art."[123] According to more advanced semiotic terminology, one could also say that he situates his "stereotypes" on the level of specific codes characteristic of different historical periods in the visual arts.

It is interesting that Hauser also addresses the question of a latent loss and distortion through stereotypes. He raises this issue not so much in terms of the ability of an image to accurately represent external reality, that is, in terms of content, but more in relation to the aesthetic problem of how to achieve individual expression by conventional means. Hauser's argument is consequently based on an "aesthetics of identity" with functional tendencies. Communication is only comprehensible "when it submits to schematization and conventionalization and . . . moves from the sphere of private and personal meaning into that of interpersonal relationships."[124] This "always has to pay the price of the content which is to be communicated losing part of its original sense."[125] One must deal with this creatively, as he rightly adds, since it is pure fantasy to think that one can ignore this fundamental relationship: "Completely subjective and spontaneous experience free from each and every conventional and stereotypical element is a just a borderline concept, an abstract idea which bears no relation to reality."[126] Therefore, one should not always consider an affinity to stereotypes a "deficit" but rather a condition of artistic creativity:

> *The process is dialectical.* Spontaneity and resistance, invention and convention: dynamic impulses born of experience break down or expand forms, and fixed, inert and stable forms condition, obstruct, and enhance each other. . . . Artistic expression comes about not in spite of but thanks to the resistance which convention offers to it. . . . This is a striking example of Hegel's *Aufhebung*: a simultaneous erection and destruction of valid conventions, symbols, schemata.[127]

In an obvious parallel to Riffaterre or to Lotman's example of the commedia dell'arte, Hauser then also refers to cultures that have an entirely different level of acceptance for schematization, repetition, and conventionality than is permitted by modernity's aesthetics. Hence, for example, in traditional East Asian culture the direct reliance on repeating visual formulas, which are substantially reduced in complexity, is considered a sign of "abstract, strictly formal art" and is thus also considered to be "more refined."[128]

From this perspective, he thus views the conflict-ridden interplay of stereo-typical and spontaneous, individual tendencies as an essential characteristic of the entire history of art—surfacing in different contexts and manners, placing highly varying emphases on the opposing poles of stereotype and difference, and resulting in very heterogeneous solutions. The play between stereotype-generated expectation and difference, which Lotman describes in a temporal dimension, is now quasi applied to the surface of the image. In Hauser's writings, the concept of the stereotype is most strongly evident in works or epochs in which simple, reduced, and conventional visual formulas tend to quite obviously dominate the concrete image in the sense of a "stereotyped style"[129] and in which this occurs in numerous similar cases; that is, formulas become conventional and stylistically definitive, as in the "stereotyping of art" in Egypt.[130]

Ernst Gombrich's use of the term "stereotype" has similar implications.[131] He also emphasized that pictorial representations of the visible world are mediated through a system of schemata in the mind of the individual artist. He too associates this with the metaphor of "the language of art": "Everything points to the conclusion that the phrase 'the language of art' is more than a loose metaphor, that even to describe the visible world in images we need a developed system of schemata."[132]

Considering this "system of schemata" or "mental set,"[133] Gombrich's argument (aimed at examining the inner processes that dictate an artist's activities) is more firmly rooted in cognitive psychology than Hauser's, which is dominated by semiotic-communicative functionalism. For Gombrich, an internal system of schemata guides artists' views of external reality as well as their creative activities. Stereotypes play a special role in this process. Repeatedly using the words "pattern" and "formula," Gombrich makes it clear that he understands stereotypes as particularly stable schemata of visual or artistic representation, which can be considered conventional within a given art-historical formation. The individual artist receives them and internalizes them as "second-hand" formulas.[134] In other words, different from a more idiosyncratic schema characteristic of *a single* artist's work (personal style), the stereotype is viewed by Gombrich as a firmly entrenched *conventional* schema.

It is worth noting that, above and beyond his cognitivistic approach, he also links the topic of the stereotype with a functional argument, namely the idea of the readymade effect. While Riffaterre, with respect to literature, talks about stylistic formulas that quasi store specific effects, Gombrich refers to visual stereotypes, which have each been specifically developed to produce a unique affective impact. In this context he introduces Aby Warburg's concept of the *Pathosformel* (pathos formula).[135]

However, also for Gombrich the stereotype is linked with a latent problem of loss or distortion, which is primarily manifested in the tension between his stereotypes and the valid visual representation of reality. The latter is one of the claims of art and a primary concern in *Art and Illusion*. He dedicates an entire chapter to an exhaustive series of examples demonstrating the deficits of stereotypes in the pictorial representation of reality. The problem is made clear from the start by the chapter's title, "Truth and the Stereotype." For example, in this section of the book he outlines how convention predominates over mimesis in visual representation throughout the history of German art. Thus the fixed idea of how a castle should look was imposed on graphic depictions of the Castel Sant'Angelo in Rome, which in reality has a quite different appearance. Lippmann's statements about the formative power of stereotypes come to mind once again, when one reads Gombrich's explanation of how stereotype and real appearance enter into a strange symbiosis in the woodcut he analyses.[136] This is not just a matter of polemics, for Gombrich dedicates substantial space to presenting a nuanced argument.

This reference to stereotypes is not only necessary in the sense that they help transport an artistic "language"—that is, in the sense of symbolic systems of depiction and information. For Gombrich they have even more significance as stabilized cognitive systems for the visual processing of the external world: "Without some starting point, some initial schema, we could never get hold of the flux of experience."[137]

Highly significant to Gombrich is the explicit differentiation between the stereotype as a specific schema in the mind of the artist, or in pattern books, and the manner in which is it realized—which he describes as "adaptation"[138]—in the process of the actual production of a work of art. Thus, for example, he differentiates between the varying degrees and ways in which images are formed by stereotypes. On the one hand, he describes cases in which representation is strictly governed by a stereotype based on a simple and highly reduced schema (as in postclassical Greek art): "The schema was not criticized or corrected, and so it followed the natural pull toward the minimum stereotype, the 'gingerbread figure' of peasant art."[139] On the other, he also refers to the possibility of a distinctly more flexible adaptation of the stereotype in more sophisticated images: "Once we pay attention to this principle of the adapted stereotype, we also find it where we would be less likely to expect it: that is, within the idiom of illustrations, which look much more flexible."[140]

FIGURE 2 Stereotypization of visual representation: views of the Castel Sant'Angelo in Rome. A series of images from E. H. Gombrich, *Art and Illusion* (1977), 61. Anonymous woodcut, 1557 (above); anonymous drawing, pen and ink, circa 1540 (center); modern photograph (below).

Again the idea is expressed that one should have a ready willingness to correct one's own stereotypes—in this case, conventional pictorial formulas. As "starting points" in the reciprocal process of perception and creation, stereotypes are seen as necessary and acceptable, given that they are subjected to a "corrective test" and are creatively adapted over the course of the artistic process.[141]

SIMILARITIES AND DIFFERENCES BETWEEN THE CONCEPTS/FOUR FACETS

Given the (highly complex) topic at hand, this overview of stereotype concepts in the social sciences and humanities is by no means exhaustive, although quite comprehensive. Following the principle of *pars pro toto*, it nevertheless does reveal trends in the conceptualization of the term, which may also ground the analysis of the discourse in relation to film.

Thus far it has been demonstrated that the theoretical use of the term "stereotype" and its corresponding concepts can neither be attributed to a single discipline or method (for example, limited to social psychology, as often claimed) nor to a clearly defined object of investigation, such as conceptions of people. The assertions as to what constitutes a stereotype and on which levels of theory it is situated are too diverse, even within individual disciplines. Over the course of this overview, however, it has been possible to delineate three fundamentally different kinds of fixed formulas or patterns, which are considered stereotypes within the individual discourses. Discussed so far in the context of the social sciences were (1) thought and attitude patterns pertaining to social phenomena, in particular formulaic notions concerning members of social or ethnic groups. Next, (2) linguistic forms in the sense of conventional lexeme connections, that is, routine verbal formulas, were addressed within the scope of the idiom. Finally, (3) we looked at the patterns or "formulas" that shape the structure of entire texts or segments of texts, whether within literature, the fine arts, or any other kind of text.

If there is a common element at least virtually shared among the various concepts of "stereotype," then it must be sought in a tendency that links activities such as perception, cognition, and communication with their material results (texts). This can only be described in very broad terms. However, a common link could be most appropriately articulated as follows: in all these interdependent spheres, more *complex, composite*[142] *forms*, structures, or patterns evolve, which are then repeatedly reproduced en bloc in similar or similarly perceived functional contexts and therefore tend to be very *persistent*.

It stands to reason that this smallest common denominator is closely related to the etymology of the word, which stems from printing technology. It is based on the compound of the Greek words τύποσ, which can be translated as "impression," "figure," or "type," and στερεόσ, which in this context means "solid."[143] Within the field of printing, the compound word was used to describe a printing plate cast in one piece, in contrast to composite plates with moveable letters. The stereotype thus unites multiple characters or lines of print in solid form. The term retained the meaning of a stable form composed from multiple elements, which could be printed (reproduced) repeatedly, when it was carried over into more general usage as a metaphor in the nineteenth century. Scientific and scholarly terminology was later based on this common usage of the word.

In and of itself, this smallest common denominator appears to be rather insubstantial. It also seems too abstract to serve as the *sole* foundation for an outline of fundamental discourses on stereotypes in film or for a definition of terms appropriate to the analysis of film. It is certainly equally important to develop a keen sense for the kinds of heterogeneous theoretical contexts in which the term is used: theoretical perspectives that—although leading to various "objects of investigation" and concepts—have almost *all been applied to film* or at least can be developed in regard to phenomena within this medium.

This approach has one very obvious implication: in regards to film or cinema (understood as film culture in general), it makes little sense to try to find a master concept, such as *the* film stereotype, to serve as an alloy of all the discursive statements associated with the term "stereotype." Here too, one must always consider the theoretical locus of any given conception of the term. From this vantage point, the very differences between the concepts discussed so far can actually offer a more precise perspective. Also, despite all the differences in the various fields of study and theoretical approaches, it is possible to identify a good number of regularities, relationships, and similarities. While these are by no means consistently articulated in each concept, as a whole they could be said to belong to a kind of family of statements, cognitive motifs, and arguments. "Family" refers to Wittgenstein's famous reflections on the "game." In light of the great variation in types of games, the latter term does not denote an absolute set of shared traits but a set of "family resemblances": "We see a complicated network of similarities overlapping and criss-crossing: similarities in the large and in the small. . . . I can think of no better expression to characterize these similarities than 'family resemblances'; for the various resemblances between members of a family . . . overlap and criss-cross in the same way."[144]

This explains why "stereotype," as a discursive entity, seems much more compact and fulsome—due to the interplay of its individual facets (its family resemblances), which are understood as clusters of similar arguments—than the paltry framework of the smallest common denominator would make it appear. This framework, in contrast to Wittgenstein's "game," does at least seem possible in this context.

The next step is to outline four such facets:[145] (1) schema, reductionism, and stability; (2) automatism and conventionalization; (3) distortion and loss; and (4) a ground for difference to emerge. In the process of fleshing out these theoretical facets, differences between them will be examined and related to methodological considerations. The resulting "theoretical web" will then be used as an orientation for the analysis of various approaches, emphases, and questions within the film-related discourse on the stereotype. On this basis it will then be possible subsequently to include statements about film that do not explicitly use the key word "stereotype" and instead operate with terms such as "pattern," "schema," "cliché," and so on, whose meanings, however, correspond to the outlined repertoire of facets in the discourse on stereotypes.

FIRST FACET: SCHEMA, REDUCTIONISM, AND STABILITY

Regardless whether one is speaking of "formulas" or "patterns," stereotype concepts are often associated with ideas and statements that are also constitutive of the term "schema." It is not uncommon for stereotypes to be explicitly described as particular schemata—whether the term refers to thought patterns about external reality or to patterns in the organization of text or textual segments. This is reflected in the *cognitive psychology* approaches of Lilli and Stephan and also those of Gombrich and Schneider. Only in the description of verbal stereotypes does the term "schema" fail to play a role.

The reference to schemata seems plausible, given that the various stereotype concepts refer to phenomena that manifest solely on the level of comparison with an individual idea or concrete textual segment, a comparison giving rise to *abstractions*. Similar to the way that schemata are formed, the analytical perception of a stereotype always necessitates the suppression of concrete information. This kind of perception is always oriented toward *reduction, simplification, and the pattern-like*. In other words, stereotypes, just like schemata, do not consist of complete passages of text or images, and they hardly consist of fully formed ideas (only the readymade formulas of verbal stereotypes could in this case be considered an exception to the rule of "incompletion"). Stereotypes are virtual entities that become viable only through comparison and abstraction. The perception and understanding of stereotypes *as stereotypes* requires a special mental effort of construction. Conversely, the actualization, reproduction, performance, or—in

Hegelian terms—"sublation" (*Aufhebung*) of stereotypes, and also of schemata, does not yield the identical but the similar.

Meanwhile, it is usually the *element of reduced complexity*, inherent to every schema, which most insistently stresses the notion of a stereotype—as soon as this reduction becomes *clearly noticeable* through specific textual performance, that is, when it concretely generates *conspicuous simplicity*. It is no coincidence that the art historians mentioned here for the most part associated the word "stereotype" with images that were *often dominated* by recurrent and simple forms or "formulas"—images whose actual composition is reduced to a *minimal stereotype* (Gombrich) displayed as a " 'gingerbread figure' of peasant art" or images, as in Egyptian art, that tend to exhibit a "stereotyped style" (Hauser). Also, in regard to literature, Ruth Amossy considered one of the "golden rules of stereotyping" to be the coupling of "the poverty of its constituents" with formal consistency (homogeneity) and redundancy.[146]

If from a cognitive point of view the stereotype, as a recurrent form of abstraction, approximates the concept of the schema, then it is necessary to defend the "schema" against a common and problematic (mis)understanding of the term. A mechanistic interpretation is often forced upon the term, because "schema" features prominently in a branch of cognitivism, which views human perception as a sort of rational machine and which is based on an ideal of perception as an objective, correct representation of an external world independent of a perceiving subject. In this context, the notion of schemata comes close to rigid matrix models, as a stable representation of a logical synthesis of invariants in the external world. This does not do justice to the *living psychic processes* occurring in discursive reality. This particularly applies to nonformalized everyday thought and communication, which tend to follow "the approximate, 'fuzzy' logic" of practice articulated by Bourdieu[147] and are certainly relevant to the question of the stereotype.

However, the term "schema" per se should not be discarded together with its logocentric interpretation. Even alternative constructivistic approaches opposing hardcore cognitivism retain the basic idea of schemata. This is true of Varela's behavioral approach to cognition, whose idea of "structural coupling"[148] seems the most plausible. Varela conceives of perceptive and cognitive schemata that guide everyday thinking as *autopoietic constructs* of human *experiential reality* and not mere representations of apparent similarities of a purely objective external world. As the former, they bear the obvious traits (of intersubjectively and socially mediated) subjective constructs and are capable of linking cognitive, affective, and associative factors of active consciousness.[149]

This preserves the most important idea regarding cognitive schemata, which Luhmann formulates as follows: "it is a question of forms which, in the ceaseless temporal flow of autopoiesis, enable recursions, retrospective reference to the familiar, and repetition of operations which actualize it."[150] They thus appear as operations of the memory, which—although they cannot be defined as *rigid* patterns—do correspond to repetitions or accumulations of similarities. They also function as forms that reduce complexity and introduce *relative* stability and consistency into our cognition, communication, and practical behavior. Simultaneously they have the quality of rules, in order to facilitate quick responses.[151] Moreover, schemata, as constituted by everyday consciousness, are not to be viewed as isolated, one-dimensional constructs but instead as organized in *emergent networks* of memory.[152] That means that they interact comprehensively, which is what enables actualizations of schemata often to become processes of interdependent associations and symbioses.

Given this understanding of the schema, it makes sense to examine the concept of the stereotype accordingly. A good number of stereotype concepts emphasize that stereotypes, like schemata, do not simply register repetitive elements of the represented, concrete world but rather integrate analogous behavioral and situational contexts. This argument is especially favored by pragmatic and functionalist approaches. If one includes communicative activity in the definition of behavior, then both schemata and stereotypes can be interpreted as *behavior-related entities*, which, as Coulmas illustrated with verbal stereotypes, *have developed in the context of different behavioral exigencies and types of situations*. This means that stereotypes do not only function as representational patterns of external reality. A good number of stereotypes can individually be considered a "formula" for meeting a typical behavioral requirement, as a proven structure for mastering a specific (communicative) situation or task.

This in itself implies that stereotypes as well as schemata by no means function solely as a means of rational orientation. As formulas of thought and conception, they have a holistic and therefore also emotional function. The idea that stereotypes are linked with the emotions appears to be a key feature of many theories. In a number of cases, stereotypes, as specific schemata of communication and textual organization, can even be interpreted as differentiated functional forms that ensure the activation of affective responses (as intended in aesthetic fictions) in the addressee. Consequently, they can be interpreted as pragmatic entities, which are coordinated with behavioral (and also communicative) contexts and which have gradually adapted themselves to specific contexts—such as the dispositions of the group of individuals addressed by certain kinds of texts. It is this unique function of stereotypes that calls for a stereotype theory above and beyond classical cognitivist approaches. Therefore, a pragmatic perspective seems inevitable.

There is another similarity: like schemata, stereotypes are also organized within the memory's *emergent networks* of experience and knowledge. Much in this manner T. E. Perkins emphasizes that the simple surface structures of stereotypes are usually connected on a deep level with highly complex caches of rational and emotional knowledge, which stereotypes access as subroutines.[153]

Finally, there is also common ground regarding the issue of stability and dynamics. Like schemata, stereotypes are not absolutely rigid patterns. However, a specific difference is relevant in this context. The term "stereotype" almost always suggests stability and inertia and does so to a much greater extent than "schema." Nevertheless, when suspicions of utter rigidity are raised, this is almost always difficult to substantiate upon closer examination. If stereotypes are, *in a heightened sense*, instances of *recourse to existing knowledge*, then they still ultimately remain "living" entities. Exhibiting the lag of pronounced inertia, they follow the dynamics of human experience, sometimes even by erratic leaps of adaptation. It stands to reason that the *transformation of the stereotype* and its successive modification are topics repeatedly raised in discussion.

Another specificity that surfaced in many of the described stereotype concepts has already been mentioned: *clarity through simplicity*. To use Eleanor Rosch's term, one could say that there is a tendency to identify stereotypes as constructs that exhibit similarities to one another on the relatively limited "basic level"[154] of abstraction. In summary, stereotypes (particularly those organizing a text) can be described as *particular* schemata. The distinctive features of stereotypes are considered to be: *a heightened affinity for demonstrative, clear performance through formulaic reduction of complexity*, on the one hand, and *an increased tendency toward repetition, in which the given form manifests an especially high degree of stability, homogeneity, and inertia*, on the other.

Of course, there is no absolute gauge for determining the moment in which both these features are present; certainly they enhance each other and often give rise to descriptions such as "formula" or "formulaic." A construct is identified as a stereotype always in relation to a *statement* expressed by a subject (an individual, group, or cultural community). This construct is dependent on experiential knowledge, and on an intersubjective level it is governed by prevailing *common sense*. It should be emphasized that the perception of simplicity and stability may itself be subject to a mechanism potentially identifiable as *stereotypization*, that is, forcing similarity within the receptive (re)construction of a pattern. Amossy's idea of *stereotyped reading* even takes into account the extreme case of a reading process in which stereotypes are asserted against the text.

SECOND FACET: AUTOMATISM AND CONVENTIONALIZATION

Although across the board almost all the various stereotype concepts address the stability and homogeneity of a repetitive pattern, they do so from two different perspectives: either by examining the significance assigned to an *intrasubjectively* rooted pattern, that is, its habitualization, or by investigating the function of an *intersubjectively* rooted schema. Two differently accentuated understandings of "stereotypization" result. While it is necessary to make a distinction between the two on a theoretical level, pragmatically speaking they substantially overlap.

From the first perspective, stereotypization is manifested in the much-repeated, automatic mental recall of a fixed pattern throughout a series of similarly perceived situations or behavioral contexts. In other words, they appear when *a schema and a type of situation are mentally coupled.*

In the 1920s, the Russian psychologist Ivan Pavlov took up the word "stereotype," using it differently from the discourse in social psychology. His concept thus serves as both a prototype and an archaic theoretical model for the association of the terminus with habitually fixed response patterns. The term appears within the context of his famous theory of conditioned reflexes, which is based on elementary stimulus-response patterns. "The dynamic stereotype of the higher section of the brain"[155] is ultimately nothing more than an enduringly habitualized and consequently automatized stimulus-response schema, which has developed due to an extremely formalized and repetitive behavioral context.

Pavlov expressly pointed to the significance of and internal link between reflexlike automatic responses and inertia. Once a stereotype has been formed, it becomes "inert, is not easy to change, and is difficult to override with a new situation or new stimuli."[156] This degree of stability can be so alleviating to an individual that a confrontation with stimuli overtly contradicting the stereotype can arouse negative reactions to the point of painful strain and even neurosis:[157]

> It appears to me that often the difficult emotions of the change in the customary modes of life, of the disappearance of accustomed activities, of the loss of familiar people, let alone the mental crises and destruction of faith have their physiological basis to a considerable degree precisely in the change, in the disturbance of the old dynamic stereotype and in the difficulty of establishing a new one.[158]

Based on intrasubjective automatization—on habitualization or conditioning—the formulation of this stability thesis has consequences that relate to Lippmann's description of stereotypes (dating from approximately the same period) as the well-protected foundations of an individual's universe. And, of course, Amossy's notion of "stereotyped reading," which demonstrates a preoccupation with déjà vu and which in principle also occurs in the cinema or in front of the television, can also be assigned to this element of accentuated intrasubjectivity of the stereotype concept, that is, an emphasis on habituality and *the pleasure derived from automatic thought processes and repetition.*

Therefore, it is certainly no accident that film theorists decidedly tend to associate the concept of the stereotype with the idea of an automatic perception enabled by a fixed acquired cognitive schema ingrained in memory. This is particularly noticeable in theoretical inquiries, such as that of Peter Wuss, which probe psychological aspects of filmic viewing and analyze "the structures of film in the process of perception."[159] Wuss is interested in stereotypes (even though he explicitly conceptualizes them as the films' conventional structures) primarily in the sense that they are manifested in the mind of the spectator as *fixed memory structures.* As stable units of information, these structures are learned by the viewer through the "repetition in multiple works of appropriated stimuli patterns"[160]— or, expressed more strongly, "a kind of continuous barrage":[161] "Stored in long-term, or tertiary memory, these structures can hardly be forgotten. Through a process of habituation they generally become matter of course to recipients, and are later, to some extent, incidentally and unconsciously apperceived."[162] Differently stated, everything amounts to an automatization of perception and an automatization of the psychic processing of repetitive patterns in a very late learning phase. For Wuss, who implicitly operates with a kind of model-reader construct,[163] these patterns can be considered "stereotype-based structures"[164] of film or respectively film's "narrative stereotypes,"[165] which thus become relevant in filmmaking.

While the *intra*subjective approach primarily examines the process through which a schema becomes firmly rooted in memory and investigates the accompanying effects of the repetitive, automatic mental reproduction of a pattern, sociological and semiological concepts of the stereotype have a greater tendency to emphasize the formation of *inter*subjective patterns. In these disciplines, the term is actually founded on how schema operate intersubjectively. Discussion here is generally concerned with the *(socio)integrative impact* of the stable distribution of a schema among a large number of individuals in a group or society. It can be said of this approach that the metaphor of "handed-down patterns" appears so frequently in the various discourses on the stereotype that it could consequently be considered a stereotype itself.

This idea of stereotypization focuses on the *conventionalization* of a pattern. It is impossible to talk about sociointegrative effects without the notion of conventionality. Conventionalization means nothing else than a standardization or codification in an intersubjective field. In the sense of producing intersubjective coherence, conventional schemata not only regulate the manner in which members of a group or society view the world, make sense of it, and create meaning; they also *standardize* communicative and immediate practical action. Thus, conventional schemata introduce stability and necessary assimilation into social (and therefore communicative) relationships. As such, an individual's identification with social roles and styles of thought and expression is paralleled by his or her orientation toward stereotypes.

Within the context of the social sciences, stereotypes are therefore often interpreted as *social standards* or *cultural models*, which steer generally accepted, normal reactions, communication, and behavior. For individuals, this kind of normality is experienced within the realm of ordinary consciousness, when conventionality overlaps with the habituality/automatic function of a stereotype.

At this point, intersubjectively established, fixed patterns of meaning and behavioral orientation become *implicit* and—quite independent from the truth aspect—are *no longer questioned*. This explains why conventional ideas and *guiding principles*, particularly those concerning people and society, feature prominently in many stereotype theories. Their common ground with discourses on ideology becomes an issue, as Roland Barthes aptly remarks: "All official institutions of language are repeating machines: school, sports, advertising, popular songs, news, all continually repeat the same structure, the same meaning, often the same words: the stereotype is a political fact, the major figure of ideology."[166]

The intersubjective aspect of stereotypization as conventionalization becomes very significant for *specific text-related concepts of the stereotype*. Here, too, the main concern is ensuring the coherence of expectations within communication between members of group—expectations based on a familiar repertoire of proven and well-rehearsed (that is, normal) forms. Producers of text have access to a repertoire of schemata that they can utilize with respect to their intended audience and its typical dispositions. Recipients are given points of reference for determining which kinds of texts or what genres should be given preference in certain situations, and during reception readers can draw on specific previous knowledge and experience. Florian Coulmas interprets his verbal stereotypes as conventional routine formulas, "in which situations, expectations, and effects are correlated with one another in a standardized [and accepted] manner and which, as such, represent an important means for the institutional control of social behavior."[167]

This idea can be easily expanded to include conventional forms of text, for instance stereotypes in (filmic) narration. Developed over time, tried and tested, and subsequently solidified, these stereotypes as textual elements can also be considered to mediate between the disposition of the audience, the authors (or filmmakers), and cultural institutions. Stephen Heath has a related view on film genres, which are nothing else than complex family groupings of interdependent stereotypes: "instances of equilibrium, characteristic relatings—specific relations—of subject and machine in film as particular closures of desire."[168] This will be discussed further in the "Genre" section of chapter 2.

A second function of stereotypization as conventionalization is at least as significant for *specific text-oriented stereotype concepts*, including those relating to film. Convention plays a fundamental role in semiotic processes, for without it there are no signs. In considering the emergence of stereotypes, particularly those in cinema, one may show through examples how a new semantic fact comes into being through the sedimentation of a textual pattern and its accompanying conventionalization en bloc and begins to take on a life of its own.

In the semantic analysis of his routine formulas Coulmas had emphasized the inadequacy of the principle of lexical decomposition and instead proposed a functional theory of meaning, which accounts for the formula's new *social meaning*—with the latter tending to obscure the original propositional meaning. This idea can also be applied to the semiotic dimension. In *Elements of Semiology*, Roland Barthes mentions "sign-functions"[169] and discusses how in the social sphere even the semantization of simple utilitarian objects is inevitable: "*as soon as there is a society, every usage is converted into a sign of itself*; the use of a raincoat is to give protection from the rain, but this use cannot be disassociated from the very signs of an atmospheric situation."[170]

This kind of *semantization through use, which consequently inscribes the customary context of use onto the repeated sign*, occurs to an even greater extent with textual formulas. As overarching variables, they undergo a *secondary semantization* and take on a referential function that points to the given context, for example, to the text type or genre in which they have developed—or also to the historical period in which they originally appeared. From the vantage point of a theory of the stereotype, this means that is possible to comprehend the gradual development of complex signs—a process that has generally been neglected in semiological studies (of film).

THIRD FACET: DISTORTION AND LOSS

Constructs identified as *stereotypes* can hardly be said to fully coincide with the beliefs or forms of expression of the individual making this identification. The act of declaring something a stereotype is usually associated with critical distanciation. In other words, another similarity between various discourses on stereotypes is that they are almost always discourses about (at least latent) distortion or loss of meaning. The stereotype hence appears as an *ambivalent* phenomenon.

This ambivalence already results from facets discussed so far. Each stereotype function indicated as productive has its "other" side. The idea of the schema amounted to a construct that reduces complexity and variation—that is, that deindividualizes, generalizes, accentuates, and thus provides "psychically reliable simplifications."[171] As necessary as this proves to be for the functioning of perception, orientation, and communication, it simultaneously presents the issue of losses and distortions in the representation of reality; these are caused by reduction, on the one hand, and the effects of stimuli classification (generalization/dichotomization), on the other. Accordingly, this problem belongs to the standard repertoire of discourses on stereotypes.

More urgent objections arise when the *conventionality* of stereotypes is at issue and when they are seen to insert themselves as *intersubjective, standardizing* schemata (in the construction of reality or the aesthetic construction of the artifact). As *second-hand formulas* that an individual receives "from the outside," stereotypes are already under the suspicion of being assimilated without passing through any checks. Hence, additional fears of alienation and manipulation also play a role, for stereotypes may correspond with social interests. This particularly applies to *very obviously* conventional ideas, which are often based entirely on projected attributions to objects not part of an individual's immediate realm of experience. For example, stereotypical ideas about foreign cultures and people largely depend on culturally transmitted illusions instead of "hard facts." Such ideas reveal more about the respective group or society authoring the stereotype than about the actual topic.

It follows that these kinds of patterns have become a popular subject in stereotype research, particularly in social psychology, ethnology, or cultural studies, and most pronounced in research that primarily focuses on the *difference* between cognitive formula and reality (or one's construction of reality). Here the theme of the stereotype is tangent to the classical concept of *doxa*, which since antiquity has been associated with appearance and belief in contrast to reality and knowledge. In his study on literary clichés, Rüdiger Kunow uses *doxa* in this sense. Following Husserl, he thus describes basic elements of how knowledge is acquired within the scope of everyday cognition: "sedimented or habitualized elements of meaning,"[172] that is, convictions one has ceased to question.

Here an additional issue factors into the discussion. Pointing out that stereotypes reduce diversity and create social interference as *second-hand formulas*, those warning of *distortion* also refer to another specific feature of many stereotypes, especially those shaping fictional narratives as schematic ideas. In many cases, these stereotypes refer to mythical worlds of the imaginary instead of factual representations of reality. Based on Wolfgang Iser's "triad of the real, the fictive, and the imaginary"[173]—a concept that I will allude to again later in this study—it can be said that stereotypes in fictional texts are often more an expression of "dreams, daydreams, and hallucinations"[174] than of representations intended to truthfully portray reality. Stereotypes thus crystallize the imaginary's transition from the vague and merely individual into an interpersonal fact, which then takes on a reality of its own through conventionality.

Similar (and also related) to *doxa* is another conflict, with a history extending back to antiquity, between a kind of *primitive thought*, forms of which Lévi-Strauss studied as myth, and the ideal of a rational worldview, which appeals to reason and claims to be a redemption of truth. It is obvious that neither manner of understanding the world—*mythos versus logos* or the *imaginary versus reason*—will ever manage to fully displace and supplant the other nor appear in pure form.

As has often been observed, everyday thought and the fictitious, highly imaginative worlds of media entertainment are particularly ruled by the principles of myth.[175] Stereotypes produced by cyclically organized representations of the imaginary can consequently be interpreted as nodes within given mythical microcosms. The critique of stereotypes and their distorting effects, which was and sometimes still is common in social psychology and in classical media criticism, is aimed at the imaginary and mythological forms of thought *behind* the cognitive schemata crystallized in stereotypes. As such, it can also be understood as part of the age-old rationalist criticism of myth.

The previously emphasized *affective dimensions* of many stereotypes and the emotional baggage that they carry are also antithetical to attempts to adequately represent reality, since such attachment intensifies inertia and habitualism.

The explicit emphasis on stability reveals another crucial aspect of the issue of loss and distortion, independent of the problem of the imaginary. The reference to stability and inertia in regard to mental or textual[176] schemata itself stresses stasis, inactivity, and automatic processes, and it is used to indicate a conflict with the *dynamics* of reality. This summons Bergson's classic loss-and-distortion problem, in which living processes are subject to mechanical retardation. According to this idea, "Our intelligence ... has for its chief object the unorganized solid"[177] and thus cannot ever fully do justice to the creative, flowing developments of life. The mind thus follows this dynamic—likened to a "cinematographical mechanism"[178]—as fitfully as frozen individual frames. This idea takes on an extra dimension in light of the persistence of stereotypes, whatever form they may take. Namely, if a stereotype, as sedimentation, is adapted to specific types of (behavioral) contexts, then it certainly is appropriate to question its adequacy, given the variable situations in which it is activated.

A second fundamental issue—in addition to the cognitive deficiencies discussed so far—is raised by the emphasis on the conventional nature of stereotypes within the *organization of a text*: the *losses affecting aesthetic or stylistic expression*. Most stereotype concepts concerned with aesthetics touch on this problem. The recourse to automatized and conventionalized schemata can ultimately be considered antagonistic to the pursuit of the most original form of expression possible. The second-hand nature of stereotypes is articulated and problematized in opposition to individuality and originality, and the "banality" of largely reproductive and redundant formulas is viewed in opposition to innovation, that is, to real information—hereby combining aesthetic with cognitive deficits. A related issue is the erosion of frequently perceived forms, in which habitual apperception causes an emotional flattening of experience and information on the part of the recipient—even to the point that one is no longer fully conscious of the perceived form. Theorists such as Riffaterre, Lotman, and Hauser have, however, repeatedly pointed out that using originality as an absolute criteria is, at the very least, one sided and, historically speaking, a quite recent phenomenon. Moreover, original and fresh ideas can result from the tension-filled and *dialectical* interplay with stereotypes.

We now have a general overview of the repertoire of classic "points of friction" that appear within different stereotype discourses in varying constellations and degrees of emphasis (in particular, these aspects of aesthetics will be discussed further on). Essentially, the perception of these kinds of frictions and instances of loss and distortion is what facilitates thinking about schematism and stability. It is the main reason why stereotypes become *conspicuous*. It seems that the condition for identifying something as a stereotype is that the given construct has somehow detached itself from the context in which it developed and functioned smoothly—automatically and adequately—and is therefore now experienced as problematic, as a phenomenon of loss and distortion.

This *detachment and problematization* of the stereotype may occur in two different basic ways. First, when a stabilized schema is applied to a different context from the one for which it was originally suited: for example, when someone (a producer or recipient of a text) attempts to meet qualitatively altered demands (such as other text types or different communicative situations) by adhering to a previously well-functioning stereotype—while being unwilling or unable to adjust. In such cases, the discrepancy between the pattern and the context can be described as *functional inadequacy*.

Second, a stabilized schema may also be *perceived* as a stereotype when it is *deliberately taken out of context and placed within a different horizon of reflection*. This is the case when a schema, which basically functions well in certain contexts, is critically investigated from the perspective of potentially more complex, or at least altered, expectations and experiences. This kind of deautomatization or denaturalization can cause the schema to appear impoverished, reductive, or cognitively distorted. This second method, of particular relevance to intellectuals' discourse on popular film, is based on a *shift in perspective*.

However, fundamental critiques of the stereotype often equate the second case with the first or, in using absolutist arguments, are not at all prepared to make this distinction. In contrast, pragmatic and functional proponents *of the value of stereotypes* generally argue on the level of inadequacy through a shift in perspective. That means that while—from the perspective of their own analysis and reflection—they stress losses and distortions, they simultaneously justify stereotypes as a necessary condition for textual functioning within the analyzed context.

To the extent that they are mentioned, cases of functional inadequacy are treated with critical distance. The latter is sometimes linguistically articulated by differentiating between stereotype (acceptable) and cliché[179] (unacceptable). In order to avoid such cases, theorists from Lippmann to Gombrich have regularly argued for a flexible, self-critical, and adaptable attitude toward one's own inventory of stereotypes. Overall, arguments in defense of stereotypes still underscore—from a *marked critical distance* and rightly—a certain *ambivalence* inherent to the phenomenon.

FOURTH FACET: A GROUND FOR DIFFERENCES

Involving an accentuation of similarity and a reflection on the power, benefits, and deficits of repetition, automatization, and convention, stereotype discourses also include seemingly conflicting ideas, namely, about the creation of difference. However, recurrent, conventional patterns essentially provide a ground for difference. It is only possible to talk about variation meaningfully if it is clear what is routine.

Every modernization results from the interaction of innovation and tradition, and every stylistic novelty is, with respect to its innovatory quality, always based on the conventional forms from which it departs or with which it breaks. Therefore, in regard to the problem of text and reception the *interplay between two (interdependent) levels upon which stereotypes rest* is always important. On the one hand, stereotypes exist as mental constructs in the minds of individuals (and in extreme cases in the minds of all members of a community), including producers and recipients of texts. On the other hand, stereotypes are outwardly manifested and communicated as particular structures or *schemata of textual organization*, for which the texts serve as a kind of physical support. These two "levels" exist in constant interaction; even a stereotype entailed in a text is not as "hard" a fact as it might initially appear.

A stereotype always transcends the immanence of an individual text and moves into the intertextual. Its perception *as a stereotype* presupposes that it is recognized as a discursively conventional schema. In other words, in order to be realized as a stereotype, the schema must correspond to the repertoire of conventions, and that repertoire ultimately only exists as a viable entity if it is present as a mental factor in the minds of the recipients.

Stereotypes are developed, articulated, conventionalized, and mentally ingrained more or less through the reciprocal interaction of these two levels. However, once a stereotype has become established, each level exhibits its own dynamics. Stereotypes as patterns of reading can be applied to texts—out of extreme satisfaction in experiencing déjà vu—that do not conform to them (Amossy's *stereotyped reading*). Alternately, stereotyped texts may encounter recipients who perceive these stereotypes as original creations, because they have not (yet) learned the appropriate mental construct or the necessary degree of critical distance over the course of their reading experience.

At the same time, it becomes possible to play with difference in a range of ways when texts incorporate well-entrenched schemata. Both Hauser and Gombrich describe a more or less simple notion of variation linked to a concept of realism of sorts; they argue for the stereotype as a starting point of creative production, in which the former should then undergo—in relation to the depicted external object—a process of correction on the part of the artist and of adaptation to the reality intended to be represented (with the stereotype being blurred and disguised for the recipient).

Lotman went even further in the deliberate play with difference by incorporating a critical stance toward the stereotype into his concept. Both in the context of an "aesthetics of identity" and an "aesthetics of opposition," the use of a stereotype directly summons an awareness of it in the viewer, which goes beyond mere habitualism. *Reflexivity* comes into play. As illustrated by his example of the commedia dell'arte, the aesthetics of identity demands, at one end of the spectrum, a deliberate presentation and reading of conventional types *as conventional types*, that is, as stereotypes. Although this lessens the propositional significance of the characters, and they are then experienced not so much as direct representations of reality but as roles played out in an imaginary world, it enhances the possibilities for freely improvising with the stereotypes. The concept of the "aesthetics of opposition" also mobilizes the specifically addressed stereotypes, *at least in absentia*, but only to build up an expectation that is unexpectedly *disappointed* or countered and refuted.

The more sedimented and conventionalized a recurrent pattern is, the more reliably it can be played upon in all kinds of configurations of difference. Something similar begins to happen outside of verbal language, which Coulmas describes with respect to his linguistic stereotypes as a shift from recurrent events in language use (*parole*) to events in the language system (*langue*).

This will be elaborated more fully in the following sections with regard to film culture and its corresponding theoretical discourses.

TWO
SOME ASPECTS AND LEVELS
OF STEREOTYPIZATION IN FILM

Completely subjective and spontaneous experience free from each and every
conventional and stereotypical element is a just a borderline concept, an abstract
idea which bears no relation to reality.

—ARNOLD HAUSER, *THE SOCIOLOGY OF ART* (1974)

Chapter 1 was concerned with the differentiation between and specification of various concepts of the word "stereotype" and their theoretical contexts. It also outlined the four facets that contain elements of a comprehensive understanding of the term. This should prove helpful in the more detailed
elaboration of aspects and elements of stereotypization in film undertaken in this
chapter, as the world of film also presents sedimented schema or patterns that are
used repeatedly in long intertextual sequences. Such patterns are intersubjectively
well established with the general audience and have long become conventional.
They seem abbreviated, in the manner of templates or formulas, and are thus often
perceived as "clichés." At the same time, they can be interpreted as functionally
adapted to their context, that is, as "canned" effects. These patterns also serve as
a constant challenge to—and basis for—aesthetically ambitious concepts relying
on all sorts of forms of play with stereotype and difference.

It is practically impossible to make *sweeping generalizations* about film stereotypes. One the one hand, stereotypization encompasses very different "levels" of
film: the construction of the characters and plot, image and sound, as well as the
acting. Stereotype theory even plays a central role in the conceptualization of
film genre. On the other hand, in part due to the kinds of stereotypes presented
in films, sociopsychological research (and corresponding stereotype concepts) is
relevant to the stereotype in film, as is research that—much like concepts previously discussed in the context of idiomatics, literature, and art history—primarily

addresses aspects of cinematic narration and presentation in film, medium-specific visual and narrative worlds, and *their* recurrent forms. In the following, the relationship between these (partially overlapping) approaches will be examined more closely with respect to characters in film.

CHARACTERS

According to the understanding of the term in sociology, social psychology, and ethnology—as previously elaborated—the "stereotype" primarily describes conceptions concerning social or ethnic groups and their members, usually "images of the Other" or, less often, "images of the Self." It seems appropriate to apply this concept to film, in order to examine how the characters in a narrative represent, influence, or shape certain conceptions about people.

Indeed, this has been, and remains, the classic interpretation of the stereotype in film analysis based on social psychology, ethnology, cultural studies, or ideological criticism. Within these theoretical contexts, this approach suggests itself to a certain extent. Understood as simply structured and stable mental images of individuals belonging to certain groups—ideas rooted in everyday cultural consciousness and therefore conventionalized—stereotypes obviously serve as important reference points for the creation of fictional characters. For spectatorship to function, it matters that a film and its characters, as the key factors of audience participation in the plot, closely relate to the world of everyday beliefs and values.

This interaction also works in the opposite direction. Popular media narratives actively affect the audience's imagination, even if only by visually shaping and concretizing current schemata of thought and thus supplying a repertoire of vivid patterns. Irmela Schneider[1] has pointed out that German conceptions about Americans (or, better said, members of certain groups in the United States) were significantly influenced by American TV series and their visual representations of typical character patterns. Much the same can be said about films, especially with a view to the pre-TV era.

This situation prompted progressive attempts to raise awareness about the perceived limitedness or distortedness of conventional "images of the Other," to create a more differentiated view, and to correct these perceptions. Such projects were also based on the (hoped-for) positive effect that films could have on audience dispositions. This became an important issue in cinema and in film journalism, particularly in the heyday of ideological criticism during the 1970s and early 1980s. Engaged filmmakers sought to intervene in the viewers' social imaginary, as did Rainer Werner Fassbinder with his film *Angst Essen Seelen Auf* (*Ali: Fear Eats the Soul*, West Germany, 1973), to name but one example. Such films generally aimed to expose negative and malicious stereotypes, especially about foreigners and minorities, and foreground the superficiality and distortedness of these prejudices. As with the character of the North African immigrant Ali in Fassbinder's film, the aim was to invoke a pattern, exaggerate it, and then take it to the point of absurdity by the staging of obvious difference—thus tangibly revealing the stereotype as a deficient, distorted image. In short, in the name of reality and humanity, the intention was to criticize such stereotypes as crystallizations of a false consciousness. Fassbinder addressed the inhuman dynamic—entrapping almost all of the film's characters—of social behavior governed by ignorant stereotypes.

Not coincidentally but part of the same discourse and orientation is the considerable number of film and media studies published in the 1970s and 1980s that emphasized, as did Steve Neale's work,[2] playing with difference in relation to stereotypical "images of the Other" and criticizing these patterns in film.

Given such interest, it is even less surprising that many film scholars and critics of other narrative media, including Richard Dyer,[3] initially adopted the notion of the stereotype as a *sociopsychological* category and then simply applied it to film characters. In such contexts, characters labeled as "stereotypes" are usually those that, *also in a narrative sense,* quite openly embody "images of the Other." These characters not only correspond to the content of stereotypical conceptions about members of certain groups, but, *as narrative or aesthetic* constructs and *conventional artifacts* in and of themselves, they are reduced to a limited number of conspicuous characteristics with multiple intertextual repetitions en bloc. As Neale states: "According to this problematic, a stereotype is a stable and repetitive structure of character traits."[4]

This is where the topic of the stereotype also comes into play as a *narrative mode*, a "mode of characterization in fiction,"[5] according to Dyer. The stereotype here functions in the broader sense elaborated in the previous chapter, beyond the limited scope of social psychology. This more general understanding emphasizes elements of automatization or conventionalization, on the one hand, and schematism and reduction of complexity on the other. In this spirit, Dyer extensively analyzed the two-faced "dumb blonde stereotype"[6]—both as an everyday idea and as a concrete character pattern of the cinematic narrative imaginary, established in the 1930s and mainly influenced by American films featuring actresses such as Jean Harlow or Marilyn Monroe.

Underlying the sociopsychological discourse on stereotypical perception and thought is always the juxtaposition of accurate, unprejudiced, and patient observations of the Other, on the one hand, and the rapid recourse to reductive and distorted conventional images, which function as prejudices or preconceptions supplanting actual observations, on the other hand. It therefore stands to reason that a similar antagonism is prevalent in narratology, which commonly distinguishes "individual characters" from "types" when discussing narrative figures.

Individual characters only become discernable over the course of the narrated story; they develop in interaction with plot events and are endowed with an individual and complex intellectual-psychological profile. Using slightly different terminology, Umberto Eco makes a similar distinction. Envisaging a character spectrum, he identifies at one end those who attain "a complete physiognomy . . . which is not merely exterior, but also intellectual and moral."[7] With reference to Lukács, Eco observes that ideally such characters can attain an "intellectual physiognomy,"[8] which readers gradually recognize as the *actual goal of the reading process.* Such characters, he argues further, "never exist prior to the work, but mark its success."[9] In other words, in such a case the narrative aims to convey to the readers psychologically layered, multifaceted figures who develop bit by bit over the course of the storyline. This is a concept of narrative and characterization, which ultimately may be realized similarly in film and literature.

At the other end of the spectrum are figures that appear as schematic constructs recognizable by a select few pronounced attributes. "When a person enters the scene, he or she is already complete: defined, weighed, and minted,"[10] writes Eco. He cites Dumas's d'Artagnan as an example of a character lacking psychological complexity and any sign of individual development. Once he is introduced, we learn nothing new about d'Artagnan beyond the exciting events that are conveyed through the vehicle of his presence in the scene, which he survives practically unscathed. "While he entertained us splendidly with his adventures, we realized that the author essentially tells us nothing about him, and d'Artagnan's adventures in no way determine him. His presence was a matter of coincidence . . . d'Artagnan serves as a pretext for the staging of events."[11] Eco's argument prompts two comments: First, as a "pretext for the staging of events," such figures are not really incidental; their construction is precisely attuned to fulfilling a narrative *function*. In other words, their specific attributes and the narrative program attached to them time and again enable and convey particular events and plot sequences. In this context, Manfred Pfister coined the fitting description of the "action-functional structuring"[12] of figures. From this perspective, the individual adventures experienced by d'Artagnan do not really sway or change him. The function of surviving certain types of adventures, of playing a clearly defined and consistent role in the plot, determines the figure through and through. If there is such a thing as self-realization for such a figure, then it comes by way of manifesting the rule.

Second, the poignancy of such figures is enhanced when they are characterized by a few particularly obvious, semantically clear and stable traits, which are further heightened by pairing the figures with counterfigures—sometimes one constant antagonist but also alternating, similarly structured counterparts of related schematic structure. Creating such pairs of opposites accentuates the unique qualities of the figures, and thus the discrepancy between them, to a greater extent than already effected by the formation of types.[13] This allows readers and film spectators to rapidly assign values and meaning, provides clarity, and propels the plot forward by creating conflicts.

Incidentally, the (figural) spectrum from individual characters to types as outlined here largely corresponds to E. M. Forster's distinction between "flat" and "round" characters: "Flat characters were called 'humorous' in the seventeenth century, and are sometimes called types. . . . In their purest form, they are constructed round a single idea or quality: when there is more than one factor in them, we get the beginning of the curve towards the round."[14] For round characters "cannot be summed up in a single phrase," and we remember them in connection with the scenes through which they "passed and as modified by those scenes"; round characters have "facets like human being."[15] Finally: "The test of a round character is whether it is capable of surprising in a convincing way. If it never surprises, it is flat. If it does not convince, it is a flat pretending to be round. It [the round character] has the incalculability of life about it—life within the pages of a book."[16]

Referring to film, Dyer makes a very similar distinction to that of Forster and Eco, which he describes as opposition between "novelistic character" and "type."[17] In doing so, he explicitly draws a close connection between the sociopsychological term "stereotype" (the image of the Other) and "type"—as a character construct in narrative fiction. Eco also originally discussed this second kind of character as a "type" only to then later favor the expression "topos," which transcends the reductive characteristics and stability of a character within a text to underscore the aspect of conventionality and the intertextual nature of such characters. Eco's "topos" largely approximates the *narrative understanding* (suggested here) of the "figural stereotype" as a conventional artifact:

> As useful and harmless as they [the "types"] are, they function as patterns of the imagination. . . . They would thus be better described as *topoi*, as places, that can be readily transferred into conventions and used effortlessly. The *topos* as a pattern of imagination is employed excellently where . . . the character recalled takes the place of a compositional act of the imagination; it relieves us.[18]

Although opposed to "individual character," "type" and "figural stereotype" (or Eco's "topos") are not a priori equivalent. A type developed in a text only then becomes a narrative topos—and thus a figural or character stereotype—when it has established itself as a *conventional figure pattern by means of repetition in the intertextual space of narration.*

Thus, the *stereotypization* of the type initially constructed by a text may occur in a second step: the *intertextual phase of type formation* produces an independent cultural fact, a conventional artifact of narrative imagination. For example, the screen vamp—whose external characteristics (primarily costume and make-up but also habitus) originally drew on the tradition of the Italian diva—underwent its cinematographic conventionalization through repeated performances in silent cinema. The vamp thus became an established *symbol of an audiovisual narrative imagination*, a figure closely related to allegory and inspiring a broad spectrum of similar film plots.[19]

Mostly, however, theoretical studies conceive "type" as fully developed stereotype: there is a general fondness for citing the standardized figures from the world of the Italian commedia dell'arte or the comparable arsenal of characters from seventeenth- and eighteenth-century French theater as particularly obvious examples.[20] The intention here is not to pursue the futile aim of reforming prevailing terminology, but it should be pointed out that the development of the kinds of *fixed* types, such as those that make up the intertextual imaginary world of genre films (for example, Westerns or swashbuckler films), concerns a second, conventionalized level of type formation; namely, it is a situation of *narrative stereotypization*, as discussed below.[21]

This differentiation also paves the way for an argument made by Stanley Cavell, who postulates that in advanced popular cinema narration is based more on types than on stereotypes: "Types are exactly what carry the forms movies have relied upon. These media created new types; or combinations and ironic reversals of types; but there they were and stayed."[22] But, as Cavell asks: "Does this mean that movies can never create individuals, only types?"[23] His answer to this question is bound to irritate anyone failing to distinguish between the character as a type or stereotype: "What it means is that this [creating types] is the movies' way of creating individuals: they create *individualities*. For what makes someone a type is not his similarity with other members of that type but his striking separateness from other people."[24]

What Cavell here claims (while discussing Panofsky, by the way) is that, since the classical phase of popular cinema, *individualities* have been more important than "stereotype"[25] figures, which migrate through films as conventional constructs of intertextually repeating characteristics and attributes—that is, as virtual readymades, much like the figures of early silent cinema. For Cavell such *individualities*, apparently created in individual films (or through a single popular character), develop first and foremost through an emphasis of difference, a figure's "striking separateness" from other figures, primarily from its coplayers or antagonists, but also from the people in the audience's everyday surroundings. One might add that such separateness is also achieved through an internal reduction of complexity, that is, through *intra*textual schematization. Insofar as such individualities are not necessarily *individual characters* in the sense described above, they are, as Cavell also states, types but not stereotypes.

In this instance, Cavell certainly underestimates the significance that figural stereotypes, established types, and general processes of conventionalization—also in terms of characters—have always had in popular film, particularly in Hollywood's genre films.[26] Studies on the presence of "stock characters"[27] in Hollywood substantiate this, should this be necessary. Then again, the differentiation between type and stereotype that implicitly emerges in Cavell's work does provide a degree of conceptual clarity. For example, it helps to distinguish between the original invention of a character type and its later (potential) stereotypization. On this basis, it is also easier to describe the differences that often exist between major and minor characters (and stock characters in particular).

So far it should be evident that narrative figural stereotypes are not a matter of mere translations or narrative-visual manifestations of the "images of the Other" as studied in social psychology under the catchphrase of the "stereotype." In fact, *two different aspects* of stereotypization can be distinguished as regards the *relationship between film characters and reality*.[28] These two aspects are interrelated and partially overlap but are not equivalent to each other.

The *social-science concept of the stereotype* (also relating to the study of film characters) raises questions such as: what sociologically relevant cultural "images of the Other," of members of certain countries, professions, minorities, or groups existing in society, are represented or influenced by film? "National types as Hollywood presents them"—the topic and approach of a study by Siegfried Kracauer from the 1950s[29]—is characteristic of the interest in the representation of such conceptions. This concerns "types" from everyday life, conventional and schematic common-sense notions about *the* Americans, *the* Russians, *the* Turks, *the* Germans, or in other contexts *the* homosexual, *the* housewife, and so on. In other words, these are ideas that—as questionable as they may be—claim a certain intrinsic validity in daily life and determine attitudes toward such groups. They can be of immediate significance for practical behavior and social interaction and are *therefore* a preferred subject of both social science and political discourses.

What needs to be set apart here is the second aspect, the *narrative concept of the stereotype*, which mainly concerns the *narrative mode* in which fictional characters are rendered. This concept does not necessarily rely on social psychology's construct of the stereotype. The narrative concept also includes character constructs intended as imaginary and common to a specific story genre, such the Western—constructs with a particular claim to validity in this context, that is, *the context of the imaginary worlds of narration.* Such constructs in fact do not bear *any* relationship (or only very indirectly) to the daily and immediate social interactions of audience members.

If stereotypes in the first sense are defined by their sociopsychological function as creations based in reality with consequences for the *world of daily life,* the second concept underscores the function of stereotypes as relatively autonomous conventional constructs serving the *intertextual worlds of the imagination.* This differentiation can sometimes prove complicated in the case of a specific character construct, since it is hardly ever possible to make an absolute distinction between even obviously imaginary narrative worlds and recipients' mental images of their daily world. For even the latter always include imaginary elements (influenced by the media). In addition, both "kinds" of stereotypes often overlap and intertwine. Hence the use of the word "aspects" to describe different forms of stereotypization that may coincide in a single figure, if the character functions both as a stereotype in the sense of the narrative mode *and* as the embodiment of a stereotypical "image of the Other" that lays claim to reality.

Here one might recall the figure of the militaristic German, which developed into a narrative stereotype of American cinema through the actor Erich von Stroheim, among others. While this figure drew on culturally established ideas, it also produced an independent, fixed narrative form, a type that soon became conventional, a "mask." Through a unique and latently comic exaggeration of traits, a certain bearing, and limited and clearly displayed attributes, this figure began to take on a life of its own in the conventional and playful realm of the imaginary. This independence was expressed by the fact that the narrative type soon managed to swing toward an amusing and almost even likeable comedy stereotype, although the figure was originally based on a clearly negative sociopsychological stereotype.

Having become conventional, narrative patterns typically exhibit this kind of independence. The same can be repeatedly observed in stereotypes of Soviet officials—for example, in the corresponding characters in Ernst Lubitsch's *Ninotchka* (1939) and Billy Wilder's *One, Two, Three* (1961). The same applies to stereotypical psychiatrists—as in *Mr. Deeds Goes to Town* (Frank Capra, 1936), *Stardust Memories* (Woody Allen, 1980), and *The Hudsucker Proxy* (Ethan and Joel Coen, 1994), among others. The "drunken journalist" is a very similar case, as Howard Good's "biography" of this figural stereotype shows.[30]

A pattern tends to become *derealized* as it gradually undergoes conventionalization. Characters first seeming to be plausible representations of reality increasingly resemble puppets in a game as they become entities of convention. In this vein, Yuri Lotman's comments on the commedia dell'arte:

> The unpitying nature of Italian (and not only Italian) folk theater is organically connected with its conventionality. The audience remembers that these are puppets or maskers on the stage and perceives their death or suffering, beatings or misfortunes, not as the death or suffering of real people, but in a spirit of carnival and ritual. Germi's films would be unbearably cynical if he invited us to see real people in his characters.[31]

Even though it is almost impossible to separately identify or systematize the complex interactions between both aspects of stereotypization, it still makes sense to differentiate between the two. For a stereotyped "image of the Other" can, on the one hand, serve as the basis for filmic characters that are much more subtly developed in the narrative mode and do not operate as character stereotypes in this sense, as fixed intertextual narrative types. These are characters whose individual configurations are "variations" on a (sociopsychological) pattern, which is superficially "reindividualized" in the narration. On the other hand, as mentioned earlier, there exists a whole range of conventionalized intertextual types (that is, stereotypes in the sense of the narrative mode), which have little to do with an "image of the Other" and are consciously perceived to be patterns of imaginary worlds as opposed to the actual world.

Such intertextual types shape the imaginary and allow it to become real as an *open imaginary construct*, a fixed communicative entity. As "fairy-tale figures," character stereotypes are stable templates of the imagination. It would be a crude misinterpretation of characters such as the swashbuckler of the adventure genre, the typage of the Western, or the stock characters of science-fiction films to automatically consider them "images of the Other" intended as realistic or worthy of criticism for their lack of reality.[32] The only frame within which the audience expects to find such characters is the imaginary, intertextually constituted *fantasy world of a genre*. Within the conventional networks of a genre, such figures are appreciated as sedimented schemata, as narrative stereotypes, and consequently as ritual entities. *This is where* their absence or fundamental alteration would not only cause confusion, but it would possibly damage or even explode a genre. In contrast, the relationship between such patterns and the recipient's everyday reality is (aside from pubescent misunderstandings) rather indirect and usually a highly mediated correspondence. It is merely the relationship that every form of imagination *ultimately* has to the world of real experience.

The expectations maintained toward the imaginary world of an individual genre stem from character stereotypes, as narrative forms, being geared toward receptive dispositions—in other words, toward needs. These stereotypes do not function as representations perceived as realistic, as vehicles of knowledge, but as personified agents of a repeatable experience of pleasure found in a ritualized, self-similar game constantly offered anew by the individual films of a genre. It is appropriate to attribute figural stereotypes with serious functions for the chosen kind of narration and its alignment with widespread cultural dispositions. The configuration of such characters is shaped and then gradually sedimented in the intertextual sphere in accordance with how successfully these functions are perceived.

Incidentally, such pragmatic thinking proves valuable far beyond the narrative stereotypes of "banal" genre film. With a view to art history, Ernst Gombrich argues for a similarly pragmatic approach to aesthetic facts, which include conventional stylistic forms: "As long as painting is conceived as serving such a human purpose, one has a right to discuss the means in relation to these ends."[33] He also observed the effect of the "idea of an 'economy of means'"[34] in classical works of art and talks about "the element of a problem solution in art,"[35] which takes place by recourse to a series of reoccurring, specific demands. The narrative figural stereotypes of film, that is, *conventional* types, can be interpreted as this very sort of "readymade" solution to a problem. They can be considered as pragmatic entities of a context- and function-based standardization of narration, as recurrent, conventional patterns of storytelling. From this perspective, they are similar to the linguistic stereotypes investigated by Florian Coulmas.[36] The pragmalinguist also understood linguistic stereotypes as pragmatic elements of situation- and function-oriented standardization.

Once the concept of the stereotype regarding the world of filmic characters has been divided into the two basic aspects already described—and having thus been emancipated from a naïve sociopsychological standpoint—it soon becomes evident that mechanisms of stereotypization factor into a whole range of phenomena affecting the world of characters in popular (film) narrative. This includes figures that would seem to lay greater claim to individuality than to stereotypy. *Popular figures* ranging from Sherlock Holmes to James Bond traverse a large number of films, which are structured around and focused on them, along with narratives in other media (literature, TV series, comics, etc.). These two characters originated in literature but only became really successful once they entered film. Such popular characters relate to the question of the stereotype in at least one respect,

insofar as behind the specific character there is a form of narrative-type development, which is embodied in the individual persona. This is the *personification* of a
relatively stable narrative figural type, which *repeatedly* appears in a large number
of texts or films: a *personification* that becomes conventional *in and of itself*—as
a concrete figure with a name—and that is copied by closely related characters
appearing in competing productions within the same genre.

Even the concept of the *star*, in which individuality paradoxically plays a central role,[37] is based on elementary facets of the stereotype. The appearance of the
star provides an object for the projection of an *imago*—a mental image emerging
from the intertextual sphere and formed by superimposed layers of (usually at first
similarly typed) characters, which are represented by different roles and repetitive
elements of the star image in media publicity.[38]

As a product of the popular media, the imago is schematically simplified in its
complexity and designed to conform to the fantasies, desires, and predispositions
of the audience. This imago has emerged from the stores of cultural experience as
a stable template of expectation. The imago is a notion that, once established and
maintained by the cult of the star, even configures an actor's *off-screen image*—
including the publicly communicated representation of an actor's "real" personality. This does not change much, even when with the advanced sedimentation
of the image—both on-screen and in media representations of the star's private
life—there occurs a usually limited play with differences, shifts, and (less often)
provocative contrasts. Even the play with differences critiquing a conventional
pattern—as expressed by the character Roslyn in *The Misfits* (John Huston, USA,
1961) in regard to the imago of Marilyn Monroe, for example—remains a possible
way of appropriating stereotypes.

EMPLOTMENT AND IMAGINARY WORLDS

A study of stereotypes accounting for the *development of stable structures of the
imaginary* must necessarily look beyond issues relevant solely to characters. Not
only figural schemata are subject to conventionalization within the intertextual field. *Situations and sequences in narrated plots*—in addition to many other
phenomena—evince very similar tendencies toward reductive schematization
and conventionalization. This is particularly true of the kinds of texts that operate more with conventional types than with individual characters. This has to
do with the fact that the types introduced are not only schematized and conventionalized on the basis of their dispositions, physical attributes, or mental
make-up; instead, they are also, according to Asmuth, constituted as "embodi-

ments of plot functions"[39] and are thus associated with specific programs of action (*programme d'action*).[40]

Figural stereotypes influence a wide field of popular narration, particularly that of genre films, television, literature, comics, and so on. Well-rehearsed patterns—also of plot—are consequently not a problem unique to film. Rather, it is a characteristic that popular narratives in the medium of film share with those of other media. As early as the mid-1920s, Viktor Shklovsky, a member of the Russian formalist circle, formulated a similar idea in response to a literary phenomenon, namely the publication of two Tarzan novels by the Soviet state press: "The mass reader loves the endless repetition of the ever-same adventures, and he enjoys when they are always overcome in the same manner."[41] In fact, this tendency toward consolidated regularities has even older origins in literature. As Joachim Paech has shown, popular film as a "legitimate heir to the nineteenth-century narrative tradition"[42] has also assumed this legacy.

Further still, one cannot say that an affinity for the repetition of incisive plot patterns is specifically characteristic of the nineteenth century, when mass-media narratives crystallized into a definitive form, although the period's innovative technologies of reproduction and the industrial culture of mass consumption did lend this tendency a resoundingly new dimension. The pleasure gained from the repetition of the similar is characteristic of much older folkloric and mythical narrative traditions. Every myth has been told and retold with hardly any alterations; it has been celebrated or has functioned—as Yuri Lotman puts it—as an "eternally repeating cycle."[43] For this reason, the phenomenon of repeating dense narrative schemata has received particular attention in the study of myth and folklore. It stands to reason that theories of popular film like to draw on this field of research.

In this respect, Vladimir Propp's structural analysis of the morphology of Russian folktales, first published in 1928, set the trend.[44] Propp described a stock of motifs and plot patterns that reoccur in the tales. He revealed a kind of abstract superstructure of narrative shared by almost all of the texts in the genre he studied. To achieve this, he reduced the surface complexity of the fairy tales to thirty-one "functions," which are essentially plot elements of similar functionality in the progression of the narrative. According to Propp, these elements reappear in the individual texts. By differentiating between constant and variable functions, the model retained a certain degree of flexibility.

Similarly to his treatment of the "functions," Propp examined a plethora of fairy-tale *figures* and distilled seven basic variations, each of which has a certain role, like the villain, the helper, the princess, and so on. These dramatis personae—whose characteristics match their roles—very closely approximate the basic types that reappear in the contemporary genre narration, albeit simply conceived as functional entities and therefore appearing less concrete. Finally, Propp also considered the functions of a tale to be associated with standardized spheres of action, to which the roles of individual figures are firmly tied. In other words, his analysis articulated a structurally ordered repertoire of schemata that are conventional within the Russian fairy-tale genre.

Joseph Campbell[45] worked from a similar basic idea when describing the "monomyth" of the "hero's journey" in the 1940s. However, Campbell's ambition to generalize went far beyond that of Propp. He universalized the approach developed by the latter within the context of Russian fairy tales and proclaimed the adventure as constitutive of ritual narrative in *all* cultures and even *all* periods of history. In doing so, he developed a "universal mythological formula of the adventure."[46] He described the "nuclear unit" of this schema, which he later expanded upon as "a separation from the world, a penetration to some source of power, and a life-enhancing return."[47]

Linked with this fundamental schema is a typology of figures. Apart from an altered scope of validity—expanded to the universal—Campbell's ideas exhibit another notable difference from Propp's theory. While the latter limited his focus to the structural organization of the phenomenon, Campbell gave an anthropological interpretation of the overarching similarities he formulated, which he tried to underpin with psychoanalysis. The element of return was seen to point to something "necessary to the psyche,"[48] which persists through time, as in the images of initiation produced by the human imagination throughout the ages: "All we find in the end is such a series of standard metamorphoses as men and women have undergone in every quarter of the world, in all recorded centuries, and under every odd disguise of civilization."[49] In the same sense, journeys of adventure, with their classic stations and figure constructs, were considered to reflect *archetypes* of the imagination. These archetypes are regarded as "directly valid for all mankind,"[50] since they are associated with the phases of the anthropological cycle, to which we all are bound, that is, the cycle of every human life from birth to death: "It has always been the prime function of mythology and rite to supply the symbols that carry the human spirit forward."[51]

Campbell cited Freud and to an even greater extent the archetype theory of C. G. Jung. Archetypes, as defined by Jung, represented the "Eternal Ones of the Dream" that have again and again "inspired, throughout the annals of human culture, the basic images of ritual, mythology, and vision."[52] For Campbell, myth was nothing more than a "depersonalized dream"[53] transcending time and culture. Consequentially, the fundamental elements of the hero's adventure portrayed therein themselves mutate into "basic elements of the archetypal pattern."[54]

The theory Campbell formulated in the 1940s was taken up again more recently and explicitly expanded to include film—a further application that seems quite appropriate given the self-proclaimed universality of Campbell's ideas. As a means of working through the basic patterns of successful American movies, the American author and story consultant Christopher Vogler[55] refers directly to Campbell's model of the archetype in his popular handbook for future screenplay authors, a book described as a "practical guide."[56] He not only discovers the hero's "eternal" journey in the adventure, action, and suspense genres, but he also finds it—by stretching the metaphoric terminology of travel and adventure extremely far—beneath the surface of melodramas.

Theories such as Vogler's might suggest that the archetypes in question could be considered hard and fast stereotypes of plot construction. A closer look reveals, however, that there are at least two distinct *differences between the concept of the archetype and that of the stereotype*. First, narrative archetypes as outlined by Campbell are based on rigid abstraction. All narrative forms associated with individual cultures and cultural segments, even those forms that are highly conventional in these cultures and that support specific cultural functions, are eclipsed by the claim of time-transcending universality. They merely appear as the material of an "odd disguise"[57] of the deeper layers of archetypes. As Campbell writes in his introduction: "There are of course differences between the numerous mythologies and religions of mankind, but this is a book about the similarities; and once these are understood the differences will be found to be much less great than is popularly . . . supposed."[58]

The archetype concept thus does not serve the idea of culturally specific patterns, which change over time or from genre to genre, but the notion of *ultimate anthropological similarity*. In contrast, theories operating with the concept of the stereotype are concerned with schemata that functionally refer to a specific *cultural* context, from which they derive and with which they then pass—at least as *viable* discursive entities.

What was previously discussed in relation to the figural stereotype also applies here: stereotypes are of interest as specific recurrent narrative patterns, which function *as pragmatic entities in the context- and function-based standardization of narration*. They can be adapted to the context of a genre as well as to an aesthetic mood—the fantasies, wishes, and dispositions—of a culture at a particular time. They are therefore not universal, just the opposite. The similarities between the texts to which the stereotype refers lie much closer to the surface of the texts and are far more conspicuous than is the case with the archetypes of Campbell and Vogler. Precisely these differences are of interest in examining films under the aspect of the stereotype: namely, how differences are manifested among different "families" of sedimented situations and plot elements (which specifically characterize individual genres—the Western, melodrama, etc.—or different periods within the same genre) and not what supposedly unites genres, and simultaneously all other narratives, on some deep level.

This relates to the second difference between the two approaches. Campbell conceived his archetypes as universal patterns that *are simply given*. His position coincides with that of C. G. Jung's inasmuch as they both uphold their attested archetypes as anthropological invariants, as eternal forms of the primal dream of humanity. Pivotal for a theory of the stereotype, in contrast, is the *process of gradual sedimentation*. In terms of narrative, this means conventionalization: a process occurring in multiple phases and allowing stereotypes to attain *relatively* stable forms with functions that each relate to a clearly defined cultural context.

This necessarily implies a different theoretical point of departure than that of the universalist anthropological concept of the archetype. The use of the term "stereotype" is oriented toward *culturally specific patterns of a conventional nature*. With respect to emplotment in cinematic narration, this means that the concept of the stereotype focuses on situations and processes of narrated stories, which at a given periods belong to the conventional repertoire of different individual types of filmic imagination. Propp's approach does seem more useful to this concept of the stereotype, as he attempted to find common schemata in *culturally linked* material—Russian folktales—in which actual, long-lasting conventions were operative.

In the field of cinema, the classical Western demonstrates a particularly pronounced concentration of repetitive forms. This genre and its continuation in television serials entails a full repertoire of plot schemata, which are conventional right down to the manner in which they are situationally, dramaturgically, and sometimes even visually broken down *in detail* and matched with types and settings. Setting aside any attempts to outline a structural or syntactic order, one need only recall a few classic elements as illustration: a threatening stranger (or group of strangers) riding into a town and accompanied by the fearful looks of the townspeople, antagonists provoking the hero at the bar in a saloon, the fistfight in the saloon, robberies of mail coaches and trains, chases on horseback, and the veritable ritual of the big pistol duel on the open street, which usually dramaturgically functions as a dramatic showdown and decisive contest. One could easily enumerate further narrative patterns.

The Western is a particularly consolidated, coherent, and quantitatively rich genre, but by the same principle, similar concentrations of stereotypical plot elements can be demonstrated in other genres. Whether in swashbuckler films, adventure, detective, or gangster[59] movies, science-fiction films, thrillers, horror films, melodramas, or slapstick comedies—in all cases a more or less conventional generic typage negotiates standard situations and routine plot sequences.

There are quite different contexts and functions underlying the development of such conventional plot patterns. They prove to be as diverse as the dispositions of the audience and the cultural needs that the films originally addressed. For example, narrative stereotypes reflect cultural knowledge, ideals, and aesthetic affinities, and they closely interact with the reservoir of conventional imagination intrinsic to a specific culture. However, plot stereotypes in particular reflect tried and true mechanisms for triggering the emotional effects desired when watching a film.

A number of these plot patterns supply a means—one that has proven successful within a given cultural framework—of activating identificatory or distant participation, achieving comical effects, or creating a heightened experience of tension to the point of thrill. These are all effects sought by the film audience. For instance, relatively concentrated narrative stereotypes have developed for creating suspense. Last-minute rescues, part of the standard repertoire of action and suspense since Griffith, have thus become sedimented in numerous genres through extended series of very similar plot resolutions, which correspond in numerous aspects, down to the mise en scène and the visual breakdown through camera work and editing (crosscutting). Similar conclusions can be drawn about other narrative formulas, regardless of whether they concern forms of suspense as described by Alfred Hitchcock[60] or, for example, the happy ending or other dramatic structures. Such formulas can be conceived of as having gradually emerged as conventionalized mechanisms for triggering emotional effects.

However, *narrative* stereotypes exhibit another trait generally characteristic of stereotypes: organization in open networks, that is, in conventionally linked repertoires. Narrative stereotypes thus appear in virtual family groups. Such repertoires can be identified and described as discursive phenomena from a variety of perspectives. As will be shown in greater detail further on, classical film genres are nothing more than open-structure repertoires of narrative stereotypes, which function as linked stores of cultural experience and knowledge. Genres represent frames for individual stereotypes, irrespective of whether they concern figural or narrative patterns. In addition, one stereotype evokes other stereotypes intrinsic to the genre.

This all results in an effect similar to that discussed in the section on characters. Through narrative genres, *conventional, fictional worlds* develop as discursive realities, which attain an internal plausibility, legitimacy, or coherence not primarily by mimetically referring to the recipients' knowledge of the world of actual experience but largely by drawing on stereotyped knowledge reservoirs of the imaginary. Thus narrative space becomes symbolic space, as constituted by the conventionalization of the intertextual sphere.

Drawing on the theory of possible or fictional worlds, one can distinguish two phases in the development of such worlds. Both speak of "possible worlds." Explicitly using the more philosophical term "possible worlds," Lotman describes the first phase, that is, their original *intratextual* construction: "One only need propose a few postulates (which can be randomly selected, by the way), and a world can be constructed upon them that is completely logical in and of itself."[61] He thus emphasizes the strength of the internal logic of the individual text in contrast to the encompassing experiential world. As a result, through the premises established by the text, we are able to comprehend a world that, as a fictional product, functions according to rules differing from those of the actual world.

Lubomír Doležel, the leading theorist in this field, also emphasizes "the sovereignty of fictional worlds,"[62] and he too refers to the philosophical framework of possible-worlds semantics.[63] In this sense he gives the definition: "Fictional worlds of literature . . . are a special kind of possible world, they are aesthetic artifacts constructed, preserved, and circulating in the medium of fictional texts."[64] In concluding his definition, he touches on the second phase of establishing fictional worlds in the interpersonal repertoire of the imaginary. This phase is based on the *intertextual* repetition of central constituents of one of these worlds in a multiple of texts, for example, of a genre. Also from this intertextual aspect, Doležel's description of fictional worlds makes sense as "ensembles of nonactualized possible states of affairs."[65] Eco comes very close to this with his definition of "possible worlds" as "a structural representation of concrete semantic actualizations."[66]

Without referring specifically to this theoretical complex, Knut Hickethier makes similar observations regarding television series. They too set up conventional figurations and rules, a phenomenon that is in fact strengthened and consolidated to a greater degree than in (not directly serialized) genre films. Instead of mentioning fictional worlds, Hickethier states that serial narratives constitute a "situationally defined framework"[67] for the actions of the characters in the individual episodes: "This framework creates familiarity, establishes the rules of the game applicable even to the characters, to whom the viewer, as a regular viewer, has become accustomed. . . . For the character many spheres of reality and actions are taboo. Many problems and conflicts, often of a very ordinary nature, are eliminated from the start."[68]

This "framework" is nothing other than a fictional world such as described here by Doležel, but in this case with a pronounced intertextual, conventional dimension. Because the repetition of a canonical repertoire, of postulates and rules as well as narrative stereotypes, determines the *actions*—the possibilities of action as well as the narrative construction of the characters, who are in many cases themselves designed as conventionalized types (that is, figural stereotypes). Vice versa, it is the repetition of these patterns that establishes the rules—and quickly lends a sense of familiarity to the framework. And one other thing results from the concentrated linkage of stereotyped elements in such a network: the individual stereotype is so strongly connected to its specific repertoire in assimilating the contexts thereof that when used alone, it summons *pars pro toto* the entire world of the genre or series with which it is associated.

Emphasizing the processes of conventionalization and habitualization, a theory of interlinked stereotypes can, moreover, explain why these kinds of fictional worlds are learned as discursive facts and gradually become parallel worlds with their own specific regularities and develop into frameworks of conventionalized patterns of the imagination. In this study, the term "imaginary worlds" is used to underscore this transition into the conventional, interpersonal repertoire of the imaginary.

This being said, at this juncture it would seem feasible to also revise the term "myth" in association with the theory of the stereotype. In contrast to Campbell's approach, "myth" in film-related literature, which today makes inflated use of the term, is used simply to underscore the both *imaginary* and *conventional* nature of narrative worlds, which are much more indebted to the crowd-pleasing perception of social and psychological functions than the reality principle. At the same time, "myth" foregrounds *regularity and repetition* and emphasizes the importance of the familiar over the new, that is, highlights what is ritually communicated and received. This rituality is the result of drawing references from the respective conventional repertoire.[69]

For example, this is how Will Wright[70] understood the term in his study of the Western. Wright positioned himself against the "transcendental flair"[71] surrounding the theoretical construction of myth the moment it is considered a universal structure. Wright's objections were not directed against Campbell, whose work is not discussed, but against the concept—more influential in film semiotics—proposed by Lévi-Strauss, who regarded myth as the mind imitating itself as object. Countering this, Wright particularly underscored that myths take on varying cultural functions in different societies.[72] In other words, his position approximates a notion of myths as imaginary worlds, where entire arrays of narrative imaginations take shape, which can each be assigned to different cultural contexts.

Wright simultaneously emphasized the reductionist structure of these imaginations, which he explains as due to the fact that mythic narratives are based on a multifaceted system of binary oppositions between characters or values. In this point, Wright's position remains noticeably related to that of Lévi-Strauss, and his work implies an understanding of mythos that seems quite compatible with the approach to stereotype maintained here.

Wright's actual aim, however, was the analysis of filmic Westerns, which contributed significantly to the creation of the Western myth. Wright's work is interesting in the context of this inquiry, because it highlights the multiple layers of the stereotype phenomenon in relation to plot while displaying a definite concern for historicity.

Wright developed structural models of narrative, which appear successively and supersede one another in different phases of the Western—with each model dominating the films of a given period. Theses structural models clearly betray the influence of Propp's method. The "classical plot" model, which dominates the Westerns included in the top-grossing list used by Wright for the years 1931 to 1955, is cited below as an illustration. Similarly to Propp's approach, the model is structured as a narrative sequence of functions (sixteen, in this case).

1. The hero enters a social group.
2. The hero is unknown to the society.
3. The hero is revealed to have an exceptional ability.
4. The society recognizes a difference between themselves and the hero; a hero is given a special status.
5. The society does not completely accept the hero.
6. There is a conflict of interests between the villains and the society.
7. The villains are stronger than the society; the society is weak.
8. There is a strong friendship or respect between the hero and a villain.
9. The villains threaten the society.
10. The hero avoids involvement in the conflict.
11. The villains endanger a friend of the hero.
12. The hero fights the villains.
13. The hero defeats the villains.
14. The society is safe.
15. The society accepts the hero.
16. The hero loses or give up his special status.[73]

Wright added three additional plot variations to this structural model, which either supplanted the classical model in the later phases of the history of the Western—as in the case of the "professional plot" in the 1960s—or coexisted with it, as did the "vengeance variation" and the "transition theme" in the 1940s and 1950s.

The advantage of developing such a model is that it indicates the multilayered nature of the stereotype problem. Not only do a large number of narrative elements (specific plot components, characters, situations, and motifs) exhibit tendencies toward schematization and conventionalization, but these tendencies are also manifest in the overarching plot structure of a text. Wright's attempt to discern an ordered substructure beneath a web of repeating plot elements and stabilized architectural models, each supporting a long sequence of narratives, is convincing in the context of the Westerns he examines.

The "classical-plot" model in particular seems to have been used so frequently over the course of a relatively extended timeframe that the years between 1931 and 1955 could almost be said to have exhibited a *conventional* plot schema. Thus the linkage between individual plot elements on a syntactical level comes close to being stereotypical—especially since Wright's model bears certain analogies to the notions of stereotype evolution and stereotype substitution. With its *historical variations* on predominant plot models, Wright's paradigm also indirectly points to the consequences of the processes of adaption and replacement (which he of course does not pursue further), as also emphasized by stereotype theory.

It is therefore no wonder that many other authors were also interested in such *patterns of plot* during the heyday of structuralism. For example, John Cawelti maintained that the trend in popular narrative toward formulas, as he emphasized, culminated in such patterns, while describing "formula" in a manner almost equivalent to "stereotype." This becomes evident when he points to the functional nature of formulas, including patterns of plot, as pragmatic entities adapted to cultural needs:

> My argument . . . is that formula stories like the detective story, the Western, the seduction novel . . . are structures of narrative conventions which carry out a variety of cultural functions in a unified way. . . . To analyze these formulas we must define them as narrative structures of a certain kind and then investigate how the additional dimensions of ritual, game and dream have been synthesized into the particular patterns of plot, character and setting which have become associated with the formula.[74]

To be sure, such consolidated and well-established schemata of emplotment cannot be found with the same degree of plausibility in all genres. In principle, however, it *is* possible not only to identify the repetition of specific motifs or the recourse to entire stereotype repertoires within certain groups of films other than Westerns, but one can also observe the influence of conventional patterns. This *possibility* has repeatedly encouraged a search for conventional "grammars of plot" (a popular topic of structuralist research). When these patterns do form a relatively stable network of stereotyped elements, the result is an impression of conventional consolidation, which places these patterns somewhat in proximity to the stereotype. The phenomenon is particularly noticeable in the serials formerly shown in movie theaters and is most obvious in contemporary television series.

ACTING, IMAGE, AND A BRIEF CONSIDERATION OF SOUND

The formation of stereotypes in film, however, can also be described from perspectives other than narratology and dramaturgy, which have been discussed so far and tend to abstract from the audiovisual mode of presentation. Here, too, it is possible to identify entrenched, conventionalized schemata of expression, which can be considered stereotypes in the sense of the four facets outlined in chapter 1. This applies to numerous forms at the level of mise en scène, including styles of acting as well as of makeup, lighting, and so on, but also occurring on the level of mise en images, that is, patterns of shot composition (framing), and, finally, of sound and the relationship between soundtrack and images.

Although the following discussion will focus *pars pro toto* on acting and the image, it is nevertheless important to mention briefly that the filmic worlds of sound are also profoundly affected by stereotypization. This is particularly true for the construction of *acoustic imaginations*, such as the atmosphere of science-fiction worlds. For example, the "sound of space" and the objects flying through it have been clearly determined by *filmic* conventionalization. The audience finds it "natural" when films conform to this standard cinematic practice. The same applies to generically specific sounds, which viewers also primarily experience as mediatized and which have become intertextually "naturalized"—as with the smack and thud of fists (which never actually sound this way in reality) in brawls or with noises made by weapons.

Sound simultaneously has a signal function. The selective use of a few, symbolic sounds is very significant in creating a specific atmosphere: for example, bells often toll to signify mourning and death. In her study on the virtual world of sound in film, Barbara Flückiger describes numerous examples, including those above, of the gradual "intertextual evolution"[75] of sound imaginations and explicitly draws on the theory of the stereotype. Following Lippmann, she argues that also on the level of sound stereotypes are generated in the world of experience conveyed by media.[76]

Corinna Dästner similarly discusses how the impression of "realism" with respect to the extradiegetic score depends on whether the film employs powerful cinematic conventions and thus satisfies automatized viewer expectations. Even the negation of convention through counterpoint (an influential concept in the theory of film music) does not affect the great power of the conventional, so that the "wish . . . to escape the soundtrack stereotype"[77] is never truly fulfilled. Similar observations can be made in light of acting and the image, aspects that will be discussed in more detail below.

In a short essay[78] from the year 1913, Herbert Jhering, who later became one of leading theater and film critics of the Weimar Republic, addressed stock forms of acting—still in the context of theater—as "habitual expressions" in stage performances. Jhering mentioned "acting clichés" and gave a number of concrete examples from his experience of contemporary theater. Below, a somewhat lengthy quote from this brief text, which was never republished:

> These are the clichés for typical situations . . . thus the nuanced gestures for bashfulness, lurking, distraction, and diversion are used repeatedly by the skilled craftsman. Should the actor, entering the stage in a baronial fur, a top hat, and walking stick, wish to direct the conversation to a certain subject after a few introductory words, then he speaks his words hesitatingly, with pauses, looking all the while at the point of his walking stick, which he nonchalantly lets swing back and forth. He is no longer Mr. X, and not his guise, but the bon vivant, *père noble*. Should a villain be plotting an evil plan that he would like to conceal, he gazes at the nails of his cupped or outstretched hand while talking. He is . . . the schemer. And whoever earns his keep with uncles and good-natured fathers is well-versed in the art of wagging a mildly admonishing finger with a "bemused smile."[79]

These and similar clichés also characterized the film acting of the same period. Especially in the early silent cinema, actors displayed a conspicuous tendency to use standard poses and gestures, and this acting style has been much discussed as a result. Erwin Panofsky, for example, amusingly described one such formula in his examination of early film: "the first kiss was invariably announced by the lady's gently playing with her partner's necktie and was invariably accompanied by her kicking out with her left foot."[80] Jhering pointedly makes a similar observation about film acting in one of his later texts: "In the very beginnings of film, acting meant a sequence of *poses*. The postcard industry had long been publishing series of pretty ladies in frozen poses and a mawkishly tinseled toilette. This appeared ideal to the cinema, and hence the movie actress was born."[81]

The silent-film star Henny Porten has often been mentioned and retrospectively contrasted to Asta Nielsen, as exemplary of an acting style based on overtly conventional poses, especially in the context of her early films (in which, for example, she presses her hands to her chest as an expression of unrequited love).[82] However, such acting is not only characteristic of early silent film. German films from as late as the 1950s featured the schemers and benevolent admonishing uncles, who displayed the gestures Jhering had previously described.

Accordingly, such representational patterns can be interpreted as acting stereotypes (in our sense of the term). They are of a conventional nature, since—as emphasized by Jhering—they are "formed by the acting tradition,"[83] that is, through the successive conventionalization of an original inspiration, which was apparently well received and also functioned semantically. Moreover, these patterns are generally composite forms and are always used in a certain type of semantic context. One can therefore interpret them as schematic patterns.

Hesitating, protracted speech, plus a gaze focused on the cane as it swings nonchalantly back and forth, plus appearing in the appropriate costume: this equaled *the* expression of the bon vivant in Jhering's example. These forms reduce complexity—in the very manner typical of schemata and stereotypes. The variety of possible representations is pared down to a repeating pattern that is soon known, accepted, and, indeed, even expected by the audience. It is a conventional pattern that has consequently assimilated its semantic context to the point of assuming a symbolic dimension.

A large number of such forms in sum thus provide *a repertoire for acting*—a specific expressive repertoire that enhances the poignancy and symbolism of the drama and corresponds to the dispositions of the viewers it addresses. Amossy points out that the phenomenon of the typified figure and the overall standardization of types was not subject to critique in the predominant aesthetic discourses of the nineteenth century,[84] and this also applies to the attitude toward such repertoires. In acting handbooks and physiognomic encyclopedias, which were related to the pattern books used by visual artists, attempts were even made to establish and systematize stereotyped forms of acting *as canonical patterns*. Such manuals gave schematic depictions of how the different emotional states to be portrayed are expressed in accentuated forms of facial expression and accompanying gesture. Together with the traditional practices of the stage, such books made a valued contribution to the fixation and communication of stereotypes.

Here too, such model forms did *not* come simply from the repetition or accentuation of patterns observed in reality, in the everyday world beyond the theater. Instead, the forms demonstrated a high degree of cultural autonomy. Just as character and plot stereotypes tend to emancipate themselves from reality and provide a structure for the imaginary in conventionalized fictional worlds, acting stereotypes originating from the practices of the theater consequently supplied the convention-based imagination of the stage with a comparable structural reservoir.

Looking at the actors' manuals on gesture, one immediately recognizes the great extent to which these stereotypes referred to the world of the stage alone

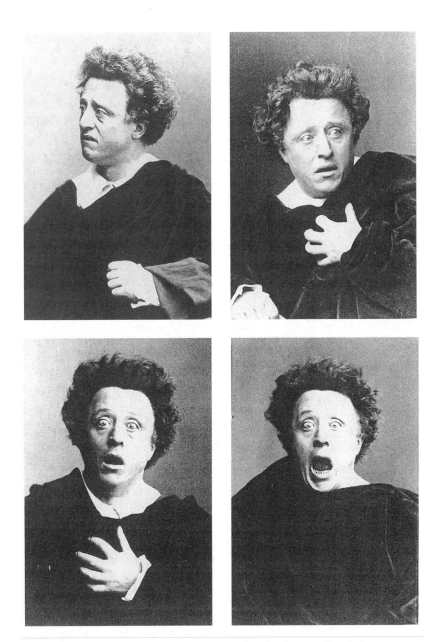

FIGURE 3 Facial expressions of "horror." Series of images from Carl Michel, *Die Gebärdensprache dargestellt für Schauspieler sowie Maler und Bildhauer,* part 1 (1886), plate XVIII, nos. 66–69.

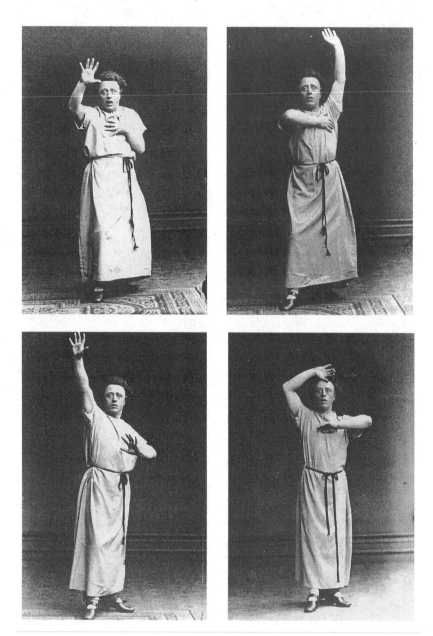

FIGURE 4 Gestures of "horror." Series of images from Carl Michel, *Die Gebärdensprache dargestellt für Schauspieler sowie Maler und Bildhauer*, part 1 (1886), plate XVII, nos. 62–65.

and how little they have in common with ordinary behavior and expression. In a corresponding standard handbook dating from 1886, Carl Michel itemizes a long list of emotional states—describing horror (*Entsetzen*), for example, as a complex schema of facial expression and gesture:

> The eyebrows are raised, creasing the brow in deep folds. The eyes are wide open in a wild gaze with protruding pupils, fixed on the object of horror. The nostrils tremble and flare, the cheeks are sucked in. The mouth, at first opened as wide as possible ... then closes and opens at various intervals as the lips quiver; the shoulders are then raised, and the raised arms are pressed tightly to the chest, similar to when experiencing great cold; the entire body folds in upon itself, crouching and trembling with one arm raised ... the fingers spread apart.... The hands may be clenched but must remain close to the body. The "ha" sound is not spoken but formed by inhaling with closed vocal chords. This all takes place at once, at lightening speed. Should the ability to speak return, then the voice is first soundless, raspy, whispering, gradually becoming louder. At the moment of the greatest fear of death, of horror, all muscles go limp, all mental faculties fail, a deathly pallor sets in, as well as labored, heaving breath and a loss of consciousness.[85]

This text obviously concretizes a complex schema of dramatic expression on the level of facial expression, gesture, and intonation. From a historical perspective, one can appreciate the great discrepancy between the standards of theatrical imagination, which today seem almost grotesque and highly stylized, and the real expression of emotion in daily life. Michel's description did in fact draw on actual acting performances, or at least this was his pretension. That Michel never questioned the conventionality of his acting formulas but apparently considered them to be "natural"—perhaps because they were so prevalent and deeply entrenched in the practices of the theater in the 1880s—throws into sharp relief the degree of formal automatization typical of the era and the level of cultural acceptance of this phenomenon.

The depth of this need—intrinsic to every stereotype—for schematic reduction and accentuation that such systems of gestures reflect becomes even more obvious when one looks at another example. The facial expressions of the actor Albert Bassermann, *the* star of the German stage at the time (and as of 1913 also a film actor) were used to illustrate schematic line drawings of the face, in a supplement of a leading Berlin newspaper. The accompanying text clearly emphasizes the significance of a schema and schematic depictions of the face for visual communication: "One might say that a picture ... of a human being is not a documentary rendering in full detail but represents nothing more than a schematization of the most important ordinary characteristics or lines of the individual represented."[86] The characteristic attitude of stage actors toward such systematization is tellingly reflected in the fact that Bassermann, who took pains to cultivate his high artistic status, apparently had no objections whatsoever to participating in this undertaking, which was published in 1914 under the title "Mimische Studien mit Reißzeug und Kamera" (Studies of Facial Expressions with Pen and Camera).[87]

Mastering physiognomic stereotypes was traditionally equivalent to mastering the expressive repertoire of an actor. This was the cornerstone of an actor's craft, and therefore in the nineteenth century this repertoire was not only widely accepted but considered professionally essential. Although the reliance on conventional frameworks of this kind became more problematic with the emergence of naturalism and realism, that is, with a proclaimed orientation toward reality, Herbert Jhering still described the actor who has mastered a fixed repertoire of gestures as a "skilled craftsman." This did have some derogatory undertones, because for Jhering such skill was just *one fundamental element* of artistic self-expression. In his choice of words he certainly emphasized the problematic side—in an aesthetic sense—of the actorial "cliché." Nevertheless, he accepted the corresponding forms. Speaking from an aesthetic position oriented toward individual expression and realistic premises, Jhering never criticized the actual use of traditional stereotypes as such but merely their *uninspired* replication.

Much like Ernst Gombrich or Arnold Hauser's treatment of stereotypes in the context of the fine arts, Jhering also argued that the creative *appropriation* of conventional schemata posed a serious artistic challenge: "Inasmuch as [the stereotype] is swept back into the personality, it returns to its origins. And true to fact and experience, when incorporated into the rhythm of an individual talent, even the most overused expression can still be unique. If the cliché is infused with personal energies, then it ceases to be such and becomes the necessary freedom of the creative artist."[88]

In thinking about film today, one necessarily questions the current relevance of the concept of the actorial cliché. Do the described stereotypes of acting and their corresponding morphologies not belong to the distant past, the culture of the nineteenth century? Have they not been gradually replaced by the advance of more naturalistic, realistic, and individualistic tendencies in the twentieth century? Was it not film itself, which—although initially influenced by theatrical forms—quickly and ultimately accelerated this breakdown through the new medium's potential for intimate psychological representation?

The shift toward naturalism at the end of the nineteenth century did in fact precipitate a crisis of traditional repertoires of expression—and of conventional aesthetic repertoires in general. In many cases, it was the order of the day to overcome what were meanwhile considered exaggerated, frozen, unrealistic, and

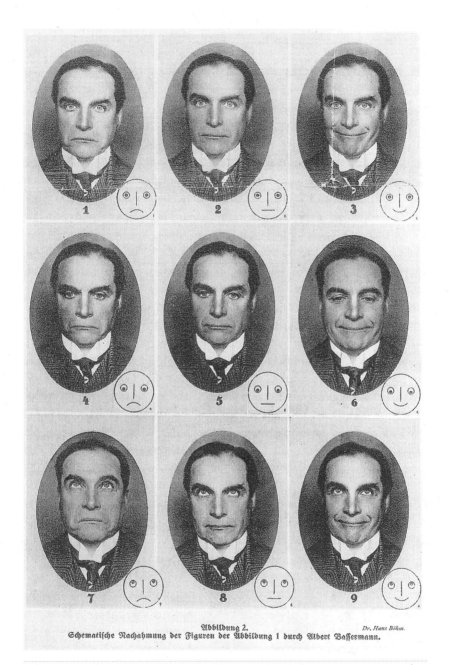

Abbildung 2.
Schematische Nachahmung der Figuren der Abbildung 1 durch Albert Bassermann.

Dr. Hans Böhm.

FIGURE 5 Study of facial expressions featuring Albert Bassermann. Illustration for Wilhelm Scheffer's article "Mimische Studien mit Reißzeug und Kamera" in *Der Weltspiegel* (1914).

implausible acting patterns. The concept of *underacting* began to take hold.[89] Underacting implies toning down *accentuated* schemata. An actor's expressiveness remains below the threshold of conventional patterns of expression in an attempt to achieve the "reduction of visible emotion, of facial expressions and gestures intended to convey inner turmoil."[90]

At the same time, psychological theories of acting emerged, such as Stanislavski's, in which any recourse to a conventional theatrical schema was considered an atrocity (at least in theory). They emphasized the process of finding an individual, authentically felt expression, to be achieved by means of everyday observation and, most of all, empathy with a character by *individually reliving an inner state.*

The medium of film provided new opportunities for such concepts, which had already been developed within the context of the theater. Film offered special possibilities for a nuanced acting style based on underacting—through photographic technology, the intimacy of close-ups showing face and eyes, and montage, the latter giving birth to the *Kuleshov effect*,[91] which was also important for reduced acting. Meanwhile, the traditional acting repertoires often considered obsolete even in the theater soon seemed particularly anachronistic in the photorealistic world of film removed from the stage (and in silent film also bereft of spoken language).

Nevertheless, the traditional repertoire remained very prevalent in early cinema, initially as a naïve visual system of expression in the silent medium. Examining Griffith's Biograph films, Roberta Pearson has shown in detail that the transition from the traditional "histrionic code" to the "verisimilar code" between 1908 and 1912 led to the presence of the two codes in this period.[92] This is repeatedly illustrated by German motion pictures from the years prior to World War I, which continue to draw on the older idiom. To cite just one striking example: when the mother figure in the melodrama short *Weihnachtsgedanken* (*Christmas Thoughts*, director unknown, Germany, 1911) learns of her only daughter's death in a road accident, the anonymous leading actress uses sweeping gestures of horror that are exceedingly similar to those codified by Carl Michel. In expressionist film and its sphere of influence, references to the traditional repertoire persist.

Even at the time, however, a number of film critics and film theorists stressed that in films actors should tone down their expressiveness and depart from the tools of theater—from the stereotypes of stage acting. The subtle signals of the almost expressionless face, which may serve as an object for the projection of the viewer's own feelings, were often upheld as an ideal of film performance.

"It is unbelievable how simple the expression [in film] must be, and how it is the gentlest of indications that have the strongest effect."[93] Joseph August Lux expressed this conviction as early as 1914, and elsewhere he added that cinema does not require "customary acting" but rather a performance style like that of

FIGURE 6 Conventional grand gestures of horror and desperation in
Weihnachtsgedanken (*Christmas Thoughts*, Germany, 1911).

Asta Nielsen, which conveys a role "through subtle insinuations of movement, through the face" and imparts the "uniquely personal" and natural instead of the conventional.[94] "Cinematic style means naturalness."[95]

Ten years later in his book *Visible Man*, Béla Balázs even based his film theory on the utopian ideal of the *convention-free* physiognomic expression in film and also lauded Nielsen in this context. Calls for an unforced acting style grounded in the everyday, rich in psychological nuances, and void of stereotypes have followed film ever since. Cinema has generally conceded to these demands (or at least tended to) when the aim has been to convey realism, psychological authenticity, and a sense of the ordinary.

The medium of film did in fact contribute to the ultimate breakdown of the nineteenth-century repertoire. Nevertheless, just as one cannot interpret the history of film acting as a "successive decline in larger-than-life gesture,"[96] neither can one consider it a continuous retreat from acting stereotypes. In surveying popular cinema, one clearly sees not only some of the traditional patterns from the last turn of the century preserved for over half a century but indeed the emergence—within the medium of film itself—of new performance stereotypes specific to individual genres and periods.

The actors portraying the gunmen in Westerns cultivated an entire palette of accentuated, conventional forms of action, with which they equipped their respective types. Time and again this genre has displayed stylized, fixed gestures: for example, how the characters walk, ride, reach for their pistols, tie up their horses, impress a crowd, behave in a saloon, pick a fight or get provoked, or how they act in a robbery or gun duel. Just as the narrative elements, figure types, and plot motifs characteristic of the Western have reappeared repeatedly and have formed a conventional world of the imagination, a static repertoire of facial expressions and gestures has been established simultaneously—giving this imaginary world *concrete visual form* while generally abandoning any sense of everyday reality or "naturalness." Similar observations can be made about other genres and periods, for example, the cast of characters of American screwball comedies, in the gangster films of the 1930s and 1940s, or concerning the acting in German comedies from the same period.

The use and formation of stereotypes is particularly apparent in the roles played by stock actors (*Chargen*), which in Germany had their heyday in the films of the Weimar Republic. The reductionist and functional elements of bit parts and supporting roles lead to actors "overplaying" their parts, that is, creating figures "stuffed and overloaded by their traits . . . wearing their characteristics like a badge."[97] This is Herbert Jhering's description from the 1920s, and he adds: "The stock actors who play bit parts lend important secondary figures clarity: through distinctive make-up, a particular tone of voice, repeated habits like playing with a pince-nez or carrying the briefcase in a certain way. . . . They serve up fine and precise individual traits and garnish them with subtle gimmicks."[98] Classical cinema's cyclical and thus also *restrictive* mode of production is another reason behind the distinctive characteristics of secondary roles, as Karl Prümm notes: "All these restrictions put actors who play bit parts at risk of being type-casted and forced into acting clichés, thus of wearing out these roles and being compelled to repeat them time and again. Given the amount of productions that require stock actors, this risk is particularly high."[99]

Nevertheless, the attraction of minor characters lies in this very threat posed by compulsive repetition, since these roles are based "on intertextuality, on intertextual effects."[100] Or as Prümm further adds: "Their countless roles are distilled into a concise text, which is continuously cited, reused, retold, and modified. . . . Autonomy, self-confidence, clarity, and recognizability are what make the performances of stock actors attractive."[101] In other words, a majority of the effects created by professional actors playing minor roles in classical cinema stemmed from the actor's individually developed repertoire of forced and particularly obvious schemata, which characterized a specific figure and came close to stereotype. This was a limited repertoire, with which actors then played in individual variations on schema and repetition. Performers also tried to arouse and confirm expectations and, less often, tried to intentionally contradict them. The art of playing stock characters demonstrates most clearly how stereotypes and individuality are not necessarily antagonisms. Rather, individuality to some extent arises from an interaction with a relatively stable personal repertoire of (cultural and individual) stereotypes.

One need not look as far back as classical film to find acting stereotypes, even though they may seem most pronounced to the eye of the beholder when viewed from the distance of time. In contemporary mainstream cinema, and here especially, one can certainly observe a great number of forced acting stereotypes. For example, the "men in black," who became an exaggerated type in the popular films and other media (such as video clips) in the 1990s, and other related gun-toting figures employ a clearly defined gestural repertoire, a range of quite obviously mannered and thus intertextually conventional affectation. This is none more obvious than in posing with weapons, which has a different look in the 1990s than in the 1980s. Not only is all realism abandoned, but such posturing lends a certain illustrative bravado to the fact that gestural stereotypes, *fixed poses*, are performed as ritual behaviors and as symbols of *coolness*.

Could anyone therefore truly claim that film exhibits an inherent tendency toward dispersing the styles of acting dictated by stereotypes?

More accurately, one could say that there are opposing stylistic concepts at play within film culture, and also in regard to acting, and that there is no single, universally established repertoire of stereotypes that needs to be generally dismantled; instead, such repertoires undergo gradual shifts and are reconfigured over time.

While Jhering still described how stereotypes, or clichés, "are handed down from generation to generation,"[102] this may be true of individual, particularly long-lasting formulas. However, this statement primarily holds true for the horizon of experience at the beginning of the twentieth century. A century of film history, and consequently a century of audiovisually documented film acting, offers a comparative overview that leaves no doubt as to the great extent to which acting stereotypes are linked both to changing cultural contexts and the specific mechanisms of mutating genres. Thus one can infer that such acting stereotypes, when viewed from a distance, can be read as signs of these genres and epochs.

To a certain extent, one may indeed argue that popular film and related audiovisual productions, which today mostly comprise TV series and video clips, have assumed the *standardizing, codifying functions* of the old gesture manuals. Current gestural patterns are created through influential films and are quickly established through repetition in numerous similar productions: they become *fashionable*. When cultural critics first became aware of this cultural mechanism—in the late 1920s—it was even said about repetition and its effects that film, as a serial and constantly reproducible commodity, contributed to the "standardization" of facial expressions. Film was thought to disseminate the "calculated, considered, cleverly devised, well-proven standardized expression" and "standardized gesture" not only in acting but even in the private sphere of individuals.[103] Apparently, film was proving to be a more powerful mechanism of pragmatic standardization than the gesture handbooks ever were.

In *Home Stories* (Matthias Müller, Germany, 1990)—a six-minute found-footage compilation—the filmmaker Matthias Müller edited shots from a selection of domestic melodramas produced in Hollywood in the 1950s. The images center on the female stars of the era: Lauren Bacall, Anne Bancroft, Doris Day, Tippi Hedren, Audrey Hepburn, Grace Kelly, Louise Latham, Dorothy Malone, Kim Novak, Jessica Tandy, Lana Turner, Jane Wyman, and others. At the beginning, after a few shots of typical interiors, we are shown a series of female figures, each in a very similar position, in segments taken from various films. All the women seem to be in a depressed state, which is conveyed through almost identical gestures. Each one is lying on a wide, elegant bed in a posh room. Müller repeatedly inserts the same image of a door, alternated by a series of close shots of the women, whose faces show strained, fearful looks and attitudes of listening. Two series of images follow, in which the women, one after the other, first sit up in bed and then get up—all throwing on similar bathrobes. Next, again in sequence, they stand with their ear to a door. Various variations follow on the opening of the door and switching lights on and off. Their faces show expressions of distress. Each then individually repeats a move to the window and opens the curtains or blinds to look outside. A series of images shot from outside now show them at the window, standing and looking out from behind the glass. It all culminates in a furious finale: multiple variations on rising up or getting up in fright, walking through corridors and passing imposing stairways in the hall; doors open and close until one of the figures is swallowed up by darkness . . .

Müller plays with his material. He selects plot situations and female gestures from this 1950s genre because they correspond to the established melodramatic roles of women. He also brings them together in a series of images that manifests the phenomenon of intertextual repetition through *an intratextual sequence*. Simultaneously, he constructs a new mininarrative: "Scenes from Hollywood melodramas are compiled in such a way that the sequential faces of the goddesses of the silver screen assume the countenance of a stereotype, the look of the classic victim,"[104] as film critic Heike Kühn aptly described.

However, the principle of the stereotype, as revealed by the serial composition of *Home Stories*, extends beyond the mere role of the victim, that is, beyond the standard plot situation associated with this role. Müller uncovers in the acting a repertoire of expressions and movements whose *tremendous conventionality* is revealed by the sequence. Fearful, strained listening, impulsively sitting up in a moment of horrified surprise, hectically getting into a bathrobe—the sequence clearly deconstructs all of this as acting stereotypes.

But the topic of stereotypization is not yet exhausted. Müller's compilation of shots points to—above and beyond stereotypical plotting and acting—complex pictorial ideas and visual structures that appear as stereotypes and can be interpreted as iconographic patterns.

The Russian cameraman Vladimir Nilsen already raised this issue in reference to American genre films in the 1930s in his book *The Cinema as a Graphic Art*. Nilsen noted the influence of stereotypes that worked together on almost every level of image composition, from costume and make-up to lighting. He observed "the establishment of standard methods of lighting and optical treatment of the visual image"[105] and the "standard compositional constructions"[106] of the shots. The staging of female faces and bodies in Hollywood films of the day appeared to the Russian cameraman to be a particularly striking case of stereotypization, which played to the desires of the male audience, as Nilsen observed at the time.

He describes a certain kind of make-up as coupled with a repeated type of lighting and a particular mise en image (framing, composition) produced by the camera. Everything is determined by reduced, conventional schemata, which is primarily aimed to generate a specific effect for the audience. With regard to close-ups of female faces, Nilsen mentioned a "type of standard beauty"[107]—a conventional, imaginary construct producing fetishistic images:

> A fetishised image of a woman is created with a clear light aureole around her head, shining eyes, clearly defined shadows from the long, painted lashes; a picture reminding one of a mannequin rather than a living human face with individual features essential to it. A soft-focus lens smoothes out all the inequality on the face, a soft, diffused frontal light destroys the relief, a strong back light emphasizes only the contoural outlines, and as a result we see on the screen "ideally beautiful" close-ups, exact copies of the picture-postcard "beauties."[108]

Nilsen emphasized a schematization effect in the final images, the reduction that results from how hairstyle, make-up, and lighting cause the differentiated texture of the face to disappear behind a mask. The facial features characteristic of an individual are partially suppressed, and in their place a kind of common mask accentuates sexual symbols such as the lips, eyes, and lashes. This optical type, writes Nilsen, is favored for close-ups, which in turn are influenced by *compositional* stereotypes. Here, too, he emphasizes the phenomenon of reduction: "The cameraman responsible for these shots knew only a single form of compositional construction for such close-ups."[109] Nilsen attempted to illustrate his observations with series of close-ups from various films. However, he did not go into the question as to the kind of filmic iconography—which is able to produce its own semantic complexes, that is, cultural icons—that results from the stereotypization of this visual layer.

Matthias Müller essentially uses the same serial principle as Nilsen, although his metafilm does not employ the same examples. But *Home Stories* too draws attention to compositional standards, in which the communication of similar emotions is linked with highly similar pictorial ideas. Thus the image of the woman behind the window, who, lost in thought, looks out into the unknown, repeatedly appears in Müller's film with slight variations. This points to the extremely frequent occurrence of this "cliché-image,"[110] as Jean-Loup Bourget calls it, within melodrama—an image whose symbolic power, enhanced by raindrops or frost on glass, was well known to classical film production, and by no means just in Hollywood, well before the 1950s: "Drops of rain run down the window pane. They are like tears that the burning eyes can no longer summon: a much-used image that belongs to the base stock of film symbolism."[111] This is a comment in a German publication from 1943 on an accompanying image of a shot from *Das Mädchen von Fanö* (*The Girl from Fano*, Hans Schweikart, Germany, 1940) showing the face of Brigitte Horney behind the window. Müller's sequential compilation thus makes one acutely aware of these stereotyped pictorial constructions as *conventional icons of the melodramatic imagination.*[112]

The ideas crystallized in Nilsen's book and Müller's film are not the same. Oriented toward the canonic values of Soviet silent film, Nilsen rejected the prevailing use of stereotypes. Within the context of capitalist cinema the stereotype appeared to contradict Soviet cinema's own artistic intentions. (Of course, he does not mention the increasing stereotypization in Russian filmmaking—for example, the constantly repeated, slightly low-angle close-ups of the fat faces of kulaks, bourgeois, and speculators.) In his own somewhat idiosyncratic opinion he viewed this practice of Hollywood as nothing more than a routinized, frozen variation of Louis Delluc's idea of *photogénie.*

FIGURE 7 Stereotypical film images: two series of images from Vladimir Nilsen, *The Cinema as Graphic Art* (1957), 178–179. Mother-and-child shots from three films of the 1930s. Six close-ups from different American films.

Müller's film avoids polemics entirely. It deconstructs the visual world of 1950s melodrama. Part irony and part fascination, his film demonstrates the roles that genre- and period-specific visual stereotypes play in the construction of this imaginary world. In doing so, he points to a cultural fact, the visual codes of a period—and relishes in playing with them on another level. What Müller and Nilsen share is an observation of pictorial stereotypes and their evidence through intratextual serialization.

GENRE AND HYBRID GENRE

In his essay "On Literary Evolution" from 1927, Yury Tynyanov, one of the theorists of Russian formalism, writes on the question of the specific characteristics of the literary genres with respect to the novel:

> The novel, which seems to be an integral genre that has developed in and of itself over the centuries, turns out to be not an integral whole but a variable. Its material changes from one literary system to another, as does its method of introducing extraliterary language materials into literature. Even the features of the genre evolve. The genres of the "short story" and the "novella" were defined by different features in the system of the twenties to forties than they are in our time.[113]

In light of these observations, he came to the conclusion (in a text written three years earlier) that "a static definition of a genre, one which would cover all its manifestations, is impossible: the genre dislocates itself; we see before us the broken line, not a straight line, of its evolution—and this evolution takes place precisely at the expense of the 'fundamental' features of the genre: of the epic as narrative, of the lyric as the art of the emotions, etc."[114]

In other words, Tynyanov developed the idea that literary genres also undergo the constant evolution that he generally considered characteristic of literary phenomena. Beyond his interest in tracing the shifts in the attribution of works to individual categories or genres, he primarily challenged literary theorists to renounce what was obviously a futile intention from the start: the construction of clearly delineated, inherently logical and coherent, transhistorical genre definitions and the articulation of sophisticated genre and category systems. Instead, he insisted: "Every term in theory of literature [sic] must be the specific result of specific facts. You cannot take your starting point from the extra- or supra-literary heights of metaphysical aesthetics and forcibly 'choose' that data that 'match' the term. A term is specific: every definition evolves just as the literary fact itself evolves."[115] "Literary evolution"—one of Tynyanov's key terms—was primarily based on the observation that certain forms and figurations within a period of literary discourse gradually become conventional (or, in accordance with Russian formalist terminology, undergo "automatization") and then degenerate and fall out of use. The final phase of this automatization is linked with the "effacement"[116] of the respective element. Thus, a struggle with different, usually more recent forms follows, and ultimately forms once common are supplanted by "the new use to which old devices are put, in their new constructive significance."[117]

Tynyanov spoke of "the moving, evolving historical order."[118] He considered it the task of literary studies to map this order—that is, the dynamics of seemingly persistent forms—but not to articulate static concepts and systems. "What is overlooked if we adopt a 'static' approach"[119] is precisely the dynamic process through which this order is formed by convention.

* * *

Although all this was already deliberated and described in the 1920s, these ideas were by no means a common assumption among the film scholars who—primarily in the United States—began to show an interest in *film* genres as of the 1960s. Instead of highlighting the relative and evolutionary nature of genres and genre concepts, many approaches initially emphasized static aspects and searched for the basic, fixed characteristics of genre.

To some extent, this is explained by the fact that the interest in film genres mainly arose in response to individual films, typically either in criticism or monographs dedicated to a single filmmaker. In such a context, the idea of genre was generally boiled down to a broad schema used to interpret a given film as an individual generic variation. As a consequence, one tended to seek dynamic and variable elements mostly through a film's specific adaptation of the genre. In contrast, genre as such was only interesting as a stable foil, not as an evolutionary phenomenon.

This situation did not change substantially even with the increasing interest in the repetitive structures of the popular as such and its specific functions. At this point, the noticeable repetitions inherent to genre films, the networks of similarities, the imaginary worlds, became a focus of attention in and of themselves, and theorists began to investigate the cultural functions of these analogous elements.

In the section on stereotypization in emplotment, it was already pointed out that anthropological concepts of myth played a significant role in finding answers to these questions. From this perspective, genre structures seemed linked to a *fundamental* human need for the imaginary—a need basically unchanged since the beginning of time, hence ahistorical, and thought to be expressed in similarly stable, repetitive, and universally valid text structures. Within the framework of this intellectual tradition, genres were especially relevant as archetypical forms.

In the United States, Northrop Frye's concept of genre[120] was especially influential among film journalists. The result: evolving or shifting elements came to be considered a mere outer layer, a surface variation of a deep and apparently immutable structure, and, as such, a topic of secondary interest at best. Even theories, such as that of Cawelti,[121] that evinced a greater interest in the cultural transformations expressed in different forms of genre still retained the basic idea of a recourse to a mythological/anthropological core. Corresponding references to antique and classical genres—compared to which all cultural changes were seen as secondary variations—belonged to the standard repertoire of such inquiries.

Apart from, or in conjunction with, this practice, there was yet another factor contributing to the resistance against a consistent evolutionary perspective. Open categories lacking clear definitions, categories not adhering to the rules of formal logic, were alien to the traditional style of thought long predominant in the humanities. Thus, film scholars vehemently adhered to the search for clear and stable indicators that would enable them to systematically pigeonhole individual film genres as fixed categories of logification.

In doing so, film theorists primarily examined bodies of films that were generally accepted as *conventional entities*: groups of films whose similarities resulted from serial trends in studio production and a degree of standardization in the types of movies produced in the studio and for which market demand existed (which shall be discussed in greater detail in the next section)—groups of films whose genre was a naturalized term in the languages of *film promotion and criticism*. This certainly seems reasonable, considering that analysis should not be guided by categories that theorists invent—logically flawless ideas but armchair constructs in which retrospectively "appropriate" phenomena are sought to illustrate "synthetic" classifications. Ultimately, the notion of genre is intended as a means of tracing real, historical processes (Tynyanov's evolving order), which have served and continue to serve as a practical orientation in the production and viewing of films.

Such attempts at studying genre showed a distinct preference for discussions of the Western, an exceptionally "compact" and long-lasting genre, which developed prior to 1910 and remained exceptionally vital well into the 1960s, with offshoots still persisting today. Many theorists were unsatisfied with defining a genre category simply through the single indicator of its name. Participants in the genre discourses of the early 1970s, such as those published in *Screen*, considered the restriction of the indicator to the genre name to be tautological. One had a general sense that there was more to the Western than purely the setting of the American West. An attempt was made to explicate genre-specific networks of similarities, which were conceived as fixed systems of invariants, such as the "filmic systems"[122] described by Christian Metz in *Language and Cinema* or the "superstructures" that Teun van Dijk[123] wished to articulate for (literary) genres.

In other words, there were many who aspired to developing the idea of genres as more or less constant, intertextual, and schematic structures. Much in this vein, Stuart Kaminsky states the following as late as 1985 in the foreword to his book *American Film Genres*: "Genre in film, if it is to have meaning, must have a limited scope, a limited definition. The films must have clearly defined constants so that the traditions and forms within them can be clearly seen and not diluted into abstraction."[124] A genre thus pertains to "a body, a group, or category of similar works, this similarity being defined as the sharing of a sufficient number of motifs."[125] Kaminsky requires "clearly defined constants" for the discussion of genre, that is, a similarity between all films within a category established by a *sufficient number of motifs* that logically define a genre.

This interest in entire networks of conventional forms, which constitute complex, interlinked repertoires of the imagination, was in fact quite productive. For if genre analyses are to be meaningful from a narratological standpoint, then they must be based upon the specific clusters of such conventional forms. However, the idea of being able to articulate a genre as a structural system of constants— defined by a necessary and sufficient number of stable indicators and not as an evolutionary phenomenon—inevitably leads in the wrong direction.

* * *

Repeatedly the elements defining established notions of genre proved to be inherently heterogeneous and dynamic. This is even far more apparent in *film* than in the literary genres of the nineteenth century, which Tynyanov studied. In cinema, shifts occur in fast motion.

The development of the seemingly stable and self-evident genre of the Western serves as a good example. In contrast to other genres, the Western is bracketed by the West: the setting of the stories on the frontier between the wilderness and the advancing American civilization.[126] In the majority of films, this is accompanied by a predilection for action-packed, suspense-filled storylines and a number of visual similarities in clothing, horses, weapons, and the handling thereof. The genre theorist Edward Buscombe tried to support his definition of genre and search for a complex of invariants with such kinds of visual similarities rather than with more closely defined narrative forms. Visual elements seemed generally more significant to him than narrative patterns, as the former ensured that completely different stories remained "part of the same genre."[127] He writes:

Since we are dealing with a visual medium we ought surely to look for our defining criteria in what we actually see on the screen. . . . There is, first of all, the setting, the chief glory of many of the films. Often it is outdoors, in very particular kinds of country: deserts, mountains, plains, woods. Or it is indoors—but again, special kinds of indoors: saloons, jails, courthouses, ranch houses, hotels, riverboats, brothels. . . . Then there are clothes. . . . Third, there are various tools of trade, principally weapons. . . . Next in importance come horses. . . . Fourth, there is a large group of miscellaneous physical objects that recur and thereby take on a formal function. . . . All these elements operate as formal elements.[128]

There are in fact a huge number of differences between the films spanning the decades from the first silent Westerns to the classical phase and then to the so-called post-Western: differences not only in the narrated, the kinds of stories and characters related, but, most of all, in the narration, that is, the dramatization, and also in the filmic-visual presentation of the material. In the section on the stereotypization of emplotment, the alterability of the narrative models of the Western was already discussed with reference to Wright's analysis of various canonical plots.[129] Hence from the perspective of an essentially static and coherently conceived definition of genre, Buscombe's comments on similar approaches were consistent: "But to use such structures as a basis for defining the genre would mean ending up not with one genre called 'the western,' but with an almost infinite number of subgenres."[130] Closer examination reveals, however, that even the external similarities favored by Buscombe are anything but static and reliable. In almost every decade since the beginning of film, Westerns have not only played out different storylines but have also had a different look. This not only concerns the visual design through camerawork and other film technologies. Even the settings, costumes (hats, clothing, weapons), and make-up vary substantially if, for example, one compares Westerns from the period just after 1910, the 1930s, or the 1960s and 1970s. The long coats and snow landscapes of the Italo-Western are merely some of the most obvious signs of such change.

Thus one cannot solve the basic problem by abandoning narrative indicators, that is, recurring patterns in plot and narration, in favor of visual indicators (such as setting and production design). The problem can only be solved by understanding genres as *openly structured, intertextual systems of stereotypes*, which upon closer examination can indeed be "broken down" into numerous, often overlapping subgenres, as systems that are also *in a state of constant change and interaction*. The coherence of the genre concepts is based on the actual evolution and cultural interaction that occurs in association with a cultural awareness of genre; it is this awareness that then groups films into a specific genre on the basis of heterogeneous and fluid aspects.

At this juncture, it is helpful to use the notion of stereotype, because stereotypes are culturally based, conventionalized schemata rooted in the minds of producers, distributors, and viewers and are mentally organized as *emergent networks*.[131] These schemata are formed in a lively process of conventionalization and then undergo processes of transformation and replacement. On this basis, one may describe genres as relying on entire networks of very different stereotypes existing on an intertextual level: figural stereotypes, plot stereotypes, even conventional story patterns, or stereotypes of visual or sound design. They form open networks, which are not frozen matrixes but are themselves continuously evolving, much like individual stereotypes.

For a certain period of time, a specific cross-linked repertoire of stereotypes appears with particular frequency and thus constitutes *a subsegment* of the genre. For instance, the great epic-heroic form of the Western emerged during the 1920s, following the variegated filmic precursor narratives of the early period. Later in the 1950s came the tales about tired and aging heroes, and even later the stories about utterly unheroic bounty hunters. The constructions of the post-Western, in particular that of the Italo-Western, stand out as the first Western form to openly recycle worn-out genre formulas by the reflexive use of stereotypes. All of these core storylines, which again cannot be neatly arranged in separate categories, were linked with complex but by no means frozen or hermetic networks of very different kinds of stereotypes.

Framed more simply, genre proves to be a vital evolutionary phenomenon, a series of generations or, in Tynyanov's term, an "order" of individual, openly structured networks (or repertoires) of stereotypes. Each generation of cross-linked stereotypes is enthusiastically performed for a period of time before it is subjected to a radical transformation. This is not only true of individual stereotypes but also of substantially less stable conventional networks as a whole. Faded and worn-out stereotypes gradually disappear from films, are "restructured," or finally become cultural signs that represent little more than their original filmic and cultural context, which they connotatively subsume. Often these stereotypes are used again in a reflexive and fragmented manner. One may see this in the retro films of the 1980s and 1990s (an example will be discussed at the end of this chapter), among others, which allude to the stereotype repertoire of classical genre cinema.

Beneath this ongoing dynamic interplay and evolution of the apparently stable lies a fundamental characteristic of genre. To once more cite Stephen Heath, genres are "instances of equilibrium."[132] They are founded on the gradual sedimentation and conventionalization of open networks of stereotypes with proven efficacy. Genres mediate between the conditions of film production (the economic interests of the studios, technical possibilities, and so on) and the dispositions of the largest possible audience (historically shaped by previous experience with film, by the sociopsychological context of a certain era, and so on). It is obvious that a change occurs in the adapted forms of film genres when substantial changes occur in this constellation—but a change also occurs when stereotypes have become so overused that they begin to morally wear down and no longer fulfill their function. This means that the dynamics of genre result from the dynamics of such (interacting) factors as the structure of film production and the mentality of the audience.

Whereas the sequential generations of a genre are therefore subject to a complex dialectic of continuity and rupture, individual "generations" can further be broken down into specific series of films and narrative cycles: for example, the epic Westerns of the 1920s and 1930s produced the two iconographic and narrative complexes of the construction of the transcontinental railroad and settlers' grueling passages to the West. Or stories centered around a city that is rescued from evil forces. All these narrative cycles come with specific stereotypes and particular clusters of stereotypes, in addition to the many patterns that they share with films in other cycles and genres.

Genres are not only intrinsically evolutionary, fanning out into relatively independent subforms within a given generation; they also lack clear boundaries. The constant incursion of what was considered specific to one genre into another was already the order of the day in the era of classical cinema. Blending of genres occurs constantly throughout film history. This allowed studios to introduce innovative elements into a genre and thus to add novelty, which also helped make films more accessible to demographically different target groups, as Rick Altman has shown.[133]

When comedies with music became common in the 1930s, American cinemagoers were presented with romancing, singing cowboys such as Gene Autry and Roy Rogers. Such figures embodied an appeal to both male and female viewers and a synthesis of the Western and the musical comedy. Once multiple studios copied these films, they developed into a kind of subform of the Western. Later, in the 1950s, proper Western musicals appeared—such as *Seven Brides for Seven Brothers* (Stanley Donen, 1954)—which combined the integrated musical with forms of the Western.

All of these aspects of instability and diffusion preempt any attempt to establish the schematic constants of a genre. This is also true of Tzvetan Todorov's structuralist efforts to match "theoretical" or "systematic" genres (that is, analytical genre models based on logical classification) with "historical" genres (that is, genres as actual historical-cultural institutions).[134] The historical evolution of genres does not comply with the criteria of logical classification. Todorov thus proposed the kind of classification described by Ludwig Wittgenstein as a "hopeless task."[135] When genre is conceived as an evolutionary, openly structured network of stereotypes, generational crossovers and the process-oriented character of genre just described are what prove interesting. Examining *reciprocities* and *processes* of this kind, that is, "the moving, evolving historical order,"[136] seems to be much more productive for an analysis of genre than the ultimately futile and highly abstract constructions entailing few instances of ultimate stability, let alone working out stable systems of genre relations.

* * *

At this point, the theoretical conceptualization of genre is further complicated by the fact that not only the development of cinema follows dynamics of conventionalization but so does the theoretical understanding of film—including the language that governs this understanding. This language shift—in other words, the innate linguistic dynamics of genre terminology—is particularly obvious in the case of the word "melodrama" (at least in terms of its American usage).

In an analysis originally presented in 1992—and often cited by genre theorists— of American film journals from the 1930s to the 1950s, Steve Neale[137] demonstrated that the emotional coloration and appeal now associated with melodrama does *not* correspond to the use of the term in that period. Today, melodrama is considered a genre that throughout film history has generally addressed women and focused on female characters, emphasizing unrequited love, sentimentality, resignation, and introversion rather than action. In his influential essay "Tales of Sound and Fury"[138] from 1972, Thomas Elsaesser wrote: "The world is closed, and the characters are acted upon. Melodrama confers on them a negative identity through suffering, and the progressive self-immolation and disillusionment generally ends in resignation: they emerge as lesser human beings for having become wise and acquiescent to the ways of the world."[139] Conversely, in his analysis of the trade press Neale came to the conclusion that in America the words "melodrama" or "melodramatic" had quite different connotations during the period from the 1930s to the 1950s, and also in the era of silent cinema: "The mark of these films is not pathos, romance, and domesticity, but action, adventure, and thrills: not 'feminine' genres and the woman's films but war films, adventure films, horror films, and thrillers, genres traditionally though of as, if anything, 'male.'[140] In another context, Neale points out that as late as 1956 an ad campaign by the *Motion Picture Herald* for Alfred Hitchcock's remake of *The Man Who Knew Too Much* (1956) celebrated the director as: "The master of melodrama, who does hair-raising thrillers."[141]

The shift from the past to the current definition of the term is obviously linked to a specific theoretical interest of the past few decades, which has placed different films at the center of film culture's understanding of this genre. One should not underestimate the significance of the previously mentioned essay by Thomas

Elsaesser, who placed the subspecies of the 1950s domestic melodrama center stage and thus broached a subject then largely defined by influential feminist discourse. From this perspective, films by Sirk and Minnelli, for example, have become predominantly associated with the word "melodrama" to the extent that they have meanwhile almost become synonymous with the generic term. Working from this redefinition, film historians then traced lines back in history, for example, Robert Lang harking back to D. W. Griffith and his films *Broken Blossoms* (1919) and *The Mother and the Law* (1919).[142] Essentially a kind of retroactive restructuring and resemantization of the genre expression took place, which has meanwhile become a discursive fact operating far beyond the confines of film theory. In other words, another level of evolution come into play.

This line of thought corresponds well with Tom Gunning's ideas, who observed that from the earliest silent films up through the Blockbuster video stores of the 1990s a downright arbitrary configuration of genre names has circulated in the film business, without the terms having much significance beyond their everyday usage: "immensely eclectic categories . . . emphasize their diversity and their rough and ready divisions which seem arbitrary from the viewpoint of genre criticism, but were most likely serviceable and pragmatic."[143] If one considers the scholarly resemantization of genre names, as in the case of the term "melodrama," which was guided by specific theoretical and discursive interests, or if one thinks about the constant neologisms of short-lived generic labels in *marketing*, in the discourse with the public, one must agree with Christine Gledhill's more general conclusion: "Genres are fictional worlds . . . their conventions cross into cultural and critical discourse, where we—as audiences, scholars, students, and critics—make and remake them."[144]

In light of these overall findings, sophisticated theories of genre have long since shifted towards openness and process. Rick Altman, one of the leading U.S. theorists[145] of film genre, thus developed his "semantic/syntactic approach,"[146] using the example of the film musical.[147] Based on a very broad understanding of the genre—guided by the term "music"—he arrives at different networks of stereotypes superseding and sometimes even competing with one other. He calls these networks *syntagmas* and describes them in detail. The evolution of such syntagmas (fundamentally independent of genre names) then becomes the actual subject of his inquiry. Altman's approach is similar to Wright's analysis of the Western, albeit somewhat less concerned with structural formalization. Altman thus describes the development of multiple conventional networks that subsequently replace one another within a given genre.

* * *

Research in cognitive theory on the formation of categories in everyday cognition was important in prompting the rethinking of genre theory,[148] which meanwhile has led to a radical paradigmatic shift, at least in English-speaking countries. Genre concepts are just such categories. Regarding genre, film theory ultimately draws on everyday concepts or complexes of ideas, which circulate in the public sphere of film culture and are then operationalized by film theory.

George Lakoff, Lev Vygotsky, and Ludwig Wittgenstein's ideas on cognition offer interesting indications as to why and in what form genres appear in cultural consciousness as relatively self-evident and even plentiful phenomena, despite their extensive lack of "basic characteristics."

Wittgenstein's thoughts on family resemblance—cited previously in a different context—seem to have been virtually written for genre theory. His ideas indicate that many everyday concepts, and also those of the humanities, are not based on clearly defined constants and a sufficient number of commonly shared characteristics but on family resemblances. Wittgenstein describes this as a "complex network of similarities overlapping and criss-crossing . . . build, features, color of eyes, gait, temperament, and so on and so forth."[149] In addition, with regard to genre this analogy suggests that the similarities (the stereotypes) are not only differently and unevenly distributed within a generation or subform but that they also change and shift from generation to generation and in connection with other families, and with new stereotypes being added. If one may describe genres as conventional networks of stereotypes, then the web of family similarities offers a viable model for comprehending such networks and the mental representations thereof.

George Lakoff has provided some additionally stimulating ideas. Already the (sly) title of his book *Women, Fire, and Dangerous Things*[150] plays a game of categorization with the reader, who often misreads a nonexistent "other" before "dangerous." This game paves the way for the subtitle *What Categories Reveal About the Mind*. Lakoff programmatically calls his concept *experiential realism* and vehemently rejects the idea that the majority of our categorizations can be interpreted in terms of the stipulations of formal logic or the *mind-as-computer* metaphor: "The classical view that categories are based on shared properties is not entirely wrong. We often categorize things on that basis. But that is only a small part of the story."[151]

He counters this with his prototype approach, which assumes "that human categorization is essentially a matter of both human experience and imagination."[152] Due to different types of active cognitive dynamics, one is everywhere confronted with indistinct categories with no basic rules or fixed parameters. Yet these kinds of concepts determine everyday cognition, are highly evident, and for the most part function smoothly, automatically, and unconsciously: "If we become aware of it at all, it is only in problematic cases."[153] These concepts are held together by processes operating in the realm of the conventional and are depicted by a cluster model based on a radial structure. A series of subcategories not characterized by universal constants is thus organized around a central case: "the subcategories are defined by convention as variations on the central case. There is no general rule for generating kinds of mothers."[154] The impression of coherence is thus generated by the dominating role that prototypes play in consciousness.

It stands to reason that David Bordwell referred to Lakoff when explaining his idea of genres as "fuzzy categories"[155] governed by particularly influential, successful, and thus prototypical films in the cultural consciousness of a respective period. This certainly seems compatible with the concept of genres as conventional networks of stereotypes that is being discussed here. One might say that the idea of the prototype emphasizes particularly successful films or those especially prominent in the media. Such films have great significance for cultural awareness of a specific genre, and they seem prototypical for a given repertoire. Just as genres undergo evolution, so do ideas as to which films are prototypical.

An observation by the Russian psychologist Lev Vygotsky provides a plausible argument for why this shifting, evolutionary, and sequential aspect does not necessarily contradict the formation of a coherent concept. He describes how the everyday cognition of adults is full of remnants of childlike thinking in complexes: "What distinguishes the construction of the complex is that it is based on connections among the individual elements that constitute it as opposed to abstract logical connections."[156] He thus develops five types of complexes, two of which seem to have provocative implications for genre theory. The associative complex is similar to what Lakoff says about cluster models organized around a central case (prototype):

> The various elements of the complex may not be united with one another in any way. The sole principle for their generalization is their empirical kinship with the nucleus of the complex. As we have said, any associative connection may link an element to the nucleus. (One element may be linked to the nucleus of the emerging complex because of its color. Another may be linked to it because of its form.) If we remember that this connection may vary not only in terms of the particular feature on which it is based but in terms of the character of the relationship between the two objects, we can begin to understand how varied, unordered, unsystematic, and un-unified the collection of concrete features lying behind complexive thinking may be at any given time.[157]

The *chain complex*, moreover, provides an elementary explanation as to why the integrity of genre consciousness is not necessarily broken by a paradigm shift in film culture. In its purest form, the chain complex can do without a central case: "The chain's final element may have nothing in common with its initial element. The fact that they are connected by an intermediate unifying element is sufficient for their membership in a single complex."[158] If one considers this not simply as a chain of three films but as a network of stereotypes evolving over an extended period in film culture, then genre consciousness can shift substantially without this change rupturing the coherence of the mental conception of the genre.

* * *

In the context of contemporary mainstream cinema, the concept of genre as open, familylike networks of stereotypes contingent upon evolution is highly significant. When dealing with a limited corpus of classical films or very specific questions, one could, under certain circumstances, still employ the notion of genre as a grid of constants without suffering a fiasco. However, this approach would ultimately break down in view of the current phenomenon of *hybrid-genre films*. In order to explain this phenomenon, it is essential that one now look at the evolution of conventional forms, the formation of evolving sequences of networked stereotypes. If one does not, then the notion of hybrid genre can, at best, be understood as a genre blend or mix. In fact, this is what often occurs. But that misses the point, however, of the actual aesthetic specificity of those recent movies for which the term "hybrid genre" was coined. Genre mixing is not an innovation of the past few decades; it was already an integral part of the film business in the era of classical cinema. I have already mentioned the examples of singing cowboys and the crossovers between the Western and the musical. A mere blending of genres cannot be equated with the novelty of the hybrid genre.

The latter's innovation lies elsewhere. The narrative structure of classical genre films—including mixed forms—was ultimately geared toward creating fictional worlds that were coherent *in themselves*. This was achieved by tapping everyday modes of perception and experiences of the real world, on the one hand, and—when departing from reality—by drawing upon conventional worlds of the imagination that had already been established (though genre) in the cultural sphere. And even in situations in which the "worlds" of two different genres were combined, the films attempted to quickly reestablish inner coherence and smooth over the fault lines between them. Usually one of the genres assumes a hegemonic role. The singing cowboy of the 1930s is placed in a situation in which the fact that he sings seems at least somewhat plausible in the context of the world of the Western—he picks up his guitar while sitting around the campfire in the evening, for example. In contrast, from the start the Western musical *Seven Brides for Seven*

Brothers asserts the logic of the film musical by integrating song and dance numbers into the storyline and carries this logic to its conclusion, while simply using the Western as a superficial milieu.

Such insistence on coherence and hegemony is foreign to hybrid-genre films, and this is what specifically defines them. No longer are the possible worlds of two genres linked and harmonized. Instead, an emphatically "artificial" diegesis is created in the individual hybrid-genre film and is pieced together from narrative or visual stereotypes, which are presented as blatant *fragments from different genre worlds* or discourses. The coherence of the original networks within the stereotype repertoire of each genre falls apart, and a conscious choice is made not to establish a new coherence or hegemonic order.

The term "hybrid" highlights this exact *disjoined or nonhomogeneous* element of linking and blending different sign systems or cultural techniques. Irmela Schneider[159] has articulated this quite clearly in a study on theoretical discourses dealing with the notion of hybrid culture. In examining aesthetic concepts and media-theoretical concepts, she refers to Bakhtin, among others, who developed the idea of "hybridization"[160] as a particular blend of languages. For Bakhtin, the "intentional hybrid" is one of three devices, which produce the "image of a language"[161]—that is, a reflexive metalanguage depicting a language. Summarizing Bakhtin's concept and comparing it with McLuhan's use of the term (which she also illustrates), Schneider emphasizes that despite all their differences, both theorists take pains to "formulate the hybrid primarily as a counter-concept to notions of uniformity and homogeneity."[162]

She also points out: "The work of Bakhtin already gives indications that the concept of uniformity [is linked] to that of centralism and absolutism, for which the hybrid serves as a counter-concept representing the manifold and the relative. Within the postmodern debate hierarchy and hegemony are largely cited as counter-concepts to the hybrid."[163] Schneider thus upholds the notion of "hybrid" as antithetical to homogeneity and related to self-reflexivity. It only follows that for the postmodern theorist Ihab Hassan "hybridization" (in a cultural and aesthetic sense) above all means the "'undefinition,' the deformation of cultural genres,"[164] which is related to Bakhtin's idea of carnival as the locus of "fragmentation, breakdown of the canon, and the loss of the self."[165]

Hybrid-genre cinema thus does not hide the fragmentary nature of the scraps of different genres it assembles but rather conspicuously emphasizes the lack of coherence between such elements. Such films do not seek to immerse the viewer in a homogeneous "possible world" of the imagination but present an exposed (in a figurative sense: metalinguistic) construct of heterogeneous signs. One could say that these films create an intentionally *impossible* world.

A key condition of the hybrid's fragmentary use of genre stereotypes (after the death of classical film genres) is their advanced stage of evolution. The patterns have long lost their original vital function and have become cultural memory's floating signs; they no longer provide a ground for the old imaginary worlds to grow along with corresponding existing cultural contexts but now merely refer to them. It would be practically impossible to follow this kind of process on a theoretical level without a concept that explains film genres as historical-dynamic repertoires of stereotypes.

Here is one example of a stereotype series. In John Ford's epic Western *The Iron Horse* (USA, 1924), which tells the story of the construction of the first transcontinental railroad in America, we encounter the following plot element: once the two lines have met, one coming from the East and one from the West, a dignitary drives a golden spike into the tie to celebrate the accomplishment. In 1939, we find the same plot element in Cecil B. DeMille's *Union Pacific* (USA). Based on these prototypes, the pattern was established as a fixed entity in cultural (and cinematic) consciousness, and from then on it belonged to the standard iconography of the American filmic narrative surrounding the construction of the railroad across the West. And according to Frank Gruber,[166] narratives dealing with the construction of the railroad are even the first of seven so-called *basic plots* of the Western.

The driving of the golden spike into the rail was by no means a simple recapitulation of the historic event at Promontory Point in May 1869, the carefully arranged setting of which has been preserved by the much-published historical photograph by Andrew J. Russel.[167] The filmic version of the golden spike ultimately became a mythic image—as understood by Barthes in his *Mythologies*[168] (which will be dealt with in more detail in chapter 7), and it in fact became a *filmic* stereotype, because not only the construction of the railroad but also the entire narrative structure of film rested on this image as a kind of conventional keystone. In Ford's film, the symbolic resolution of all the film's conflicts runs parallel to the ritual of hammering in the spike. The couple whose love story has dominated the romantic plot line unites with a kiss in close-up. And in DeMille's film, too, the ritual of the spike is accompanied by the main characters kissing.[169] A highly complex, repetitive narrative pattern.

Furthermore, both of these films develop a very similar visual staging of the event. A long shot based on Russell's photograph is standard: two locomotives facing each other on the same track and bracketing the decorated site of the spike ritual, which is encircled by a crowd of people. Other standard elements include cutting to protagonists on either side, the close-ups of the kissing couple, and the close-up of the spike as it is being pounded into the tie.

FIGURE 8 The ritual of driving in the spike as visual and narrative stereotype: (above) *The Iron Horse* (John Ford, 1924); (right) *Union Pacific* (Cecil B. DeMille, 1939).

Key moments of this staging remain in place as the stereotype resurfaces yet again in the hybrid-genre film *Wild Wild West* (Barry Sonnenfeld, USA, 1999). However, here all the old narrative links have been severed, which had therefore allowed individual details to recall classical narrative patterns. The narrative make-up of the film has little to do with the transcontinental railroad. Instead, the focus is the comically staged fight between two gunmen and a tyrant whose legs have been amputated—an allegorical personification of evil with the telling name Mr. Loveless, who wants to destroy America. The fictional world of the high-action movie assembles stereotypes from various genres as well as from completely different periods and presents them as pure semantic fragments. Numerous patterns

stem from the repertoire of the Western, and an equal number are taken from *fantasy*. The film additionally draws on all possible sets of cultural signs.

The spike ritual reappears as one such fragment and provides a particularly telling example of hybridization. The conventional and potentially coherence-generating contexts of this stereotype are shattered. First, since the film is not about the construction of the railroad, the nail-pounding ritual pops up quite randomly along the heroes' way through an absurd *fantasy* world of signs. It is called up from the cultural repertoire and made recognizable as a conventional entity, which is then arbitrarily combined with other signs to the point of overload. The spike ritual now takes place in Monument Valley, itself an iconic site of the West—but

FIGURE 9 The ritual of driving in the spike in the hybrid-genre film *Wild Wild West* (Barry Sonnenfeld, 1999).

not one originally associated with stories surrounding the construction of the railroad. This already indicates that the nail ritual is used in order to be decontextualized and broken down.

Although we see the classic shot of the two locomotives facing each other with the festive space of the ceremony between them (now in wide-screen format and extremely elongated horizontally), something else then happens that does not adhere to the rule, in which the hammering of the spike is followed by the cheers of the onlookers and a kiss in close-up. Here the spike refuses to go into the tie. Each time the president is about to hit the spike, it topples. These kinds of mishaps are commonly used for protraction and suspense. Several characters in DeMille's movie also have trouble hitting the spike. But in *Wild Wild West*, strong tremors in the ground are the cause. As the camera pans away from the spike and the ceremony, we discover the source of the tremors: the grotesque *fantasy* construction of a towering giant spider robot made of metal. This is Mr. Loveless's vehicle, which turns threateningly towards the president. The railroad context is then abandoned.

The original generic context of the golden spike is only retained as a fragment, which is presented, on the one hand, as (film-)cultural sign, which—like the tip of the iceberg—symbolically and fleetingly recalls its genre. On the other hand, its fragmentary nature is displayed by the radical removal from the original context and its insertion into a new context of the absurd.

Tynyanov discussed the "new use" of old "effaced" forms with a "new constructive significance" within the late phases of an "evolving historical order"[170]—largely within the context of the parody[171]—as a variation on the indirect use of a spent, that is, semantically or emotionally worn out, form.

The example of the gold spike illustrates how the fading and reuse of visual-narrative stereotypes currently function. What finally remains is a conventional image, into the meaning of which the original genre context is inscribed. In hybrid-genre films, this image is not only laid bare but also detached from its original context, from its former conventional network. As a depleted, free-floating entity, it becomes a mere toy element.

Wild Wild West is not a unique example. It was accompanied by a large number of hybrid-genre films, the best-known certainly being Baz Luhrmann's film musical *Moulin Rouge* (USA/Australia, 2002). It is a virtuoso combination of stereotypes, quotations, and references to specific hypotexts from a wide range of styles, genres, and periods into one great hybrid hypertext, a patchwork celebration of artificiality and disjointedness.[172] Luhrmann's film does this both in terms of narrative and image as well as in the tonal world of the music. The specific characteristics of such generic hybridity would be impossible to grasp without a theory of genre that addresses the evolution of stereotypes instead of trying to identify stable schemata of constants.

THREE

THE INTELLECTUAL VIEWPOINT VERSUS
THE STEREOTYPE IN MASS CULTURE

That which is past and proven appears over and over again in kitsch; in other words . . .
it will never take its vocabulary of reality from the world directly but will reapply
pre-used vocabularies, which in its hands rigidify into cliché, and here is the nolito,
the rejecting of goodwill, the turning away from the divine cosmic creation of values.
—HERMANN BROCH, "EVIL IN THE VALUE SYSTEM OF ART" (1933)

W orking through the concept of the stereotype against the backdrop
of its highly diverse conceptualizations from an array of scholarly
disciplines and schools (in chapter 1) has already called attention to two things.
First, from the standpoint of pragmatic analysis stereotypes are *functional entities*, indispensable phenomena that ultimately shape every form of cognition
and communication. Given a degree of analytical distance, one can even discern the stereotypical behind even the most subtle artistic expressions. Second,
as instances of reduced complexity, (intrasubjective) stability, and (intersubjective) conventionality, they always have a "downside." This is most apparent to the
"external" observer, when contexts have shifted or patterns have become worn out,
that is, when automatic perception or the habituality of the stereotype is at least
partially suspended.

The structuring of communicative messages through stereotypes is by no
means unique to popular film or the audiovisual media texts originating from
the cinematic tradition. Nevertheless, this phenomenon has been debated with
particular intensity in the context of film, and for a long time in an exceedingly
polemical and occasionally extremely contentious tone.

In part 2 of this inquiry, the conceptual motifs that have shaped the intellectual critique of the stereotype in film since the 1920s will be discussed at length.
The participating theorists and critics highlighted cinema's particular affinity for
the stereotype as indicative of a cultural and aesthetic development gone awry. To

begin with, one can ask why stereotypes were and continue to be so pronounced in the field of popular cinematography and in succeeding audiovisual media, especially since structuring based on stereotyped forms is not restricted to this object. What made the stereotypes of these media so conspicuous to those engaged in these critical discourses? Why have so many intellectual observers objected—and in some cases continue to object—to *these particular* stereotypes?

These questions will be explored from various perspectives. On the one hand, explanations can be found in the special characteristics of specific films and in the conditions governing their production and reception. For this reason, the specific coordination performed by stereotypes within this framework (of production, distribution, and reception) shall be examined first. On the other hand, the main reasons behind the particular conspicuousness of stereotypes in popular cinema only become obvious when one closely examines the dispositions of the intellectual observers engaged in the critical discourse. The specific salience and relevance of the phenomenon is only revealed in the interplay between these two sides, that is, in the antagonism between the intellectual viewpoint and the popular product.

COORDINATING FUNCTIONS
FOR THE CULTURE INDUSTRY'S PRODUCT

From a pragmatic perspective, stereotypes can be interpreted as *instances of equilibrium*, as *factors of functional mediation*. This also applies to the figurations used or formed by cinema.

The cultural-industrial fact of "the film" is inscribed with its function as a *mass* medium. From an economic standpoint, this is already dictated by its expensive mode of production, which (at very least) requires an amortization of investment. The technical possibilities of mass distribution, of reproduction, provide the basis for this. Film is thus presented with the task of mutually aligning its content and form of presentation with the expectations and desires of a mass audience. This also involves strategies for promoting efficient production within the operations of the culture industry. For it is the latter that largely mediates the production and distribution of popular-media products, including film (this particularly applies to the studio era).

Relative to the question of stereotype functions, this first of all necessitates a two-sided approach. First, stereotypes contribute to the coordination of content and form with the dispositions of a wide range of viewers, that is, the coordination of the films *with the audience*. Second, the well-rehearsed patterns have an impact on the economic efficiency of production processes; they help coordinate the structure of the product *with production and distribution.*

* * *

On the reception side, films perform a kind of *sociopsychological calibration.* They interact with the needs, wishes, and desires, as well as the viewing habits and the capacities that unite major target groups. Ideally in the era of classical cinema they corresponded with the dispositions of an actual mass audience.

The media sociologist Dieter Prokop once described the tendency toward a *common denominator* for large groups of viewers as a tendency toward "modal fantasy values," that is, toward "generally common fantasies, meanings, moods."[1] These fantasies are connected to viewers' real experiences but primarily also to their imaginative reservoirs, and they are associated with a form of spectatorship that is—normally—assigned the functions of "play" and "self-affirmation" or the role of a counterbalance to everyday experience.

Once they have been developed, both formal and content-based solutions tend to be repeated, as least in terms of their structure. These solutions are manifested in stereotypes as soon and as long as they harmonize with viewer dispositions and function smoothly. Numerous stereotypes that have become established in popular film consequently appear as sedimented product structures, which have gradually become articulated over time through an interchange with the dispositions of a wide audience. Hand in hand with these stereotypes came the development of *crystallizations of filmic fictions coordinated with a mass audience* in popular cinema—"effective formulas" both from an aesthetic-psychological and socio-logical standpoint.

In today's postclassical cinema, the spectatorship is no longer a "mass" audi-ence in the maximized sense·of the word, which traditionally implied something close to a cross-section of the population. Instead, the viewers are predominantly a youth audience, which, however, is still not sociologically further specified. This certainly does not alter the basic principle of sociopsychological coordination, except that it is now primarily oriented toward *this* target group. Despite *this new context*, stereotypes remain pragmatically interpretable entities adapted to the "modal" dispositions of the viewers they address.

The coordination with viewer dispositions is a reciprocal process. Develop-ing schemata affect the horizon of the viewer's imagination through the learning and adaptation that accompany repeated perception and cultural sedimentation. This means that stereotypes do not only represent preexisting fantasy values; they also actively participate in the formation and structuring of the reservoirs of the imagination. They structure the audience's fantasies. As Wolfgang Iser writes: "In our ordinary experience the imaginary tends to manifest itself in a somewhat diffuse manner, in fleeting impressions that defy our attempts to pin it down in a concrete and stabilized form." Only the fictionalizing act overcomes this diffuseness, "endows the imaginary with an articulate gestalt," and provides it with the "determinacy of the real."[2] Based on this, one could say: stereotypes of fiction lend the imaginary not only concrete form but also sustainability and thereby provide a particularly high degree of determinacy. They allow their underlying patterns of the imagination to become intertextual and intersubjective entities. Through the process of conventionalization, stereotypes become powerful cultural instances.

* * *

If one now looks at the production and distribution side of the issue, then one sees how *economic aspects of the coordinating functions performed by stereotypes* come into play and how they were largely constitutive of the cultural-industrial institution of cinema. In his famous study on film as commodity from the 1940s, Peter Bächlin specified two basic phenomena intrinsic to the profitable production of films. In principle, they can also be applied to more recent forms of audiovisual production (for example, TV series). The two phenomena were *first* "minimization of sales risk [by] achieving maximum use values" and, *second*, "minimization of production risk [through] the most rationalized form of production possible."[3]

For Bächlin, the term "standardization" was central to both of these aspects. Orientation toward the tastes of the audience in itself already "forces the production to typify, to standardize the film commodity."[4] Product structures that are standardized and thus coordinated with the dispositions of large target groups reduce sales risk. They ensure the specific use value of the films for the audience. A certain "uniforming of taste"[5] is a by-product of the mass consumption of standardized film commodities. This instance of homogenized audience dispositions is then a beneficial source of reference for further production.

In trailers and other marketing materials, signalized references to stereotypes—such as those indicating the advertised film's specific genre—provide potential consumers with clues facilitating the decision whether or not to watch the film. As key stimuli of stereotypization, only a few signal-like visual and narrative fragments are needed in order to activate complex semantic subroutines. Viewers can thereby gauge what sort of product to expect and whether it is one with which they have already had positive experiences. Vinzenz Hediger uses the word "stereotype" much in the same way in his study of American film trailers. He primarily considers highly familiar story patterns: "Trailers boil the film material down to the story stereotype and thereby offer a quality guarantee."[6]

From an economic perspective, stereotypes can also help ensure consistent sales. They may not only be viewed in the sense of sociological or sociopsychological coordination but are *simultaneously* of economic significance. They function as *product standards*, which help guarantee the use value and sale of the film commodity.

These conventional patterns are also useful in terms of the second aspect of economic efficiency: reducing costs through a *rationalized form of production*. Bächlin believed that in addition to other factors, "standardization in the interest of economic production"[7] is necessary for the greatest efficiency of film production. This is understood as the standardization of production processes and technologies in the creation of a film with the goal of rationalization. As with any kind of mass production, across-the-board similarities in product structures facilitate the standardization of production processes. Conversely, this standardization is expressed in similar product structures—and thus also in stereotypes.

Although the *metaphor* of "assembly-line production" is common in the discourse on *stereotype and film*, naturally the production of narrative films does not literally resemble factory production. Identical products were never the aim but rather films that foster a tension between similarity, stereotype, or norm, on one end of the spectrum, and difference, and even spectacular novelty, on the other. Which way a film leans depends on the type of production (for example, A-pictures versus serial films). Nevertheless, the "excision of differences *superfluous* to the use value of the commodity"[8] is essential to every major and, in the long run, commercially oriented form of film or media production.

In regard to the classical film business, Bächlin points out that the phenomenon of standardization has contributed to the fact that expensively equipped locations, set constructions, decorations, costumes and materials, stock film excerpts, and so on are preserved for repeated use. In the staging and realization of individual films it is possible to fall back on well-rehearsed patterns of narrative and well-proven forms of visual composition, on "readymade solutions"—type repertoires, special effects, music, lighting, camera and montage techniques, that is, standard elements of all kinds. This accelerates production and serves its efficient organization as a cyclical process based on the division of labor. These are techniques that were used excessively primarily in the period of the classical Hollywood studio system and were employed somewhat less intensively in European studios.

In her study[9] on the history of Hollywood cinema, Janet Staiger has comprehensively shown how this institution, which in its classical period became synonymous with the "culture industry," had from the very start always sought new means to achieve this kind of economic standardization: "It is accurate to define the Hollywood mode of production as mass production and detailed division of labor, its organization most closely approximates serial manufacture, allowing some collective activity and cooperation between craft workers."[10] The discourses of film advertising and craftspeople (cameramen, screenwriters, and so on) served as authoritative influences on communication aimed at the creation and establishment of norms—as did manuals such as *How to Write a Pictureplay*, which were more common in the United States than in Europe from the very beginning.

As early and intensively as this tendency—particularly pronounced in genre films from 1907 forward—emerged, the B-picture productions of the 1930s and 1940s are today the best known aspect of an overtly standardized cinema. *B-pictures* differ from A-cinema primarily in that the former were initially created as somewhat shorter movies for the double features then common in American cinemas. Shot with low budgets and at regularly scheduled intervals, B-movies appeared as explicitly standardized products, and they were much less concerned with a *distinctive* aesthetic style, the spectacular, *production value*, or the literary quality of the original story than were the expensive A-pictures. However, the latter also consistently displayed the use of standard techniques. This principle of standardization culminated in genre films, serials, and series, which constituted the core of the B-pictures. Bächlin wrote about the development of "standardized film genres"[11] and of "stereotyped film serials"[12] as possibilities of organizing a cyclical mode of film production highly reliant on the division of labor: film production uniformly structured according to a fixed scheme and whose results openly show all signs of being a mass product.

The core of cyclical production has long since shifted to television and its output of narrative series, where the basis for this kind of production was substantially expanded. Television replaced cinema as an everyday medium, and the films nowadays intended for release in theaters cultivate an A-attitude, even if mediocre productions, in promising a special attraction through the PR-created aura of the momentous. However, this does not abrogate a dependence on popular stereotypes, which now are often immediately established on an intermedial level, largely in interaction with television.

It is important to note that once manifested in films, the standards of rationalized production then also function as stereotypes in the minds of the viewers. As soon as they come into being—established as the normed skills of the trade and aesthetically reflected in the product—these standards also influence the spectators' conceptions of the world of film and shape their viewing habits. Such standards also create a kind of viewing norm and "standardize" not only the reservoirs of the imagination and aesthetic experience but simultaneously also the structure of demand. Staiger touches on an essential component of this interrelationship with her observation that standards do not simply introduce elements of "regularity or uniformity" into the mode of production and its output but also serve as "norms of excellence"[13] for the audience and ensure use value. Differently put, the need for rationalized and cyclical production not only enhances a tendency toward stereotypes but also influences the nature of the interpersonal world of stereotypes and notions of filmic quality.

This demonstrates that stereotypes of popular cinema have a double-sided optimizing function as mediators between the need for efficient production (minimizing production risk), on the one hand, and viewer dispositions (minimizing sales risk), on the other. Thus they necessarily play a role in the formation of a sedimented intersubjective imaginary.

OBSESSED WITH THE STEREOTYPE: INTELLECTUAL AND CONVENTIONAL FORMS OF THE POPULAR

For those involved in the critical discourse on the stereotype in film, practically the entire set of relationships just elaborated must have posed a startling challenge, if not provocation, to their intellectual self-image. This challenge is ultimately the reason why stereotypes in film (and subsequently in audiovisual media more generally) were so pronounced in the eyes of intellectuals, who were confronted with a phenomenon imbedded in functional contexts and "expectations" of use value obviously *different* from their own aesthetic discourses. Crystallized in the stereotypes of popular cinema and popular media as a whole are cultural tendencies at odds with traditional basic tenets of aesthetic thought. This concerns ideas about the role of art in *perception and knowledge* as well as about *aesthetic uniqueness*.

The progressive notion that art contributes to the transparency of the world— by providing a trajectory above and beyond ordinary, everyday perceptions and ideas by ultimately fostering intellectual maturity—was an expression of at least two concerns in twentieth-century thought, as indicated by the catchwords "deautomatization," "defamiliarization," and "demystification."

As early as 1916, Viktor Shklovsky specifically emphasized the idea of *defamiliarization* in his definition of art. In the essay "Art as Technique,"[14] he described this effect in relation to everyday perception and thinking. Shklovsky not only drew on a principle that was well aligned with predominant ideas on aesthetics at the time but also on a psychic "mechanism" that interested psychologists of the era and that also has a number of implications for stereotype theory. A few years prior to Shklovsky's essay, the psychologist Richard Avenarius had exhaustively studied the tendency toward habitual apperception and explains it through "the principle of minimal effort."[15] Avenarius noted that in "habitual apperception," the "impression made by external stimuli on the soul and body [is] attenuated," which "relieves the activity of the soul."[16]

Shklovsky subsequently emphasized the problematic aspect of this effect of psychic automatization for aesthetic perception: "After we see an object several times, we begin to recognize it. The object is in front of us and we know about it—hence we cannot say anything significant about it."[17] He described the consequences as follows:

> Habituation devours works, clothes, furniture, one's wife, and the fear of war. "If the whole complex lives of many people go on unconsciously, then such lives are as if they had never been." And art exists that one may recover the sensation of life; it exists to make one feel things, to make the stone *stony*. The purpose of art is to impart the sensation of things as they are perceived and not as they are known.[18]

Therefore, for Shklovsky the central task of art is to "remove objects from the automatism of perception,"[19] even to "remove the automatism of perception,"[20] and counter the blinding effects of habit.

The artistic technique that performs this function, defamiliarization (in Russian, *ostranenie*), is intended as a means of making the world immediately visible once again; a description or depiction consciously avoids or breaks through worn-out, habitual imagery and much-used linguistic terms, that is, all automatisms—thus allowing us to once again have a sensitized "vision" of reality "instead of serving as a means for knowing it."[21] Shklovsky found a practical application of this approach in the work of Tolstoy, whose technique "makes the familiar seem strange by not naming the familiar object. He describes an object as if he were seeing it for the first time, an event as if it were happening for the first time. In describing something he avoids the accepted names of its parts."[22] The purpose is to create a difference between the accustomed workings of the everyday world of perception and communication, on the one hand, and the artistic pictorial world, on the other, that is, between the conventional language of the ordinary and the language of poetry.

The notion that such a discrepancy can reclaim what had become unconscious because of habitualization influenced very different concepts of art, above and beyond Shklovsky and the circle of the Russian formalists. It represents a *guiding notion of modernity*. Brecht's concept of estrangement, or V-effect (*Verfremdung*), also rests on the basic idea of a defamiliarized and distanced view of the known (although this concept is linked with quite different implications in the context of his theory of theater). For Brecht, estrangement is achieved by partially robbing what we commonly encounter—such as the gestural and linguistic stereotypes from everyday life that refer to social contexts—of its familiarity and putting it on overt display. In addition, ideas relating to the revelation of the "optical unconscious,"[23] as Walter Benjamin described, are ultimately founded on this notion. Such ideas then also came to characterize theories of film art. Thus the idea of recovering the poetry of visual reality through the defamiliarizing effect of the filmic image unites the otherwise very different theories of Béla Balázs, Rudolf Arnheim, and Siegfried Kracauer.

The mechanism of the stereotype, on the contrary, *spontaneously* aims in the opposite direction. By their very nature, stereotypes are based on habitualization. Far from disrupting the latter, the primary effect of the stereotype is geared toward the enjoyment of repetition and the confirmation of the familiar. Stereotypes offer spontaneous self-affirmation, not estrangement and irritation.

In popular cinema, with its tendency (in a broader and narrower sense) toward incorporating serial forms that are conventionalized among the general public and its tendency toward providing psychic relief, the genuinely habitualizing mechanism of the stereotype is especially apparent. It is no wonder that Shklovsky emphasized how the *popular* narrative products of literature and cinematography display an inclination toward the repetition of structural forms—a tendency that aroused his disdain. In 1923, clearly prior to the topic having been taken up by the German film-theoretical discourse, he ironically described a "machine that produced plots"[24] for scriptwriters working in the American cinema. A year later, he expressed the following opinion about storytelling in popular literature: "Look at Burrough's eight or ten novels, which take place on Mars. . . . John Carter fights. He chops the heads of the planet's inhabitants as if they were cabbages, white, red, black, green, and yellow, and even a purple one would likely experience the same fate. . . . All his adventures are as similar as one egg is to another—only the colors of the Martians change."[25] And: "The mass reader loves the endless repetition of what is always the same adventure, and he likes it when it is surmounted in always the same manner."[26]

The opposition of *habituation and defamiliarization* is related to another antagonism. The term "defamiliarization" is used to describe an uncontrived, immediate, and fresh appropriation of reality similar to the idea of *demystification or demythologization*, which aims at perception and thought being based on reason. As noted in chapter 1, this conflict between two classic principles of thought—between the principle of myth and the ideal of a rational worldview—has a history dating back to antiquity. The stable nature of this conflict is clearly due to the fact that both modes of appropriating the world, *mythos* and *logos*, are engaged in an ongoing cultural struggle, in which the one is never able to supersede or replace the other.

Intellectuals of the Enlightenment tradition see themselves as apologists of reason. For example, in 1919 Max Weber stated that "the world is disenchanted" (*entzaubert*) as a result of "intellectualist rationalization, created by science and by scientifically oriented technology,"[27] and in 1927 Siegfried Kracauer proposed the historical process in the modern era as an advancing "process of demythologization" or "a stage in the process of demystifaction" (*Entzauberung*).[28] Their statements suggest how central this idea is to the self-image of intellectuals, particularly at the time of the incipient debate on the standardization of film.

Kracauer considered the "limited number of typical themes"[29] that recurred frequently in the average popular movie of the 1920s and early 1930s to be an alarming relapse into the realm of "mythological delusions."[30] Most of these films and the stereotypes crystallized therein gave form to fantasies, in which unreal desires, wishes, and sensibilities were expressed. These fantasies, according to Kracauer, are largely based on the desires of the (then new) class of salaried employees. Kracauer considered such imagination as coming before an impartial, open view of reality—and coming before reason. Representing a "relapse into mythology," these fantasies served the "ideological needs of an audience oriented towards the political Right."[31]

Kracauer thus was one of the first critics, if not the very first, to articulate this aspect of the intellectual antagonism toward the stereotypes of popular film—which ultimately boils down to the objection that the fantasies congealed in these patterns tend toward wish fulfillment and contradict a rational, factual, truthful view of the world. Later deception theories were linked to this basic conflict, which became particularly salient in view of the manipulative practices of fascism. The most famous of these theories stems from Max Horkheimer and Theodor W. Adorno and, by no coincidence, deals centrally with the topic of the stereotype (or "schematism" of mass culture).[32]

As also stated by theorists in more recent discourses, everyday thinking and the conventional fictional worlds of media entertainment are especially subject to the principles of myth.[33] Those stereotypes, which are generated by the cyclically organized imaginary and upon which they are based, may be interpreted as "crystals" of mythic microcosms. However, today the principle of the myth[34] and its sometimes ritualized fantasies are also accepted by scholars of media as a cultural fact *in its own right* that is on equal footing with the principle of reason, *logos*. Nevertheless, the latent conflict between these two forms of consciousness persists.

This is part of the reason why stereotypes in popular audiovisual media continue to be so obtrusive to the critical gaze. The critique of the stereotype, or its distorting effect, which was and (partially still) is common in both social-psychology texts and in classical media criticism, has often proved to be a rationalist critique of the imaginary and mythological thought patterns that underlie conceptual schemata. It can be understood as part of the age-old rationalist critique of myth.

A third aspect of the criticism of stereotypes in film as a mass medium is informed by the dichotomy between individuality and the mass audience. "What is peculiar to phantasy is its *optional character*. And therefore, speaking ideally, its unconditioned arbitrariness."[35] Edmund Husserl thus formulated an axiom of a form of aesthetic thought insisting on radical individuality. Since the romantic period, if not before, the original, unique work of art appearing as the free self-expression of idealized individuality has been considered an unquestionable, fundamental tenet of art. There could hardly be a greater contrast to this ideal than the notion of the cyclical, standardized production of intellectual and aesthetic goods based on industrial structures and unabashedly complying with the requirements of the market. The culture industry does not merely produce genres and series; it also forces the phenomenon of fashion to assume utterly new proportions. The stereotypes of popular cinema emerged as signs of this overarching development.

The fact that commercially produced films are so powerful and ubiquitously available due to their industrial basis and mass-media status, that they sometimes flatten cultural differences due to their worldwide distribution, and that as (certainly initially) predominant parts of mass culture they pervade almost all aspects of cultural existence and socialize the fantasies of masses of people, thereby regulating the individual "from without" on a grand scale—all this tremendously enhanced the conspicuousness, and even provocative dimension, of the stereotypes of popular cinema in the eyes of the champions of individuality. As a result, the mass-culture stereotype advanced to a *symbol of the anti-individual.*

Throughout history, individuality has always been articulated at the juncture between *social* discourses and on the basis of preexisting languages and socially mediated semantic systems, that is, always in a—charged—interchange with an interpersonal world of stereotypes. This nevertheless did not hinder advocates of what was conceived as the absolute autonomy of the individual from emphasizing the real tension between individual fantasies and those produced by the mass-market industry and from presenting them as absolute opposites.

From a sociological perspective, Pierre Bourdieu reflected on intellectuals' desire for radical proclamations of individuality and a corresponding fundamental skepticism toward anything mass produced, and he articulated an interesting underlying dimension of this phenomenon. In light of the social and cultural role of intellectuals, a cultural "distinction value"[36] is of virtually existential importance, since their capital is largely of an intellectual nature and based on intellectual distinction. In this context, overreactions against homogenizing tendencies advanced by mass culture that partially characterized the discourses on filmic stereotypes seem logical, for they have a kind of symbolic, demonstrative function.

In the logic of this argument, it follows that analyses of historical discourses have often identified the confirmation of a threatened cultural "exclusivity"[37] as the reason behind fundamentally critical intellectual attitudes. This is also suggested by the fact that the critique of stereotypes is generally not concerned with the immediate patterns of the intellectuals' own specialized and expert discourses but rather with an (at least partially) extrinsic discourse. This latter is rooted in the modal fantasy values of large groups of people and relates to the experiences, preferences, and fantasies of these viewers, which is why it may appear "trivial."

One could certainly continue enumerating and specifying the points of friction between the stereotype and traditional intellectual standpoints. In fact, the subsequent analysis of the discourse of film theory will do just that. However, here it suffices to simply hold in mind that the stereotypes of popular film serve as antipodes to multiple concepts viewed as positive by critics: as the opposite of individuality/distinction, as counter to the defamiliarization of the perception of reality, and as antithetical to the principle of demystification, to name just three of the most significant. This naturally has made stereotypes even more conspicuous and into symbolically negative entities in such discourses.

The latter is most noticeably apparent in Hermann Broch's writings on "kitsch." For Broch, the essence of kitsch is crystallized in the mechanism of the stereotype, or, in his words, the "cliché." All of the above mentioned aspects of the clash between the ideals of art and the stereotype are basically reflected in his argument. According to Broch, art is based on the "autonomy of the ego"[38] and is guided by "the ethical demand made of the artist, as always, to produce 'good' works."[39] Doing good work means inspiring "new forms of seeing"—a thought closely related to the fresh perspective afforded by defamiliarization—and "the discovery of new insights."[40] Broch's programmatic rejection of everything mythological reads as follows: "This always concerns, even in music, the portrayal of an inner or an outer world, a representation that must, first of all, be unmediated, and therefore unswervingly truthful."[41]

Broch's concept is distilled in the notion of a "vocabulary of reality" (*Realitäts-vokabel*), which is "the actual material that art works with."[42] The imperative is to consistently create something new, to build on a continued rejection of what has come before. Jochen Schulte-Sasse thus characterizes Broch's standards of art as a "genuinely created vocabulary of reality."[43]

Kitsch runs counter to all such standards. Kitsch is nothing less than "evil" in the value system of art.[44] It creates a system of imitation, which—instead of adhering to ethical standards—is oriented toward pure emotional gratification, which is achieved through a reliance on conventional formulas. In kitsch thus "even the vocabulary of reality from the immediate historical past was replaced by prefabricated clichés."[45] And:

> The means employed for effect are always "proven," and . . . that which is past and proven appears over and over again in kitsch; in other words . . . kitsch is always subject to the dogmatic influence of the past—it will never take its vocabulary of reality from the world directly but will apply pre-used vocabularies, which in its hands rigidify into cliché, and here is the *nolito*, the rejecting of goodwill, the turning away from the divine cosmic creation of values. [46]

In his analysis of the intellectual critique of popular fiction, Jochen Schulte-Sasse considers Broch's objection to the stereotype, that is, the cliché, one of the fundamental arguments of this discourse.

Given the complex constellation of opposing ideas, it is not surprising that Ruth Amossy identifies a critical hypersensitivity among intellectuals and artists of the twentieth century, the century in which mass-media culture developed, toward all determinate forms. She describes a genuine obsession with the stereotype: "une veritable obsession du stéréotype."[47]

She points out that whereas in nineteenth-century France there was not a comparable aversion to stereotyped forms, whether as fixed collocations or (stereo) typical figures, certain fundamental indications thereof can be found in Flaubert's *Dictionnaire des idées reçues*. However, Flaubert was aware, Amossy notes, that even great antipathy toward the stereotype does not permit one to actually go the full lengths of abandoning it altogether. This would ultimately only lead to an even greater reliance on it. Nonetheless, the "obsession with the stereotype" is basically an obsession with the idea of being able to free or at least partially emancipate oneself from it.

WAYS OF EMANCIPATION FROM THE STEREOTYPE

Against the backdrop of what has just been outlined, the stereotype presents a constant challenge, and not just for theory. It poses a challenge both to theoretical analysis and to the praxis of filmmaking, at least when the process is driven by aesthetic ambitions and a desire for individual expression. Both groups, filmmakers and theorists, have thus repeatedly sought ways of freeing or emancipating themselves from the stereotype, or at least a means of gaining an upper hand.

Despite the exceedingly diverse array of such attempts, one can outline three basic tendencies common to film theory and ambitious cinematographic approaches to the stereotype. These avenues of emancipation can be described as follows: (a) *radical critique and renunciation*, (b) *individual appropriation*, and (c) *celebratory revelation*. The three are in conflict with one another and warrant closer examination.

RADICAL CRITIQUE AND RENUNCIATION

This first tendency, a fundamental criticism of stereotypes in popular cinema, initially characterized *theoretical* discourse. Critics perceived the stereotype as the very opposite of their own cultural and aesthetic ideals. Although they sensed that they could not break the cultural power of the stereotype, critique was deemed to have one effect: the critic could thereby assume an external, superior position and claim to have seen through the mechanisms of stereotypization. At least in this way critics could claim a stance of superiority. The critical discourse on film can thus always also be interpreted as a vehement effort to defend intellectual autonomy against the culture of the stereotype. The logical site of this discourse is the position of radical exteriority, a fundamental renunciation of the logic of commercial mass media. This stance is rooted in an underlying similarity between critical and avant-garde concepts, as described by Peter Zima: "The concern shared by modernism, the avant-garde, and critical theory . . . was something beyond the given circumstances, something that soon assumed aesthetic . . . soon political . . . soon religious dimensions."[48] Both as an entity of economic regulation and as sedimented structure, the stereotype represents the principle of the already established. It conspicuously presents itself as a kind of symbolic anticoncept[49] of this common aim (Zima). The "stone of stereotype"[50] and the "schema of mass culture"[51] are consequently at the heart of Adorno and Horkheimer's critique of the culture industry.

The critical and *utopian* nature of this mode of thinking simultaneously implies that it is *practicable* only within a limited scope. These limitations are not only due to the fact that stereotypes underlie *every* kind of perception and communication. As Miriam Hansen aptly stated, given a cultural situation in which mass-media culture provides the "horizon of public self-understanding, within which—and in contradiction to which—all public spheres are constituted,"[52] any attempt to assume an autonomous, external position becomes questionable.

According to Hansen, the same applies for Horkheimer and Adorno, whose *Dialectic of Enlightenment* is still considered the most important manifesto of this theoretical stance. Popular media's permeation of cultural reality no longer permits anyone to truly and consistently remain "outside." Not only does it offer no means escape from the mechanisms of the stereotype as such, but it also hinders any determined renunciation of the stereotypes of audiovisual mass culture.

This is all the more apparent regarding the production of feature films. The theoretically outlined notion of radical difference corresponds to two fundamental practical concepts of cinema: one, the aim to renounce popular stereotyping by accessing reality as closely as possible, and, two, the (reflexive) filmic critique of such patterns.

One of the most prominent concepts in film theory to advocate the *elimination* of stereotypes is to be found in Siegfried Kracauer's *Theory of Film* from 1960. Kracauer indirectly argued for the avoidance of stereotypes. He was interested in making the "real" world, which had been distorted by conventional abstractions and ideological *patterns*, visible and discernable once again. The "redemption of physical reality" was to be achieved through a form of filmic depiction and narration, which avoids all the conventional-schematic constructs of filmic language in directly and inductively probing reality from its immediate physical surface, "from bottom to top."[53]

Kracauer's basic idea is closely related to Shklovsky's thoughts on artistic defamiliarization as a function of art. Whereas Shklovsky sought to deactivate automatic processes of perception through the use of unconventional artistic means, in order to achieve a resensitized "vision" of reality instead of a "means of knowing it,"[54] Kracauer's aim was to escape the ideological abstractions that determine our perception[55]—namely by having the camera take on "revealing functions."[56]

Accordingly, the camera should impart an undistorted view of reality, different from the narrative and pictorial patterns of popular film in revealing "things normally unseen."[57] The filmic image should transform "familiar sights into unusual patterns,"[58] for example, by means of the close-up. For Kracauer it was precisely the mechanical nature of the photographic recording process that held potential for this, since it conveyed direct evidence[59] of the depicted physical reality. It was his hope that the preformed world of an artist's ideas, which has always meant abstraction and conventional form (and also, stereotypes) and which thus engulfs the raw material of "reality," could thus be kept out of film by the technical possibilities of the medium.

As generally agreed today, this manner of thinking was misleading from an epistemological point of view, not least because the stereotype mechanism remained unaffected in the viewer's minds. Even if some films do not activate this mechanism to the same degree as do others, it still structures perception. Retrospectively speaking, one strength of this concept, however, is that in spirit and aesthetic sensibility it resembled the underlying attitudes of the contemporary neorealist cinema. It is no coincidence that Gilles Deleuze formulated one of the main aims of neorealism as "tearing a real image from clichés."[60]

The neorealist filmmaker Roberto Rossellini expressly stated his variation of the movement's aspirations. "What mattered to us was the investigation of reality, forming a relationship with reality"[61] and the "need to tell of things as they are, to take account of reality in an uncompromisingly concrete way."[62] The world itself should serve as the immediate subject matter of neorealist cinema: "It rejects formulas and doesn't pander to its audience."[63] According to Rossellini: "In the beginning I am guided by the resolute desire to avoid the commonplace by penetrating the inner core of things. . . . Cinema must teach people to know themselves, to acknowledge each other, instead of always telling the same stories. Otherwise one just produces variations on the same theme."[64]

He wanted to cut through blinding habitualization and make reality directly visible: "Everything has lost its real significance. One must try, I repeat, to once again see things as they are, not as malleable material, but as real material."[65]

Rossellini's films did in fact break with the conventional repertoire of the cinema of the period. Their success benefited from the atmosphere of the early postwar era, among other things. For a brief period, there was uncertainty among Europe's existing mass-culture institutions and the world of stereotypes that they provided. The public was open to new directions. Within this context, Rossellini did in fact attempt to demonstratively set his films apart from the conventional imaginary worlds of commercial genre cinema—as did Italian neorealist cinema as a whole—and particularly from the spectacular films of the Mussolini era and their routinized forms. Unlike these films, Rossellini's dealt with subject matter corresponding much more closely with people's everyday world of experience in postwar Europe—also in the way they were structured—than was common in ordinary commercial cinema, which, as Rossellini aptly noted, relied heavily on fantasies that had already been molded by previous films.

In contrast, Rossellini made films deliberately focused on the everyday reality of the period, and his work provided crucial inspiration to European cinema. Examining these films more closely, however, one realizes that they are more concerned with an emphasis on difference than with the assertion of an absolute ideal. Lotman hit the nail on the head in his assessment of neorealist cinema: "Its active elements were always 'refusals': refusal to use a stereotyped hero or typical film scenes. . . . Such a poetics of 'refusals' can only be effective against a remembered background of cinema art of the opposite type."[66] It would be hard to understand the full aesthetic attraction of neorealist cinema without the contrast it provided to commercial cinema and its world of stereotypes as a powerful cultural factor whose *absence is felt*, so to speak, in the films, which makes one aware of the differences between these two types of cinema.

From the defamiliarizing perspective of history—which allows what was once hidden to become gradually apparent—it is obvious that even neorealist films never completely managed to circumvent narrative or dramatic stereotypes. Rather, they incorporated and used them at least partially. Despite their cinematographic lyricism of the ordinary, they ultimately did not reflect an unadulterated reality; they were created for a wide audience and could therefore hardly escape the influence of the established forms and techniques of popular cinematic narratives. For example, in *Germania Anno Zero* (Roberto Rossellini, Italy/Germany, 1947) one cannot overlook the conventional patterns of melodramatic staging that characterize entire scenes of the frame story or that the film included character types—regardless of the great disparity between this film and the stereotype world of Mussolini-era cinema.

Mentioning these character types should not be taken as a criticism[67] of the film but merely of Rossellini's theoretical credo, which aimed at reflecting an *immediate* reality through film without conventional forms of narration, visual presentation, or thinking intervening between reality and the filmic diegesis. Incidentally, neorealism did in fact gradually return to the use of more conventional forms, in great part due to the pressures exerted by the competition and the audience.

This example highlights that even the emancipation from stereotypes as sought by neorealist cinema was invariably a matter of degree. Particularly when the cinema targets a wide audience, it is not possible to completely abandon the stereotypes of popular film. Approaches to film concerned with radically eliminating stereotypes and conveying an immediate external reality, ultimately—consciously or unconsciously and with varying emphases—boil down to the inscription of *relative* differences.

The latter is even more pertinent to films employing the other type of radical difference, namely films using a reflexive mode of critiquing cinematic stereotypes. Examples include Robert Altman's antigenre films from the 1970s. His *McCabe and Mrs. Miller* (1971) and *Buffalo Bill and the Indians* (1976), which critically deal with the myth and stereotypical world of the Western, are analyzed in detail in the final part of this book as key examples of this type of filmic self-criticism. At this point, it will suffice to say that these films also do not radically transcend stereotypes into the world of reality per se. Instead they remain symbolically rooted in the very patterns that underpin the central critical motifs of the films. Even if one does not share Deleuze's deprecatory stance toward the films of Altman and the former's call for a real "new image" of reality above and beyond all stereotypes, one thing is certain: neither the cinematic critique nor the parody of the cliché manages (and presumably never intended) to show us a truthful image: "the rage against clichés does not lead to much if it is content only to parody them; maltreated, mutilated, destroyed, a cliché is not slow to be reborn from its ashes."[68] Here Deleuze at least approximates the core of the stereotype's cultural power.

INDIVIDUAL APPROPRIATION

The second basic tendency of emancipation from the stereotype takes into account that a freedom from stereotypes can only be based on graduated, relative difference. Instead of renunciation or critique, this approach adheres to a more *dialectical treatment* of the stereotype. The aim is not to eliminate conventional patterns but to appropriate them in an individual manner. This is more or less what Herbert Jhering meant in writing that when one encounters a talent "even the most overused expression can still be unique."[69]

This means using stereotypes of filmic composition and creatively combining them with something new, partially revising them, giving them different nuances, or adding a layer of originality. The latent aesthetic imperative is thus served by selectively inscribing a structure governed by the stereotype with instances of difference, either to make conventional patterns of the imagination permeable to reality and thereby doing justice to the demands of *realism* or to introduce formal innovations that characterize the personal ideation or "signature" of an individual filmmaker.

One can read the film-*theoretical* discourses of the 1930s—such as those of Rudolf Arnheim and Erwin Panofsky—in this way: as *concepts of mediation* between the popular stereotype and individual expression. While expressing high expectations as to the originality and uniqueness of the photographic image and deploring conventionality on this level, they in fact accepted the use of popular stereotypes with respect to storylines and diegetic characters. Panofsky even called for their use in characterization and plotting (which will be discussed more thoroughly in part 2). More influential even today is another concept, which emphasizes a more narrowly *dialectical* approach to potentially *all* levels of popular cinema's established forms: *auteur theory*. It originated in France in the 1950s within the circle of the *Cahiers du cinema* critics. In one of his articles for this journal, André Bazin helped coin the phrase of "politique des auteurs."[70] The intellectual context was the desire of the *Cahiers* critics to take a stand "against the subjugation of film to the dominant role of literature as an expression of traditional literary culture's dismissal of cinema,"[71] writes Joachim Paech. The title of "author" (*auteur*), which was accorded great prestige in literary culture, was conferred on film directors, who were upheld as the true creators of the audiovisual text called film, whereas the writers of the literary sources were assigned a subordinate role. The solution was not considered to be an art cinema adapted from books with literary prestige but a form of cinema that took its own culture seriously.[72] This approach brought with it a revision of the traditionally disparaging view of Hollywood and even of its *genre system of stereotypes*. André Bazin wrote: "The American cinema is a classical art, but why not then admire in it what is most admirable, i.e., not only the talent of this or that film-maker, but the *genius of the system*, the richness of its ever-vigorous tradition, and its fertility when it comes into contact with new elements."[73]

Top directors such as Hawks, Hitchcock, Ford, and Ray were considered *auteurs*. They had succeeded in asserting their own personal voice, their own "signature," *not so much in contradiction to* the conventional system of Hollywood but rather through an interaction *with the genius of the system*—through their individual manner of appropriating conventional forms. It was thought that when placed in the hands of an auteur with a sense of innovation and a unique subjective perspective, studio-cultivated stereotypes would demonstrate their fertility over and over.

"Auteur" was a label of esteem, and someone could only be an auteur if he or she took the conventional system seriously but simultaneously brought to it a personal mode of expression consistently apparent in the resulting films: "The *politique des auteurs* consists, in short, of choosing the personal factor in artistic creation as a standard of reference, and then assuming that it continues and even progresses from one film to the next."[74] Bazin subsequently qualified this definition: the status of auteur could lead to sterile films, when based on formal intelligence alone. For a film to truly be an aesthetic event, Bazin required "social truth."[75] For Bazin, the question of the author was not exhausted by the personal factor as a formal standard of reference: "*Auteur*, yes, but what *of*?"[76]

This aspect was constitutive of Bazin's aesthetic thought. To him, film was always a medium for the revelation and reflection of nonfilmic reality. However, this idea receded decidedly into the background when auteurism became popular in America in the early 1960s. Adapted by Andrew Sarris,[77] it gained a more pragmatic dimension. Now called auteur theory, it was thus more oriented toward "formal intelligence," to quote Bazin, than social reality and soon developed into an ideal tool for tracing the development of artistic signatures *within* the Hollywood system.

The fundamental notion that was retained—that artistic individuality does not demand a radical breach with the system of mass culture and its stereotypes but can in fact be manifested in the personal and nuanced manner in which ready-made patterns of cinema are used—permitted the identification and aesthetic appreciation of a great number of *auteurs* in Hollywood. Soon this included second-tier studio directors, since the theory could explain how such directors had created original films out of conventional narrative and visual patterns by introducing distinctive personal characteristics and how they had thus developed an individual aesthetic profile. In this context, Bazin's original idea hardly played a role any longer—the notion of social reality made visible through the interplay of individuality and conventional forms, a condition for designating someone a *major* auteur.

The *politique des auteurs* thus underwent changes similar to the shift of Shklovsky's concept of defamiliarization in the neoformalist film theory of Kristin Thompson. Shklovsky was concerned with (at least in the previously cited text "Art as Technique") with the ability of art to penetrate habitualized, everyday perceptions of reality and thus to "recover the sensation of life,"[78] which, in the context of verbal descriptions, means eliminating customary terms and "accepted names,"[79] that is, conventional patterns. As already explained, Shklovsky's concept thus belongs to the first type of theories, which seek to regain reality through consistent renunciation of conventional forms of representation. For Kristin Thompson, who draws on Shklovsky's text, defamiliarization is also the be-all and end-all for assigning the value of "art." "Defamiliarization, then, is the general neoformalist term for the basic purpose of art in our lives. . . . Defamiliarization must be present for an object to function for the spectator as art; yet it can be present to vastly varying degrees."[80] However, Thompson's use of "defamiliarization" does not so much describe the recuperation of (non-filmic) reality but instead implies the recovery of stereotypical artistic forms.

> But if a series of artworks uses the same means over and over, the defamiliarizing capability of those means diminishes; the strangeness ebbs away over time. By that point, the defamiliarized has become familiar, and the artistic approach is largely automatized. The frequent changes that artists introduce into their new works over time reflect attempts to avoid automatization and to seek new means to defamiliarize those works' formal element.[81]

In other words, here the emphasis is not on the defamiliarization of everyday perceptions of reality by means of new artistic forms but on the *defamiliarization of conventional artistic forms*, which thus repeatedly, and at least partially, escape the mechanism of the stereotype. "Clichés and stereotypes" of artistic representation certainly also serve as an artist's "basic material."[82] Tending toward a reinterpretation or extension of Shklovsky's idea of defamiliarization, Thompson (like Sarris) shifts to an overtly more formal level, which within the framework of Russian formalism is actually closer to Tynyanov's concept of "differential quality"[83] of artistic forms in relation to the "the moving, evolving historical order"[84] than anything else.

Nevertheless, Thompson's theory is, like neoformalist theory as a whole, highly characteristic of a consciously partial emancipation from the stereotype through individual appropriation, that is, variation, shift, and defamiliarization, in short, through the estrangement of conventional forms. All other differences aside, her work thus exhibits the same fundamental dialectical pattern of aesthetic thought as all the variations of auteur theory. As a result, her theory could be equally subject to backlash from proponents of the idea of *fundamental* difference.

An example of such backlash stems from Pauline Kael, who sharply criticized Sarris's American version of auteurism. For Kael, "Sarris with his love for commercial trash" assumes "an anti-intellectual, anti-art role" by "suggesting that trash is the true film art."[85] Mast, Cohen, and Braudy cite another fierce reply to Sarris in which Kael articulated the subsequently prototypical objection "that there is something perverse about admiring an artist for managing to make an artistic silk purse out of the sow's ear of Hollywood trash. Isn't the true artist responsible for the choice of his materials and for finding an appropriate form for his chosen subject?"[86]

Based on *partial* difference and playing creatively *within* the system of established patterns of the popular imagination, this dialectical approach to the relationship between individuality and stereotypical conventionality must necessarily—irrespective of the question of formalism—remain unsatisfactory to proponents of *radical* difference. The latter tend to see the stereotypes of popular cinema more like "the sow's ear of Hollywood trash" (Kael) than the "genius of the system" (Bazin).

CELEBRATORY REVELATION

A third way of emancipation consists of a concept that is as radically conceived as the first, but in the opposite sense. According to this approach, dialectic attempts to "rescue" artistic individuality from the stereotype make almost as little sense as the desire to radically renounce conventional forms. Underlying this third set of considerations is a fundamental skepticism toward any kind of ideal as cultivated over the last few decades mainly under the banner of postmodernism. This skepticism questions both the romantic concept of individuality and the notion of perceiving reality as such.

Concepts such as those promulgated by radical constructivism[87]—a theory of cognition, in which the behaviorally determined, active dynamic of human perception and communication governed by schemata, or stereotypes, is much more decisive than the appropriation of reality in and of itself—have contributed to the belief that traditional questions of "truth" are obsolete. According to Fredric Jameson, postmodernists take this one step further in that they consider "the very concept of 'truth' itself" as "metaphysical baggage."[88] Jean Baudrillard, a leading voice in postmodern philosophy, is even convinced that reality is no longer tangible in the age of modern media. "Today the whole system is swamped by indeterminacy, and every reality is absorbed by the hyperreality of the code and simulation. The principle of simulation governs us now, rather than the outdated reality principle. We feed on those forms whose finalities have disappeared. No more ideology, only simulacra."[89]

Such skepticism toward "truth" and even "reality" per se often goes hand in hand with the conviction that the original Renaissance idea of individuality—based on the free will of the individual subject—is hardly more than an imaginary construct given the fragmented but interdependent social and mental world of today. Postmodernity thus assumes "the end of the bourgeois ego."[90]

Where the traditional ego ends, there also terminates the drive for originality. Much in this spirit, Vilém Flusser regards the drive for originality as futile—in the context of the media age (or, as he calls it, the "information age")—and he responds to still persistent aesthetic longings for the individual and the unique with irony and mild ridicule. He uses the example of art typographers, who "certainly must have a rough time with the rising flood of hard, monotonous stereotypes."[91]

A great ingenious artist created a marvelous, unique "capital B" character. The evil automatic printing machine saw this as a prototype and flooded us with millions of its clones, indistinguishable capital Bs. The typographer enters and at the last moment wrests the unique capital B from the grasp of the machine. He then sits down, looks at the capital B from all sides, and, lo and behold, at the creative hands of the typographer the capital B takes on a different character. . . . However, even the typographers cannot prevent the machines from coming and insidiously making stereotyped prototypes out of their redesigned capital Bs. The typographers simply hope that their B is so illegible, that only a few of them actually make the rounds.[92]

Thus the culturally predominant world of the mass-culture stereotype is ultimately grounded on social or psychological functions and in the media age does not permit individual escape. From this perspective, the question presents itself as to why one should still hold onto guiding ideas that are now obsolete, such as the expression of individuality or originality and the revelation of (physical) reality? From a postmodern standpoint, this is all a phantom cultural drive, which has long been obsolete.

What value could there still be in wishing to break with or transgress stereotypes, if this is merely a phantom notion? In the place of a call for a more or less radical exposure of reality, for critical deconstruction, the logic of postmodernism sets up an almost equally radical avowal of the stereotype as a component of omnipotent simulation. For cinema, this primarily means radically acknowledging of the world of media stereotypes, including the conventional patterns of popular film.

Nevertheless, despite all its consistency and the almost "heroic" acknowledging of the realities of the mass-medial "stereotype mechanism"—a stance that might also be criticized as cynical—from the moment films de facto reveal a specific aesthetic concept based on an avowal of stereotypes, this position proves hardly any more practical than its counterpart, the negative aesthetics of Horkheimer and Adorno.

This is because there is always something else that surreptitiously reenters the picture: the phenomenon of difference, the *partial* emancipation from the stereotype. Without it there would be no means to identify any degree of aesthetic distinctiveness, which is indeed necessitated by the logic of the current media economy. Speciality entails marketability and product differentiation. And it is distinctiveness that predominates in the minds of the filmmakers. Not only is the principle of stereotypization, that is, Flusser's machine, part of the media game, but so is the principle of continuous individuation and innovation, which are mutually dependent. Returning to Flusser's image, one could say that the typographer who constantly creates new forms is not a fool; he is simply no longer conceivable outside the context of the media game. Instead, he is constitutive of it, even if, or precisely because, this game constantly requires prototypes of the most useful forms for another round of stereotypization.

Hence, it is no wonder that meanwhile even postmodern cinema's star directors that are closest to the mainstream, such as Tarantino, Besson, Lynch, or the Coen brothers, are deemed *auteurs* and specifically staged and marketed as such. However, this sometimes occurs as a semi-ironic media game. This indicates how the prototypical aesthetic solution is used to display partial difference while celebrating the stereotype in a postmodern context. It involves the reflexive, "improper" treatment of stereotypes. Conventional patterns are employed unhesitatingly and are even exaggerated, but not in a manner that paints an overall picture or creates a homogenous whole or a coherent and consistent diegesis, which might claim the experiential character and illusionary immediacy of an alternate, coherent, fictional world. Instead, conventional patterns are incorporated into compositions of a dual nature. Such films do not really eliminate the gratification that the stereotype provides in its original functional context; they deliberately bank on it. At the same time, they reflexively reveal stereotypes as prefabricated constructs, as forms taken from an established repertoire.

Films of this kind—as different as *Wild at Heart* (David Lynch, 1990), *The Hudsucker Proxy* (Joel and Ethan Coen, 1994),[93] or *The Fifth Element* (Luc Besson, France/USA, 1997), to name only three—present fictions that certainly and absolutely do not refer to an "authentic reality"; they are fictions that no longer aspire to or feign the impression of realism, which had been a predominant concern of classical cinema. Instead, they emphasize and flaunt their reliance on prefabricated patterns of the imaginary and conventional, fictional worlds, that is, their operation with "second-hand" motifs—and often stereotypes.

This form of *self-referentiality*[94] is, on the one hand, accompanied by the "waning of affect," the "decorative exhilaration," and the "new kind of superficiality," which Jameson sees as "perhaps the supreme formal feature of all the postmodernisms."[95] On the other hand, an element of difference comes into play: a difference from the original, unmediated, "home-grown" use of the stereotype. Although the audience is once again provided with the gratification of the stereotype, this difference—as a quasi intellectual or aesthetic supplementary offering—presents a defamiliarized, reflexive view of enmeshed stereotypes, which is offered up as a play of signs and is by no means to be enjoyed only by an intellectual audience (as for instance with the previously mentioned hybrid-genre films).

The phenomenon of distance effects a sense of conscious individual superiority over the stereotype and one's pleasure derived from it. As a result, one is at least given *the feeling* of a deconstructed world of stereotypes. This effect is enhanced by many films assuming an ironic, sometimes satirical tone, occasionally even straying toward the absurd or grotesque. The intent is not polemical parody (as with Robert Altman's stereotype-critical films of the late 1970s) but a hyperaccentuated pastiche of stereotypes, which for all its irony once again allows the enjoyment of the patterns, sometimes even pushing the fascination that they hold to the point of mystification. One alternates between a monument to and a carnival of stereotypes.

Viktor Shklovsky once noted: "History shows that, as forms develop, both the baring of the device and the parody of a phenomenon signal the end of a given cycle."[96] Thus it stands to reason that the celebratory revelation of popular cinema's stereotypes has played such a dominant role in the era of postclassical film of the past three decades—at a relatively late stage in the development of film culture. Nevertheless, it is not a trend limited to this particular phase but a basic technique that had been used previously. For the most part, it was comedies that offered an appropriate context for elements of this technique. The film musical *Singin' in the Rain* (Stanley Donen, Gene Kelly, 1952) is a good example. The self-irony of this take on the genre did not ruin the pleasure provided by conventional genre forms, which had at that point been worn down by two decades of film musicals; on the contrary, the partial distance and irony "saved" and reinvigorated the genre.[97] It is no surprise that this technique later gained such cultural significance, particularly in a period when essentially all film genres were dead (having met their final demise together with the classical Hollywood film industry in the 1960s) and when genre stereotypes seemed worn out and faded.

* * *

This first overview of the three fundamental ways of emancipation from the stereotype demonstrates that aesthetic standards and a mastery of conventional forms can be asserted in different, and even opposing, ways. All three approaches individually reflect facets of the stereotype, all three offer specific concepts for playing with stereotypes and difference, all permit the theoretical articulation of unusual aesthetic concepts, and all have thereby produced very different films. None of these provides "the solution," the royal road free of inherent contradiction. Although consummated in theory, the fundamental elimination of the stereotype appears to be as impractical as its pure affirmation. When the stereotype is dealt with in a sophisticated manner, then almost anything is possible—except for one thing: its *unconsidered*, unreflected use.

These three variants of the push for emancipation from the stereotype have touched on fundamental ideas in the discourses of film theory. Part 2 of this book will subsequently examine in more detail how the stereotype has been considered by selected theories in the history of cinema.

PART II

A DISCOURSE HISTORY

The Topic of the "Stereotype" Throughout
Film Theory

FOUR

PRELUDE: WALTHER RATHENAU'S
CULTURAL CRITICISM, HUGO MÜNSTERBERG'S
EUPHORIC CONCEPT OF FILM AS ART, AND
THE NEGLECT OF THE STEREOTYPE

Writing in 1927 under the pseudonym Arnold Höllriegel, the Viennese author Richard A. Bermann voiced the conviction in his *Hollywood Bilderbuch* (Hollywood Picturebook)

that American film cannot be considered "art," for it is a consumer product for the prodigious masses, much like the canned meat goods which ... the people strolling down Broadway eat in the thousands of "cafeterias" there, perhaps ham and beans, perhaps chicken, perhaps a magnificently extravagant turkey, *always the same stuff prepared from the can in prodigious amounts for the prodigious masses.*[1]

At roughly the same time, Egon Erwin Kisch stressed the ever-same nature of the mass product of film even more explicitly: "The audience does not notice that it is seeing the same story with the same pictures, as long as the cowboy is the latest cowboy, the hero of all boys, large and small."[2]

Both passages indicate the great currency of the idea of film as a stronghold of the stereotype in the critical discourse of the late 1920s and how this was considered a direct reflection of the industrial, mass-cultural production of film in opposition to art. Both quotations offer an initial indication of how the debate on the stereotype in film—which emerged, at least in Germany, in the mid-1920s—had by the beginning of the 1930s not only developed into a conceptual topos much used within the narrower context of film theory but had also become a firmly established conceptual and narrative motif in cultural journalism on cinema. As a narrative motif, it functioned to highlight *the* principle antithetical to artistic individuality and originality.

How films were aesthetically judged was influenced by cultural criticism, as the latter saw itself provoked by the changes that occurred under the banner of the new media culture—or, more generally speaking, the industrialized mass culture of modernity as a whole. The assessments made in the two spheres of discourse, that is, cultural criticism in general and the aesthetic critique of cinema, were based on the same axioms. As will be elaborated more thoroughly in the chapter on the discourse of standardization around 1930, the great popularity of the topos of the *mechanization of life* in cultural critique from the mid-1920s on largely explains why the stereotype—considered an expression of mechanization—became a viral topic in writings on film aesthetics of the same period. The descriptions around 1930 of established film stereotypes as "standardized," "canned," or "readymade" suggest this correlation. Hence, a world of metaphors predominated, which interpreted the aesthetic phenomenon that critics perceived as stereotypes mainly as a result of the mechanical-industrial mass production ruled by standards: the use value of such production was oriented toward mass consumers, production volume was high, and production was rationalized by the principle of repetition so as to offer prices suitable to mass demand. The assembly line served as a leading cultural metaphor. The 1920s are regarded as the decade that ushered in the era of full mechanization, in which the assembly line played a decisive role and consequently assumed a symbolic dimension.

The social and cultural effects of this development were particularly apparent in Germany. Given the country's interrupted development due to the cultural upheavals of war and postwar crisis, social and cultural changes were unusually erratic during the phase of economic stabilization and across-the-board modernization. It is therefore no wonder that in Germany more than anywhere else a complex discourse developed on the cultural consequences of the modernization process, which many intellectuals perceived as the "mechanization" of the entirety of social existence. Opposing standpoints evolved: mostly euphoric variations of New Objectivity's celebration of rationalism and new technology, on the one hand, and a deprecating, skeptical, and even pessimistic viewpoint, on the other. Those subscribing to the latter tended to invoke the submission of the living to the specter of a dead, soulless machine producing ubiquitous uniformity.

The discovery of the stereotype as a topic related to cinema was—in the second half of the 1920s—largely owed to the same sensibility that had spawned the overarching discourse of cultural criticism. After all, cinema was in fact shaped by mechanisms of standardization or a certain seriality. Cinema was backed by an industry, and its films were made for the masses. In the mid-1920s, there was also a surge of rationalization in the German film industry, which attracted further critical attention.

A question presents itself, however, regarding the period leading up to this: All these developments took place in the mid-1920s to an unprecedented extent and degree, but they were not truly novelties of the decade. Both the debate in cultural criticism on the mechanization of life as well as industrial mechanization itself were clearly older phenomena, as were the implications that they bore for culture and cinema. Even America, the ultimate symbolic locus of modernity for German intellectuals of the 1920s, had already long represented this trend, which is why Americanization did not first become a topic of discussion with the emergence of New Objectivity but already prior to World War I was alternatively embraced enthusiastically or painted in a terrifying light.[3] Prior to the war, film production had also already exhibited clear tendencies toward standardization.

The question then arises as to why the issue of standardization or stereotype in film attracted attention relatively late, that is, in the second half of the 1920s. An answer one can eliminate is that the theoretical discourse on film only first emerged in this period, because by this time film theories had been developing for a decade. In effect, intellectuals had been debating cinema in the press since 1909—a discussion substantially colored by cultural criticism. This prelude to the discourse on stereotypes in film and especially the question of possible causes of the initial neglect of the issue—discussed so vehemently a decade later—therefore merit closer scrutiny.

* * *

The history of the mechanization of production and even of the assembly line extends far back into the nineteenth century. The basic components of this trend developed gradually. On the one hand, mechanical reproduction emerged with the processes of punching, embossing, casting, printing, and so on, accompanied by the standardization of machinery and product and the interchangeability of parts. On the other hand, the work invested in a product was divided into the separate, sequential, and standardized—that is, optimized and then repeated— tasks of a process, which were then synthesized and merged into a cyclical procedure through comprehensive organization and the introduction of the assembly-line principle. As described by as Sigfried Giedion,[4] major slaughterhouses, first in Cincinnati and then soon in Chicago, had already introduced the assembly-line concept (in this case, conversely, the disassembly line) into the organization of their operations a half a century prior to Ford, who began the assembly-line production of automobiles in 1913/1914. By 1915, his assembly line in Detroit was in full swing.[5]

Highly industrialized Wilhelminian Germany was of course affected by this powerful drive for extensive mechanization, even if somewhat less spectacularly than in the case of Ford. At the time, intellectuals already believed that transformation had far-reaching implications for culture; it was considered an essential process of modern capitalism and was discussed—predominantly accentuated by cultural criticism—already prior to World War I.

Walther Rathenau, himself a prominent industrialist, dedicated an entire book to the topic of the mechanization of the world in 1912.[6] It pervasively and critically concludes that the primacy of accelerating mechanization had comprehensively altered all aspects of life and the structure of society, from the sphere of production to people's leisure activities, intellectual life, and the arts. Rathenau developed a remarkably panoramic critique of civilization, which for him amounted to the *form of mechanized life in the modern era*. Even capitalism and its money economy appeared to him a "side-effect of mechanization itself."[7]

The extent to which his panorama of the mechanization of modern life was influenced by the antitheses of "culture versus civilization" and "community versus society" prevalent among German intellectuals of the time[8] becomes apparent in his outline of mechanized modernity against the backdrop of a mythical precivilizatory world in which still "the soul and mind of the community" predominated.[9] He regarded the mechanical as the core characteristic of a new social and even spiritual state.[10] The mechanical is used in a partly metaphoric and partly metonymic sense as an embodiment of everything antithetical to the origins of life, the organic, and to the search for meaning in life, spiritual depth, and contemplative emotionality. Rathenau saw the new world of industrial society as driven by whizzing flywheels, its highest law being: "Acceleration, precision, minimized friction, uniformity and simplification of types, minimization of work."[11]

In other words, his writings from 1912 include almost all the elements of what cultural critics described as the "age of mechanization," which would surface again in the 1920s in the cultural-criticism discourse on the standardization of life—and on film. Rathenau lamented the simplified and simplifying effect of mechanical production: "It creates extracts, monocultures, norms. But such products have no life of their own."[12] Like the many cultural critics who would follow him, he deplored the uniformity incurred by standardization, which remained unaltered even if "mechanized fate, fashion, [knocks] on the door"[13] and brings wavelike phases of change.

There are also hints of the notion—later important in Siegfried Kracauer's "The Mass Ornament"—that an alienated organization rules over people, even dominating them on a global scale. A "mechanized organization" spreads its "invisible nets out over every inch of the world."[14] In concert with reconfigured forms of production, society, and the world, it has an effect on every single life, on the circumstances of the individual. Through the standardized production processes mechanization not only turns people into "living machinery . . . mass-producible and replaceable . . . capable of extremely rapid and uniform movement."[15] It affects the very essence of the individual, both mentally and physically, above and beyond the actual sphere of production. What had already taken place as the human adaptation to the social demands of the production process was considered by Rathenau a simple linear extension of mechanization: this adaptation creates "new ideas, tasks, worries, and joys" and forms "the personality much in the way a machine properly sequences the workings of its parts."[16]

Thoughts repeatedly voiced in the media age about the change in perception caused by mechanical reproduction are already present in Rathenau's writings. The mechanical and millionfold reproduction of the image leads to "Bilder-flucht,"[17] or "fleeting images," which for viewers is equivalent to a "flood of unrelated impressions."[18] With its speed and diversity, mechanical production facilitates rapid, emotionally superficial perception. What Walter Benjamin later gave a decidedly utopian accent through the catchword "distraction" (*Zerstreuung*)[19] Rathenau described by emphasizing aesthetic impoverishment: "No time remains for contemplation, remembering, or reminiscing."[20]

Articulating another topos of contemporary criticism, Rathenau saw this as meeting the needs of the modern "working person," which "are as extensive as his work."[21] What results are "amusements of a sensational nature, rushed, banal, gaudy."[22] They correspond to a life that seems to be a "cyclical routine without a goal."[23] Rathenau regarded the arts as the opposite of such enjoyments, but once the former get caught in the gears, they too relinquish that ideal function so important to him. According to Rathenau, the arts had "lost their transcendental, their religious, their spiritual content."[24] To him, the secular and confidently nonideal art of modernity appeared to be "the art of the unbridled senses," which takes the "path of carnivalesque and travestying fashion"[25] and forms the deplorable "art ideal of mechanization."[26] That is to say, even the structural transformation of the public sphere[27] going hand in hand with new media and the accompanying changes in art introduced by technical reproducibility were considered effects of the mechanization of the world. Mechanization thus became *the* synonym for the modern era.

It is not surprising that reference was also made to the cinema in this context. Inasmuch as the following could be considered one of Rathenau's axioms, "Art enriches the soul, amusement belies its impoverishment,"[28] he viewed this new leisure institution as an example of the new trend toward amusement culture, as a "mechanical rival" of art or a "mechanical spectacle."[29] He wrote: "One symbol of an utterly inverted sense of art [is] the gangster film of the cinematograph. But even in this madness and over-stimulation there is something mechanical."[30] Here a conceptual construct appears that has resurfaced repeatedly since about 1911 in the debate on cinema. For German intellectuals of the period, film and cinema were veritable *symbols* of the new civilization. Thus even among authors who made opposing arguments as to the *cultural value* of film (and the modern age), as did Franz Pfemfert (anti) and Egon Friedell (pro), there was still agreement that cinema was the symbol of modernity.[31] Like Rathenau, in 1913 Alfred Kerr also stated that cinema and art have nothing in common and subsequently emphasized the mechanical character of film: "A field unto itself. Plays a role in mechanical developments."[32]

Nevertheless, as emphatically as cinema was understood to be a cultural emblem of the age of mechanization, as vague remained the references to what the films actually showed. The medium seemed to represent a symbol of modernity largely because it was perceived as a metropolitan institution oriented to the needs of the masses, a medium based on a mechanical, electrically driven apparatus, technical reproducibility (photo technology), and an industry. Additionally, it was obviously a business segment in the world of capitalism and also corresponded to the new urban dynamic of perception.

In contrast to the discourses of the late 1920s, however, the real "mechanization" of film production was *not* an issue at this time—that is, the cyclical mode of production based on the division of labor, the accompanying standardization of the medium's means of expression and of filmic narration, and the correspondence of visual and narrative structures to stereotypes. The tendency toward consolidated repetitive patterns, as in various film genres, for example, went uncommented and did not yet enter into reflections on the "uniformity" of mechanized culture and its worldwide leveling effect.

At first glance this seems perplexing, since Rathenau's discourse on the mechanization of life seems to lead directly to this question. Also, at the time the production of genre films was in full swing, as was their global distribution. That means that the phenomenon was certainly apparent but simply not yet an issue.

Film historians today agree that standardization was consciously implemented already in the early years of the film industry, particularly in America but also in Europe, even if less intensively. Standardization was already a factor in the era of short films, prior to the transition to longer formats (*feature films*) in 1910/1911 in Europe and in 1912/1913 in the United States. It was especially pronounced as a trend toward genre films and even more so with serials. It is therefore only logical that important studies on the history of film, and particularly American film, notably by Eileen Bowser[33] or Janet Staiger,[34] retrospectively focus on the issue of standardization in films after 1907.

This obvious trend toward conforming to certain norms can be explained by the program formats common in early cinema, which consisted of a selection of different short films. The weekly program change in cinemas, already then typical, resulted in a high quantitative demand for such programs. In 1911, the U.S. market alone had a demand for thirty new films per week.[35] Film producers were thus faced with the challenge of systematizing, typifying, and cyclically organizing their output, so that a consistent number of productions left the studio on a *regular* basis—and corresponded with tried and true types of films. This mode of production encouraged the trend toward standardization on all levels, including film style, and culminated in the distinctive mode of *genre* and *serial* films. The genre film

> as a standardized product would be one that . . . would be reliably available on a regular schedule, that the exchange and the exhibitor could count on; one that would draw the consumer to brand names, that would be familiar; and one that would be under the control of its producer. The standardized film would make it possible to rationalize production methods and would be more profitable for the producer.[36]

Between 1909 and 1914, the standardization of production and product was accompanied by a precise internal division of labor,[37] the development of individual departments, and the establishment of a large number of specialists contributing to the production of a film who were organized in an overarching hierarchy. The ultimate shift from small, artisan film production to the "film factory" had taken place. Thus a contemporary observer described his impression of the Selig film studio in 1911: "The Selig plant is an enormous art factory, where film plays are turned out with the same amount of organized efficiency, division of labor and manipulation of matter as if they were locomotives or sewing machines."[38]

The fact that American studios soon even created the position of "efficiency engineer"[39] in order to reorganize production processes illuminates the extent to which this idea of rationalization, so typical of the era, had taken hold in the new industry of filmmaking.

However, the topics of genre, standards, or stereotype and film played as little a role in American film theory and criticism as they did in German debates on film and culture, although American genre films even circulated on the German market. Considering the German cultural criticism à la Rathenau that generally prevailed in journalistic debates on cinema, the reasons for this situation probably were that the phenomenon of cinema as such was so scorned that contemporary film programs or production processes hardly merited the closer examination of cinema's detractors. Criticism was leveled at the cultural institution of cinema and its apparatus rather than at the specific structures of films. In other words, cultural critics of cinema at the time did not take the pains to carefully examine the films they deplored from the outset and thus made rather sweeping arguments. Hence, the issue of the standardization of film itself initially eluded them.

The period's typical blindness toward this issue seems all the more peculiar in the case of the German-American Hugo Münsterberg, who published *The Photoplay* in April 1916,[40] the first systematic study on the psychology and aesthetics of film. In preparing this survey, which is distinguished by a precise knowledge of contemporary techniques of filmic narrative and celebrates the new medium, Münsterberg watched a vast number of films, which means that in contrast to many other journalists expressing their opinions on the medium, he had a precise knowledge of the film practices of his era.

As the founder and trailblazer of applied psychology in the United States, Münsterberg was also known for his sharp sense for economic interests and relationships. Within this new discipline, he considered it his task to develop specific psychotechniques (*Psychotechnik*) for a wide range of life contexts, particularly for industry. Influenced by F. W. Taylor's ideas on rationalization that were characteristic of the period and based on improving the efficiency of the *physical* organization of labor, Münsterberg thus sought to further enhance efficiency through a better mastery of subjective, *psychological* factors.[41]

Apart from his treatise on film, Münsterberg was therefore certainly interested in the topic of standardization and its translation into the area of psychology and communication. The critique and skepticism found in Rathenau are completely absent in Münsterberg's work, which is dominated by a pragmatic approach. In his book from 1914, *Grundzüge der Psychotechnik* (The Fundamentals of Psychotechnique), indicative of the psychologist's self-image as a technician, he even expressly recommends "certain standard forms of communication"[42] for business life. For Münsterberg, the communicative dimension of business (for example, conversations with customers or advertising) was still ruled too extensively by "momentary impulses" and showed "hardly any signs of the mechanization processes of our time."[43] The language used in conversations with customers was compared to "a psychologically developed use of the future form, like skilled labor to factory operations."[44] Whereas Münsterberg considered the solution to be obvious: namely, the application to communication of Taylor's scientifically optimized standardization of workers' movements in production:

"Once the right form of suggestion or argument has been found, this must be retained and practiced, if one wishes to achieve psychological economy and accuracy."[45] Münsterberg described four aspects of standard communication forms that enhance efficiency:

First, "psychological economy" is achieved by formulating the "right form of argument." This represents an *automatization effect* for the speaker, who is thus "psychologically relieved, since he can proceed automatically instead of exerting effort."[46]

Second, one can improve "accuracy" by adhering to the "right form of suggestion," that is, by an *adaptation effect* oriented toward the recipients of the communication.

Third, a kind of *reciprocal adaptation* occurs on the part of the consumers, a learning and recognition effect important for product advertising: a "factor in retention [is] the frequency of repetition."[47]

Fourth, this is supplemented by what could be described as the *pleasure of repetition*, which is associated with a "warm sense of familiarity"[48] and therefore positive emotions. "The sheer memory value, however, is all the more important for the task at hand, because according to a well-known law of psychology, the pleasure gained from pure repetition is readily transferred to the recognized object."[49]

Interestingly, these four aspects regularly resurface in reflections of subsequent theorists on the causes of aesthetic *standardization of film*. Münsterberg indirectly outlined the basic repertoire of thought on this question—without considering film in this context.

For all intents and purposes, Münsterberg's aim was also to develop quantifiable "psychotechnical rules" for art. The *pleasure of repetition* is an important topic, also explored in the context of his "experimental aesthetics of form"—which is obsessed with the idea of quantification—for visual art. In an extensive series of experiments, his Harvard laboratory investigated "the degree to which the repetition of a form is pleasing and the conditions under which genuine pleasure still may be fostered by partial repetition."[50]

In this context, it is more than reasonable to suspect that this interest in standard forms of communication would also have been clearly reflected in Münsterberg's study on film. Especially since he as a psychologist also demonstrated an astute understanding of the needs of the film industry, with which he cooperated. For example, in an incidental remark he matter-of-factly explained the contemporary producers' lack of interest in *newsreels*: "It is claimed that the producers in America disliked these topical pictures because the accidental character of the events makes the production irregular and interferes too much with the steady preparation of the photoplays."[51]

Whereas decades later Adorno explicitly described "psychotechnique"[52] (to him negatively connoted) at work in the Hollywood film industry, Münsterberg as one of the very founders of psychotechnique does not mention standard forms of communication, stereotypes, or the pleasures of repetition. The reason behind this contradiction can most readily be explained by the fact that *The Photoplay* is dominated by a strategy of argumentation—typical of the film theory of the period—not served but hindered by such considerations.

The basic aim of Münsterberg's aesthetic reasoning in his survey was to *justify the viability of film as art*. This certainly was aligned with the intentions of the film industry at the time, whose marketing strategies were oriented toward elevating its products to art. Both in the United States and in Germany, nationwide advertising campaigns for elaborate major productions—from German "author's films" (*Autorenfilme*) as of 1913/1914 to American special features and *The Birth of a Nation* (David W. Griffith, 1915)—invoke the distinctive value of art. The tension between standard and difference assumed a new dimension with these films, which were emphasized as being unique works. Production and advertising value of difference, that is, of artistic singularity, increased.

Not least against the backdrop of the film industry's confident ambitions to henceforth produce *art* it seems logical that the beginnings of a more sophisticated film theory coincided exactly with the rise of long feature films. It is also no coincidence that this theory began as a project seeking to assert cinema's potential of being an *art* form capable of adhering to the *traditional* "laws" of art in new ways specific to the medium.

The Photoplay is a characteristic and outstanding example in this respect. In his wish to validate the artistic potential of film and to ambitiously place cinema in the ranks of what was already accepted as fine art, Münsterberg tended to rely on a range of traditional aesthetic standpoints, as previously formulated in his philosophical work *The Eternal Values*, in relation to the classic arts.[53] These ideas do not spring from the generally American and pragmatic orientation of his psychotechnique but were in the thrall of the idealist thought of German neo-Kantianism. Emphasis is placed on the integral world (*selbstseiende Welt*) of the work of art, in which the plurality of all parts come together as a whole in complete harmony, as an ideal experience transcending practical interests. Thus corroborated, Münsterberg's groundbreaking psychological account of central aspects of the film viewer's disposition—which made *The Photoplay* a classical text of film theory—takes its place in the film-as-art approach, as discussed elsewhere in greater detail.[54] Münsterberg renders an image of a perceptual instrument that absorbs spectators with an all-encompassing hold on their attention, places them in an aesthetic world of perfect harmony and isolation, and makes the everyday world seem far removed. Film is "a new form of true beauty in the turmoil of a technical age, created by its very technique and yet more than any other art destined to overcome outer nature by the free and joyful play of the mind."[55]

His attempt to reconcile an idealist theory of art with a technically and sociologically new medium brought out the *inconsistencies* that the pragmatist John Dewey had already criticized in reference to Münsterberg's *The Eternal Values*. Dewey stated that such discrepancies were inherent to any philosophy "that professes Ultimates, Absolutes, and Eternals."[56] To the classic tradition of aesthetics and cultural philosophy of the era, the notion of standardization was inconceivable as anything but an absolute antithesis to art and individuality. The moment that Münsterberg adopted the idealist patterns of argument, he precluded all ideas of the standard or stereotype in favor of proclaiming the continuity of art. And he did so even though his psychotechnical categories seemed to call for just the opposite. On this point, the aesthetic idealist won out over the psychotechnician.

This emphasis would typify the film-art theories of the following years. Whatever motif of the traditionally accepted arts and art theories such inquiries chose to rely on, they consistently sought to prove the new potential for the realization of art that the technical medium afforded. Celebrated exceptional films with distinct artistic ambitions were upheld as forerunners of the burgeoning culture of film. In contrast, the frictions between the idealist approach and the mass-culture reality of film as a popular medium with industrial origins were barely mentioned in the emphatic proclamations of film as a new art form. There was also a failure to recognize that the new mass culture of media—driven by film—was to change the very nature of art itself. The stereotypes of popular cinema and the tendencies toward standardization in film were persistently ignored.

FIVE

BÉLA BALÁZS'S NEW VISUAL CULTURE, THE TRADITION OF LINGUISTIC SKEPTICISM, AND ROBERT MUSIL'S NOTION OF THE "FORMULAIC"

For words now obscure things. Hearsay has consumed the world. . . . And so
a desperate love has been awakened for all the arts practiced in silence.
—HUGO VON HOFMANNSTHAL, "EINE MONOGRAPHIE" (1895)

SALVATION FROM CONVENTIONAL LANGUAGE: THE MYSTIFICATION OF GESTURE

Münsterberg had validated cinema's potential as art, largely by celebrating the psychological power of the medium to create an intrinsically harmonic and hermetic, aesthetic world of appearances. In doing so, he had ascribed to an idea central to traditional definitions of art. However, film theory soon shifted, particularly in Germany, toward a different line of thought in high-culture aesthetic discourse:[1] an anthropomorphic perspective based on physiognomy.

This thinking predominated in the premontage era of German film theory (until approximately 1926) and had continuing influence thereafter. Writers such as Béla Balázs[2] and Rudolf Harms[3] advocated cinema as an artistic medium, now arguing that its silent motion displayed a particular affinity to gesture, to human expressive movement. They regarded gesture as the true aesthetic material of film and thought that even the world of objects could convey gestural-emotional expression—either through an appropriate composition of mise en scène or the photographic framing of a certain perspective.

Anthropomorphic concepts grounded in physiognomy were particularly prominent in contemporary theories of the humanities. In their commentaries on Balázs, both Gertrud Koch[4] and Hanno Loewy[5] have convincingly illuminated these theoretical contexts, particularly the distinct influence of Georg Simmel's work. Joseph Zsuffa illustrates similar correspondences by means of biographical links.[6] Also, it hardly needs to be pointed out that Expressionism—whether in the visual arts, literature, or the, not incidentally, acclaimed *Ausdruckstanz* of the period—was driven by the desire for an immediacy of expression above and beyond traditional forms. However, it is important to bear in mind that the prevailing psychological aesthetic of the time and its related theories of empathy (*Einfühlungstheorie*) were based on the concept of expressive movement (*Ausdrucksbewegung*)—as with the aesthetic thought of Theodor Lipps and Johannes Volkert, who as the academic teacher of Rudolf Harms and an inspiration to Ernst Iros[7] certainly had a substantial, if indirect, influence on film theories of the era.

The expressive movements embodied in a work of art were considered by proponents of the psychological aesthetic to be a central mediator between the artistically created artifact and the receptive experience. Expressive movements generated an involuntary response on the part of the spectator. By recognizing human expressive movements in the visual structure of the work (including inanimate objects thus anthropomorphized), recipients could associate emotions they themselves have experienced with these movements and project them into the world of the artistic work.

The artistic experience was considered nothing other than "empathicizing into" the expressive movement present in the structures of the work of art. Readers and spectators empathically endow a material framework with emotional content. A work of art only becomes a living entity when a receptive subject transforms it in this manner. Taking this further, Theodor Lipps believed that aesthetic enjoyment resulted from the pleasure of experiencing expressive movement in the fictional realm of the work itself, even independent of its emotional coloration: namely, "the aesthetic pleasure of expressive movement comes from the pleasure aroused in me from this sort of voluntary, inner engagement of an inner reaction, which for me immediately lies in the expressive movement. . . . Simply stated, this is the pleasure of 'empathy.' "[8]

Given the great influence of the aesthetics of empathy, it stands to reason that the theory of film as art was informed by such a prominent paradigm as that of expressive movement, especially since the poignancy and originality of visual gesture were also devotedly cultivated in the more advanced segment of German silent cinema, both in acting[9] and décor.[10]

Münsterberg's theory had omitted the topic of the stereotype and all its facets, because it did not directly support his argument. A theoretical reflection on conventional and seemingly reductive repetitive forms would not have served but instead opposed and detracted from the objectives of his analysis. As described below, the same is true to a much greater extent regarding the physiognomic theory of film.

In the cinema debates around 1910 and after, cultural criticism had deplored the new visual medium's "explicitness crippling to the imagination"[11] and even its "lethal effect on the imagination,"[12] because the image, particularly the moving image, did not offer the spectator's imagination the space afforded by *linguistic abstraction* but instead took "the place of the imagination."[13] Just at the point when, as Friedrich Kittler describes, "the ability to record sense data shifted the entire discourse network circa 1900,"[14] breaking the monopoly of the book, critics of film's new cultural influence foreboded its harmful effects on the practice of art and intellectual life. Their main objection concerned the elimination of linguistic abstraction.

The physiognomic theory of film art simply inverted this argument and used it in its favor. These theorists considered the medium of film potentially superior to language-based arts, *for the very reason* that it did away with the abstraction of linguistic semantics and once again taught the viewer to truly see. Thus one can understand Béla Balázs's proclamation of a utopian *new visual culture* as emerging with cinema in his programmatically titled book *Visible Man*, published in 1924.

Neither film's incapacity for language nor its focus on the image was the source of cultural impoverishment. According to Balázs's premise, the emerging culturally preeminent medium of cinema promised—precisely because of these unique features—to compensate for the harm that the language-dominated age of Gutenberg had inflicted on human beings' direct sensual relationship to their immediate surroundings.

Historical research on film theory has shown that this argument too was informed by the literary discourse of *Sprachskepsis*,[15] or linguistic skepticism, prevalent in the decades around 1900 and with precedents dating back even further. Physiognomic film theory's pretensions advanced the photographic film medium as the very solution to what linguistic skeptics considered the essential deficits of language.

In the field of literature, it was Hugo von Hofmannsthal who most notably articulated this sense of deficiency. Although certain excerpts from his writings, in particular his fictional "The Lord Chandos Letter" of 1902,[16] have often been quoted in historical studies on film theory, it is worthwhile to examine the conceptual construct of linguistic skepticism somewhat more thoroughly than it generally has been in such contexts. In the process, one discovers that the linguistic skeptics' critique of their medium was not so far removed from the objections raised by critics of the stereotype and later film critics.

Thus, parallels and common intellectual roots between linguistic skepticism and language criticism on the one hand and the critique of the stereotype on the other become obvious. Hence, in retrospect it almost seems paradoxical that the physiognomic theory of film actually celebrated the medium, which would soon be declared a "stronghold" of the stereotype, as the cultural solution to the supposed deficits of language. It follows that within the celebration of film, aimed at theoretically legitimizing film as art and incorporating arguments of language criticism, a discussion of stereotypes in film would not only have hurt but fundamentally counteracted its line of argument.

In expressing their sense of language's essential deficits in adequately reflecting and articulating both the external world and the inner self, linguistic skeptics ultimately drew on three interdependent specifics of language: *abstraction*, *automatism*, and *conventionality*—terms that are familiar from the facets of the stereotype outlined in chapter 1.

The fundamental starting point is the phenomenon of *abstraction* inherent to any language and its necessarily generalized terms. Terms are based on summations of similar, not identical entities. Linguistic skepticism emphasizes that abstraction cannot grasp and convey anything close to the true richness of concrete reality. For this reason alone, the linguistically expressed appears as a barren reflection of reality's actual abundance, which is why "it beggars all words."[17] Hofmannsthal lets his character Lord Chandos articulate the poet's own sense of the inadequacy of language: "the abstract words that the tongue necessarily shapes when passing any kind of judgment simply fell to dust in my mouth like decaying mushrooms."[18]

A second objection, linked to abstraction and heightening the first, concerns the phenomenon of the *automatization* or habitualization of language. Achieved through repetition, the automatization of an abstraction, a cognitive formula, and the accompanying reinforced semantic link with a signifier necessarily lead to a reduction of initial psychic activity. This is the function of automatization.

As indispensable to the function of language and thought as this may seem, as problematic it appeared to linguistic skepticism, given the successive detachment of an abstraction from the primary intellectual-emotional process, the original psychic activity of experiencing meaning, and thus also from perception (and the mental image); automatization promotes deconcretization and leads to semantic reduction. From the standpoint of language criticism, the pool of existing terms or concepts (*Begriffe*)[19] is standardly faulted as being a reservoir of faded meanings no longer truly felt and judgments long gone unreflected.

This effect is further exacerbated by the necessary *conventionality* of language, because conventionalization simultaneously shifts the process of expressions emerging and wearing out into the intersubjective realm of the language community, and thus also into linguistic history. This is the basis for the often-deplored obsolescence of terms, that is, the fact that cultural change places them in new contexts that often deplete or displace their meanings. However, with the intersubjective basis of terminological formation being a condition of communication—as enabled by convention—and with the relatively independent dynamic of language, a third objection arises: namely, society's intervening in the individual subject through terms that are not the self-created property of the individual but "something that has entered from without, a conventional sign,"[20] as Hofmannsthal wrote as early as 1895.

Hence, speech does not convey the speaker's sensibility; instead, terms function as instances of a depersonalized and depersonalizing force. The subject's social dimension appears as the antithesis of a "pure" self, and the intersubjective phenomenon of language appears as an overpowering façade obscuring the subject or as an interference from without. Thus the "real" inner self remains inexpressible. This is the essence of the dilemma described by Hofmannsthal:

> I understood their ideas [*Begriffe*] well enough, but I found their amazing interrelationships rising up in front of me like glorious jets of water tossing golden balls into the air. I could examine them from all sides and observe their interactions; but they only bore meaning for each other, and my own most profound, most personal thoughts remained forever banished from their circle. Among them I was overcome by a feeling of awful solitude.[21]

Within a social environment perceived as foreign, the conventionality of language became a symbolic agent of alienation. And many intellectuals indeed felt alienated by the world of cultural and social upheaval around 1900 and thereafter. It is therefore not surprising that someone like Walther Rathenau too took pains to include arguments from linguistic skepticism in his critique of the "age of mechanization" (which was nothing but a formula expressing the sense of alienation in modernity). He described the phenomena of abstraction and conventionality as problematic aspects of contemporary language in particular and counterposed them against the mythic fiction of concrete expression in antiquity: "more recent language itself, with its countless formulas of abstract interrelationship, forms a powerful vehicle of mechanistic thought. . . . We know almost everything that is written before we read it."[22] Whereas to Rathenau this constituted an alienation from the metaphysical principle of the soul, Hofmannsthal (similarly) reflected on the alienation from the true self. No one was anymore able to "say what he feels and what he does not feel."[23] This longing for a "true" position of subjectivity seemed more satisfiable on the level of *direct feeling* than linguistic discourse, for feeling was (deceptively) understood as a phenomenon remote from language. The internalization of alien words, however, went so far as to not only make one's own true feeling inexpressible, but it even corrupted it: "thus the ghostly connection between words wins out over the naïve expression of the people. They then perpetually speak as if playing 'roles', with mock feeling, with feigned opinions, feigned attitudes. They manage to be perpetually absent from their own experiences."[24]

Like the "true" inner self, the external world remained inaccessible. Because the terms that one absorbed shaped both expression and thought, they were not only held responsible for reduction, stiffening, flattening, and falseness, but were also considered to transport conventional ideas (reflecting the *zeitgeist* or ideology), which then governed cognition and impeded true knowledge: "The inexhaustibly complex lies of the time, the dull lies of tradition, the lies of the bureaucrats, the lies of the individual, the lies of science, they all sit like a myriad of lethal flies on our poor life."[25] Thus Hofmannsthal wrote in 1895, and later he permitted Chandos to conclude that every opinion expressed in language is "so undemonstrable . . . so false, so hopelessly full of holes. . . . Everything fell into fragments for me, the fragments into further fragments, until it seemed impossible to contain anything at all within a single concept [*Begriff*]."[26]

Beneath this skepticism lies a palpable longing for the absolute, for the "true" perception of the external world as a "thing unto itself," and a mutual longing— even more relevant to the intentions of art (*Kunstwollen*)—for the valid, deep expression of true, unfeigned interiority, of *original and genuine feeling*, in which the contours of an absolute position of subjectivity begin to emerge. Contributing to this was the romantics' yearning for a harmonic unity of the true self with the holistic world, for totality and harmony.

Among the frequently reflected insights that have, certainly since Nietzsche, precipitated a sense of crisis and general decay is the notion that such absoluteness and totality are no longer a conceivable reality for the modern intellectual, who is guided by positivist rationalism. This idea, however, persisted as a *longing* consciously understood as utopian. Nevertheless, it has also proven inspirational, playing the role of an ideal foil for a critique of reality and serving as a focal point of modern mysticism, which is particularly expressed in a form of artistic imagination described by Walter Benjamin as "secularized ritual."[27]

Linguistic skeptics regarded—and still regard—a lack of absoluteness primarily as an inadequacy of language. Consequently, Hofmannsthal let Lord Chandos, who served as the mouthpiece for most of the objections outlined here,[28] cease writing and fall silent. However, linguistic skepticism also permitted less absolute reactions. For example, there is the work of the linguist Fritz Mauthner, whose influential work *Beiträge zu einer Kritik der Sprache* (Contributions to a Critique of Language), published in 1901/1902, can be attributed to the scholarly branch of the same discourse.[29] He also emphasized that words are only "conventional current values," "images of images of images,"[30] and "never a perception of reality,"[31] but he insisted more explicitly than Hofmannsthal on the ultimate futility of such expectations. The linguist underscored "the relative nature of human knowledge of the world"[32] as a fact not worth lamenting. He even considered it his task "to explain why objective truth is [to be] sought only in language, why it is nothing other than the common usage of language."[33]

In contrast, the linguistic skeptics who did not want to relinquish the absolute, on the one hand, but who were unable to simply remain silent, on the other (the literary figure of Chandos decides to fall silent, but not his creator Hofmannsthal), were presented with the challenge and dilemma of using language against what was perceived as the inadequacies of language, of at least approximating desired absolutes despite all hurdles. The proclaimed "solutions" were as diverse as they were fragmentary and tended to have a mystical bent.

Essentially, the main concern was always a *partial deautomatization* of language. This went as far as radical expressionist attempts to break the boundaries of conventional understanding and its worn-out meanings by destroying syntax. The attempts made by the *Sturm* author August Stramm are an extreme example. According to his basic idea, the poet should put words into unspent structures departing from conventional syntax, so that they may be read in a new and unusual way.[34] Hence, Stramm's work anticipated the theoretical concept of deautomatization through defamiliarizing or "making strange" (*ostranie*), as developed by Shklovsky soon after, but in radical form and applied to the automatism of the conventional system of language.

However, even for authors with a much less radical approach, like Hofmannsthal himself, the neoromantic desire to consistently lend fresh expression to a direct experience of the world was central to their thinking. The imperfect approximation of this desired result seemed briefly possible only in places yet untouched by the formulations of language, where expression did not yet begin to become automatic and conventional.

If language was to retain its communicative function, then it was not possible to question its fundamentally abstract and conventional nature. Hence, more moderate concepts concentrated their criticism and defense on *particularly obvious readymade linguistic formulas*, which were less essential to the basic function of language than were elementary terms. As abstractions, automatisms, and conventions not yet operating on the level of the language system, such forms were considered in any case avoidable.

Blatant antagonism was aroused—particularly in the aesthetic discourse—by the use of fixed stylistic formulas, conventional lexeme connections, fashionable terms emphasizing abstraction,[35] and by tropes (particularly metaphors), which were beginning to become conventionally consolidated through repetition but were not yet at the point of being *completely* worn out, that is, inconspicuous and seemingly elementary.[36] Even the relativist Mauthner assumed an unrelentingly normative stance and ranted against the "mechanical metaphors"[37] in poetic texts, although at the same time he was perfectly aware that the repetition and fading of metaphor belonged to the fundamental mechanisms in the historical development of language.[38] His opinion prototypically expressed a common stance of the period:

> Metaphor becomes mechanized in the development of language whereby one is no longer consciously aware of the comparison and the word seems to gain a new meaning. In poetry, where the pictorial should not fade from consciousness, this kind of mechanization is always vulgar. . . . For the poet forms metaphor from his ideas of the moment and individual mood; just as he would not assemble a poem from quotations, so he ought not repeat *mechanical and not yet commonly used* metaphors.[39]

This is a fundamental idea used in the aesthetic defense against a linguistic syndrome that, by the way, often provoked the term "stereotype." The stereotype was thus seen as a halfway consolidated linguistic form, which critics, for this very reason, paradoxically regarded as the most extreme contrast to the *direct* expression of experience and the freshness of language—because the form was not yet so consolidated and conventionalized as to already belong to the foundations of language that remained seemingly unchanged over time. Languages that have gradually developed such foundations are but a historical development with a high degree of consolidation. Linguistic skepticism thus assumed a frontal opposition in language criticism's moderate critique of the "mechanical" on a first level, or, as one could also say, of the linguistic stereotype. This opposition was retained in many fields of literary discourse well after the period and even to this day, as it considers its relevance consistently validated by the modern language practices of the media. Decades after Mauthner and Rathenau, Roland Barthes formulated a quite similar premise of his own: "The stereotype can be evaluated in terms of *fatigue*. The stereotype is what begins to fatigue me. Whence the antidote, cited as far back as *Writing Degree Zero*: the *freshness* of language."[40]

The physiognomic film theory of the early 1920s was both more radical and more naïve than the moderate variant of language criticism focused on the stereotype. Guided by the film proponents' aim of advancing the aesthetic-theoretical status of the medium, it tended to promote film as a far-reaching solution to the basic longings of the linguistic skeptics, as the means for *a genuine* renunciation of conventionality and abstraction in language-based communication.

Whereas in 1895 Hofmannsthal, not yet thinking of cinema, proposed a "desperate love for all arts . . . practiced in silence"[41] as a counterbalance to the dubious nature of language and in 1921 attempted to explain the popularity of film as due to people's fear of "language the tool of society,"[42] Egon Friedell used this construction as early as 1913 in his ambivalent apology of cinema. "Words gradually lose some of their credibility,"[43] he stated, in contrast to his praise of cinema's expressive capacity for the subtlest facial expressions and gestures: "The flutter of the eyelashes, the narrowing of the eyelids, and an entire world moves. . . . The human gaze, a human gesture, a person's entire bearing is today sometimes already able to say more than the human language."[44] A year earlier, Alfred Baeumler had considered film in a similar light:

> The stage of film is intimate. All the subtlest shifts in the features of the face . . . the most expressive gestures, the gentlest movements of the hand and the lips are sharply and clearly visible. A world of expression opens up. The innumerable possibilities of the soul to show or reveal itself, to become visible with a wince or a shutter, are strikingly manifested by film. A new culture of physiognomy and play of facial expressions is emerging.[45]

The basic elements of a physiognomic film theory foreshadowed here flowed directly into the film-theoretical discourse of the first half of the 1920s, which was dominated by the physiognomic paradigm.

As a kind of trace left by reality, the *photographic image* was thereby considered a *direct* process of reproduction, free from the abstractions of language and its conventional signs. Most importantly, however, the human expressive gestures captured by silent film, and especially the subtle facial expressions, which Balázs later called *microphysiognomy*,[46] were interpreted as providing *direct access to the inner workings* of the human soul—to "genuine" feeling, the verbal expression of which linguistic skeptics so urgently sought but considered so problematic.

Whereas language was regarded as a combination of abstraction and conventionality, expressive movements seemed immanently concrete, absolutely unconscious and physical, as *naturally inscribed* on human behavior.[47] Physiognomic film theory was seamlessly connected with established notions about expressive movement in empathy theory (*Einfühlungstheorie*), namely as the *absolute opposite of language as conventionally and symbolically mediated*. Theodor Lipps had specifically articulated this in his description of the semantics of eye movements: "It is not as if I see a shift in the eyes and then imagine a feeling of pride, rather this pride is immediately manifested to me by this shift to the extent that I can say I see pride in the eyes."[48] In other words, even before film theory, expressive movement had the reputation of being *immediately* and, in a sense, *naturally* joined with the inner self without the intervention of convention. This idea would circulate among film theorists for a long time. Thus, Maurice Merleau-Ponty still insisted that "we cannot say that only the signs of love or anger are given to the outside observer and that we understand others indirectly by interpreting these signs: we have to say that others are directly manifest to us as behavior."[49]

The basis for this manifestation is not the successive conventionalization resulting from automatization but a metaphysical "being thrown into the world"—a "natural bond"[50] between expressive movement and emotional content.

Whereas Theodor Lipps spoke somewhat vaguely of a "peculiar inwardness"[51] (of gesture), the writer Carl Hauptmann openly transfigured this idea in an influential essay on film from 1919: "Gesture, that is the primal realm of all mental impartation."[52] He continues with expressionist pathos:[53] "The meaning of film, its most inner means of expression, is primal communication through gesture."[54]

Béla Balázs took up this line of thought: "The culture of words is dematerialized, abstract, over-intellectualized,"[55] whereas film, in contrast, creates a new visual culture that "involves the direct transformation of spirit into body."[56] Balázs regarded the inner and the outer, the soul and the body as directly united in film, far removed from any form of abstraction and conventionality. All the desires of the linguistic skeptics seemed fulfilled:

> For the man of visual culture is not like a deaf mute who replaces words with sign language. He does not think in words whose syllables he inscribes in the air with the dots and dashes of the Morse code. His gestures do not signify concepts at all, but are the direct expression of his own non-rational self, and whatever is expressed in his face and his movements arises from a stratum of the soul that can never be brought to the light of day by words. Here, the body becomes unmediated spirit, spirit rendered visible, wordless.[57]

One of Balázs's central ideas was the *unmediated* visibleness of the spiritual in the physical, and this was closely connected with the notion of a corresponding *visual resensitizing* of the individual through the filmic image, through which "we finally see things with our eyes, that would cause us to close our eyes if appearing in reality,"[58] as he wrote elsewhere.

For Balázs, film taught one to once again see the "visual spirit"[59] and "the visual corollary of human souls immediately made flesh."[60] It made the human being visible in a new way and once again fostered the capacity of *seeing*, which had atrophied under the influence of the culture of words. Film was particularly able to achieve this by means of the close-up, enlarging and isolating the expressive subtleties of the human face. Film did in fact enhance what Balázs's teacher, Georg Simmel, had emphasized as the "aesthetic significance of the face."[61] However, Balázs attributed film with the power to unveil dimensions of the visual, which he believed would *not* ordinarily pass through the predominating perceptual filter of abstract and conventional thought, that is, "the sieve of words and concepts."[62]

"Existence within the image is a transfiguration of existence. Raised to the sphere of the other-worldly, of the illusory, the flow of the present has such a strong effect, that we have the sense of only being able to understand this existence when it is played out before us . . . here . . . we are able to enjoy it purely for its own inherent value."[63] Alfred Baeumler, whose thinking—like that of Balázs—was grounded in phenomenology, thus had already formulated the theory's central logic of the *revelatory power of film* achieved through the processes of recording and disassociation. In his 1925 essay on the "Dramaturgy of Film"[64] (inspired by *Visible Man*), Robert Musil recalled the roots of such ideas—essentially oriented toward achieving a shift in perception through partial deautomatization—in romanticism. Musil writes that "impressions become overvalued and estranged, as soon as they are separated from their customary setting,"[65] and this leads to "that transformation of our consciousness, to which Novalis and his friends owed their great and wondrous experiences."[66]

The concept that the revelatory power of the visual is based on the medial isolation of a segment of perceived reality from its accustomed context—an idea clearly indebted to the romantic tradition and now applied to film—introduced a mode of thought that would have implications far beyond the physiognomic period. It is especially relevant to all forms of cinema emphasizing the poetry of the visual surface.

It is no coincidence that in this context one can plausibly draw parallels between Balázs and the roughly contemporary French discourse on *photogénie*.[67] The notion of the revelation of an "optical unconscious,"[68] as fittingly termed by Benjamin, served as a construction used against the blinding effects of the conventional and continued to appear right through the last classical film theories.[69] Even Siegfried Kracauer's *Theory of Film* from 1960 deals with, quite centrally, the *redemption of physical reality* simultaneously through the indexical power of film and the medium's ability to deautomatize perception. Through their theories of visual immediacy, both Balázs and late Kracauer attempt to reinforce their preference for a poetic-realistic cinema and their dislike of intellectual, symbolic, or "language-like" film concepts—for example, of "hieroglyphic film"[70] such as Eisenstein's *October* (*Oktjabr'*, USSR, 1927).

* * *

Nietzsche's statement "when skepticism and yearning are paired, mysticism is born"[71] can be applied to many aspects of the physiognomic-anthropomorphic discourse on cinema. The role of mysticism in the suggestion of film as the antipole to the culture of language—painted in a radical light by skeptics—is most apparent when the anthropomorphic concept of the filmic revelation of (what Balázs called) the "face of things"[72] or landscape as "physiognomy"[73] broadens into an avowal of the myth of cosmic, universal harmony, in which the self and exterior world merge.

The metaphoric idea that things and the landscape have a "face" does not constitute a mystical idea per se. To a limited degree, prefilmic and filmic compositions do allow an emphasis, through accentuation and displacement, of structural similarities between human expressive movements and things and the landscape, so that on this basis *among others* these objects achieve symbolic expression. This similarly applies to the dynamics of masses of people: "The movement of the mass is a gesture just like that of an individual."[74] In the period of Expressionism, German cinema is concerned with both of these ideas, the face of things and the mass gesture.

These anthropomorphic ideas, like much of Balázs's thought, are not focused around a coherent and stringent theoretical argument but served more as means of loosely bracketing the wealth of observations made by the film critic about cinema.[75] Correspondingly, Lotte Eisner considered *Visible Man* largely an interpretation kindred to the "rather confused stipulations"[76] of Expressionism. In this sense, these anthropomorphic ideas can be interpreted as referring to *compositional tools*—inspired by empathy theory and present in contemporary films—for filmmakers, who may thus, for example, exaggerate the depiction of their characters by surrounding them with an "aura"[77] of inanimate objects within the filmic image. Herein lies the intellectual and even poetic appeal that Balázs's text still has within the context of expressionist film. True to the romantic tradition, Robert Musil also identified the creation of an aura as a capacity of the medium—which Balázs overestimated, as he adds—to summon effects bordering on the mystical: "One could in fact call this symbolic face of things the mysticism of film, or at least its romanticism, if it played more than an episodic role in the shadowy realm of living photography."[78]

However, the work of other authors, such as Carl Hauptmann and Rudolf Harms, exhibited such a lofty anthropomorphism that *their ideas* clearly crossed over into the mystical. As Iampolski[79] has illustrated in great detail, for them the expression of inanimate objects was apparently based on a notion of transcendental meaning arising out of the depths and penetrating the manifold nature of being.

For Hauptmann and Harms, the longing for the metaphysical totality of the self and the world, the "cosmic principle"[80]—a yearning encountered so often since the romantic period, and not only among the literati of linguistic skepticism—was fulfilled in film. Film becomes a "cosmic drama."[81] For Hauptmann, the medium had the capacity to reveal that not only the human body but "the whole wide world . . . is a great realm of meaningful gesture,"[82] in which gestures can "objectify and isolate these universal elements of spiritual communication from the entire cosmos."[83]

Film thus was attributed with a kind of revelatory effect, which in truth boiled down to anthropomorphic projection and approximated what the author Paul Scheerbarth was attempting to do in 1904, when he completed ten "portraits"[84] of planets and comets inspired by telescope photographs. In much the same manner, Rudolf Harms spoke of an "organic ring" to be shown by film: "Film places the human being and the cosmos in relationship . . . cosmos and individual respond to one another with the same means of expression. *Breath, not language!* Gesture is the binding agent of organic unity."[85]

ROBERT MUSIL AND THE FORMULAIC NATURE OF THE VISUAL

The mystical tendencies in the physiognomic argument for film as art thus climaxed in the motif of the cosmos. This mysticism had fundamentally deeper roots in the idea of the spirit's unmediated visibility in gesture, which formed the basis of the celebration of film as a supposed alternative to the fundamental abstraction and conventionality of language.

Siegfried Kracauer remarked on the latter in his review of *Visible Man* in 1927 and criticized the linguistic skepticism underpinning Balázs's argument: "His underestimation of language—without which human culture would be unthinkable—leads Balázs into terrible blunders in the opposition of the arts of film and language."[86] Although Kracauer thus objects to this "cornerstone" of Balázs's concept, he regards its details, such as Balázs's treatment of the "the little things of life"[87] or the "face of things," quite favorably. Kracauer, who, like Balázs, assumed an anticapitalist stance at the time, objected to the insinuated link between social emancipation and what Balázs described as the "yearning for the concrete, nonconceptual, immediate experience of things"[88] that Balázs believed constituted the "nature of film"[89] and was constrained by the culture of capitalism. This—rightly—seemed too mystifying to the young Kracauer (1927), against which he defended the value of language: "The new visibility of man displayed by film is so completely the opposite of a shift towards true concreteness that it instead merely validates and clings to the poor rationality of capitalist thinking. Radical change comes only from the knowledge actuated by language."[90]

Working from very different premises, Robert Musil was also bothered by Balázs's juxtaposition of abstract language and the direct embodiment of the spirit in film. In his previously cited "Dramaturgy of Film," Musil focused his main argument against Balázs's film theory on this opposition. Nevertheless, his own ideas about the purposes of art came rather close to the metaphysical objectives of physiognomic film theory, which is why he was quite taken by it. He did indeed yearn for the "other spiritual condition," in which "a secret rising and ebbing of our being with that of things and other people"[91] is manifested. He considered this a heightened relation to experience that can be attained through art only momentarily—a half-conscious fiction. This intensification of experience overrules "the individual's practical, factual, normal condition"[92] and particularly the "formulaic nature [*Formelhaftigkeit*] of existence."[93] Art is realized in these moments of contemplation.

But Musil rejected the idea that the filmic image and the gestures visible therein are per se superior to language or literature in this regard. Like Kracauer, he considered Balázs's antagonism toward language and thought (as a linguistically structured procedure) to be "an oblique angle of attack that does not aim at the center of the problem."[94]

Deeply influenced by the emerging ideas of Gestalt psychology,[95] Musil decidedly rejected the idea that human perception, and also expressive movement, is free of abstraction and convention.

> Above all, we must remember that not only our intellect [*Verstand*] but also our senses are "intellectual." It is common knowledge that we see what we know: ciphers, signs, abbreviations, summaries, the principal attributes of a concept [*Begriff*]: imbued and sustained merely by isolated dominant sensory impressions and a vague outline of the rest. . . . This goes so far that without preformed stable representations—and these are concepts—really only a chaos remains; and since on the other hand concepts are dependent on experience, there arises a condition of mutual formation.[96]

In other words, Musil was conscious of the fact that in the process of perception, that is, during the processing of sensory impressions, regardless whether of reality or film, aspects of abstraction and convention are at work and that cognitive schemata are formed at the juncture of the two, which he called "stable representations" (*stabile Vorstellungen*), "concepts" (*Begriffe*), and "formulas." Only the latter enable us to organize the chaos of what we perceive into preformed patterns and lend it meaning. Musil thus was working from a basic constructivist idea, which still has currency in perceptual theory today. In addition, he apparently also understood that neither perceptions nor filmic images are mere mirrorings and that even the (prefilmic and filmic) composition of such images is influenced by and relates to such formulas.

These formulas appeared to him to be closely related to concepts, first because they are of an abstract nature—given that the recognition of form (*Gestalter-kennung*), like its configuration (*Gestaltung*), is associated with summarization, reduction of complexity, and selection or accentuation. What is more, once these "formulas" have served as a basis for the configuration, they often become openly symbolic and conventional forms: as ciphers, signs, and abbreviations. To distill Musil's insightful position, regardless of the differences between the two, without such formulas and without symbolic forms neither language nor nonverbal communication (such as expressive movements)—nor even simple perception—can function.

To him, the basis for the process of symbolization was discursive repetition, which allows symbolic conventions to become rooted in the interpersonal. As Musil understood, just as linguistic signifiers become linked to complex conceptual processes and charged with semantic fields (or the reverse) through repetition in discourse, the same occurs with repeated visual impressions, particularly the perception of gestures: "It is . . . simply the need for practical orientation that drives us to . . . [the formulaic (*Formelhaftigkeit*)] . . . to formulas for concepts (*Begriffe*) no more than to formulas for *our gestures* and sense impressions, which fall asleep after a few repetitions just as do the representational processes that are tied to words."[97]

The idea of the unmediated presence of the spirit in gesture and the physiognomic language games based thereupon were regarded by Musil as untenable. He emphatically insisted upon the *symbolic* nature of gestures as conventionally mediated forms. Thus, unlike Balázs, he clearly emphasized "the *symbolic* face of things."[98] His thinking shows indications of a modern understanding of symbols, which does not assume a singular act by which convention is arbitrarily formed by agreement (as even Saussure understood linguistic convention) but instead grasps the quality of a symbol as resulting from a successive, *discursive process of conventionalization*. This has been described more recently and thoroughly in relation to language and film by Harmut Winkler,[99] who is indebted to the work of Bühler.

Musil thereby introduced a way of thinking that can be readily applied to the visual forms shaped by repetition and employed in the composition of film and to repetitive narrative structures. All of these can be interpreted both as cognitive schemata (as proposed by Bordwell) and as symbolic forms, each of which evoke more complex semantic fields.

In this regard, Musil touched rather cursorily on fundamental ideas for a semiotics of the visual, specifically of film, that would not *definitively* become part of semiotic theory until the late 1960s and early 1970s, as, for instance, in the work of Umberto Eco, who was committed to questioning commonly accepted notions about the iconic sign free from convention, "'natural expressivity', the immanence of meaning in the thing,"[100] or also in gesture. Beneath the ostensibly direct manifestation of meaning Eco revealed the conventional and symbolic nature of visual codes: "Gestures are not 'natural' . . . in contrast they are convention and culture. . . . Gestures and body movements are . . . not instinctive to human nature but learnable human systems of behavior, which markedly differ from one culture to another."[101]

Musil was not inclined to pursue this direction any further. His interest in conventional forms was clearly negatively motivated—and in this context closely related to the interests of the linguistic skeptics and very different from Eco's. It was focused on the most far-reaching defense of aesthetics *possible* and not on an analysis of the potential functions of conventional formulas reducing complexity. The question of how one could creatively use culturally determined symbolic forms as aesthetic material would have radically contradicted his thinking.

Musil's argument on physiognomic film theory sought to reject fiction glorifying film as being per se—due to the special characteristics of the medium—farther from the abstraction and conventionality than literature as had been problematized by the linguistic skeptics. However, he primarily used his refutation to clearly demonstrate that film thus faced the *same aesthetic challenges* as writing, namely to resist the formulaic *to the greatest extent possible*. Film confronted the *same* dilemma of abstraction, conventionality, and automatization as linguistically based literature: "Film realizes its destiny not as a deliverance from literature, but as sharing its destiny."[102]

If aspiring to a form of art, film must also transcend the "individual's practical, factual normal condition" and thereby its own expressive repertoire in the sense of attaining the "other condition."[103] That means: "the formulaic limitation of sensation and concept [*Begriff*]"[104] characteristic of the individual's "normal," everyday condition must at least be partially shattered by *artistic* means: "Intermediate shades, oscillations, modulations, gradations of light, spatial relationships, axes of rotation; in literature the irrational simultaneous effect of words that illuminate each other: as in an old painting, when it is varnished, events emerge that had been invisible, so these things escape the dull, confining picture and the formulaic nature of existence."[105] Such an aspiration, which reveals a demonstrative interest in the flowing texture of the visual and in unveiling what has become optically unconscious through the conventionality of the everyday, was closely related to Balázs's thinking but could never be *fully* realized. However, the dilemma articulated by the linguistic skeptics remained a *constant challenge* to any art form—including film: "In this way art frees itself from the formulaic limitation of sensation and concept [*Begriff*], but this condition cannot be 'stretched' to totality. As little as mystical experience can without the rational scaffolding of religious dogmatism, or music without the scaffolding of teaching. Thus is condemned the essence of all-too-optimistic attempts at 'liberation.'"[106]

This clear insight as to the impossibility of *completely* disabling elementary formulas in perception and communication, including gestural communication, thus crystallized in a hostility toward the formulaic (*Formelhaftigkeit*), which has not yet attained the basic, inevitable, and *fully automatized* stage and is thus particularly conspicuous.

This has obvious parallels with the ideas of moderate linguistic skepticism. Whereas the latter focused on a critique of conspicuous repetitive forms in language, especially on partially automatized but not yet utterly blind formulations in the language of literature, such as "mechanical metaphors," within the context of film Musil's critical attention was largely focused on the kinds of repetitive patterns that were based on particularly conspicuous reductions and accentuations in visual symbolism. Most of all, so it certainly seems, he is concerned with patterns (also of facial expression and gesture) that have developed specifically for the staging of films (or other media), that is, that can be interpreted as specific patterns of *secondary staging*.[107] He considered this sort of *narrative or visual-stylistic* stereotype of medial staging a "coarse indicator"[108] of life in film, which even surpasses the existing coarseness of everyday human perception and communication.

With the transgression of this threshold—ultimately indefinable since it is in constant flux and determined by the viewer's horizon of experience—the term "formulaic" becomes a *vehicle of fundamental critique* and operates on an intermediate level resembling that of the linguistic stereotype attacked by linguistic skeptics. Musil logically also wished to strictly ban the formulaic and used the incendiary word *kitsch* much like Mauthner spoke of the "mechanical metaphor." Indirectly criticizing Balázs's euphoric model, Musil saw kitsch as inscribed on the whole of film and particularly on its specific repertoire of gestures: "The pretentious quality of formulaic gestures constitutes the greater part of kitsch in film. . . . What is unbearable in film and dance . . . begins where anger becomes rolling of the eyes, virtue is beauty, and the entire soul is a paved avenue of familiar allegories."[109]

In his aesthetic preferences, Musil sees utterly eye to eye with Balázs, who celebrated Asta Nielsen for her "natural" style of acting. Nielsen no longer employed but certainly underplayed the "acting clichés" (to return to Jhering's words) of the conventional language of gesture inherited from nineteenth-century theater— and thus became a forerunner of an emerging trend in the medium.

However, Musil did not associate film in and of itself with a programmatic emancipation from the formulaic, an idea that repeatedly emerges, somewhat shrouded in mysticism, in Balázs's euphoric ideal construct. In contrast, he placed much greater emphasis on the *artistic challenges posed by formulas*, and in his perspicuous realism he recognized the beginnings of certain trends in film, which, he thought, pointed to a new manifestation of the formulaic. But Musil also sensed that in the silent, unifying monochrome visuality of black-and-white film lay *the opportunity* for lyricism and for a special kind of deautomatization of perception: "When we look at a film, it unfolds the whole infinity and inexpressibility possessed by everything that exists—placed under glass, as it were, by the fact that one only *sees* it (there are exemplary instances of this in Balázs)."[110] Then again, in complete contradiction to Balázs's utopia, he affirmed that film did not actually have less but more affinity to crude formulaic elements of style than literature (that is, the literature he considered literature): "In making connections and working out relations among impressions . . . film is apparently chained more strongly than any other art to the cheapest rationality and platitude [*Typik*]."[111] At this juncture, Musil employs an implicit and sociologically tinged argument, which is not further elaborated: the *popular* medium exhibits extensive formulaic tendencies, because it must meet a greater demand for understandability, and as "the comprehensibility of the action increases, the more undifferentiated it is. . . . Thus the expressive power increases with the poverty of expression."[112]

Whereas Balázs linked his vision of the ideal nature of film with romantic aspirations for the medium as a new form of folklore, "the *popular art* of our century,"[113] and a new, because directly manifested "penetration of the ordinary material of life by the human spirit,"[114] to Musil the conventional figurations of the popular in film, as instances of a new formulaic tendency, were particularly pronounced; thus for him they overstepped the threshold of aesthetic taste from the outset. In accordance with his logic, such figurations represented the sustained antithesis of the attempt to attain that "other spiritual condition" which insistently calls for a distancing from reductive, conventional forms. Film was thus not an art form but a distraction, which, as someone who went to the cinema almost daily, Musil himself apparently enjoyed.[115]

* * *

In summary, Robert Musil's position presents a nuanced picture. Unlike proponents of the physiognomic theory of film, he did not recognize film and the cinematographic representation of gesture as a cultural trend or media-based opportunity promising convention-free communication or a truly nonabstract expression of the human spirit. Instead, he clearly recognized that also in cinema expressiveness and perception are grounded on what has been previously formed—on patterns that emerge from processes of abstraction and conventionalization or symbolization. Musil, however, was *not* interested in the aesthetic benefits of such "formulas," but he pondered their implications within the scope of a fundamental aesthetic critique. In art he criticized the "formulaic" quality of expression that exceeds the established and unavoidable degree of abstraction and conventionality necessary for any perception or communication.

Translating Musil's idea of the formulaic, to which he added the notion of kitsch, into the terminology of this inquiry, one could say: as one of the first authors to reflect *on film*, Musil made the critique of the stereotype a central element of his thought.

With his statement, "this tendency toward rigid formulas [*Formelhaftigkeit*] is the enemy of the saint as well as the artist . . . "[116] Musil formulated an aesthetic axiom—no longer questioned in the context of his and related ideas—of an incipient fundamental-critical discourse on the stereotype, which was to broadly shape areas of theoretical thinking on film in the following decades. From this discourse the fears and arguments previously expressed by linguistic skeptics would then be transferred to the system of expression inherent to the new popular medium of film.

It is revealing that Musil actually voiced the conceptual basis for his judgmental attitudes toward the stereotype. As constructions rooted in the romantic tradition, these attitudes were retained in principle as premises in later theories of film as art, even where theorists were less willing to express them openly. The focal point of Musil's critique of the formulaic could be considered to be the construction of the fluid "*other condition*," described in many facets—a condition that borders on a moment of mysticism and constitutes the ideal aim of any practiced art. The formulation of this "other condition" entails the exalted expression of a desire implicitly or explicitly shared among many film-as-art theorists to approximate a state of harmony between an absolute notion of self (soul) and a true perception of the world.

The formulaic, the always preformulated, the reduced and accentuated, the foreign, that which comes from without, in short the stereotype, fundamentally only arouses aversion when viewed from this perspective. The stereotype appears to be a latent but never completely eliminable disruptive factor that inserts itself between the self and the consciousness of the self, between the self and the world.

Hence, the attitude toward the stereotype had oddly come full circle. The first film-as-art theories avoided the issue of the stereotype, although it was actually clamoring for attention given the common practices of the cinema and traditional ideas about aesthetics that contradicted these practices. However, bringing up what was considered a problematic phenomenon would have conflicted with strivings to proclaim film as art. Even when observations from specific films were introduced into the discussion, theorists were ultimately concerned with an *ideal film*, with proving the medium's validity as a form of art per se.

However, as soon as authors like Musil began to accept this view of the medium as a valid art form and take the aesthetics of film seriously, there emerged an awareness of the fragility of the apologists' argument and the different nature of the *reality* of film. Cinema began actually to be judged by the traditional aesthetic criteria that early film theory had demanded. As a result, a critical consciousness emerged, in which one began to see stereotypes everywhere in films.

Only a few years later, the critical perception of film as a stereotype machine was a mainstream idea among intellectuals, as was the critique of "standard gestures and standard facial expressions."[117] In accordance with the skeptical view common by around 1928, cinema was considered a new institution, which had "standardized gesture and facial mannerisms by virtue of conformity and conventionality,"[118] even implementing on a massive scale its "standardized" facial expressions in the private lives of the audience: "If mass psychosis can lay claim to a sphere of activity anywhere, then it is here [in film], in standardized feeling, in standardized gestures, in the standardization of the play of the facial features: the plain language of film."[119] Such a statement is the complete inversion of the former utopia of the anticonventional and nonabstract gesture in the cinema.

Marking an *important moment* in this turnaround are Musil's thoughts on the formulaic dating from the spring of 1925, in which he took film seriously as a potential art medium but in light of his own criteria for art remained skeptical—especially toward the utopias of physiognomic theory.

SIX

THE READYMADE PRODUCTS OF THE FANTASY MACHINE: RUDOLF ARNHEIM, RENÉ FÜLÖP-MILLER, AND THE DISCOURSE ON THE "STANDARDIZATION" OF FILM

The "industrialization" of the American cinema has already led to the conveyer-belt method. . . . The final product is a shapeless mass, for even the best theme, after it has passed through so multifarious a filter, loses its form and originality. Industrialization is threatening to destroy the hopes which awakened in us the day the world of pictures was born.

—RENÉ CLAIR, *REFLECTIONS ON THE CINEMA* (1951)

AMERICANIZATION, RATIONALIZATION, FILM CRITICISM

A marked shift toward a widespread awareness of the stereotype in cinema took place in the second half of the 1920s and was prompted by the increased interest among journalists and theorists in the topic. This primarily occurred under the aegis of fundamental critique. By this time, key theoretical positions on film as art were fully developed. Based on these positions, the film criticism in the feature pages of daily newspapers and in cultural journals was widely established. There was a powerful sense of discrepancy between the theoretical imperative—particularly pronounced in Germany—to apply the traditional romantic vision of art to the new medium of film, on the one hand, and the actual practices in the mass medium, on the other. This discrepancy could not longer be simply ignored or dismissed as a mere transitional phase by authors and critics who had become film enthusiasts and knowledgeable moviegoers.

Critics and theorists now began to problematize the stereotype. They were less interested in pursuing the origins of the phenomenon in aspects of spectatorship and recipient dispositions than in examining the circumstances of production within the film industry. Economic considerations, traditionally regarded as purely external factors in contrast to aesthetics, became an increasing subject of interest. They were considered an *impediment* to the realization of artistic ideas, disruptive factors in the production of aesthetic goods—while appearing to grow steadily in influence. The new mass culture's mode of operation as a culture industry was considered an *aesthetic aberration*, a trend irreconcilable with true art. The predominance of the economic approach to the question of the stereotype was even reflected in choices of language: it inspired metaphors such as "standardization" and the "readymade film," in German *Konfektionsfilm*.[1] Such terms clearly underscored what was considered a clash of opposites, between the aesthetic ideals of individuality, genuinely fresh expression, and vitality, on the one side, and the mechanical, the serial, the standardized, and cyclically produced, on the other. With respect to cinema, the term "standardization" had distinctly polemic undertones—which it does not have today among certain film historians (for example, Janet Staiger).[2]

Contemporary developments in film theory and criticism alone, however, hardly suffice to explain the introduction and rapid gain in popularity of this new theme. Two concomitantly developing trends of the 1920s also played a role. On the one hand, the discourse on the standardization of cinema was massively influenced by an overarching cultural discourse, by no means simply restricted to film, in which "assembly line" or "conveyor belt," "rationalization," and "standardization" functioned as catchwords. This discourse was influential during the Weimar Republic, and in literature studies it falls under the rubrics of "Americanism" or "New Objectivity." On the other hand, underlying this line of thought was a trend toward widespread rationalization in the business sector, which also included the film industry and hence provided additional impetus to the debate on the stereotype in film.

After a world war, economic stagnation, and hyperinflation, Germany underwent a surge of modernization during the phase of economic stabilization (1924–1928). This led to a wave of rationalization, which pervaded the entire economy and was driven by the American money flowing into the country with the Dawes Plan. In many respects, the United States was considered an economic role model. It emerged as an increasingly strong competitor on the German market, and American efficiency was considered to be the benchmark.

The American industrialist Henry Ford became a figure of almost mythical proportions, a paragon of the new rationalization trend. Published in German in 1923, his biography was a bestseller.[3] The technocratic vision it expounded, that efficient management was simultaneously the solution to social problems, fell on fertile ground in Germany. The war, the collapse of Wilhelminian society, and the many years of crisis had led to a state of emotional shock, a veritable implosion of traditional values and certainties that had left behind a spiritual vacuum. This made the segment of the public open to modernity also receptive to what was deemed a radically new spirit of objectivity.

Proponents of this thinking upheld the technological, utilitarian, unemotional, and effective aspects of modern industry's mechanical production—as championed by Taylorist and Fordist ideas of rationalization—as a beacon of hope. In the spirit of Ford they glorified technocratic illusions. As Helmut Lethen states in his standard work on New Objectivity, society was intended to function as a depoliticized "apparatus" operated by experts.[4]

The "steely nature" of the engineer[5] emerged as a literary topos. A great concentration of metaphors based on mechanics, machines, and apparatuses began to pervade both narrative and visual imaginations. It is certainly no coincidence that during this period the science-fiction genre ultimately achieved full form in cinema (for example, *Metropolis*, Fritz Lang, Germany, 1927).

Ford's assembly line took on special significance. Together with the success of the automobile in the 1920s, the principle of the *assembly line*, which dictated the radical standardization of parts and labor, began its incredible triumph and became a pervasive idea. As Sigfried Giedion wrote in *Mechanization Takes Command*, it became "almost a symbol of the period between the two world wars"[6] and undoubtedly served as a guiding cultural metaphor for the new age of fully mechanized mass production.

The currency of this topic among the general public is apparent in that the interest in, and indeed fascination for, this new phase of modernization (and the use of corresponding metaphors) was by no means limited to technocratic or progress-oriented authors. The discourse included much ambivalence in addition to affirmation, and it had another side, a resolute cultural criticism often paired with anticapitalistic attitudes held by conservatives. Many intellectual critics felt especially challenged by the new "expansion of capitalistic rationalization into areas that had thus far seemed unaffected, into the consciousness of the liberal sphere,"[7] as Lethen wrote.

Topics such as seriality and standardization, including of *culturally and aesthetically relevant products* and in particular those oriented toward mass consumption—such as cinema—became a focal point of interest. This fueled the controversy about serial principles of production taking over artistic products, a trend perceived as ubiquitous and thus making incursions into a field that the literary and cultural intelligentsia had considered its special domain.

Modernists applauded the new rationality of Fordism as a purge of the obsolete, a form of cultural demystification, and democratic progress.[8] The art theorist Adolf Behne, for example, had leanings in this direction. In 1929, he regarded the principles of constructivism as realized "in the daily use and daily consumption"[9] of urban poster advertising (particularly for motion pictures) and considered shop-window decorating cultural progress, although he maintained a slightly

FIGURE 10 Adolph Behne refers in 1929 to this satirical series of images from *Punch*.

ambivalent attitude. For Behne, the introduction of constructivist principles into the quotidian realm of the city street elevated "the masses to a new artistic niveau,"[10] and in reverse this meant: "The painters forced into a bitter struggle for survival learn from film, from today, from the moment, from the season, *from the series*, from the cut, from montage, from the close-up, and from the happy end. This all applies to the niveau, the serial production of the new man."[11] Somewhat self-deprecatingly, Behne supplements this with a series of pictures caricaturizing the cinematic stereotype.[12]

In contrast, critics of Fordism vehemently deplored "Taylorism, standardization, and readymade production"[13] in the cultural sphere. These made even the human body into a "body type"[14] by destroying individuality and cultural distinctiveness. Whereas critics engaged in the prewar debate on film regarded cinema as a threat to art, because it provided a forum for coarse, garish sensuality and banal mass sensibilities and because it was feared that cinema would economically undermine traditional arts such as the theater,[15] the critics of this later period viewed the serial mechanism of the global mechanical operations to which film had also succumbed as the main threat to art. Many cultural critics viewed cinema as an agent of this threat. The new guild of film critics viewed this threat, interestingly, as posing the greatest danger to their proclamation of film as *art*.

In 1925, Stefan Zweig's attestation of "the monotonization of the world"[16] was virtually programmatic. For Zweig it created a new "uniformity" and was much too powerful to be meaningfully combated. Meanwhile, every conscious individual was to reject it "with their soul"[17]—namely also, and especially, through art: "the fine aroma of the particular in cultures is evaporating, their colorful foliage being stripped with ever-increasing speed, rendering the steel-grey pistons of mechanical operation, of the modern world machine, visible beneath the cracked veneer."[18]

Just as Henry Ford was regarded as a figure symbolizing the new, fully mechanized civilization, America became its symbolic land. Zweig asks: "What is the source of this terrible wave threatening to wash all the color, everything particular out of life? Everyone . . . knows: America."[19] Almost everyone, regardless whether enthusiast or detractor, spoke of the *Americanization* of German culture, or also *Americanism*, when referring to the new rationality, although these developments were inherent to the logic of Germany's own economy and culture: "From the mid-decade it was the German-elaborated concept of 'rationalization' that dominated discussions. . . . German spokesmen, however, still credited the United States with originating the underlying ideas."[20] Economically powerful and indeed more advanced in the trend toward efficiency, America was considered a nation without history "lacking the retarding elements of old European societies"[21] and thus also lacking any inhibitions toward worshipping the machine as well as technology, efficiency, and commercial success. Here the "mechanization . . . of all aspects of life"[22] was pursued in its purest form. Peter Wollen remarks on the subject: "the central idea of 'Americanism' was provided by Fordism."[23] America appeared as the place where one could already observe the hoped-for or dreaded future of one's own culture.

The German public's interest in the United States increased exponentially. There was a flood of travel reports, news stories, and features from the mid-1920s onward. Between 1923 and 1928, even the number of articles on American literature increased by 400 percent.[24] "Never before had so much been written about

America within such a short period,"[25] Erhard Schütz concluded, and "in the Weimar Republic America and the machine [became] synonymous."[26]

In addition to the Ford plant in Detroit and the slaughterhouses of Chicago, Hollywood's film studios were among the sites most frequently visited by reporters and travel writers.[27] Whereas Ford's automobile factory attracted the literati, because here they could encounter the almost mythological place of full mechanization— and not simply of a production plant but of a whole set of life circumstances (which Ford himself had described)—in Chicago the mechanized slaughter and processing of live animals into a standardized product, that is, canned meat, was a source of fascination. The view of the American film world was also guided by the motif of a mechanized and "perfectly standardized civilization."[28] Full of ambivalent fascination, Arnold Höllriegel (who had been the co-author of the legendary Expressionist *Kinobuch* in 1913 and author of one of the first novels to be set in the film milieu)[29] described his first impressions of his visit to the Californian film city in 1927 much in this vein: "When one comes to Hollywood, one immediately notices that this place belongs to the machine, not the dirty machine of the factories, but the beautiful, appealing machine."[30] Therefore, one realizes right away, he writes in another passage, "that American film cannot be a matter of 'art,' that it is rather a commodity for the prodigious masses, just like canned meat products."[31] Bernhard Goldschmidt, another literary visitor to Hollywood, was one of few to express his outright admiration for the calculated efficiency of its film production: "Here too ... the American has demonstrated an ability to extensively mechanize work flow by introducing ingenious machines, in order to economize on expensive human labor."[32]

The motif of efficiency is even more pronounced in the writings of critical visitors. When Egon Erwin Kisch talks about the uniformity of genre films, such as the "collegian picture" and the "western picture,"[33] in his reportage novel ironically titled *Paradies Amerika* (1929), his attention and criticism focuses on the standardization, or stereotypization, of the films. Kisch sarcastically speaks of "individuality produced on the assembly line."[34]

* * *

The origins and culture-critical background of the discourse on the standardization of film are undoubtedly to be sought in this context—reportage about America and Americanism. American genre films and the symbolic place of Hollywood were subjects also often included in later accounts of the standardization of cinema.

Contemporary sources and historical research do in fact corroborate that, in keeping with the trends of other production sectors, the American film studios of the 1920s implemented division of labor, systematization, and cyclical production far more extensively than did German studios. Kristin Thompson[35] and Thomas Elsaesser[36] have researched to what extent German practices allowed directors more creative freedom. In contrast to most of their colleagues in Hollywood, German directors retained much greater control over the entire production process. They could influence and alter scripts. They had the authority to determine the visual breakup of scenes and could even use this freedom in order to develop completely new, experimental solutions in cooperation with cameramen and set designers. The final cut was naturally controlled by the director. He was the master of production. In America, by contrast, the main responsibility clearly lay in the hands of the producer, who oversaw a much more comprehensively standardized production process divided into specialized tasks. Whereas the director hired by the producer had authority over the actual shooting, the final editing process was, for example, passed on to an *editor*, who was no longer answerable to the director. The editor compiled a montage of the shots, which had been produced according to a largely standardized process of visual composition. The editor also followed a so-called continuity script, to which the director was also bound and which structured and predetermined the entire production down to the breakup of individual scenes. Thomas Elsaesser describes the continuity script as a kind of cinematographic "blueprint equivalent."[37]

It goes without saying that this form of organized production entailing greater standardization, together with an overt tendency toward specific genres, aesthetically shaped the majority of films produced. However, the trend toward an increasing convergence of narrative economy and industrial efficiency did not remain limited to American cinema and thoughts entertained about it—and even less so to travel journalism alone. In the mid-1920s, German cinemagoers were able to see large numbers of American films with their own eyes. In the face of this new, powerful competition, the German film industry made exerted efforts toward rationalization, in line with the logic of the culture industry.

Although first the war and then later the weakness of the German currency during the period of inflation had largely protected the German market from imports, including film, during the so-called *Stabilisierungsjahren* (stability period) of the Weimar Republic the German film industry was confronted with an unprecedented wave of American exports. This played no small role in the impression of German culture being Americanized. In his study *Hollywood in Berlin*, Thomas Saunders describes a "cultural invasion without parallel since the age of Napoleon,"[38] which began with the Dawes Plan in 1924.

In 1920, German cinemas were almost exclusively in the hands of domestic productions. In the following year, the market for imports gradually opened up.

In 1923, the ratio of American to German feature films shown was already 102 to 253. In 1924—after the stabilization of the currency—it was 186 U.S. to 220 German productions. In 1925 and 1926, this ratio was then inverted, with 216 American films on the market in each of these years compared to only 212 German films in 1925 and 185 in 1926. In terms of short films, which included slapstick productions, German products were almost completely crowded out.[39]

Given these figures, one understands that not only outstanding works but also many average films made their way over to Germany. Looking back twenty years later at the American cinema of the period, Peter Bächlin wrote: "The danger of clichéd production ignoring all individual characteristics was clearly demonstrated in the American cinema after 1926. At the time the impetus for the large scale 'mechanization' of film production came from the . . . banks."[40] The banks had good reason for doing this, for to a certain extent the standardized productions established their own kind of quality, which was related to the mechanism that also functioned with other consumer goods. Patterns became reliable and thus sought after by the public. But the glut of American products on the German market seemed disconcerting. Thomas Saunders writes of an "overexposure to average American films"[41] in terms of the productions exported to Germany and the boom of "assembly-line entertainment."[42] This gave rise to a certain weariness and to some extent aversion among members of the German public, especially critics. At the time, Siegfried Kracauer responded much in this vein: "Indeed, more than any others, the American products that have made their way to us recently—with the exception of a few astonishingly fine achievements—would have done better never to have left."[43]

That the topic of standardization was taken up by German film journalism and criticism and became a leading metaphor during precisely this period certainly was significantly influenced by these changes in the films on offer—and to an even greater extent by the impact this had on German film production. After the uninterrupted business during the war and postwar periods, the German film industry experienced a considerable economic crisis[44] due to the powerful competition from America in its domestic market.

Close to bankruptcy, the leading German film company Ufa was forced to come to terms with the competition. The alliance of Ufa with Paramount and Metro-Goldwyn under the logo Parufamet was considered by contemporaries to be another symbol of Americanization. Attempts followed to curtail imports through quotas and to expand markets through European alliances. There was also an effort to organize domestic film production more efficiently and to make it adhere more strictly to economic criteria. Ufa reorganized its production processes and division of labor. This was demonstrated, for instance, by the introduction of the post of production manager in 1927/1928, whose role, based on the model of the producer, was to oversee the production of a film from an economic perspective.[45] The result of these changes was an obvious approximation of German products to the American model—also in aesthetic terms. Kristin Thompson aptly remarks: "Of all silent films, there are probably none that so consistently resemble those of Hollywood as the ones produced by Ufa in the late 1920s."[46]

In 1923, that is, at the height of euphoric film-art conceptions, the writer Rudolf Leonhard had still proclaimed in his essay "Zur Soziologie des Filmes" (On the Sociology of the Film) that "industry does not necessarily need mass products."[47] Even if the word "industry" consistently has "overtones of the enormous, utterly organized, rational, and planned, ultimately also as something affecting the public at large," in essence it solely means "that one has to use a machine for production."[48] That film therefore did not belong among "the 'pure' arts" could only be claimed by someone who "would also deny organ music, the performance of which certainly requires a complex apparatus, the status of art."[49] For Leonhard, the concept of "art" was not sociologically altered by film (with its appeal to the masses and its context of culture-industrial production) but rather the other way around. Film changed industry, "because as a *work of art* it is in fact sociologically classified in a different way than is a plain consumer article."[50]

In light of the developments that had taken place by the end of the 1920s, such utopias and hopes for a continuity of art within the film industry definitely culminated in a crisis. However, the crisis was not perceived by the critics as a crisis of their own film-art concepts but as an aesthetic crisis of cinema. "Film-Krisis" (Film-Crisis), the title of a debate carried out in *Das Tagebuch* in 1928 by reputable film critics,[51] became a ubiquitous catchphrase. Critics aligned with the idea of film as art understood the crisis against the backdrop of existing economic difficulties primarily in an aesthetic sense. Film was perceived to be at an artistic low, which was explained as due to attempts to reorganize and raise the efficiency of domestic production, as driven by the banks. "The enormous consumption of film ideas was naturally greater than were new creative possibilities available in response; artistic stagnation was the inevitable result, over and over the action in films circled ad nauseam around increasingly watered-down variations on story material with proven financial value."[52]

In 1929, Herbert Leisegang thus described his perception in recent years of the "crisis of film." Similarly, Willy Haas identified the source of the aesthetic crisis as the "Taylorization" that "has swept . . . the entire film world."[53] For Haas, the trend had negative connotations leading him to believe "that film, the first purely, inherently, and truly natural collective art, can by no means thrive in the cramped conditions of private enterprise."[54] For this reason, the author, who was otherwise considered a liberal democrat, called for aesthetically salvaging film by socializing the film industry or through "further incorporation and monopolization." For Haas, both solutions would make it possible to satisfy immediate economic concerns and pursue an aesthetic "politics over the long term."[55]

In the same year, Siegfried Kracauer also addressed the trend toward standardization. In a critical resume of the most recent German film productions of 1928, he emphasized the "employment of genre clichés [*Typisierung des Filmes*]"[56] as one of their most noticeable characteristics: "Parallel with the consolidation of various narrative genres, a ready-made manufacturing technique has become established; screenwriters, more or less experienced directors, and their assistants use it unhesitatingly."[57] In other words, the economic crisis and the accompanying pressure toward enforced standardization exacerbated the clash between traditional romantic notions of art and the pragmatic efficiency of media operations. Many critics still retained the hope that the crisis would pass or that the public could be aesthetically educated. But instead during this crisis—which was also one of the critics' ideas—a *fundamental conflict* between traditionally conceived art criteria and the culture industry's practices simply revealed itself more fully. At this time, film criticism developed questions, a cognizance of specific problems and perspectives, which drew on fundamental cultural developments of the media age, above and beyond the immediate situation. This included—as one of the then most prevalent metaphors for the stereotype—the definitive establishment of "standardization" as topic of film theory.

THE "STANDARD" AND THE "READYMADE": NEW METAPHORS OF FILM CRITICISM

Although the new catchword of "standardization" certainly carried positive associations in a number of cultural discourses (for example on design and architecture), there was initially hardly a film critic willing to attribute anything positive to the phenomenon.

One might say that Siegfried Kracauer ventured the farthest in this direction. His sense of film aesthetics reflected perspectives from sociology and cultural analysis. In his essay "The Mass Ornament" from 1927, he did not criticize the new rationalization in an antimodern reflex but rather embraced it as a step in the historical "process of demythologization"[58] or "a stage in the process of demystification [*Entzauberung*]"[59] in the sense of Max Weber. However, he perceived the capitalist rationale as incomplete, "murky reason,"[60] because it did not take people into consideration: "Everyone does his or her task on the conveyor belt, performing a partial function without grasping the totality."[61] It entailed a tendency toward relapsing into myth, into the "mythological delusions"[62] and not enlightenment and reason, that is, "serving the breakthrough of truth."[63] This caused people to subordinate themselves to the alienating organization of capitalism.[64]

This dialectical position may explain why Kracauer's film criticism was not (at this point in time) opposed to popular cinema's tendency toward seriality and genre as such. Instead, he demonstrated a nuanced view of economic rationalization, an understanding that—compared to other reputed film critics of the time—probably went the farthest: "the variation of specific patterns is in fact preferable to indiscriminate experimentation, and, besides, even the biggest firms cannot deliver new and original models week after week."[65]

However, Kracauer criticized the "low standard of such operational procedures"[66] and what he perceived as the backward attitudes of many films that drew on reactionary ideologies and myths and thus produced delusions. Most of all, such films nourished conformist illusions among the new class of white-collar workers regarding their social status. Standardized structures and recurring motifs did not only appear to him as constitutive of popular culture, but they interested him to a much greater extent as signs of deeper underlying ideological schemata, as indicators for critical ideological analysis, which he considered the central task of film criticism (and later of his film historiography): "In the endless sequence of films, a limited number of typical themes recur again and again; they reveal how society wants to see itself. The quintessence of these film themes is at the same time the sum of society's ideologies, whose spell is broken by means of the interpretation of the themes."[67]

That Kracauer was able to review three important books on cinema in a single article of 1932,[68] which discussed the industrial nature of film production and the standardization of its products, bears witness to the significance that the theoretical motif had meanwhile attained in the discourse on cinema[69] as well as to the different, and indeed contrary, perspectives it inspired.

Ilja Ehrenburg's reportage novel from 1931, *Die Traumfabrik*[70] (The Dream Factory), alludes to this theme already in its title, as did the essay *Die Phantasiemaschine*[71] (The Fantasy Machine) by the Viennese essayist René Fülöp-Miller. Rudolf Arnheim also entitled two chapters of his famous film-theoretical analysis *Film als Kunst*—the third book Kracauer reviewed—"*Schematisierung*" (Schematization) and "*Zur Psychologie des Konfektionsfilms*" (On the Psychology of the Readymade Film).[72]

Both *Die Traumfabrik* as well as *Die Phantasiemaschine* bear clear relationships to reportage on America. One can hardly overlook the affinities between

Ehrenburg's book and Kisch's ironic reports from America and Hollywood, and, appearing in the United States (at approximately the same time), the (more concentrated) original version of Fülöp-Miller's essay had even been published as a firsthand account of American cinema in a book on theater and film coauthored with theater scholar Joseph Gregor.[73]

The comparison of the three texts shows that Ehrenburg, unlike Fülöp-Miller and, more significantly, Arnheim, barely touched on film's aesthetic dimensions. The question of aesthetic quality or art seemed apparently pointless to him, given his vision of the efficient operations of the film industry, which was exclusively concerned with profit and dominance through manipulation. In a capitalistic world full of alienating assembly-line monotony, standardized dreams are produced by means of film for moviegoers who "after [performing] unpleasant work want to forget as quickly as possible."[74] He adds: "We produce films on the assembly line. Ford automobiles, Gillette razor blades, Paramount dreams,"[75] and "the wasteland, the horrible consuming wasteland. That is film."[76]

Hence, through a strategy of offering distractions from social misery, films promised not only to maximize profits but also to make the masses compliant. Writing from a Marxist perspective, Ehrenburg brought together the then (to some extent also among conservatives) widespread thought motifs of capitalist critique, exaggerated to apocalyptical dimensions, in a hermetic scenario of leftist cultural criticism. In contrast to Horkheimer and Adorno's later critique of the culture industry, the Soviet author is certain of a historical solution: as an ominous reminder of the otherwise omnipotent capitalist machinery, *The Battleship Potemkin* repeatedly crosses the pages of the book. Kracauer's insightful assessment in 1932 of Ehrenburg's *Traumfabrik* reads: "visions of dark grandeur" that neither penetrate the "heart of the circumstances criticized" nor reveal "the constructive forces perhaps present in Europe and America beneath the surface."[77]

At first glance, Fülöp-Miller seemed to play with similar images. He painted a picture of the Hollywood film industry as "this extraordinary machine which made it possible to take entertainment rolled up in strips, like canned meat in tins, and ship it to the most distant settlements. The moving picture engenders the pleasure that comes of manufacturable goods and permits the industrial satisfaction of spiritual needs."[78] Correspondingly, Fülöp-Miller also emphasized the commercial basis of film production and its affinity for standardized forms. However, in contrast to Ehrenburg he "goes about it more carefully, without the stamp of ideology, which is genuine content,"[79] according to Kracauer.

Especially Fülöp-Miller's interpretation of the "readymade" metaphor of film production interested Kracauer, who himself sometimes used this metaphor, which was prevalent at the time and which paraphrased the motif of standardization.

Arnheim too employed the term as a matter of course, however with a quite a different accent. When Fülöp-Miller used the term "readymade," he was mainly thinking about the emergence of filmic stereotypes through adaptation to common dispositions of the public. That means that he emphasized a (semio)pragmatic and simultaneously economic aspect with respect to reception: the reciprocal adaptation of product and consumer as the basis for a functioning production of goods. The garment industry (*Konfektion*) served him as a provocative comparison. Just as it had been possible in the readymade production of clothing to reduce customers' different body sizes "to a few types," so the film industry used stereotypes to create "common denominators for the wishes, feelings, temperaments, and philosophies of life of all mankind," which made it possible to "to satisfy the spiritual needs with a standardized article which would not only be manufacturable but which would also offer each customer something that suited him."[80] Thus, the fantasy machine of cinema prefers to draw on emotional motifs, since common ground between people is found more on an affective level than an intellectual one. Cinema adheres to "everything that instinct and passion awakens," to "the primeval myths that are a part of the sensibilities of a whole people"[81]—and naturally to sexual desires. The latter only really assume visual form through film, with its "standardized erotic types."[82] Thus "men with insufficient imagination" get their "ready-made dream-pictures."[83]

In their overarching structure, films accommodated the widespread receptiveness of the audience for illusionary "wish-fulfillment."[84] The happy ending, an "unvarying form"[85] for concluding a film, Fülöp-Miller considered as the culmination of an omnipresent compensatory tendency toward overcoming the limits of the everyday: "the film story permits itself to be completely guided by the wish."[86]

Finally, he interpreted the reduction in narrative complexity (and the stereotype) as another form of adaptation to an international mass audience: "the film plot followed quite rudimentary themes which in their simplicity could be understood the world over, and their motives, which the action of the performers established, corresponded to the impulses of an instinct and inner life common to all men. Characters as complicated as the average normal man were not clear enough even for pictures."[87] Popular cinema's affinity to the development of figural types appears to result from the trend toward reduced complexity: "Only characters with one trait could be used—characters who through their very externals and through their behavior are easily recognized as being good or wicked."[88] Both a learning effect and the pleasure of repetition played a role in reception, since "stereotyped figures"[89] were gradually memorized: "Through constant repetition, these figures have gradually come to be recognized as conventional forms in whom the public can readily place its trust; like magic signs and symbols."[90] This "endless repetition of the same impressions"[91] made reception additionally appealing.

Fülöp-Miller's book is not only a—largely though undeservingly forgotten—crucial document of the incipient discussion of cinema's culture-industrial contexts, in which film is compared with other industrial products rather than the traditional arts. In addition, it is the first book in the history of the theoretical discourse on film to lend central importance to the pragmatic interpretation of stereotypes as *factors coordinating the commodity of film with the dispositions of a mass audience*. This also inspired Kracauer's praise for the book, which "in an outstanding manner derives the origins of contemporary film from the deep insights about the universal emotional reactions of the public, of which precisely the profit-oriented creative minds in the business were capable."[92]

Above all, it is this first elaboration and identification of the pragmatic connection between the stereotype and audience dispositions that earns Fülöp-Miller's text its rightful place in the history of film theory. This is not much changed by his often ambivalent or even ironic perspective on the phenomenon, which sometimes assumes the tenor of cultural criticism.

While *Die Phantasiemaschine* invokes the metaphorical "readymade," or the stereotype, respectively, as the mutual adaptation of film and widespread dispositions of the mass public, Rudolf Arnheim gave the metaphor a different emphasis in *Film als Kunst*. He used the terms "readymade product"[93] to point to the film industry's automatization effects and thereby sought to characterize the routine nature of film production, against which he delivered an aesthetically based polemic: "the fastest, most effortless fabrication . . . a minimum of intellectual effort."[94] The "industry film," as he described the majority of cinema offerings, provides endless mechanical combinations of prefabricated elements taken from a conventional repertoire, that is, from stereotypes. Indicative of Arnheim's emphasis of the readymade metaphor was the comparison he drew with serial architecture:

The architect Walter Gropius once had the idea to build *serially manufactured* houses, which were not all the same, and even looked quite different, but were all constructed from the same elements; he wanted to manufacture these elements in series. The film industry produces its goods according to this very principle. Elements are predetermined and are then always fabricated in the same fashion, although they are combined in very different ways, so that new films continually result from the same material. Time and again one sees a disguise, a last-minute rescue, competition for a woman, red herrings, inheritances, chase scenes—it would not be difficult to create a chart onto which each of these films could be entered and which, much like the periodic table of the elements, would help identify gaps and make it possible to calculate which film plots were still to be invented.[95]

This idea does resurface regularly in later writing on film, sometimes as polemical critique, as with Buñuel[96] or Shklovsky,[97] sometimes as a serious attempt to actually construct such systems. Arnheim observed this sort of combination of prefabricated elements not only with regard to subject matter, milieu, story, and character types. He regarded the entire narrative structure of film down to the individual shot as determined by "schematized, preformed gimmicks":[98]

> The grandfather clock on which the hours are sped up, the name plate on the apartment door, the revolver pulled out of nowhere, the keyhole, the kicking silk-stocking legs with no upper body, the telltale man's hat on the clothing hook, the death notice set in the center of the newspaper page, the monocle falling out of the eye, the champagne glass crashing to the floor, the tuxedo worn in the morning, the stage box at the variety theatre, the ashtray full of cigarettes . . . [99]

From the perspective of Arnheim's Gestalt aesthetics, the frequent repetition of such visual ideas with established function were the most striking and, for him, the most annoying fact about the readymade. This opinion is close to the attitude of the cameraman Vladimir Nilsen, previously cited in a different context. Nilsen too expressed a particularly negative view (somewhat later than Arnheim) regarding the "standard compositional constructions"[100] of film images.

When fifteen years later the film economist Peter Bächlin investigated rationalization tendencies in the film industry, he articulated, as elaborated in chapter 3, two specific trends apart from technical innovation: "1. saving work time by omitting variation superfluous to the use value of the commodities, and 2. . . . a typification of the end product in regard to the commodity's use value."[101] In examining Fülöp-Miller and Arnheim's interpretations of the readymade and standardization, one notices that Arnheim primarily discussed the first tendency mentioned by Bächlin, whereas Fülöp-Miller's ideas tended instead to circle around the second.

STANDARD VERSUS ART CONCEPT: ARNHEIM AND FÜLÖP-MILLER

Both Rudolf Arnheim and René Fülöp-Miller brought a culture-critical perspective to bear on the topic of the film industry's tendency toward standards.

Nevertheless, as differently as they each used the metaphor of the readymade product, their views of the relationship between the standardization of film and aesthetic or artistic criteria were equally at odds.

From the very first, Arnheim's view of the readymade film and its standards served purely as a negative foil for his theory of film as art, namely as a phenomenon unworthy of further investigation. His idea of film as art emphasizing freshness, individuality, and unique expression was directly opposed to his vivid outline of the film industry's routinized game with building-block components: "Regularity is not odd when it concerns the production of small cars. In matters of art, however, standardization seems like a bad joke."[102]

This view remained fundamentally unaltered by the insight that the conventional regularities of the "average" film are not truly static but gradually shift due to the constant integration of innovation: "The average production does not remain the same in its use of filmic means of expression. It lags an appropriate distance behind forerunning developments: what is today a bold outsider statement will be common property in two years. . . . *Only that novelty becomes banality as soon as it is considered domesticated and legitimate.*"[103] The idea consistently predominates that artistic quality is defined by a *maximum* distance from repetition and convention and thus also by novelty and an aversion to the everyday, hence by aesthetic exclusivity.

Influenced by Gestalt psychology,[104] Arnheim could have certainly shown an interest in stereotypes as a variation of repeating, incisive patterns. Gestalt psychology underscored visual perception not as compiled like a mosaic of multiple individual entities but as guided by preexisting, familiar structures—so-called *Gestalten*, hence the discipline's key term. These structures reduced complexity and ensured a consistency of perception. It would have suggested itself to apply the—ultimately—constructivist basic idea of the approach[105] to the interpretation of conventional forms, in particular to visual stereotypes.

However, Arnheim did not do this. Despite all his interest in basic forms, his later reflections on art and visual perception were also shaped by the notion of aesthetic development being rooted in a process of progressive differentiation. Dialectical ideas about the stereotype, like those proposed by Ernst Gombrich, another theorist of visual perception (in which conventional and reduced standard forms are indispensable to every single creative process as initial, stabilizing schemata, as starting points which are individually taken up and partially transgressed, or "suspended"),[106] were not relevant to Arnheim. Thus, a Manichean pattern of thought particularly dominates the theoretical passages of *Film als Kunst*: creativity, originality, and exclusivity are the *absolute* opposites of conventional form, mechanization, and banality.

"Artistically speaking, an expression become formulaic no longer bears fruit"[107] was his dictum. Against this backdrop, even the use of symbols seemed unacceptable to him. The reasoning behind this aversion recalls Mauthner's objection to "mechanical metaphors":

> A symbol in most cases is the representation of an abstract object or process through a concrete object or process. However, and according to the use of the word this is indeed the nature of a symbol, this representation is one that has been long customary, is universally known, not brand new; and very often the significance of the symbol cannot be discerned from simply looking, rather one must have learned it by experience. . . . Thus it follows that symbols are not instruments of art. . . . The artist must create his symbols himself, and such symbols are not called "symbols."[108]

Arnheim was most bothered by "the fixed clichés" of symbolism "common in *mass fabrication*,"[109] for example the "skeletons, sand glass, people in animal cages"[110] in *Lied vom Leben* (*Song of Life*, Alexander Granowski, Germany, 1931). This can largely be explained by—apart from serial aspects of production or the opposition of familiar versus new—the fact that these forms and films were generally addressed to the masses and their dispositions and not to a public of sophisticated art connoisseurs. This had to bother him, given how he claimed early on in his introduction to *Film als Kunst* and later often repeated that film as art "operates according to the same age-old laws and principles as all the other arts."[111] *Sociologically* based shifts in ideas about art did not play a role in Arnheim's thought.

Aesthetic products with different sociofunctional accents and responding to mass needs, for example, "distraction" (as it was termed by Arnheim and many of his contemporaries), from the first did not deserve the quality seal of "art" at all. Overall he found few offerings in what the film or culture industry produced for mass reception that met his criteria. The presence of standardized forms, simultaneously adapted to the mass public, only made this discrepancy more pronounced. For Arnheim, the bond between art and popular culture had plainly been severed.

In contrast to some other prominent film critics and intellectuals of the time, who hoped that precisely film could in fact close the perceived gap between the two realms, for example through education, Arnheim clearly stated his lack of faith in such hopes already in 1928. At the time (in contrast to later on), he was even opposed to the influence of any educational ambitions regarding the public in matters of art: "The quality of higher intellectual achievements should not continue to be called into question by the already hopeless attempt at popularizing them."[112] He drastically concluded: "Let us separate, particularly in film and theater, the amusement industry from art, so that artists are not . . . impeded by the demands of those in need of distraction."[113] Traces of such intellectual reservations about popular culture can also be found in *Film als Kunst*, and they overtly characterize his indictment of all tendencies toward the stereotype.

Kracauer, who sympathizes with Arnheim's material-aesthetic approach in his previously mentioned review of 1932, criticized this type of thinking: "At the very least his [Arnheim's] interpretation of the 'ready-made film' is not original, he is still lacking in the necessary sociological categories."[114]

Taken to its ultimate consequences, a theoretical approach to film as art that from the outset regards viewers' needs for entertaining narratives as alien or even antagonistic to art means excluding the majority of the medium's offerings from "art" and thus also from examination in film studies, which Arnheim always considered a discipline of art history.

It stands to reason that Arnheim, a film critic for the *Weltbühne*, was hardly in a position to rigidly maintain this stance toward the realities of popular film. He ultimately depended upon identifying positive aspects of popular film, and, being sufficiently obsessed by cinema to do so, he would discover them primarily on the level of visual form.

Film als Kunst evinces a double-layered conceptual model, which was frequently employed in the film criticism of the period: a distinction between the narrative content, on the one hand, and the more formal aspects of visual design and film technique, on the other. Arnheim was tolerant toward narrative plot structures. He was certain that "the (kitschy or reasonable) 'action' is not so relevant, but one must look at how the individual image, the individual scene is composed, photographed, acted, edited; Stendhal writes: *il n'y a d'originalité et de vérité que dans les détails!*"[115]

On this level, Arnheim tacitly accepted the orientation toward stereotypes, for example, recurrent plot elements, as an unfortunate condition of film's economically necessary popularity. In an article praising the stock actor, he even celebrated the interplay of reduction, accentuation, and repetition, that is, the principles of the stereotype in regard to characters and acting.[116] On a visual level, however, particularly in terms of camerawork and montage, he was never as equanimous. At the time, almost all critics, quite rightfully, associated the specificity of film, especially silent film, with its *visuality*. After all, precisely in the era of silent film the development of narrative cinema was dependent on the evolution and cultivation of *visual* techniques. Against this backdrop, Arnheim advocated a strict formalism of the image. True artistic stylization was achieved through the techniques of *visual* expression specific to the medium: "In terms of plot, film must, at least over the short term, make concessions to the instincts of the masses, who wish to be excited, moved, surprised. But, as always worth repeating, no concessions may be made in terms of technique!"[117] This almost ideal-typical statement stems from Kurt Pinthus's contribution to the film-crisis debate. However, in terms of content it could have easily originated from Arnheim, and it conveys his same two layers of thought. The creative development and use of visual possibilities of expression—namely those offered by the "apparatus," the technique of the camera—was the aspect of film that truly fascinated the young Gestalt psychologist, who would explore problems of artistic expression in the visible throughout his life: "All the characteristics of the camera and of film footage, framing, two-dimensionality, black-and-white reduction, etc., become in the course of their development positively applicable artistic devices."[118] His thought on film centered on this basic theme, the use of these reductive elements of the filmic image in comparison to unmediated visual perception of reality. What he emphasized about these *deficits* is that they provide the opportunity for subjective intervention in the photographic process, which otherwise occurs independently, and thus also room for creativity and interpretation: "It is the very gap between the filmic image and reality, the reduction of bright colors to black-and-white values, the projection of a three-dimensional image onto a flat surface, and the selection of a specific segment of reality through the rectangular frame that make it possible not simply to mirror but compose reality through film."[119] On this level of visual design, and less in the visual composition of the mise en scène, Arnheim perceived the special aesthetic challenge presented by the medium. He thus ascribed to a concept of aesthetics within a German tradition dating back to Lessing's "Laokoon oder Über die Grenzen der Malerei und Poesie."[120] The idea conveyed therein is that every art medium has its specific material of expression associated with specific mimetic deficits. This is the origin of the distinct and specific aesthetic challenges, compositional tasks, and limitations pertaining to each medium.

Along these lines, Arnheim systematized the most important means of expression of camera and montage that had been developed by 1930 in *Film als Kunst* and thus produced a formal-aesthetic summary of the visual expressive techniques employed in silent film. Herein lies his undisputed achievement.

From this perspective, the question of art was for Arnheim primarily a question of form in relation to the dynamic, photographic image. If the "deficits" of the film image were to be used productively in an artistic sense and in continuously new ways, then originality and innovation *on this level* were for him essential requirements for a designation as "art." In contrast, narrative content and the quality of the intellectual examination of the real world remained secondary

from the perspective of art—even if their political tendencies may have sometimes bothered him. According to Arnheim, the history of the visual arts was not
lacking in great artworks with tendencies worthy of criticism: "The question of
a film's subject matter is greatly overvalued, particularly by intellectuals . . . the
example of Jacques Feyder's 'The New Gentleman' demonstrates how one can create a magnificent work of art out of material with objectionable tendencies. And
art history is not lacking in such examples."[121]

Arnheim, who had studied art history in addition to psychology in Berlin, is
thus rooted in the tradition of formal pictorial analysis, which largely pervaded
the art history of the period and which was undoubtedly a major influence on his
work, as was Gestalt psychology.

In response to the "crisis of representation,"[122] art scholars such as Alois Riegl
and Heinrich Wölfflin identified the *intrinsic nature of art* purely with visual
form. Much in the way that avant-garde visual artists pursued a path of increasingly radical abstraction, scholars who sought emancipation from the objects of
representation also moved toward an autonomous history of human visual perception and pictorial forms. For example, Wölfflin had distilled these ideas from
solely representational images; he studied pictures as purely visual and structural
phenomena, and the content of the images essentially no longer played a role in
his history of form.

Arnheim applied this approach to the dynamic visuality of film and brought it
together with his interest in the possibilities of film technology, which he derived
from the difference between the film image and the perception of reality. The idea
of pure visual form ultimately enabled his compromising attitude toward the content and stereotypes of popular narration that underlay his double-layered model.
The idea also offered a variation on the compromise with the stereotype, or from a
different perspective, one might say the *partial emancipation* from the stereotype.

* * *

For Fülöp-Miller, more cultural analyst than art theorist, the question of art was
far less significant. His interests did not lie in elaborating an aesthetic concept of
film art even roughly comparable to that of Arnheim's. And what does emerge in
terms of his immanent ideas about art is anything but coherent and sometimes
contradictory; it resists systematization.

Nevertheless, the tension between industry and art is expressed repeatedly.
To Fülöp-Miller it seemed evident that the industry's commercial interests, its
orientation toward "clichés . . . in place of the rich variations of real life,"[123] and a
reticence toward "anything that the mass intelligence may not comprehend" have

"robbed the film of the possibility of developing a genuine artistic form."[124] Without further addressing the question of "how," Fülöp-Miller declares, however, that in cinema "constant attempts at the artistic also have been made, despite the numerous arbitrary conventions, the stifling necessity for typ-ing and the formal 'happy ending.'"[125]

Aside from such commendatory remarks, Fülöp-Miller's explanation of the readymade principle was, even in terms of approach, not primarily concerned with drafting a polemic counterimage for art. His real interest lay in interpreting the film industry and films as a "cultural pattern of our time,"[126] and he obviously took pleasure in doing so. Incidentally, he identified one type of film that particularly fascinated him and that in its narrative structure used the intellectual technique he himself employed of distanced, ironic observation: namely, *slapstick comedy*.

In the chapter on the poetry of this genre, an ideal notion of popular film emerges, which is far removed from romantic ideas about art and from the concessionary stance of Arnheim's double-layered concept. Fülöp-Miller's attitude indeed recalls Balázs's glorification of the naïve, as articulated in the film-crisis debate and elsewhere. Countering Pinthus, Balázs had asked: "But does Chaplin buy his popularity with concessions?"[127] The concessionary attitude thus condescendingly masked the true aesthetic challenge of popular film: "the magic of simple storytelling, meaningful and poetic without intellectual complexity."[128]

For Fülöp-Miller slapstick was a form of such naïve poetry, in which individuals combat a hostile material world, a struggle intended to be watched by the viewer, not compelled to identify with the hero, from a perspective of pleasurable detachment. The majority of the figures revealed "fiendish, inimical mechanics independent of human intelligence."[129] With the playfulness of the situation made clear from the beginning, the spectator could enjoy the freedom of the action, which with great comedians always boiled down to the victory of the human spirit over lifeless mechanisms.

This recalls Brecht's statement from the same year: "It is *not* right that the cinema needs art, unless we create a new idea of art."[130] Especially since Brecht considered the explicit use of stereotyped characters to be of exemplary significance: "For the theatre, for instance, the cinema's treatment of the person performing the action is interesting. To give life to the persons, who are introduced purely according to their functions, the cinema simply uses available types . . . the person is seen from the outside."[131]

Admittedly, Fülöp-Miller agrees with Brecht only in the rather external motif of the pleasure afforded by an overtly displayed stereotype that is not cloaked in empathy (at least in the slapstick film). However, this was not an insignificant trend in the intellectual zeitgeist, even if a recessive one. In the film-music book written by Adorno and Eisler (a project directly preceding Horkheimer and Adorno's *Dialectic of Enlightenment*), one even reads:

> As in many other aspects of contemporary motion pictures, it is not standardization as such that is objectionable here. Pictures that frankly follow an established pattern, such as "westerns" or gangster and horror pictures, often are in a certain way superior to pretentious grade-A films. What is objectionable is the standardized character of pictures that claim to be unique; or conversely, the individual disguise of the standard pattern.[132]

In contrast to this motif, rather typical of New Objectivity, not only Arnheim but also Fülöp-Miller associated the readymade film with a state of regression. As expressed ten years earlier in the writings of Hugo von Hofmannsthal, the notion of cinema as "substitute for dreams,"[133] now a prevalent idea, is present in Fülöp-Miller. The escape into pleasant dreams, the return to an easily understood, simple world with clear values, which functions according to wishes lodged deep in the spectators' subconscious, to Fülöp-Miller as well as Arnheim appears to be the true core of what the play of standards in the film narratives offered. But again, both authors approached the idea from different perspectives.

For Fülöp-Miller, cinema as a whole was an apparatus of regression sui generis. Therein lay the essence of its success, which was already facilitated by its technological apparatus. One is clearly reminded of Münsterberg's theory of film perception, in which he described how through close-ups and editing the "machine" itself guides viewers' attention and thought processes and relieves them of mental work whenever possible.[134] Fülöp-Miller rounds out this picture with a description of narrative stereotypes as vehicles of mental relief and regression par excellence. Continuing in this train of thought, his text seems to anticipate Jean-Louis Baudry's thesis:[135] "Thus we see that every conceivable effort is made to enable each spectator to realize his wish-phantasy in the most effortless and comfortable fashion, so that he has nothing to do but watch the screen in complete relaxation, freed from the eternal necessity for watchful care that real life occasions, freed from the strenuous effort of attentiveness, of the obligation to think."[136] That this orientation toward regression, combined with the search for "common demoninators,"[137] led to "primary functions of the human soul,"[138] that film narratives had assimilated whatever aroused the instincts and the passions (even if moderated by convention)—for Fülöp-Miller all this constituted their very nature.

Adorno would later polemicize against such regression, claiming that in the context of the culture industry it was pernicious: "The renunciation of resistance is ratified by regression."[139] Fülöp-Miller, in contrast, limits himself to simply mentioning the phenomenon. Beneath the surface, a fascination even shines through that recalls the provocative declarations from the ranks of the avant-garde during the cinema debate in the years prior to World War I. Such proclamations were aimed at rejecting attempts—made under the banner of the *Autorenfilm*—to elevate the status of cinema to a recognized art form (in the sense of traditional concepts of art). The intellectuals were in fact fascinated by cinema's garish *visual pleasure* and its perception as a *space of delightful regression*.[140] In 1913, Lukács appreciatively wrote: "the child that is alive in every person is liberated here and becomes lord over the psyche of the viewer."[141]

Arnheim emphasizes clearly different ideas. Having committed himself to an extensive "excursion in extra-aesthetic regions"[142] of the psychology of the ready-made film, he too considered it beyond question that the stories consistently asserting the triumph of a naïve sense of justice ultimately addressed the unconscious wishes and desires of the spectators. This, however, gave him a sense of unease, and he felt compelled to wield his pen against the image of the "psychology of the average man," which successful films revealed to him—"much like the psychologist can uncover the structure of a patient's soul by the recounting of an insignificant dream."[143] It showed the extent of the prevailing "stale air in the unconscious": "the readymade film gratifies the sluggish creature of habit within the individual,"[144] and it reveals the secret "taste for small-mindedness and backwardness."[145]

In the context of 1932, the film critic of Carl von Ossietzky's *Weltbühne* also identified a political dimension, in that the stereotypical wish fulfillment of contemporary cinema could promote social passivity and a reactionary mentality. Film makes it possible "that dissatisfaction does not incite a revolutionary act but instead fades into dreams of a better world. It serves up the things worth combating as sugar pills."[146] Nevertheless, for Arnheim too this pleasure in the regressive unexpectedly (and without consequences for his later thinking) broke new ground:

> Cinema wonderfully fills our imagination with the bogeymen that children both love and need and that they procure from one place or another. Thus we associate with cinema the same tender gratitude we feel toward our old children's books. . . . Today we will sometimes go to the eighty-cent cinema on the corner, and, delighted and moved, we experience the "Lord Gray's Night of Horror" and the "Rapture of Sin."[147]

This last thought again strongly recalls the previously discussed paradoxical arguments, which were characteristic of the intellectual fascination for the non-intellectual, the "primitive," the "childlike," which originated in the early period of the medium and which soon became a topos, albeit recessive, in the intellectual discourse on cinema.

THE STANDARD AS A TOPIC IN EXILE:
ADORNO, ARNHEIM, AND PANOFSKY

When many of the intellectuals in Germany who had contributed to the debate on the standardization of film were forced to emigrate in the 1930s and 1940s, the discourse was continued among these émigrés in the United States. The basic structure of the arguments adhered, for the most part, to the framework already established by around 1930. However, the discourse did undergo a pronounced radicalization and polarization, not least because the theorists encountered—much like the reporters of the 1920s—an even more driven and overtly commercialized media business, which belied all illusions of a temporary "crisis."

Theodor W. Adorno later recalled that it was in America where he first truly realized "to what extent rational planning and standardization had permeated the so-called mass media."[148] Contributing to this was certainly the fact that he began his career in exile with the Princeton Radio Research Project, as did Arnheim somewhat later. The project brought the new arrivals in close contact with the American media business: Adorno was responsible for music studies, and Arnheim, of all people, was commissioned with examining the successful narrative formulas of *daytime serials*, that is, radio *soap operas*.[149] Hence, it is not surprising that the standards of popular culture became a leading topic in the years that followed.

The function of this motif, again as a focal counterpoint to a positive aesthetics, was already distinctly articulated in Adorno's essay "On the Fetish-Character in Music and the Regression of Listening,"[150] published in German in 1938 and providing a skeptical response to the technological optimism of Benjamin's theses on the work of art. This motif remained unchanged[151] until the publication in 1947 of Horkheimer and Adorno's *Dialectic of Enlightenment*.

In today's cultural memory, this book functions as a paradigm of left-wing criticism of the culture industry. The text was, however, not without precedent but rather picked up the threads of the discourses of the late 1920s and early 1930s, including the discourses on the standardization of film. The book also marks the height of the culture-critical discourse on the stereotype. For Horkheimer and Adorno, the set of problems that they criticized in the culture industry culminated in the tendency toward the stereotype: "Despite . . . all the gesticulating bustle, the bread on which the culture industry feeds humanity, remains the stone of stereotype."[152]

They emphatically raised the issue of the constant repetition of conventional, "banal" aesthetic patterns in Hollywood films and in the products of the culture industry as a whole. Nevertheless, they did *not* situate the core problem foremost on the level of aesthetic appearances, and in this they diverged from most of the opinions dating from around 1930. Instead, their criticism was aimed at the *schematism* dominating the individual's relationship to the world and underlying aesthetic form:

> The senses are determined by the conceptual apparatus in advance of perception; the citizen sees the world as made *a priori* of the stuff from which he himself constructs it. Kant intuitively anticipated what Hollywood has consciously put into practice: images are precensored during production by the same standard of understanding which will later determine their reception by viewers.[153]

> The active contribution, which Kantian schematism still expected of subjects— that they should, from the first, relate sensuous multiplicity to fundamental concepts—is denied to the subject by industry. It purveys schematism as its first service to the customer.[154]

In "The Schema of Mass Culture," Adorno regarded the genuinely distinctive element of this *filter* as operating in concert with the reified state of a society subjugated to commodity fetishism: "Perhaps the gesture of the narrator has always had something apologetic about it, but today it has become nothing but apology through and through."[155]

The power of the "predigested"[156] rests on the omnipresence of patterns: "the totality of the culture industry. Its element is repetition."[157] Following this train of thought, the pointedly described standardization of aesthetic appearances remains a derivative phenomenon functioning as a metaphor for the deeper-lying filters of *deception*.

Since for Adorno and Horkheimer the contradiction between the idea of individuality and the reality of mass culture seemed insurmountable, *stereotypy*— developed as a counteridea to individual expression—assumed omnipotent proportions. In this sense, they shared the Manichaean axioms of theorists such as Arnheim. However, in contrast to the former film critic of the *Weltbühne*, who attempted a certain degree of aesthetic nuance with his double-layered model, the two cultural theorists remained hermetic in their critique. Similar to many of the polemical reporters on America in the 1920s (such as Kisch), they considered cinema little else than the return of the "unending sameness"[158] of the a priori banal. "Every film is a preview of the next, which promises yet again to unite the same heroic couple under the same exotic sun: anyone arriving late cannot tell whether he is watching the trailer or the real thing."[159] From this perspective, every individual trait, every novelty, every talent becomes a mere external guise of schematism, in which change merely means adapting to changed circumstances. But is the "Lubitsch touch"[160] truly nothing more than "pseudoindividuality" or "a fingerprint on the otherwise uniform identity cards"?[161] This negative hermeticism eliminates a priori stereotype concepts in the spirit of *Dialectic of Enlightenment* from differentiated analyses of popular film.

* * *

Arnheim's pessimism also became more pronounced around this time. In his study on radio *soap operas* he concluded: "The effects of commercial control are well known from what motion picture producers and pulp writers offer to their customers. Any admissible means to exercise a strong appeal is welcome, and since generally the strongest and widest appeal can be secured by the crudest means, commercial art production tends towards lowering the cultural level."[162] He hardly saw any more chance for the realization of his idea of film art. He had meanwhile given up his hopes that, as claimed in 1931/1932, the standardization tendencies were merely the expression of a temporary crisis. Taking stock in the essay "Il cinema e la folla" (Cinema and the Masses) for the Italian magazine *Cinema*, he explained in 1949 that film is ultimately bound to providing a modern "spectacle for the masses"[163] due its high cost of production and commercial-industrial base.

> In the meantime, film production continues to industrialize, and the type of small producer who attempts to unite commercial interests with honest artistic ambitions is on the verge of disappearing. Production tends to create grand things, solely on the basis of precise calculations made from the current tastes of the audience and the processes of a rationalized and standardized mode of production.[164]

With the exception of a few atypical cases, the attempt to make cinema into an art fostering individual, nonstandardized expression was necessarily deemed a failure against the backdrop of the "continuous, enervating friction between the creative imagination and commercial intentions"[165] intrinsic to the media economy.

In 1934, Arnheim had once described such an atypical case, Erich von Stroheim. Whereas "in Hollywood the mechanization and commercialization of human creativity have been carried to the most violent consequences . . . because the tendencies of modern industry have been applied to the most recalcitrant object, namely, art," Stroheim's work had demonstrated "the rebellion of a strong and exceptional personality against the rules and the norms."[166] By the late 1940s, Arnheim did not mention such exceptions anymore. The fact that around this time he definitively turned his attention to questions of aesthetic perception in the field of modern art and from then on barely addressed topics of film (or radio, which he had studied in the 1930s), is already prefigured in this resume. "Il cinema e la folla" is a document of departure from film. It already indicates an outside perspective.

It is interesting that in this text he explicitly takes up the topic of mechanization one more time, which, placed at the beginning of the text, serves as its central idea: "The spirit thus resists the tendency of mechanizing the relationship between the individual and reality to the extreme."[167] Two types of mechanization play a role in film: the mechanics of the photographic reproduction technology, on the one hand, which is predisposed toward technical verism, and the mechanism of the stereotype, on the other, which is likened to the task of the architect "who is to fabricate a building out of standardized construction elements."[168]

In respect to the first kind of mechanism and the resulting "conflict between artist and machine,"[169] Arnheim argued for a dialectical concept, a "considerate verism,"[170] in which artists (in accordance with the concept of *Film als Kunst*) use the "deficits" of the mechanical procedure in order to assert their subjectivity without breaching the verism of the photographic process. However, he remained uncompromising toward the second type of conflict, which resulted from the transfer of "popular theater into a phase of industrialization"[171] in the commercial medium of film. Here he did not use a dialectical approach to reflect on the way that standards were handled, although he did at one juncture even mention that innovation can be allied with commercial interests. Nevertheless, like Adorno, he too considered this as pseudoindividualization.

Ultimately, the problems in his aesthetic theory of cinema become transparent at this final juncture, a theory precluding all cultural sociological change and guided by a "pure" understanding of art, which, removed from the standards of mass production, was oriented toward the "eye of the connoisseur," the exclusivity of the "happy few,"[172] as Arnheim expressly stated—and (now exclusively) toward the experimental avant-garde.

* * *

But also the antithetical and instead optimistic side of the discourse was represented by a film essay by Erwin Panofsky, a German émigré art historian.[173] The origins of this study are related to the prominent scholar's support of the New York Museum of Modern Art in establishing a film department. To this end, he held the lecture "On Movies" in 1934. First published in 1936, the text appeared in 1947 in its final and substantially revised version under the title "Style and Medium in the Motion Pictures."[174]

Noticeable from the first is that Panofsky, like Arnheim, also pursued a double-layered mode of thought and distinguished between narrative content and visual presentation in the photographic medium. However, his points of emphasis differed from those of Arnheim's *Film als Kunst*.

He turned his attention to the world of popular narrative not simply as a gesture of conciliation or critique. More clearly than hardly any other theorist of film as art, Panofsky acknowledged a form of filmic narration, which "appealed directly and very intensely to a folk art mentality."[175] This mentality was expressed in films that adhered to a "primitive sense of justice and decorum" and "plain sentimentality" and that satisfied a "primordial instinct for bloodshed," "a taste for mild pornography," as well as a "crude sense of humor."[176]

Panofsky responded with genuine fascination to the stereotypical structures of pictorial narration, which he mainly described in the context of silent film. Known as an iconologist, the famous art historian spoke of the "introduction of a fixed iconography"[177] for characters and standard situations in early film, that is, of recurrent conventional patterns. In a manner comparable to the pictorial art of the medieval period, this iconography "from the outset informed the spectator about the basic facts and characters, much as the two ladies behind the emperor, when carrying a sword and a cross, respectively, were uniquely determined as Fortitude and Faith."[178]

For Panofsky, the well-known character stereotypes of film, for example the "Vamp" and the "Straight Girl" ("identifiable by standardized appearance, behavior, and attributes"),[179] were "perhaps the most convincing modern equivalents of the medieval personifications of the Vices and the Virtues."[180] He saw the effects of a "fixed attitude and attribute principle"[181] everywhere in cinema but considered them especially pronounced in early film.

A checkered tablecloth meant, once and for all, a "poor but honest" milieu; a happy marriage, soon to be endangered by the shadows from the past, was symbolized by the young wife's pouring the breakfast coffee for her husband; the first kiss was invariably announced by the lady's gently playing with her partner's necktie and was invariably accompanied by her kicking out with her left foot. The conduct of the characters was predetermined accordingly. The poor but honest laborer who, after leaving his little house with the checkered tablecloth, came upon an abandoned baby could not but take it to his home and bring it up as best he could; the Family Man could not but yield, however temporarily, to the temptations of the Vamp.[182]

In early film melodramas "events took shape, without the complications of individual psychology, according to a pure Aristotelian logic so badly missed in real life,"[183] and the films regularly tended to have a happy ending. This was their special charm. In this context, Panofsky explicitly argued against the aesthetic development of filmic narrative contrary to "a primitive or folkloristic concept of plot construction."[184]

Here the topos of the intellectual fascination for the nonintellectual, the naïve, and the regressive was far more immediately apparent than even in the work of Fülöp-Miller. There are obvious parallels with early positions from the cinema debate that cultivated this thought motif, such as Walter Hasenclever's apology for cinema from 1913, although Panofsky's avowal of the folkloric seemed less paradoxical and ambivalent. Hasenclever had written:

> [Film] is not an art in the sense of theater, no sterilized intellectuality; it is by no means an idea. For this reason it resists (repeated attempts at) inoculation with ethereal music: it still would get smallpox every time. The movies remain something American, ingenious, kitschy. That is their popular nature; that is what makes them good . . . for their modern character is expressed in their ability to gratify idiots and intellects alike, but each in a different way, each according to his mental make-up.[185]

Panofsky saw the beginnings of media-compatible popular narration in cinema in the same light—prior to "attempts at endowing the film with the higher values of a foreign order":[186]

> The legitimate paths of evolution were opened, not by running away from the folk art character of the primitive film but by developing it within the limits of its own possibilities. Those primordial archetypes of film productions on the folk art level—success or retribution, sentiment, sensation, pornography, and crude humor—could blossom forth into genuine history, tragedy and romance, crime and adventure, and comedy, as soon as it was realized that they could be transfigured—not by an artificial injection of literary values but by the exploitation of the unique and specific possibilities of the new medium.[187]

The difference from Arnheim's ideas is obvious. Whereas the latter tolerated the content and dramatic forms of popular narrative as *extra-aesthetic* factors and later even deemed the evolution of cinema into a "theater for the masses" responsible for what he felt was the aborted artistic development of film, Panofsky emphatically affirmed these elements of popular narrative.

This *explicitly* included stereotypes, or "archetypes," of narration. Panofsky showed none of Arnheim's strict aversion to the universally known and conventional. And naturally (as an iconologist) he had no objections to the symbolic as based in the conventional, and there were no signs of the fundamental rift between art and mass production. While culture criticism viewed the bonds between these two spheres as long severed, Panofsky avowed their renewal in, of all things, popular film—certainly a provocative stance: "The 'movies' have reestablished that dynamic contact between art production and art consumption which, for reasons too complex to be considered here, is sorely attenuated, if not entirely interrupted, in many other fields of artistic endeavor."[188]

Whereas Arnheim later, in keeping with his views, preferred modern abstract art as exemplary material for his psychology of art analyses of pure visual form, Panofsky was precisely interested in the continuation of representational imagery afforded by film and the medium's inclination toward stereotypes and the symbols that Arnheim distrusted. Panofsky's iconographic method was oriented toward, and even dependent on, these two phenomena, which is why Thomas Levin regards Panofsky's acknowledgment of the popular as "profoundly antimodernist cultural politics."[189]

> Panofsky's seemingly progressive endorsement of film's mass appeal, of its "communicability," may well have as its hidden agenda an attack on modernism and modern art, a resistance to abstraction that can be traced quite consistently from the early 1930s (at which point Panofsky felt that he could still integrate Cezanne and Marc into his universal iconological model) through the mid-1940s. . . . Film . . . restores the legitimacy of the iconographic method, and the model of immediate experience and transparent perception upon which it depends.[190]

Levin further points out that Panofsky, who accepted the commercial basis of the medium without any reservations—as a phenomenon with an extended history in the production of art—formulated what was in many respects "almost point-for-point the exact antithesis to Adorno and Horkheimer's contemporaneous 'culture industry critique.'"[191] This assessment holds true much to the same extent as Panofsky delivered a side blow to the abstract art of modernism with comments that described, for example, film as "the only visual art entirely alive."[192] Nonetheless, one should also not overlook the antimodern tendencies underlying the fundamental cultural criticism of media production, not only in the work of Arnheim but also in the astute observations made by Adorno and Horkheimer.

Panofsky did at least draw on a second layer of reception and expression in the sense of the double-layered concept, in order to provide validity to different aesthetic criteria. In this meaning, the plot with its narrative standards merely has a grounding function. Film's artistic substance "remains a series of visual sequences held together by an uninterrupted flow of movement in space."[193] For Panofsky this was an established fact, and he added that a sound film first and foremost "remains a picture that moves and does not convert itself into a piece of writing that is enacted."[194] For the art historian, the core artistic challenge lay in the creative handling of the "unique and specific possibilities" of the medium, "defined as *dynamization of space*" and the "*spatialization of time*."[195]

In accordance with the photographic nature of the medium, it was important "to manipulate and shoot unstylized reality in such a way that the result has style."[196] Even if Panofsky did not go into further detail in regard to visual expression, unlike Arnheim (whose uncontested strength lay in this area), and although Panofsky's argument was more heavily focused on content,[197] the two art theorists nevertheless shared a double-layered mode of thinking, which emphasized (at least in terms of art) the level of visual-photographic style.

STANDARDIZATION AND CLASSICAL FILM THEORY: CONCLUSION

The discourse on the standardization of film emerged in Germany during the film crisis of the second half of the 1920s, when increased competition gave rise to a new wave of rationalization in the film industry and when there was an influx of a large number of more thoroughly "standardized" (than at the time customary in Europe) American genre films. The new theoretical motif was carried and shaped by the cultural debate on Americanism, whose main topics included "mechanization" and "standardization" of society and the cultural sphere.

An interpretation that regards the discourse on standardization only as an expression of these cultural changes, that is, merely as a response to novel practical developments (or even solely to a temporary crisis) is too limited in scope.

The discourse was the concrete historical manifestation of film theory's "discovery" of the stereotype as a topic. The contemporary crisis created a particularly acute awareness of the role of cinema as a cultural industry—although this was the result of developments having taken place over the course of two decades and having reached a highly advanced stage. This awareness came together with deeper-seated developments in the logic of the film-as-art theory, which previously had tended to downplay the topic of the stereotype in order to promote film as a valid art form. In addition, a certain fundamental understanding of art largely contributed to the blind eye that was initially turned toward altered sociological conditions and the economic or industrial production contexts of film. Instead, there was a desire to demonstrate that in essence "in film one continues and will continue to work with the same tools as . . . customary in the recognized arts"[198]—however on the basis of the medium's own material specificity.

Concepts no less euphoric aimed to admit film to the ranks of these recognized, venerated art media. Once these positions gained influence and film criticism, meanwhile an established institution, became concerned with using such aesthetic criteria in a serious assessment of the range of existing films, it was inevitable that the discrepancy between romantic ideas about art and the "average" film would become prominently apparent. The "film crisis" of the period simply accelerated and exacerbated these circumstances.

The basic tenor of the standardization discourse was substantially colored by disappointment about the industrial realities of the medium, which had taken a path divergent from romantic concepts of art. Stereotypes or standards were regarded as crystallizations of this unwelcome development and were therefore on principle almost always considered antithetical to artistic quality. Since most theorists, not only Arnheim, now viewed film primarily as the *pictorial* art of the camera and editing, they attempted to save film from standardizations on the visual level, even if compromises had to be made on the dramaturgic level of the plot in regard to the popular medium.

Then again, the thinking of a number of intellectuals was shaped by ideas emphasizing in cinema a sort of exoticism of the plebeian or the pleasure gained from regressive, naïve tendencies. This was certainly only an undercurrent. Balázs's idea of film as a new folk art (still based on preindustrial models) belongs to the ambit of such modes of thinking, as does Panofsky's celebration of archaic folklore. The iconologist even went as far as not only tolerating the visual-narrative stereotype in the mise en scène and in the structure of plot, but he also felt it to be constitutive of film as a popular medium. Nevertheless, when aesthetic quality or the specific aestheticizing possibilities of the medium was at issue, as a special presentation to the expert eye, then for Panofsky too the art of the cinematography became relevant. As vague as his formulations often were, such as his description of shooting "reality in such a way that the result has style,"[199] it remained clear that stereotypes did not belong on this level. Herein Panofsky was in agreement with the classical German theory of film as art.

SEVEN

THE STEREOTYPE AS INTELLIGIBLE FORM:
COHEN-SÉAT, MORIN, AND SEMIOLOGY

At an intermediary level, we see "stereotypes" crystallize: typical objects, typical characters, typical gestures. The screen universe is thus Aristotelianized: objects, characters, and stereotyped gestures make their intelligible essence appear: they are entities of reason.

—EDGAR MORIN, *THE CINEMA, OR THE IMAGINARY MAN* (1956)

THE STEREOTYPE AND THE LANGUAGE OF CINEMA:
THE FILMOLOGISTS

The culture-critical discourse on the stereotype continued through the end of classical film theory[1] and even persists today, although it is no longer a dominant approach. In parallel with this line of thought, a fundamental shift in theoretical attitudes toward the stereotype began to emerge in the postwar period. These new ideas remained very influential, above and beyond later film semiotics, and introduced a new type of thought.

The roots of this change lie in the 1940s and 1950s. It was largely authors from the ranks of French *filmologie* and its circle of influence who began to show an interest in the stereotype as a productive entity within film composition, *precisely because of its conventionality*. In his 1946 *Essai sur les principes d'une philosophie du cinéma*,[2] Gilbert Cohen-Séat, considered the founder of filmology,[3] expressed the view that filmic stereotypes were a source of specific possibilities of expression. Ten years later, in 1956, the cultural anthropologist Edgar Morin (who at the time was affiliated with the Institute of Filmology) pursued this idea further in his book *Le cinéma ou l'homme imaginaire*.[4] Whereas up to this point the stereotype had been reputed as being a manifestation of the banal and the worn out, or at least of the naïve and the regressive, the two authors now upheld the stereotype as a condition of a particular and now desired *intelligibility* of the medium.

This reevaluation of the term signaled a changed theoretical interest in film, a new aspiration: "The cinema frees itself, then, from the cinematograph to constitute itself in an intelligible system."[5] And "film fulfills itself and blossoms into rationality,"[6] the motto of this new rationale as articulated by Morin. It is not without reason that he followed this with a seemingly cognitivist idea: "The intelligence proceeds by the projections of abstract 'patterns' and identification with these patterns."[7]

Most film theorists, positioned between physiognomy and poetic realism, had—sometimes in parallel with the aversions of language skepticism and in opposition to language—affirmed the immediacy of the image in film, the poetry of the photographic, the immediately visible, the nonabstract, the unconventional, the nonformulaic of the visual. In contrast, the new desire for an intelligibility of images fueled an interest in and revaluation of the obviously *non*immediate. There was general fascination for breaching this immediacy and, indeed, for a language-like approach to images.

Arnheim had even rejected the symbol on aesthetic grounds, due to its abstraction, conventional mediacy, and roots in what had long become customary, familiar, and understood by experience: "Thus it follows that symbols are not instruments of art."[8] But precisely this was interesting according to the new perspective. This reassessment also applied to formerly disreputable terms, such as "abstraction," "automatism," "conventionality," "formula," or "pattern," and also the stereotype—a new emphasis with far-reaching consequences for the thought of the following decades.

Although it may initially seem paradoxical against this backdrop, Morin was in fact greatly indebted to Béla Balázs. That he chose a quotation by Balázs as an introductory motto to his book[9] was not an expression of misunderstanding but of reverence. The manner in which Morin draws on Balázs, however, exemplifies the underlying shift in emphasis, especially where he resolves one of Balázs's theoretical incoherencies.

To recapitulate, Balázs had ascribed a decidedly instinctual character to the notion of expressive movement, which was so important to his aesthetics, and he had celebrated the nonconventional visibility of the spirit, the "direct transformation of the spirit into the body"[10] through gesture. However, this theoretical train of thought did not hinder him from occasionally describing certain gestures as having "their own vocabulary of 'conventional,' standard forms,"[11] which exhibited national differences. The international dimension of the film market contributed to the "normalization" of gestural language and to a "universal language of gesture, which had to be comprehensible in all of its nuances from San Francisco to Smyrna."[12] In other words, Balázs had very well observed that gestures tended to be subject to *conventionalization*.

Morin identified the contradiction between Balázs's two arguments and, in contrast, underscored the aspect of conventionalization. That means that he explicitly argued against the idea of the immediacy of gesture and against the convention-free degree zero of expressive potential entailed in a primal gesture:

> If it is not true, as Balázs believed, that the silent film revived a perfect sign language [*un langage mimique parfait*], abandoned by man since prehistory, for the very good reason that gestures, the smile, even tears *have distinct meanings according to civilizations*, it is nevertheless true that the American film has spread across the globe a veritable new sign language, a gestural Esperanto that is easy to learn and whose universe, under the sway of cinema, from then on knows the vocabulary. There is a "degree zero of sign language" . . . but thanks to the cinema.[13]

Significantly, unlike Balázs's basic idea of *immediate* emotional expression in film (as a medium of salvation from conventional, mediated language), Morin and, prior to him, Cohen-Séat did not deny analogies between film and language in respect to the *phenomenon of conventionality or abstraction*. On the contrary, both favored a "linguistic conception of expression,"[14] as Cohen-Séat called it, and they thereby primarily had in mind the elements of abstraction and conventionality constitutive of every language. Different from Robert Musil in the mid-1920s, whose thinking was closer to Morin than Balázs, both French theorists now showed a *decidedly positive interest* in such analogies. Thus, it is not by chance that they began to programmatically use the terms "film language" in their new interpretations, instead of setting film apart from linguistic conventionality and abstraction in the tradition of language criticism.

This *new* interpretation of the term should not be overlooked, for "film language" was by no means a neologism within the film-theoretical discourse of the period.[15] The metaphor had, independent of the topic of the stereotype, been popular since the 1920s. Even Balázs, in another contradiction, sometimes spoke of the "language of film," but he conceived it in essentially antilinguistic terms, free of abstraction and convention. Such vague and incoherent meanings, which suggest little more than that language and film are communication media, were (and still are) common, for example in Spottiswoode's *A Grammar of the Film* (1935).[16]

Another theoretically more influential interpretation of the language metaphor sought syntactically based analogies between the sequence of words in language and the filmic editing. This articulation of the metaphor was particularly important in the film writings of the Russian formalist school. Under the spell of Soviet cinema's montage aesthetic, the formalists had developed a theoretical concept of "film language."

In 1927, Boris Eikhenbaum assigned the metaphor of the "language of film" a significant theoretical function,[17] which he explained as being the most thoroughly relative to the discourse of the period. The analogy between language and film underlying his comparison was based on the succession of individual shots linked through montage to form larger meaningful syntagmas, just as words are joined to make sentences and sentences to make text. Eikhenbaum took this analogy far. He even spoke of the "cine-phrase" and described film sequences as the "linking of phrases."[18] Just as with the reading of a written text, the recipient thus translated the succession of images into "the language of his own internal speech."[19] Very much in the spirit of the legendary Kuleshov experiment,[20] Eikhenbaum emphasized that the syntactic sequence within this translation effected far more than merely adding up the meanings of each shot. As in language, this translation produced its own meaning, a *context-based meaning* that is more than the sum of the parts: "The basic semantic role belongs . . . to the montage, since it is the montage which colours the frames, beyond their general meaning, with definite semantic nuances."[21] This is Eikhenbaum's core statement. Similarly, Sergei Eisenstein's understanding of film had, after his experience with *Bronenosec Potemkin* (*Battleship Potemkin*, USSR, 1925) and, above all, its lion experiment, entered a new phase around 1926, as he himself stated: "The phase of approximation to the symbolism of *language*. Speech. Speech that conveys a symbolic sense . . . through something that is uncharacteristic of the literal, through *contextual confrontation*, i.e. also through *montage*."[22]

This insight ultimately had fundamental significance for Eisenstein's cinema and particularly for his later concept of intellectual montage. The closeness of Eisenstein's ideas and Eikhenbaum's concept attests to what Wolfgang Beilenhoff identified as the "convergence of theoretical discourse and artistic practice in the 1920s."[23]

Whereas the language metaphor as soon as it became more concrete mainly alluded to the phenomenon of linking shots through montage, that is, to an *intratextual* and *syntactical* aspect of the analogy, the writings of Cohen-Séat and Morin primarily focused on the *process of conventionalization* of filmic images and narrative *patterns*, that is, on an *intertextual* aspect. What in 1946 generally interested Cohen-Séat about the reference to language for film was the fact that as a result of lengthy processes of conventionalization, film commands a deep-layered repertoire of well-defined and intersubjectively known semantic elements, which point toward a *language system*. He therefore deemed the conventionality of filmic facts more significant for the abstracting potential of human utterance than the intelligibility of montage. Thereby the stereotype, the conventionalized visual or narrative pattern, became the focus of the language metaphor.

The discursive development and use of fixed schemata on all levels of the filmic diegesis would gradually seep into the consciousness of the participants in cinema's discourse as semantic, readymade structures, which would be accumulated as a "tacit 'dictionary' of images,"[24] as Cohen-Séat put it, conscious of the inherent paradox. That, in effect, is what the filmologists' linguistic analogy aimed toward: "It is easy to foresee that the assimilation of filmic facts [*faits filmique*] to 'words' and the entirety of these signs to a linguistic conception of expression cannot occur without a fundamental change in thinking."[25]

One result of this shift in thinking was a changed attitude toward the stereotype. In view of the new accent given the language metaphor, the stereotype became *a fixed semantic entity* and thus, in a sense, a distant relative of the word, a productive building block in the expressive capabilities of film.

It was the conventionality of the sign, established in filmic discourse through the stereotype, which first offered the possibility of "rediscovering the lessons of conventional language in the brimming agitation of filmic images."[26] This half sentence was programmatic for Cohen-Séat in 1946. In his eyes, the ideal was a film that had abandoned the "age of visual and auditory echoism,"[27] mimesis, and the *direct attachment to physical reality* (as well as to the task of revealing it) and suggested a reading of the "text of film from the image to the idea."[28]

Remarkable about this interest of the theorist in film as "a process of our logification"[29]—as an indicator of the comprehensive shift in emphasis in one area of contemporary film aesthetics, especially in France—is that it to some extent shared the tenor of the famous utopia that Alexandre Astruc extolled soon thereafter (in early 1948) as the agenda of a new film avant-garde. His concept of the "caméra stylo," or the "camera-pen," represented as a major advance in the impact of film, aspired to nothing less than asserting the shift from the (seeming) immediacy of the image to a semantics (conspicuously) based on abstraction. Astruc prefaced his brief essay with a quotation from Orson Wells: "What interests me in the cinema is abstraction."[30] Astruc himself wrote: "[The idea of the caméra-stylo means] that the cinema will gradually break free from the tyranny of what is visual, from the image for its own sake [*l'image pour l'image*], from the immediate and concrete demands of the narrative, to become a means of writing just as flexible and subtle as written language. . . . What interests us is the creation of this new language."[31]

However, Astruc did not go beyond this proclamation. He remained very vague about the basis of this language and how such abstraction was to be attainted, and he did not explore the dimension of conventionalization as a fundamental principle of every language. Cohen-Séat, however, took up this topic. To him it was essential that the medium of film, aspiring to abstraction, develop a repertoire of specific conventional forms. He discussed how in the intertextual field of film a "conventional stylization"[32] was operating to the effect of assigning "every sign a certain established expressive power."[33]

One might argue that in the 1920s Eikhenbaum had already arrived at this assumption: "Cine-language is no less conventional than any other."[34] However, he was primarily concerned[35] with preexisting conventions employed in the medium of film. For him the determining idea was: "The basis of cine-semantics is made up of that stock of expressivity in mime and gesture which we assimilate in everyday life and which is 'directly' comprehensible on the screen."[36] In relation to the filmic metaphor, or in his words "cine-metaphor," to which he dedicated substantial attention as a montage-based phenomenon, he emphasized that it was always the visual translation of an afilmic conventional form: "The cine-metaphor is as it were a genuine realization of a verbal metaphor implemented on screen."[37] Eikhenbaum thus touched on precisely the kind of filmic metaphor that Eisenstein concomitantly took to extremes in his film *Ten Days That Shook the World/October* (*Oktyabr*, USSR 1927) and that Balázs rejected.[38]

In contrast, Cohen-Séat's new perspective on "the forms of conventional language"[39] of film emphatically addressed the *conventional forms developed by the medium itself* as a starting point. What he evidently meant was that stereotypes that had emerged within the "discours filmique"[40] (a term that Cohen-Séat introduced to film theory through his language of metaphoricity) had become distinct and conventional and could therefore address a corresponding semantic consciousness[41] en bloc.

Even if Cohen-Séat only rarely used the term "stereotype" explicitly, his text bears witness to him being conscious of the extent to which conventionality was grounded in the process of discursive (intertextual) repetition. Consequently the study of the language of film or "*filmography*," as he writes, "reveals certain types of repetition. It may be treated as language only if it entails such repetition."[42] These repetitions must be "methodically investigated to be defined and classified."[43] Repetition's pragmatic origin in the imitation of structures already proven successful with the audience and now deemed "serviceable" bothered him as little as the tendency of these structures toward reduced formulas:

> Thus it is not impossible that one might discover a natural selection of the means and procedures of filmic expression. This selection arises from the need of making oneself understandable and from the ability to do so with the help of what is entailed in "fixed" signs and expressions. The immediate or gradual assumption of comfortable or suitable forms to express certain things occurs quickly through use. In the process this or that type of sign is assigned a more or less

precise accepted meaning. This determination extends beyond the single sign and also applies to the application and synthesis of the signs. In a word, the happy discoveries of film [*trouvailles du film*] would correspond to those of any language or to the rhetoric of all languages. Isn't a metaphor that has established itself a good example? What is here called the discoveries of film . . . contagiously inspires imitation. The sign takes on a role and crosses into the conventional.[44]

Cohen-Séat explicitly went on to elaborate that he did not understand the "discoveries of film," "signs," or "fixed expressions" (which he all used synonymously) as concrete images but as *schematic-structural phenomena* in the sense of the stereotype, which are individually actualized as the repetition of a new idea from a specific film. He did not conceive of repetition as a reproduction of the same but as a production of the similar, and herein he again made recourse to the language metaphor:

> Whereas discoveries in common language are commonly repeated in their original form, in film they stabilize almost immediately and adapt to its form. In film, in which exact repetition is as impossible as it is useless, contagion occurs through a closeness and similarity to a new idea, which does not detract from the enrichment and perfection of the sign. The retouches undertaken with each repetition are also similar to the inflections of language.[45]

Even more vividly than Cohen-Séat, Edgar Morin described his observation of how "a general tropism"[46] in film leads to new "discursive signification"[47] and intelligibility.

Interestingly, there is a parallel to Rudolf Arnheim, which, as in the previous comparison with Balázs, once again illustrates the fundamental shift in perspective at this time. Whereas Arnheim in 1932 in *Film als Kunst* had regarded the frequent use of metonymic images, such as "the grandfather clock on which the hours are sped up . . . the kicking silk-stocking legs with no upper body . . . the ashtray full of cigarettes,"[48] and so on as mere banalities, because what were once original film ideas had undergone flatting and wear through imitation, Morin now found precisely in this "abrasive effect of repetition"[49] an enhancement of the semantic abstraction that he so valued, because it more closely approximated conceptualization. The examples he enumerates to support his observation are astoundingly similar to Arnheim's list of negatives: "the withering bouquet, leaves flying off the calendar, the hands of a watch spinning around, the accumulation of cigarette butts in an ashtray: all these images that compress time have become symbols, then signs of time passing. The same for the train speeding into the countryside, the plane in the sky (a sign that the film's heroes are traveling), and so on."[50] Morin consistently asserted the, for his concept, productive side of the automatization, conventionalization, and, above all, the accompanying *abrasion* of intertextually repeated patterns. Sedimentation and wear become conditions no longer for an immediate but an *abstract* and *semiotic reading* of filmic images. A reading that thus detaches itself from the surface of the visual as a mere photographic index of the represented. The flattening effect of repetition is reinterpreted as a condition for what one could exactly call, in the context of Astruc's writings, the release from the tyranny of the concrete or immediate and what Cohen-Séat had described as the "path leading from the real and syncretic thought to understanding . . . to reason, and ultimately to language."[51]

Under the heading "From Symbol to Language,"[52] Morin writes:

> The process is the same as in our verbal language, where marvelous metaphors have slackened and ossified into "clichés." In the same way, cinema "stereotypes" are symbols whose affective sap has turned wooden. They accordingly better assert their signifying role and even initiate conceptualization: they are . . . quasi-ideas (the idea of time passing, the idea of the journey, the idea of love, like the idea of the dream, the idea of memory) that appear at the end of an authentic intellectual ontogenesis. Consequently, we can grasp the continuity that goes from the symbol to the sign.[53]

Here Morin quite explicitly names the process of stereotypization and the accompanying wearing out of forms as a basis for special processes of sign formation. "In some cases, stereotyping ends up in the crystallization of veritable grammatical tools."[54] He viewed "stereotypes"[55] that had become fixed signs as crystallizing on all levels of filmic diegesis, and he attributed the same effect to all of them: "At an intermediary level, we see 'stereotypes' crystallize: typical objects, typical characters, typical gestures. The screen universe is thus Aristotelianized: objects, characters, and stereotyped gestures make their intelligible essence appear: they are entities of reason."[56] And: such "techniques of the cinema activate and solicit processes of abstraction and rationalization that go on to contribute to the constitution of an intellectual system."[57]

The positive accentuation given to the "abrasive effect" of repetition and conventionalization as the basis for a particular sign formation in cinema undoubtedly represented a new and highly productive idea for contemporary film theory. It became an integral component of the film-theoretical shift in emphasis toward the nonimmediate and enabled a positive view of conventionality and abstraction in conjunction with the reinterpretation of the "language of film" metaphor.

* * *

What interested Morin and Cohen-Séat most about the stereotype-become-sign was therefore its function as a semantic building block. More precisely, its function as a *semantic structure* commonly used within a communicative group, a structure no longer needing to be pieced together bit by bit by recipients, but functioning en bloc in a manner comparable to the idea of *Gestalt* (as understood in Gestalt psychology) and beginning to take on a semantic life of its own as a new unit. In the words of Cohen-Séat quoted above, important were "comfortable or understandable formulas" of expression, upon which not only film composition but also reception could rely. Underlying this idea was the aspiration that film could develop a kind of repertoire of signs coming with a system of references distantly recalling the mechanisms of the language system—even if less complex and far more fluxionary, despite all relative sedimentation.

With all their references to the language metaphor, on this point the ideas of the two French theorists coincide with Panofsky's largely figure-oriented thesis, according to which in popular film, much like in medieval art, a "method of explanation was the introduction of a fixed iconography which from the outset informed the spectator about the basic facts and characters."[58] Panofsky, however, was grounded in a different theoretical tradition, not in the linguistically oriented thought of semiotics but the discourse of iconology based on the pictorial arts and associated with the idea of the power of the conventional.

For Morin, the postulate of semantic elements originating from stereotypes served as a basis for an additional train of thought addressing the idea of abstraction. He noted that, once established, such readymade structures facilitated a particular *acceleration of storytelling*. The language of film was able, not least on the basis of stereotypes, to establish "shorthand notations" activating an "excess of speed" in filmic narrative, a tendency toward "elliptical multiplications."[59]

This was an unquestionably accurate observation, since acceleration is in fact made possible through the repetition of highly conspicuous forms within a specific narrative context, which is then gradually subsumed by these forms (in the audience's perception). It then suffices to only show the conspicuous form, in order to summon the standard context, even in absentia. This is a fundamental mechanism of sign formation and language acquisition.

Against this backdrop, it is to be understood that the development of filmic narration, from the beginnings of the medium through subsequent decades—and hand in hand with processes of conventionalization—was accompanied by an almost steadily increasing elliptical form. This remains unchanged by the fact that opposing stylistics have regularly been employed to offset this trend.

Morin's interest in abbreviations and the *pars pro toto* may be explained, on the one hand, as arising within the context of the French traditions of film and film theory (for example that of Jean Epstein). On the other hand, through linking these interests with the topic of the film stereotype he prefigured discourses on the analogy between film and language, which the semioticians of the 1960s vehemently debated. His interest in abbreviation thus parallels the overarching new discourse on intelligible formulas and signs.

Characteristic of the language-analogy trend is a text worth mentioning in this context, little known today despite the later prominence of two of its authors and stemming from the German branch of the "film and language" discourse. In an essay for the journal *Sprache im technischen Zeitalter* from 1965, Edgar Reitz, Alexander Kluge, and Wilfried Reinke explored the question of whether one could achieve the abstraction-based "expressive effects of highly organized language"[60] with film images. The question was in line with the idea that Cohen-Séat had put forward twenty years earlier, of developing a linguistic conception of expression for film. Part of the inquiry also addressed the question of whether film could similarly accelerate, condense, or metaphorically compose its imagery in the manner of prose. The answer, too, reads as if borrowed from Cohen-Séat or Morin: "If narrative forms were to be used in film . . . for a longer period of time, then after a while one would probably have a filmic world of metaphor, which would facilitate an abbreviated mode of narrative, as do the worlds of metaphor and ideas in language."[61]

Reitz, Kluge, and Reinke desired such a fixed world of signs specifically for auteur cinema, which would only thus be "able to develop generalizations and distinctions similar to those of literature."[62] But they also identified such patterns as conventional forms—mainly within American "commercial film" and especially in Westerns—which they immediately associated with the topic of the stereotype (or the "cliché"). By taking recourse to stereotypes as medially "prefabricated conceptual forms" that corresponded to the "prefabricated jargon"[63] of mass literature, for instance, the Western had created the necessary "notional world in the minds of the viewers,"[64] that is, a kind of interpersonally operating *system of reference*:

> Most new Western films live from references to the old Western cliché. The mail coach, the entrance into the saloon, the beginning of the *showdown*, the new sheriff, the almost masochistic situation of the drunken judge, the Western hero's list of motives, and the canon to which all are bound are phenomena in which the total aura of all Westerns is present in any individual Western.[65]

On this basis, forms of variation, ellipses, and synecdoches may then be developed in genre cinema. Moreover, Hollywood film could visually employ "concrete clichés," in order to supply the audience with similarly generalized inspirations and "mental directives . . . such as those transmitted by the terms 'pretty as a picture.' "[66]

However, true to the German tradition of critical theory, the three German cineastes viewed commercial genre cinema with deep mistrust and were imbued with the ambition of *Neuer Deutsche Film* to portray radical difference.[67] With overriding normativism they therefore rejected the use of the described possibilities for not being aesthetically "legitimate."[68] What the three sought instead was the emergence of *independent* conventional forms, a world of conventions specific to auteur cinema, or, ironically speaking, "good stereotypes."

The notion of the legitimate norm was alien to Morin, whose writings on the potential of stereotypes suggested yet a second perspective in addition to the possibilities presented by automatization and abbreviation. This second perspective also led down the path originally laid out by Cohen-Séat, "from the image to the idea."[69] Namely, the stereotype acquires a special symbolic quality, above and beyond the primary semantic function it performs en bloc.

This idea surfaces only briefly, but it is so significant that it is worthy of serious examination. It means that visual stereotypes function as signs—as extensively quoted in the examples of the airplane lifting off into the sky or the close-up of a kiss—but not merely as simple semantic facts or shorthand notations stating that the heroes are going on a journey or that they love each other. Instead they may be read as elevated to a concept of essential meaning, as "quasi-ideas (the idea of the journey, the idea of love . . .)."

The effect is all the more pronounced the greater the "abrasion" of visual immediacy, which, as previously elaborated, Morin viewed as strengthening the intelligible, mediated reading of images. Morin thus addressed a phenomenon that, with respect to film characters, may be understood as the transition from type to allegory or, in more general terms (since Morin himself did not exclusively think about characters), as a *transition from the stereotype to the emblem.*

This idea also came to play an important role in 1960s film semiology (by no means as an outgrowth of Morin's minor comment). In his 1968 book *Signs and Meaning in the Cinema,*[70] Peter Wollen discussed this emblematic dimension of cinema at length. For Wollen it was characteristic of the emblem to go beyond the initial iconic meaning of images and unfold its more general meaning, heightened to the symbolic, quasi on a metalevel, where, however, it had a fragile and basically connotative character almost impossible to verbalize. This is the tipping point at which the heightening of what Arnheim would have described as banality, that is, the heightening of the stereotype, definitely becomes intelligible. A point where a new reading, a new sensibility emerges.

Given the logical consequence of this point for Morin's intelligibility-oriented theoretical perspective, the casual mention it receives is almost surprising. Morin's observation is indeed not far removed from the thoughts that Roland Barthes (far more systematically and comprehensively, if only peripherally related to film) elaborated one year later in 1957 in his book *Mythologies*. What Barthes writes about "myth" follows a similar idea, up to a point, and can be applied to the film stereotypes that Morin had in mind.

Inherent to Barthes's understanding of the visuality of modern myths (he considered cinema a site of the modern world of myth) was the idea that an image that already carried meaning would in toto take on a second, more abstract and distilled layer of mythological significance, for which it then becomes a *key cultural sign*. A layer of meaning where the image crosses over into symbol and displays "*a second-order semiological system.*"[71]

Barthes was hereby not thinking of traditional symbolic constructs but of a kind of image that presents itself as a "spontaneous, innocent, *indisputable* image."[72] A well-known example of this is the Basque house in Paris, which, similar to one aspect of the process of stereotype formation, accents and inherently unites in pure form the conspicuous traits belonging to the iconography of the Basque house style. In the process, these traits are separated from their original technological order. To Barthes, the house not only seemed to convey an "an imperious injunction to name this object a Basque chalet: or even better, to see it as the very essence of *basquity*."[73] According to Morin, one could translate "basquity" as the "idea of basqueness" and place it alongside the "idea of love" and the "idea of travel." Much in this vein, the face of Garbo, conventionalized and reduced to a mask-like form, that is, approximating an "archetype," revealed to Barthes "a sort of a Platonic Idea of the human creature."[74]

Barthes viewed this kind of hidden essentialism, "hiding behind the fact, and conferring on it a notifying look,"[75] from the critical perspective of enlightened reason. The phenomenon produced mythical thinking and allowed the underlying ideological discursive motifs to appear "natural." Morin, in contrast, did not problematize his observation. He was primarily interested in the tendency of symbols to be formed out of stereotypes, presumably because it supported his idea of the intelligibility of filmic effects.

However, Morin and Cohen-Séat viewed the need for mythic imagination and ritualized fantasy with at least as much import as Barthes assigned it. Independent from the semantic argument just presented, they regarded it as an anthropological constant. A need satisfied by different media over the course of history, and now in modernity cinema was simply the next in line.

Reason, the counterconcept to mythical thinking, could therefore not serve as the sole interpretative criterion in the reception of film. Morin described "the semi-imaginary reality of man"[76] and stated that the task facing the film theorist was therefore to articulate the ambivalent complexity of the effects of film as posed between mythos and logos and grasping "the profound continuity between magic, sentiment, and reason."[77]

Cinema offered a virtual space for the imagination, which crosses into the magical with its visions of yearning and desire, into a participation in the "ghost."[78] Much in this sense Morin placed great value on the detailed elaboration of the close relationship between film, on the one hand, and the imaginary, the dream, animism, and ritual, on the other. Even the "anthropo-cosmomorphism"[79] formerly asserted by German physiognomists reappeared (which also had a distinctive tradition in France), but now as a phenomenon openly interpreted as grounded in "projection-identifications."[80] The following train of thought is typical of Morin:

> Our whole practical world is surrounded with rites, superstitions; the imaginary is still latent in symbols and reigns in the aesthetic. . . . The cinema effects a kind of resurrection of the archaic vision of the world in rediscovering the almost exact superimposition of practical perception and magical vision—their syncretic conjunction. It summons, allows, tolerates the fantastic and inscribes it in the real.[81]

The characters that populate this world without differentiating between the imaginary and the real must consequently function as cyclically appearing, prominent stereotypes and not as distinct, unique individuals from the realm of daily life. If they are to do justice to their purpose as fantastic masks in the ritual-imaginary game, then they too must acquire superimposed layers of empirical experience and the "magical vision" (of desires and idealizations) in the form of stereotypes and must function as formulas reduced in complexity. Morin made an interesting distinction in this respect:

> A strange process of decantation distinguishes the primary and secondary roles. The latter, rationalized according to average age, type or genre, veritable "stereotypes," are "bit parts," reduced to the rank of objects endowed with vague subjectivity. By contrast, the . . . heroes. The latter constitute the archetypes of a glorified humanity. . . . The Star System makes these idealizations blossom into divinations.[82]

There is an obvious conceptual parallel between the image of the star and Barthes's view of Garbo, which also ultimately boils down to the archetypical.

Morin considers a number of particularly distinctive characters in the ritual game to be a very special kind of stereotype, which become archetypes (a form of heightening the essence of the stereotype into the realm of the elementary and symbolic) of reactions to certain formations of desire or idealization. This brings his ideas full circle to what was previously said about the transition to allegory.

The extent to which Cohen-Séat worked from similar premises becomes clear when one reads, for example, that cinema not only establishes the conventions of film language worldwide but simultaneously pursues a common global "elaboration of myths which *are going to please* groups of people, which correspond to the anthropomorphism of dreams and the human desires of an epoch."[83] And Cohen-Séat stressed the role of the stereotype in *this* particular effect of film: "this warpage of a manner of behavior, which is reduced to the most simple, which is endlessly turned and shifted, universally imitated and thus stereotyped."[84]

If one places Cohen-Séat and Morin's anthropological ideas (implicitly) invoking the ancient need for myth and the imaginary in relation to Horkheimer and Adorno's fundamental critique oriented along the ideas of enlightenment and radical reason, an *antinomy* with a long philosophical tradition is revealed, which at this point, if not earlier, also began to shape traditions in film theory.

In its basic outline, it returns in the polarized theoretical approaches to American genre cinema and its stereotypes, which influenced the film-genre discourse of the 1970s and 1980s, especially in the United States.[85] Here too the advocates of a ritual-based approach were opposed by proponents of ideological criticism. The former understood genre cinema's world of stereotypes as a space of sedimented symbols, which, similar to an archaic ritual, were cyclically received and therefore could not be said to meaningfully or directly refer (in the realist sense) to afilmic reality but to mythical needs. In contrast, the latter tried to identify the deceptive, manipulative, illusionary aspects of films and to join the critique of the stereotype with criticism of the culture industry, society, and their dominant ideology.

Cohen-Séat and Morin (now almost forgotten and not even acknowledged by this discourse) are clearly part of the prehistory of the later concept of ritual, which would later primarily refer to Lévi-Strauss and his structural research on myth. At least with Lévi-Strauss reference was made to a thinker whose influential research on myth had, by no coincidence, its origins in the same climate permeating French cultural anthropology in the 1940s and 1950s that also influenced Cohen-Séat and, in particular, Morin.

With respect to these two thinkers, it should be remembered that they essentially developed important basic concepts pertaining to cinema that would later reappear in the *ritual approach*, although they themselves did *not yet* employ a structural analysis of the individual mythic worlds of specific genres. John Cawelti,

Will Wright, and Thomas Schatz, among others (following Lévi-Strauss), later did. As generally characteristic of filmology,[86] they instead limited themselves to the explication of the idea of *situating popular film and its stereotypes per se in the realm of myth.*

* * *

It stands to reason that the new view of stereotypes, the reinterpreted metaphor of film as language, and the reference to myth went hand in hand with a fundamentally changed attitude toward *popular* (film) culture. And it seems no coincidence that the arguments of both Cohen-Séat and Morin were primarily *anthropological* and only then, against this backdrop, aesthetic. Cohen-Séat provided a very vivid description of the difference between two possible approaches to cinema.

> The cinema can develop out of its own substance, building upon the original, i.e. naïve and universally valid, elements it contains; but it can also place itself at the forefront of our instruments of expression and their subtlety. Should such "culturism" gain the upper hand, one would not need to change a single word of the formulas that have not been molded to film. Then we would find ourselves in the process of creating the "style of decadence" . . . which aging cultures bring forth under the light of their setting sun.[87]

There is no doubt that Cohen-Séat's (and Morin's) sympathies rested with the first variant. This is already apparent in the way that the alternative is proposed and described in this example. Striving for an intelligibility of expression did not coincide with the aspiration toward a cinema for intellectuals, an *anti-Hollywood*—in contrast to the culture-critical thought of Reitz, Kluge, and Reinke.

Cohen-Séat valued the worldwide popular culture that cinema had produced for its global "community-building function,"[88] the core of which he regarded as the worldwide establishment of *common* myths. His statement that cinema had created "the most extensive group of people resembling one another in the history of the world"[89] does not convey the fears of commodification, standardization, and lifelessness, which once characterized the German debate on standardization, but instead an almost *euphoric counterconcept.*

Nevertheless, an affinity of his choice of certain words with the culture-critical model of mass humanity is clearly apparent, for example when Cohen-Séat pointedly describes cinema's international community of viewers: "They are all one and the same man."[90] But instead of deploring the leveling of specific cultural characteristics, he celebrated the progressive internationalization of culture with the argument (quite common today in the age of globalization and a worldwide TV and Internet culture but already present even in the work of Balázs) that global cinema overcame "intellectual provincialism" and "philological particularity."[91] Cinema thus would enable a global, collective form of worldview.

Ultimately this avowal of modernity itself verges on the utopian and mystifying in moments of exaggeration: for example, when Cohen-Séat evokes the constitutive role of film in a "planetary conscience."[92] Whereas in the debate on standardization the reference to the stereotype was a crystallization point for the cultural and aesthetic critique of cinema as mass culture (produced by the culture industry), in the context of this later paradigm the avowal of the stereotypes of popular cinema was a clear indication as to the reevaluation of the mass cultural sphere.

The anthropological premise, however, did not simply dismiss the aesthetic pretension or the question of aesthetics but instead situated the aesthetic challenge within the functional fabric of popular culture. Based on a position oriented toward the need for myth and the universal, that is, the conventional—a stance in which the stereotype was regarded as constitutive—a view emerged that implicitly pointed in the direction of the *aesthetics of identity* later elaborated by Lotman.

Lotman viewed the principle of the aesthetics of identity as characterizing entire art-historical periods, for example the Middle Ages, and especially the folklore of all cultures. Rather than emphasizing radical difference to the stereotype, the aesthetics of identity was committed to the stereotype and a playful treatment thereof: "Rituals of narration, strictly defined possibilities for plot combinations that are known in advance, and *loci communi* (whole pieces of frozen text) all form a very special artistic system."[93] Artistic activity takes place *within* this system. It is interesting that in this context Lotman (writing in the 1960s and 1970s) referred to the effect of reduced immediacy, as did Morin, which was owed to the *flattening* impact of conventionality:

> The films of Germi . . . shock the audience with their merciless "cynicism." But we need only recall the language of the puppet theatres and the *commedia dell' arte* in which death can be a comic episode, murder—a buffonade, suffering—a parody. The unpitying nature of Italian (and not only Italian) folk theatre is organically connected with its conventionality. The audience remembers that these are puppets or maskers on the stage and perceives their death or suffering, not as the death or suffering of real people, but in a spirit of carnival and ritual.[94]

For Morin as well as Cohen-Séat the challenges posed to artistic creativity were laid out within a quite similarly conceived framework. The two filmologists were concerned with the kind of creativity expressed in an imaginative approach to the stereotypes of popular cinema, in which these stereotypes, as formulas, remain intact. Another comparison suggests itself, if one returns to the linguistic metaphor of the "film language." One could also say that Cohen-Séat and Morin aimed for a treatment of stereotypes closely resembling what the linguist Karl Bühler had once described in his *Theory of Language* in reference to conventionalization in language:

> But it may be, indeed it must be the case that in some points language (*la langue*) departs from the stage at which it has an amoeba-like plasticity from speech situation to situation, that it abandons this plasticity in order to make it possible for the speaker to be productive in a new way and on a higher level; the implement of this higher productivity is that which has congealed or solidified . . . [thus becoming fixed linguistic "structures"].[95]

Particularly in Morin's text one senses a pervasive enjoyment of "the implement of this higher productivity" as "congealed and solidified": a pleasure in ellipses, synecdoches, shorthand notations, and metaphors, all only enabled by a reliance on stereotypes, as well as the flash of pleasure that appears in reading a second layer of meaning in allegories and other emblematic forms. This coincides with dialectical ideas about the treatment of stereotypes. The following is typical of Morin's thought: "*the art* of the mise-en-scène consists in struggling against the impoverishment that the necessary abstraction involves."[96] And in a similar vein, Cohen-Séat had already stated:

> The stylization, the proposed convention, *the intention* of the system simultaneously produce inner impoverishment (the system no longer has the freedom to signify everything or anything it entails) and a relational enrichment (the communicative value is enhanced, the targeted understanding hits its mark more directly and precisely). What remains is a lasting mixture of animosity and exchange between the regime of this stylistic order and the independence of the concrete.[97]

A framework was thus established for the workings of creativity, a framework referring to a fundamental paradigm shift. In the context of cinema, Cohen-Séat and Morin dismissed the absolutism of a creativity primarily seeking a true inner self, the "other condition," or the genuine representation of physical reality in aspiring to the maximal opposition of creativity and the universal and conventional, or, at most, a compromise between them.

Their *dialectical approach*, which developed a kind of "aesthetics of identity," replaced this type of thought. In retrospect, their approach in this sense recalls the parallel logic predominant in auteur theory. Also originating in France in the 1950s, this theory too was ultimately concerned with a dialectical idea, namely the assertion of a personality and its aesthetic identity *within* (and *not* primarily against) the world of stereotypes of classical film genres.

* * *

Situating both works of Cohen-Séat and Morin in an overarching context illuminates the wealth of new accents that they placed and the theoretical complexity of the manner in which they supported the *paradigm shift in relation to the stereotype*. Both succinctly brought together a series of arguments, which would be elaborated in later film-theoretical discourses and in some cases were even expanded into veritable guiding ideas. Both texts developed a preliminary history not only of the later ritual or myth approach in genre film theory; the new approach to the metaphor of the *language of film* also forms part of the early history of semiology.

STEREOTYPES FORM CODES: FILMOLOGY AND SEMIOLOGY

There is general agreement among historians of film theory that the concepts and terminology of filmology can, in many regards, be considered precursors of the semiology of cinema. Christian Metz, the central figure in French film semiology, himself explicitly acknowledged this fact in an obituary of the filmologist Etienne Souriau (apart from Cohen-Séat and Morin, another key figure of filmology): "Ultimately filmology was in certain respects a very direct precursor of the semiology of cinema."[98]

Edward Lowry considered the "scientific distance"[99] that filmology maintained to its subject of study, the cinema, a fundamental indication of a continuity extending through the semiology of the early 1960s. One expression of this was the fact that more consideration was given to fundamental sociological, psychological, and semiological questions *pertaining to the medium* than to individual films. Frank Kessler recognizes that "perhaps the most important legacy of filmology"[100] for later film theory lies in the vocabulary that filmologists developed, through which they established important analytical terms still relevant today. He particularly refers to a project directed by Souriau[101] on the vocabulary of film theory, which coined the pair of terms "*afilmic/profilmic*," among others.

What Cohen-Séat and later Morin had written about the *language of film* struck a chord with fundamental ideas of the semiological concept that began to emerge in the 1960s. However, the connection was by no means seamless. Whereas "film as language" formed the main overarching paradigm of early film semiology, there was an obvious discrepancy between the emphases of different semiologists. Prolonged controversies developed about what was meant by "language" in this context.

However, semiologists did implicitly agree on one fundamental insight, which Umberto Eco articulated in the late 1960s as follows: "even there where we presume vital spontaneity, there exists culture, convention, system, and code."[102] These codes, which may be interpreted as conventional systems of communication, consequently became central objects of study in the semiology of film, to the extent they were relevant to film's multilayered system of expression.

Hence, it is not surprising that there is a correspondence between the metaphor of filmic "discoveries" in the sense of Cohen-Séat and Morin, which grow out of the stereotypes semanticized en bloc within larger groups of films, and what Christian Metz, using different terminology, described in 1971 in *Langage et cinema*[103] about the "sub-codes" in the "cinematic language system."[104]

For Metz, cinematic subcodes were codes that did not refer to cinema as a whole but had developed in the context of certain groups of films and genres. The parallels between Metz and the filmologists rest on the fact that Metz also regarded cinematic codes as based upon consolidated, conventionalized structures of films, and with respect to subcodes he obviously envisioned family groups of stereotypes, as did Morin: these were narrative or visual film "patterns," which had become standardized in the context of certain groups of films or genres.

In contrast to Cohen-Séat or Morin, the semiologists usually just assumed the existence of codes. In other words, they were initially less interested in the cinematic *process* of conventionalization, how something *became* conventional, for example the process of the *codification* of images, which only become cinematic stereotypes and thus also cinematic codes by being imitated multiple times within the film medium. Instead, for a long time they concentrated on ordering and classifying different types of codes within film's pluricodic system of expression, whereby only relatively seldom were individual stereotypes discussed as elements of the codes. Hence, it is to the credit of the two predecessors, whose work was explicitly oriented toward the stereotype, that they called attention to the *process* by which new semantic patterns were formed and the role that the *process of conventionalization* played therein.[105]

In retrospect, that they used *the metaphor* of the "language of film" in a casual and open-ended manner simply as one theoretical motif among others and with the language metaphor did not aspire to a systematic, semiological theoretical model (more closely aligned with linguistic categories) is *not merely* a shortcoming of their work. At least this saved them from some of the possibly unavoidable excesses of their successors. Because fully intent on the order of the code and influenced by structuralism, film semiology suffered, particularly in the 1960s, from the tendency to forcefully impose fixed systems of organization—usually drawn from linguistic categories—onto a complex audiovisual semiosis in flux, which was replete with grey areas, shifts, and blurred boundaries.

One example is Metz's overemphasis of the defining idea of cinematic specificity in the mid-1960s. Another is Pier Paolo Pasolini's rather idiosyncratic interpretation of linguistic concepts in relation to film. Both are revealed in one of the famous arguments that Metz carried out with Pasolini in 1966 about the semiological status of cinematic visual stereotypes. In his lecture "Le cinéma de poésie"[106] held in 1965, Pasolini had chosen as an example of a visual stereotype (which he did not term as such) the image of the wheels of a moving locomotive in a cloud of steam.[107] This was a close shot much used in classical cinema and hence conventionalized, and since the 1930s at the latest it appeared with a certain regularity and symbolic force when the narrative of a given film entailed a journey by train.

Much in the vein of Cohen-Séat and Morin's idea, Pasolini discussed how such conventionalized images, which he called "stylemas," tended to lead to a filmic language and form "a kind of dictionary."[108] The latter was much more ephemeral than an actual dictionary but nevertheless genuine "common patrimony."[109] This quasi-lexicon was then linked to a grammar of style.

Metz responded to Pasolini in 1966 with a counterargument typical of the period,[110] in which he pointed out that, first, a semantic element such as the image of the wheels has nothing to do with cinematic language in a narrower (specific) sense, that is, nothing to do with "properly cinematographic codes";[111] second, it was not a grammatical phenomenon. He argued his first objection as follows: "for the image of the wheels of the train (and similar images) most commonly represent *cultural stereotypes*, which if they are picked up—or even partially varied—by the cinema are picked up and varied by other forms of expression as well."[112]

This thus concerns "in our period, a fixed and codified figure" that "belongs to the iconography and iconology of our society much more than to cinematographic language."[113] He refused to call the image of the wheels "specifically cinematic," because the content of the image as a filmed motif was associated with afilmic reality and therefore could also be conveyed by other media.

But this image had indeed undergone *conventionalization* as a fixed filmic image, as a visual-narrative stereotype, *within the context of cinema* from the

1920s through the 1950s. Sensational railroad films, such as *La roue* (*The Wheel*, Abel Gance, France, 1923), *Das Stahltier* (*The Steel Beast*, Willy Zielke, Germany, 1935), *La bête humaine* (*The Human Beast / Judas Was a Woman*, Jean Renoir, France, 1938), or perhaps also *Pacific 231* (Jean Mitry, France, 1949) helped define the shots of wheels and piston rods immersed in steam that were almost automatically employed (usually as a short, symbolic segment) in classical cinema—from neorealism to genre film—when train rides, speed, train departures, or good-byes at train stations were to be depicted.

In 1966, Metz did not yet accept this progression from conventionalization to established visual formulas of filmic narrative within the context of cinema, a procedure that Cohen-Séat and Morin had considered so important, as a criterion of cinematic specificity. Not until *Langage et cinéma* did he seem to carefully correct this rigid stance in remarks on cinematic specificity with respect to similar codifications: "Above all, we must, in this regard, make it clear that the only entities capable of being or not being unique to the cinema are codes (systems), so that these codes are only (or at least primarily) manifested in the film, or that the film, to the contrary, is content to 'adopt' them from other cultural units."[114]

Pasolini had, however, paved the way for Metz's polemic by identifying the image as a conventional formula in filmic discourse, on the one hand, while simultaneously referring to the existence of the image in reality, on the other, and tending to hold forth on "reality *as Language*."[115] For Metz (at least in 1966), only the pure structural principles of linkage between segments, that is, *syntagmatic* relationships, were specifically cinematic. In this he was close to the montage tradition, and at the time his interests were oriented toward different variations of the "stabilized syntagmatic orderings"[116] of filmic images. He associated these orderings with the (metaphorical) term "grammar." Namely: "Grammar has never dictated the content of thought that each sentence should have; it merely regulates the general organization of the sentences."[117] And: "Cinematographic grammar does not consist in prescribing what should be filmed."[118] Metz's second, more plausible objection to Pasolini's argument originated from this idea. The image of the locomotive wheels was not a *grammatical* fact, as the latter had claimed, but a conventional image, a visual stereotype.

Underlying this reduction of the specificity of cinematic language to the syntagmatic was, on the one hand, Metz's main interest in the principles behind the sequencing of film shots, that is, the elaboration of *la grande syntagmatique* (great syntagmatic system),[119] through which he attempted to formalize the montage codes of narrative cinema from the classical period. The *grande syntagmatique* is considered his most important achievement in this phase of his theoretical work.[120] Then again, it is apparent that he wished to exclude from the analysis of "actual" film language (*langage*) the problematic questions of judgment accompanying the stereotype: "*A grammatical fact can be neither a cliché nor a novelty*, unless it is so at the moment of its first historical occurrence; it exists beyond the level where the antithesis cliché/novelty even begins to have a meaning."[121] In contrast, the use of the wheel image in film encouraged working with "*the categories of originality and triteness*."[122] Hence, for Metz, this image is neither "grammatical" nor, as it once again follows, does it have anything to do with the "specific" language of cinema.

But Morin and Cohen-Séat had been interested precisely in the reevaluation of "banal" and conventional patterns such as the stereotype (or cliché) as the basis of a specific *intelligibility*. They explored the banal as a potential foundation for originality.

＊ ＊ ＊

Much in the way that Cohen-Séat and Morin avoided the danger of overextending the specificity of cinematic language (something that still occasionally resurfaces in semiological inquiries today), they also escaped another tendency common among some later film semiologists and film grammarians: namely, the tendency of taking the metaphor of film language too literally, of engaging in what are ultimately and extensively self-serving discussions about the applicability of all sorts of linguistic concepts to film, and thereby all too rigidly applying the model of language to film,[123] whose complex semiosis is ultimately not comprehensible by means of overly narrow analogies with language.

The debate on the double or triple articulation of film and the search for the smallest unit of meaning point in this direction. Looking back, one has the impression that sometimes the metaphor of film as language underwent what Fritz Mauthner had once described in his critique of language as a typical fate of metaphors in theoretical discourses. As metaphors, they initially often signify "something relatively clever" until they become "something conventional." "The former symbol was good as a play on words, but now the word is taken literally. One has forgotten its meaning and therefore takes it mindlessly earnest."[124] Cohen-Séat had still quite consciously reflected on how he *played* with the "language of film" as a metaphor: "We like to place new things in familiar categories, and we trace the unknown back to the known. But we are also aware of such gyrations and thus analogical reasoning has been able to win many adherents."[125] And also Morin's thought (on individual, symbolic stereotypes), which was not further specified, seems even more compatible with the flexible point of view that Barthes later advocated when describing *Codes* and their fluidity:

Hence we use *Code* here not in the sense of a list, a paradigm that must be reconstituted. The code is a perspective of quotations, a mirage of structures . . . the units which have resulted from it . . . are themselves, always, ventures out of the text, the mark, the sign of a virtual digression . . . they are so many fragments of something that has always been *already* read, seen, done, experienced; the code is the wake of that *already*.[126]

A third problem specific to the film semiology of the 1960s was not spared its two "predecessors." Their theory of the sign-become-stereotype was primarily conceived in terms of semantics, or certainly always then when it was connected with the language metaphor.

Their thought comprised the "adoption . . . of comfortable formulas for the expression of certain things."[127] This is closely aligned with Metz's idea of the objective of semiotic study: "*The fact that must be understood is that films are understood.*"[128] Pragmatic considerations, such as how stereotypes or other filmic structures are simultaneously coordinated with the psychological needs of the viewer (that is, once these needs have been emotionally activated), were initially[129] ignored by film semiologists interested in processes of comprehension. In the work of the two predecessors, this tendency of concentrating the language metaphor on processes of comprehension and rationality were compensated by the fact that this metaphor represented only one approach among others. Morin, who argued primarily along the lines of anthropology and not semantics, thus additionally explored the "technique of affective satisfaction"[130] and "aesthetic imaginary and participation."[131] However, he did not pursue the implications for the stereotype as conveyed in his statement: "The cinema . . . has adapted itself to all subjective needs."[132]

* * *

In his essay *L'actualité du saussurisme*[133] from 1956, the same year Morin's book on cinema was published, Algirdas Greimas criticized Merleau-Ponty for underestimating average behavior and collective structures in a literary study and for instead emphasizing individual, anormal qualities of the creator. In her study on the history of semiotics, Anne Hénault considers Greimas's critique of Merleau-Ponty an early indication of a burgeoning paradigmatic shift in the discourse of literature and literary studies: "this is probably the first time in French literary thought that an awareness of the institutional, the stereotype, the code, the automatization of representation . . . was so clearly formulated."[134] The relativization indicated by the intelligently inserted "probably" may serve here as an indication that the advance made by Cohen-Séat and Morin, from a position of fundamental critique to positively tinged interest in the stereotype, was highly representative of the intellectual discourse in France in the mid-1950s. The date given by Hénault for a shift in literary thought additionally indicates that Morin and his book—and certainly Cohen-Séat, who had published his position already in 1946—may undoubtedly be regarded as forerunners of this new trend. This is worth emphasizing, since it was largely forgotten in the period following the semiology boom of the 1960s.

Incidentally, it seems only logical that it was film theorists who made this transition so early. Doubtlessly the paradigm shift was propelled by the overwhelming cultural presence of the mass culture or culture-industrial medium of film. It is no coincidence that the film theorists of the 1920s and 1930s considered the popular "average" film the ultimate stronghold of the stereotype. But in retrospect one wonders why this change did not occur sooner and why it took place at a relatively late stage in the development of the medium.

Much suggests that first a certain threshold in the experience of film and the development of film culture had to be crossed, that a quantitative accumulation of stereotypes needed to be present, also in the awareness of film theorists, before the paradigm shift and the search for an also theoretically positive interest in and confident approach to stereotypes could emerge.

In this sense, it is certainly not just mere chance that the discovery of the stereotype *as intelligible material* by Cohen-Séat approximately coincided with the final resignation of someone like Arnheim, who—given the ongoing cultural accumulation of stereotypes—in the late 1940s finally laid to rest his idea of film art as based on a fundamental opposition to the visual stereotype. It had become ever clearer that a view of film rejecting basic characteristics of the actual development of the medium, whether this be the influence of the culture industry, the "theater for the masses," or the stereotype, could only have limited relevance as the basis for a theory of film, regardless how productive individual observations may have been. The power of the facts as they stood called for a new theoretical orientation toward a theory of film that no longer regarded the stereotype as a purely negative entity.

Finally, the new paradigm, the initial phase of which was marked by the work of Gilbert Cohen-Séat and Edgar Morin, corresponded well with late classical genre film, the culturally predominant film type of the 1940s and 1950s. While Hollywood genre film had already developed large families of stereotypes of the most diverse nature, it now played with these patterns with steadily increasing confidence. In many regards, the mainstream cinema of the 1950s demonstrated a heightening to the point of the symbolic, also through recourse to stereotypes. What theorists discussed, the way meaning was taken to the extremes of the archetypical, became generally palpable.

EIGHT
IRONY AND TRANSFIGURATION:
THE POSTMODERN VIEW OF THE STEREOTYPE

Camp—Dandyism in the age of mass culture—makes no distinction between
the unique object and the mass-produced object. Camp taste transcends
the nausea of the replica.

—SUSAN SONTAG, "NOTES ON 'CAMP'" (1967)

ONCE UPON A TIME IN THE WESTERN:
REFLEXIVITY AND SELF-REFERENTIALITY

In *All That Heaven Allows* (1955), director Douglas Sirk conveys the emotional
nadir of his female protagonist Cary as follows: we see her standing alone at a
window and looking out. The reverse angle shows a view into a cold, snowy world
bathed in blue light. Daily life, the bustle of the Christmas season, which Cary is
no longer part of, continues outside and carries on matter-of-factly without her.
She is hermetically sealed off from this world by the cagelike lattice of the window, through which we see her in the next shot, now from the outside. The camera slowly moves in on her face until it is all we see in the frame of a windowpane.
Her face is surrounded by frost patterns that have formed on the window lattice.
The camera lingers for a few moments on this key image.

The wealth of symbolism inherent in this passage is obvious. Multiple symbolic layers overlap simultaneously. This is heightened by the stereotype of the
prototypical woman-behind-the-window composition.[1] Although on the surface it appears as an immediate image seamlessly incorporated into the carefully
designed realism of the diegesis, as a stereotype of melodramatic staging, the
image ruptures this immediacy through its conventionality and formulaic character: an essentialized image as sign that recalls a conventional meaning en bloc.

According to Cohen-Séat, this could be read as one of the "happy discoveries" of film; according to Barthes or Morin as an *emblem of the "idea of loneliness."*

Here the stereotype becomes symbolic. However, at the same time it remains integrated within the diegesis and subordinate to a "realistic" motivation, which is intended to give *an appearance of immediacy and spontaneity.* In terms of symbolism, this approach to stereotypes is characteristic of classical genre cinema, not only in Hollywood. This applies to the Western as well as the melodrama.

At the beginning of *High Noon* (Fred Zinnemann, 1952), for example, the three men who ride into the little town to then camp at the train station embody clear (character) stereotypes. As soon as they enter the scene, we know how we are supposed to view them. This is not only explained by their difference to the other characters, who react to the riders with expressions of fear and alarm, but also because we are already familiar with similarly constructed characters with comparable external traits and a similar set of behaviors from a large number of films of the genre, that is, we know that they adhere to a stereotype. We would not have needed the reactions of the people along their path to comprehend the three riders as *allegories of evil.* This visual motif is subject to a similar symbolic multiplication as in the Sirk scene. And *High Noon* too is concerned with seamlessly integrating symbolism into a diegetic world at least externally committed to scenic realism, an *appearance* of immediacy, and a certain psychological verisimilitude in the behavior of the characters within the rules of the imaginary world of the Western.

The concepts and conceptual models elaborated in the previous chapter suffice for the analysis of such use of stereotypes in classical cinema. Around the mid-1960s, however, a different approach to the use of the stereotypes of popular film began to emerge with increasing prominence, in cinema itself. This new approach demanded farther-reaching ideas and a new attitude toward the stereotype. Briefly stated, the shift was characterized by conventional patterns such as those just described no longer being integrated into an illusionary diegesis ruled by scenic realism and psychological coherency. The performance of stereotypes was now more intently focused on creating a nonliteral or allegorical reading, on breaking down the appearance of immediacy, and on emphasizing *artificiality.*

The tendency to openly reveal stereotypes as such became more influential. Using Christian Metz's interpretation of the term *énonciation* as applied to cinema,[2] one could also say: in the popular cinema of the mid-1960s a style arose that openly revealed the enunciation, that is, demonstratively allowed a film to be recognized as "enunciated," by *making the conventional nature of stereotypes identifiable through the manner in which they were employed* and thereby attempting

211

to raise awareness as to their *stereotypical quality*. In other words, a *reflexive* or *self-reflexive*[3] treatment of stereotypes became more important.

Reflexivity is understood as the quality of a text to refer back to its status as a text, to display this status by emphasizing medial or artificial elements instead of cloaking it in illusion. The *demonstrative presentation of stereotypes* is *one* crucial instance of reflexivity that has barely been dealt with in relevant scholarship on reflexivity/self-reflexivity. Although long common in comedy, this mode of reflexivity rapidly gained importance in the 1960s, far beyond the comedy genre. A systematic treatment of this topic in film theory, however, did not emerge until later, and for a long time—and for the most part still today—it is not associated, or only indirectly, with the concept of the stereotype.

It has been left to this inquiry to remedy the situation and to develop a *theory of reflexive stereotypes*. Elements of existing theoretical studies can provide a basis for this, ideas developed—not only in respect to film and pertaining to areas outside the narrower scope of film theory—in the 1960s in keeping with a theoretical sensibility paralleling developments in film. Under the circumstances, it therefore makes sense, in contrast to the previous chapters' historical approach to theory, to first discuss the practical phenomenon in detail by means of an exemplary, a symptomatic example, in order to then analyze the related conceptual and theoretical models of contemporary discourse, which will subsequently be incorporated into the concept of the reflexive and self-referential stereotype. *Once Upon a Time in the West* (Sergio Leone, Italy/USA, 1968) will serve as the case example, a key film of the new tendency.

A comparison between the previously described opening sequences of *High Noon* with those of *Once Upon a Time in the West* immediately illustrates the difference between the two films. The superficial realism of *High Noon* means that the visual staging of the film relies directly on the audiovisual modes of presentation conventionalized and automatized in classical cinema, while the film simultaneously draws on the habits of perception and the referential framework of daily life. In contrast, *Once Upon a Time in the West* systematically breaks with an entire series of such habits already in its first sequence.

To be sure, there are definite similarities between the openings of the two Westerns, and indeed the later film alludes to the earlier. Like Zinnemann, Leone too presents a trio of gangsters waiting at the station for a passenger arriving on the next train. The three are even more explicitly recognizable as bandits than those in *High Noon*. In *Once Upon a Time in the West* the constellation—already reduced in 1952—clearly undergoes further *reduction*. Here there is no ride through the city past a row of frightened people along the street. The train station of Cattle Corner is far removed from any settlement, and the scene begins directly with the entrance of the bandits into the station house. The display of terror and fear is focused solely on the station master whom the bandits encounter. This figure is defined by almost caricature-like emotions. An Indian woman, apparently stoically and silently watching the scene, is the only other person present, but she prefers to quickly leave the station. The film forgoes the presence of any other participants in the scene.

Sitting or standing, the men wait for a long time in the empty station, barely moving. The surrounding flat expanse of landscape appears empty; the tracks stretch into the horizon. This simple act of waiting is shown for over six minutes, and the film virtually *demonstrates* how (stereo)typing involves a reduction of character to a few accentuated traits. The three waiting men are shown in alternation. Each one of them has a quirk, which he stoically performs and each of which is presented in a series of at least three prolonged shots. The most extended shot shows the leader of the group, who sits dozing in the sun while grudgingly and unsuccessfully defending himself against a fly that has landed on his mouth (three long close-ups of his face). Without raising a finger, he tries for what seems like an eternity to shoo away the insect by blowing on it. The second bandit cracks his knuckles with abandon, while the third, whose face is cropped at the bottom of the shot, listens stoically as drops of water fall and collect in the brim of his hat. Finally, in a slow movement he removes the hat and drinks the water. The only spectacular microaction in this passage occurs when the first bandit traps the fly, having landed on the wall, with his revolver in a surprisingly fast movement.

The visual and auditory design play a significant role in the reductionism of the situation. Neither film music nor atmospheric sound accompany the extended, often cropped close-ups of the faces or the inserted shots of the fly and the water drops. Instead, highly amplified individual sounds alternate without overlapping: the buzz of the fly, the crack of the knuckles, the impact of the drops. Only the monotone creaking of a windmill, not yet visible, intervenes in the sound composition.

After minutes of waiting the train approaches. The three men rise to make their appearance, which has clearly been rigorously choreographed. The entering train is seen in a carefully staged tableau, a depth shot showing in the foreground the monumental figure of a gunman in a long dustcoat, his back to the camera. The departing train later appears in another depth shot with a similar foreground-background composition. No one gets in or out; the station remains empty. When the door of a boxcar opens and a large packet is thrown out, we see in response a new series of medium close-ups of the startled and searching glances of the men. As the train is pulling away—the bandits have already turned to leave—"Harmonica" appears behind their backs on the other side of the train after a dramatic delay, announcing himself with his harmonica motif. Although the latter is superficially motivated as diegetic, it is unmistakably studio-produced sound. Then for the first time—after thirteen minutes—a few bars of nondiegetic music are introduced to accompany the confrontation between the men.

There is an extensive exchange of glances and a brief exchange of words, which takes the well-known laconism of language in Westerns to the extreme, again through reduction:

HARMONICA: Did you bring a horse for me?
BANDIT: Looks like we're shy one horse.
HARMONICA: You brought two too many.

Then guns are pulled, shots are fired, men fall. There is a rapid succession of close-ups, mostly of the faces, and panoramic tableaus, long shots or medium long shots. Among them is a shot showing the bandits from behind immediately before the gunfire: reduced to silhouettes by the back light (and shown at a slightly low angle), they tower formidably over the empty, wide-open landscape. The three meet their end. The windmill, now filling the screen, creaks imperturbably in the silence that follows, now the only sound. "Harmonica" also has fallen to the ground. But then he gets up with some hesitation, one arm hit by a bullet, in a landscape now appearing even emptier. He picks up his bag and walks away. The full duration of the thus concluded sequence is well over fifteen minutes.

Almost everything is geared toward a pronounced stylization, which "de-realizes" or deillusionizes the stereotyped characters and conventionalized Western actions and, indeed, the entire audiovisual world of the film. The artificial character of the whole is emphasized and the actions openly celebrated *as rituals*. How does this occur?

Many of the images and actions of the opening sequence and later of the entire film seem to be reduced to the core set or basic structures of the stereotype world of the Western. They seem to be models in their purest form, stripped of all inessentials—all the reality-conjuring accessories of classical Westerns—in order to display their abstract nature: stereotypes presenting themselves as archetypes.

The skillfully composed tableaus of the shootout at the train station with the figures reduced to silhouettes in front of the empty landscape are visually incisive examples. The plot of the opening sequence is another. It tells the story of an entire Western, which has been "pared down" to an "ideal" stereotype structure, a pure schema: the arrival of the gunmen, waiting for the opponent, his delayed arrival, a short provocative exchange, showdown, death of the bandits, the "right" man survives and walks away. This reductive totality is again enhanced and topped off by the fact that two of the bandits shot already in the first sequence are played not by insignificant minor actors but by prominent actors in the Westerns of the period, Woody Strode and Jack Elam, whom by experience a viewer would have identified as protagonists of the entire film.

In addition to reduction, a second fundamental technique of reflexive stylization is the pronounced slowing down of movement. In later scenes, these were in part coordinated directly with the extradiegetic film score during the shoot. As with the reduction, the principle of deceleration not only applies to the opening scenes but the film as a whole. As is so often the case,[4] the film's beginning sets the tone. Initially, movements within the diegesis are slowed down. This goes hand in hand with reduction, since facial expressions, gesture, and language seem to be boiled down to a minimum, as are the repertoires of character and plot. The selected movements, performances, and actions are thus celebrated with slow, deliberate care, with the exception of the exchange of fire.

Analogous to movements within the image, the overarching rhythm of images is also substantially slowed down. The length of the takes seems as extended as the sequences. Against the backdrop of the image and plot rhythms customary in classical cinema and particularly in classical Westerns, this prolongation seems extreme. The emphasis of this differential quality, the defamiliarization achieved through elongation, draws on a device from the auteur cinema of the 1960s,[5] which is here applied to popular cinema.

Other techniques of audiovisual staging contribute to the openly artificial, stylized nature of the film. Ritual is further pronounced in that gestures or actions are subject to the principle of multiple repetitions, with only slight variations. In the first sequence, the previously described series of images featuring the men's startled, searching expressions attest to this.

The visual composition of the individual shots contributes its part. Carefully composed tableaus, which appear on screen for a long time and sometimes display their depth of focus in an accentuated contrast between especially close elements in the foreground and the extreme depth of the background, emphasize their own artificiality. One example is the close-up of the face of one of the gunmen in profile. It fills the left half of the widescreen image, while in the right half the train approaches from the depth of the landscape and (after the shot has been interrupted by the insert of a gun being loaded) expands to an almost all-encompassing scale.

The hyperrealism of the extreme close-ups of cropped faces has a similar effect. The initial sequence already shows details that seem especially dramatic when enlarged to the cinemascope format. Harmonica's eye filling the screen, or extremely enlarged skin surfaces, pores, and stubble have no analogy in extramedial perception, without the mediation by photographic technology. Therefore, they in turn emphasize their artificiality (at least to the extent that they have not become conventional pictorial devices). This procedure corresponds with the selective use of individual sounds (drops of water, cracking knuckles), which seem filtered and amplified as extreme audio "close-ups."

For the mainstream audiences acquainted with classical Westerns, the abrupt transitions between half shots and total shots and the extreme close-ups or details shots were uncustomary. This and the unmistakable studio sound of the diegetic harmonica and Ennio Morricone's music score in general all worked to the same effect of enhancing the stylization.

As a result of *reduction/selection, enhancement, deceleration, repetition, and hyperrealistic display,* a distanced view of an artificial sphere emerges, which allows the "mechanics" of the genre to become visible through defamiliarization. This "world" *itself calls attention* to the fact that it is not inhabited by "real" or even only seemingly real people but by masks of the imaginary, by artificial beings referring in extremely reduced form to a long line of predecessors and their patterns of behavior. It is a world that does not attempt to create an appearance of realism but indicates that it celebrates a game regulated by conventionalization and based on the system of the Western.

Roland Barthes remarked on myth: "It abolishes the complexity of human acts, it gives them the simplicity of essences."[6] The essence of stereotypes that constitute modern myths, such the Western, is brought to the fore in *Once Upon a Time in the West* (as in other Italo-Westerns). Incidentally, in 1969 Sergio Leone described this as his intention in an interview with Horst Königstein: "There are now different possibilities of expressing oneself in a Western than before. I approached the main characters of the Western as symbols; for me they are archetypes like the characters of the Homeric epics. And that's how I told my tales: I eliminated the old—American—form of storytelling."[7]

And in the same year, the German film director Wim Wenders described his cinema experience of seeing Leone's film much in this sense, if with a touch of abhorrence:

> I realize that this film . . . no longer shows the "surface" of Westerns, but rather what lies behind: the *inner side* of Westerns. The images no longer only mean themselves, something else glimmers through; they are threatening without making their threat visible, they turn the acts of violence into symbols of violence, into primal Western scenes. A close-up of Charles Bronson in this film becomes a close-up of a *personification*, whose story is no longer that of *a* revenge, but rather that of *revenge* itself.[8]

Once Upon a Time in the West not only provides structural references to the genre's repertoire of stereotypes, which the film discursively examines, but also a many-layered complex of *innuendo* or direct *allusions*[9] to individual Westerns. The three gangsters waiting at the station clearly refer to *High Noon*, as already mentioned. The form of the train station itself also alludes to this film, although its staging is more monumental, with its large, prominent water tank, the fearful station master, and the stereotypical image of the train tracks stretching into the horizon. Another indication is that the absent boss of the bandits is in both cases named Frank.

Similarly, the impressive panorama shot depicting the drive through Monument Valley in a later sequence can be easily deciphered by any Western aficionado as a reference to John Ford and a classical landscape of the genre. The list of examples could be continued.

Bernardo Bertolucci, the co-sceenwriter of the film, recalled his original intention: "I wrote a huge treatment—about three hundred pages long, full of 'quotes' from all the Westerns I love."[10] And in his book about the European perspective on the Western Christopher Frayling comments: "The final version of the film is so crammed with 'quotes' from Hollywood Westerns that it is difficult to imagine how many more Bertolucci could have fitted in."[11]

This question aside, intertextual[12] games such as these do in any case contribute to the laying bare the enunciation, or in the words of Brecht, " 'something to construct,' something 'artificial,' 'invented.' "[13] Metz[14] himself had already indicated this, even if only in passing.

It is interesting that despite such demonstrative heightening of conventional forms and precedents, the balance does not tip into the comical. No sense of parody arises, or at least the underlying tone of the film is not primarily aimed at mocking generic forms. This, however, does not preclude humorous nuances. The gangster's trapping of the fly in his revolver seems to travesty the mythic swift-handedness of the Western's dueling men. Apart from such examples, the generally predominating tone is one of pathos.

The solitary individual confronting fate and the magnificent expanse of landscape: this is a carefully staged visual leitmotif carried throughout the film, a familiar, and indeed conventional, motif from famous Westerns that here was also systematically singled out and heightened. In the visual arts, this motif has served as a fundamental romantic pathos formula (*Pathosformel*),[15] at least since Caspar David Friedrich's painting of *The Monk by the Sea*.

Instead of a parody, Leone created a distant and simultaneously devoted pastiche.[16] He approached the conventional patterns of the genre with the confidence of knowing the *stereotype world of the Western*, presenting it as such, and *loving it for what it is.* The result is a congealed déjà vu, a *monumental memorial to the Western*.

A comment by Wenders on the film relates to the impact of a monument as a mummifying resume: "This one is the limit, the end of a métier. This one is deadly."[17] This statement lends an unintended double meaning to the distribution title of the German dubbed version, *Spiel mir das Lied vom Tod* (in English, Play Me the Song of Death).

This monument achieves two things at once: it is reflexive and openly reveals the stereotypes of the genre; it robs their performance of any semblance of immediacy in deconstructing while simultaneously transfiguring them. This produces a dual effect upon an audience versed in Westerns. On the one hand, the film aims to convey a superior feeling of being able to see through the generic world and its stereotypes, that is, a confident enjoyment of experiencing the conventional patterns that have, for all intents and purposes, long become worn out. On the other hand, the film again provides a—now reflexive—echo of the original pleasure that the stereotypes once provided and the fascination that they held. This double effect of reflexivity is further raised to the level of a memorial by the powerful pathos of the images and music, and the (sometimes manipulative) game played with our expectations adds refinement to the film as a whole.

Favorable reviews and analyses of *Once Upon a Time in the West* from the 1970s or early 1980s often emphasized the film's *critical* commentary[18] on the Western. Bernhard von Dadelsen still insists on this point in *Fischer Filmgeschichte*. He characterizes the story of the construction of the railroad as a "fable of capitalist critique,"[19] and he sees in the "conflict between Frank and the Mexican Harmonica a glaring allegory of the US exploitation of Latin America."[20] Dadelsen explicitly associates the supposed critical potential of the film with the (approximately contemporary) genre-critical cinema of directors such as Robert Altman or Arthur Penn, whose *Little Big Man* (1970) "once and for all destroyed the form of the Western and its affirmative ideology."[21] He refers, among other things, to a comment that Leone made in an interview: "As always, I used conventional cinema as a basis. Then I focused completely on playing with its codes and destroying them. I wanted to confront all the existing lies about the history of the settlement of America."[22]

Independent of this comment, in looking at the film one is hard pressed to see it as an attack on the deceptive nature of stereotypes, let alone on the ideology of the Western, or as an invocation of historical truth.

Let it be said that *Once Upon the Time in the West* no longer boasts the perfect heroism of settler myths, which characterized the epic Westerns of the 1920s and 1930s but had already long become an anachronism by 1968. In the development of its story, the film certainly engages with the critical common sense of the late 1960s. However, characters such as the railroad magnate, who intends to see through his plans with the help of a posse of gunmen, do not represent a new truth, a biting critique of capitalism, or an ideological criticism of the genre but instead had already long belonged to the Western's conventional repertoire. Also, the replacement of the overarching national ideals that formerly propelled the heroes of the epic Westerns by decidedly nonidealistic factors, such as money, power, or revenge as key character motivations, even of the protagonists, is certainly no longer a novelty *within* the genre, that is, *within* conventional cinema, by the late 1960s. This contrasting variation of the outmoded imaginary world of the genre had certainly already been introduced by the wave of Italo-Westerns directly preceding the film, if not before.

Irrespective of this shift, Leone does not develop a (counter)world of historical truth, a critical response to the "deceptive" stereotypes of the genre, but rather a celebratory composition based on historically altered premises of *common sense*— on *genre consciousness*—and plays with a repertoire of stereotypes *as a repertoire of stereotypes*. The film takes its (stereo)typization *farther than* any prior film and thus makes it visible.

The capitalist, for example, becomes a lurid type, a cripple with fantasies of omnipotence. This is a type that has appeared in films ranging from Fritz Lang's banker Haghi in *Spione* (*Spies*, Germany, 1928) to Kubrick's Dr. Strangelove (in *Dr. Strangelove, or How I Learned to Stop Worrying and Love the Bomb*, UK, 1964) and that today still belongs to cinema's stereotype repertoire, as demonstrated by the character of Dr. Loveless in Barry Sonnenfeld's *Wild Wild West* (1999). With his glaring attributes, the character hardly connotes a reference to some "true" story; instead it is nothing more than the exalted figure of an imagination long become conventional. The protagonists as a whole remain "ahistoric schemata,"[23] in the historical no-man's land of the genre, as created by conventionalization. Christopher Frayling described this as follows:

> Rather he [Leone] chose to portray America's first frontier using the most worn-out of stereotypes: the pushy whore, the romantic bandit, the avenger, the killer who is about to become a business man, the industrialist who uses the methods of a bandit. These stereotypes, which, in Leone's and Bertolucci's hands, become fictional "emblems" of a sort, are taken from the dime novel, the Wild West show, the Hollywood film, the pulp magazine, the comic-strip, rather than from American history—parts of a "fixed terminology" or "code" of the fictional genre.[24]

Leone's comment—incongruent with other statements made by the director (as above the comment on the figures of Homeric epics)—is possibly attributable to the prevailing rhetoric in the discourse of the late 1960s and early 1970s, which asserted social or ideological criticism as central paradigms of judgment. This same mechanism still echoes in Dadelsen's writing. The film itself hardly functions in this sense, and this argument *against the text* fails to understand the film's aesthetic incentive and thus also its film-historical significance.

Paradoxically, opinions that come closer to understanding the uniqueness and significance of the film are those with a dispraising tone—arising from the same discourse of ideological critique—toward these very qualities. One such voice was the *Cahiers du cinéma* reviewer Silvie Pierre, who in 1970 aptly remarked that *Once Upon a Time in the West* is basically not interested in history or ideology but most of all in the genre's system of stereotypes as a repertoire of variation. Her assessment read: "cinematic narcissism, a cinema only interested in itself and its own mythology."[25] Despite clear undertones of criticism, this formulation describes the aesthetic constitution of the film much more precisely than did the superfluous attempts at refashioning the film as a work of generic and historical critique.

Once Upon a Time in the West is *reflexive* cinema. The film not only lays bare the generic world of stereotypes it uses. It does more in that its actual theme is the reflection of genre stereotypes *as stereotypes*. It "addresses" the stereotypes it employs. Stripped of their immediacy, these set pieces serve as both the material and topic of the new composition. Hence, the film is not only to be characterized as reflexive; it is also *self-referential*, in Kay Kirchmann's[26] sense of the word: "One could categorize a . . . film as self-referential which *no longer displays references* an 'outside'—whatever form this may take—of its own filmic context for which *no antecedent mimetic principle* is any longer constitutive."[27] If one applies Kirchmann's formulation (somewhat tempered) to *Once Upon a Time in the West*, then one is confronted with a film whose references are predominantly based on other films, in particular on the stereotype repertoire or the imaginary world of the Western genre. Any pre- or extramedial (historical) reality lying beyond this medial-discursive reality has become *meaningless* to the viewer. Through its reflexive, stylized, and artificial treatment of stereotypes, Leone's film makes clear that it is neither meaningful nor really possible to relate the conventional schemata of the imaginary world of the Western to an original historical "West" or any other reality beyond the Western's imaginary.

This transparency created by the skillfully produced artificiality of the whole distinguishes the film to a degree from classical Westerns. As strict genre films, the latter were themselves based on the conventionalized fictional world of the genre. In this sense, they had de facto also long been self-referential. However, for the most part they were not yet deconstructive in raising the issue as such. Instead, their illusionary staging was primarily focused on the *appearance of immediacy*.

The epic Westerns of the 1920s to the 1940s even simulated claims to reconstructing historical reality, as in the voiceover framing *Dodge City* (Michael Curtiz, 1939), for example.

In contrast, the gesture of artificiality, of *reflexive* self-referentiality, is fundamental to Leone's film. The metaphor for the Western as a "horse opera" is attributed to William S. Hart, a pioneer of Western films. This traditional opera metaphor takes on additional meaning in view of the new type of openly self-referential and even monumental artificial world stylized with genre-nostalgic pathos. This is what Silvie Pierre was probably referring to in her assessment of "cinematic narcissism."

The overt self-referentiality of the film and the disclosure of the stereotype *as stereotype* were, however, viewed positively by other theorists. Writing in 1971, Horst Königstein, for instance, who explicitly uses the term "stereotype," identified a latently emancipatory dimension. Following Horkheimer and Adorno, he equated commercial cinema (by nature) with alienation, deception, and the mechanism of stereotypization. Within the framework of existing social reality there was hardly a chance for viewers to escape the dominant stereotypes by which they are conditioned. Therefore, an emancipatory, political cinema must be concerned with "initiating [the audience] into the political substance of the medium."[28] An initial step of sorts was to develop an awareness of the all-powerful stereotypes. He regarded the stereotype-conscious Italo-Westerns and particularly *Once Upon a Time in the West* as at least close to such a cinema, precisely because they presented bare stereotypes and made them recognizable as such but simultaneously refrained from creating any sense of ideal coherence. They can "only discharge viewer into emptiness"[29] and so at least avoid gestures of affirmation. Thus this cinema reveals "a 'shitty' world, and contempt and cynicism plague any attempt to bring lies into harmony at the end."[30] However, stereotypes are incapable of social anticipation.[31]

At the time quite common, this fascinated, left-wing reading of the Italo-Western underscores—and this is perhaps the most interesting point—the previously discussed ambivalence, openness, and integrative power of reflexively presenting genre stereotypes with respect to different audience groups.

The section "Ways of Emancipation from the Stereotype" outlined three basic variations or means of emancipation. One was entitled "radical critique and renunciation," another "celebratory revelation." The latter was largely associated with the retrocinema of the 1970s to 1990s, a cinema meanwhile frequently labeled as "postmodern."[32] Today, this much seems clear: at least in terms of its approach to generic stereotypes, that is, their celebratory revelation as a central and consistent aesthetic principle, *Once Upon a Time in the West* is an *early, pivotal film marking the transition to this influential tendency*. In other words, it is an important model case of the reflexive stereotype, and *herein* lies the film's significance within the history of the medium, regardless whether one may like the film or not.

This significance tended to be obscured by the misinterpretation of the film as a critique of stereotypes or ideology, especially when viewed in context with the example set by Arthur Penn and Robert Altman, who distinctly represent a *different* tendency in the approach to stereotypes, namely critique and renunciation.

Considering cinema since the 1980s, especially what Fredric Jameson described as "the so-called nostalgia film (or what the French call *la mode rétro*),"[33] the relationship to Leone's Western becomes obvious. Examples include *The Sting* (George Roy Hill, 1973), *Hammett* (Wim Wenders, 1982), *The Cotton Club* (Francis Ford Coppola, 1984), *Wild at Heart* (David Lynch, 1990), *Pulp Fiction* (Quentin Tarantino, 1994), *The Fifth Element* (Luc Besson, France/USA 1997), almost all of the Coen brothers' films since *Miller's Crossing* (1990), and, of course, Leone's own *Once Upon a Time in America* (1984). As different as they prove to be in detail, all these works share the practice of revelation and the celebratory reflexive display of genre stereotypes. And one could easily compile a much longer list of films.

Following a trend toward hybridization, in the 1990s the remnants of scenic realism still retained in *Once Upon a Time in the West* were even more radically broken down. The constant search for new means of defamiliarizing or deautomatizing existing patterns played no small role in the process. In *Natural Born Killers* (Oliver Stone, 1994), right at the beginning of the film, the protagonist couple drive a convertible not through the landscape of an imaginary reality but through a collage of conventional film and media images, whose material status *as* media images and their hybrid connections are signaled through new digital technologies of image processing and internal montage. A new gesture of revelation and surrender to the medial patterns of the digital age.

Another sequence in Stone's film, in which the couple meet for the first time, kill their parents, and drive off, functions similarly. Placed in the middle of the film, the sequence is staged as a parody of the American sitcom *I Love Lucy* and uses the conventional forms and stereotypes of this TV genre, including canned background laughter. Its fragmentary character is not only marked by the abrupt shift of the narrative code at the beginning and end of the sequence but also through an insertion of the opening and closing credits (of the *sitcom*) in the middle of the film. The interpolation of this sequence, a diegetic non-sequitur, is a particular form of integration that Metz called the "symbiotic type."[34] The sitcom is not a logically bracketed film within a film, for example, a television program within the diegesis, but: "*the film within the film* [in this case the sitcom] *is the film itself.*[35] The main characters pass through constantly changing worlds of medial code, which clamor loudly for attention. This world is literally a media world. Through a constant shift in code *Natural Born Killers* repeatedly highlights the inhomogeneous, the hybrid, and its imagination as pieced together out of disparate preformed patterns.

Morin had even talked about certain sedimented film images being used as signs representing the "ideas of love," the "idea of loneliness," or the "idea of evil," hence enabling them to be read as a form of symbolism in classical cinema, such as Douglas Sirk's image of the window in *All That Heaven Allows*. However, in view of the newer type of cinema, it is necessary to systematically include another level, that of *open self-referentiality*. The reflexively staged stereotypes in films ranging from *Once Upon a Time in the West* to *Natural Born Killers* no longer represent the *idea* of evil, love, and so on. Instead they present themselves as references to the *film*-idea of evil, love, and so on, or the *media*-idea thereof. An empirical world of experience behind the imaginary patterns of the media no longer seems detectable. The intertextual and increasingly intermedial "reality" of the medial stereotypes serves as the sole material reality.

The conceptual stereotype models elaborated in the previous chapter lead the way from a critique of the "standardized cliché" toward an appreciation of the stereotype as a basis for abstraction and symbolism. Although these ideas may still serve as a useful foundation for the interpretation of this kind of reflexive and self-referential cinema as grounded in the revelation and reflexivity of stereotypes, they are no longer fully sufficient.

More or less concomitantly with this new type of cinema, theoretical discourses emerged—as expressions of the same cultural sensibility (even if outside film theory in the stricter sense)—which articulated further-reaching ideas on the approach to stereotypes.

THE NONLITERAL, DUAL TONE, AND
THE TRANSFIGURATION OF THE COMMONPLACE

Cultural consciousness develops in waves. Whereas in the early 1920s film theorists avowed the immediacy of gesture as salvation from the conventionality and stereotypical aspects of language—within the context of the discourses of expressionism and empathy theory—in the second half of the decade and at the turn of the 1930s, disillusionment predominated in association with metaphors such as "standardization," the "readymade," and "assembly-line" film production. All of these circumscribed the stereotype and were bracketed by or part of contemporary discourses of Fordism/Americanism and New Objectivity. Later, the emerging contexts of semiology, or semiotics, gave impetus to the filmologists' modified reflection on stereotypes as intelligible forms.

Over the course of the 1960s—against the backdrop of an altered relationship to the conventional—other ideas gained significance, linking the (indeed largely indirect) reflection of the stereotype with a new celebration of nonliteral reading and the transfiguration of the commonplace. Such thinking did not immediately form a dominant tendency but was expressed in a large number of theoretical and artistic statements of the decade, and it paved the way for what would soon become the highly influential discourse of postmodernism, the founding texts of which already stem from this period, such as Leslie Fiedler's "Cross the Border— Close the Gap."[36]

How might one more closely describe these two motifs, the *celebration of non-literal reading* and the *transfiguration of the commonplace*? Is there a connection between the two, and what is the source of their new significance in the 1960s?

A text published by the German writer Peter Schneider in 1965 is illuminating. Although entitled "Vom Nutzen des Klischees" (On the Use of the Cliché), a more appropriate title might be "On the Pleasure of the Cliché." Schneider vehemently argues against all attempts, both in film criticism and film production, to enhance the status of genre films (he writes about the Western) *in contradiction to* the stereotypes of the genre, whether this take the form of incorporating substantive historical references or serious real-life problems familiar to the audience or recasting stereotyped figures as individual characters: "Such attempts fail to understand what makes the Western unique: that its subject matter is only enjoyable as self-confident cliché. Any ambition of enhancing the shell of its plot through articulated content is a betrayal of the original Western."[37] And he adds:

If one takes the Western seriously and sheds even one genuine tear for the hero who has been shot through the leg scissors maneuver, then one misses out on all the wonderful minor aspects of the Western, i.e., the leg scissor maneuver. The Western, and also the high-class Western, is then denigrated to the level of the third-class social problem film and immediately swings towards becoming overbearing.[38]

Schneider therefore favors an attitude toward the genre that takes pleasure in the inherent value of playing with stereotypes *in and of itself.* "It [the Western] proves its worth in its very renunciation of novelty."[39]

Hence Schneider regards the only appropriate approach to conventional patterns as one that makes no secret of being detached from all meanings above and beyond the conventional, imaginary world of the genre. He writes: "Over the course of sixty years the Western's continuous appetite for repetition has removed the plausibility of all its documentary elements, even if occasionally preserved."[40] And: "Everything that serves as a motif in the Western at some point experiences the cold shower of the *pars pro toto* jargon, which declares the entire world of feigned immediacy to be *pure playing material*."[41] In other words, Schneider, like Shklovsky or later Lotman,[42] refers to the derealizing effect of conventionalization, the fading and shifting of meanings, and the tendency toward ellipsis. Stereotypes could and should be experienced as free and open imaginary factors, as fixed patterns of a pure play world, as in the reflexive manner of *Once Upon a Time in the West*. He regards questions pointing beyond the artificial world of the genre as meaningless and even as fundamental misconceptions. Such references would only impair the beautiful regularity of the conventional.

Just as the connection to reality is suspended, so too is the relationship to the customary schemata of aesthetic judgment. Here quality has nothing to do with the exploration of the real or critical reason. It is instead rooted in the regulated use of effects and a particular kind of style. To the extent that the imaginary world develops into a repertoire of specific repetitive forms, which present themselves in an "understated distance from dead earnest,"[43] so the expert eye appreciates the sometimes grotesque departures of conventional forms from the real. Schneider's delight is associated with apparent mannerisms (the "leg scissor maneuver"!). The special quality and stylistic challenge of the Western lies in imaginatively varying these mannerisms and celebrating them.

That means that the posited artificiality of the conventional world here provides the condition of affirmation: of the transfiguration of the stereotype. A special aesthetic realm emerges with its own rules and specific criteria. According to Schneider's dictum, the subject matter of the Western is "only enjoyable as a self-confident cliché."[44]

Here one might interject that similar statements have been penned by intellectuals in the past. Isolated remarks pointing to similar constructions appear early on, some of which have already been quoted. For example, with respect to stereotyped character patterns Erwin Panofsky argued against the cultural refinement and distinction of popular patterns in film, as did a number of preceding avant-garde writers involved in the early cinema debate (but *without* reference to the stereotype topic). Also Adorno and Eisler discussed (only marginally and with little consequence for their own concept of film music) how the productions that "follow an established pattern" are in fact superior to "pretentious grade-A films."[45]

However, a new quality marked the situation in 1960s. Statements such as Schneider's now assumed a much more conceptual character, and, most significantly, they now played out within a discursive field and media reality increasingly characterized by similar ideas and techniques of cultural production rooted therein. The celebratory play with the nonliterary reading of stereotypes and the open self-referentiality of genre forms constituted one of the decade's highly conspicuous cultural tendencies, and its influence was felt beyond this period.

It is no coincidence that Schneider's essay shares key conceptual motifs with a far more famous text, Susan Sontag's "Notes on Camp." Writing in the United States at almost the same time as Schneider, Sontag described in 1964 the kind of aesthetic sensibility that she called "camp." The first characteristic of camp ultimately boils down to nonliterary reading: "Camp sees everything in quotation marks. . . . To perceive Camp in objects and persons is to understand Being-as-Playing-a-Role. It is the farthest extension, in sensibility, of the metaphor of life as theater."[46]

Like Schneider's experience of genre film, camp is also described as types of experience "that have not been brought under the sovereignty of reason"[47] but define a special realm in which "the good-bad axis of ordinary aesthetic judgment"[48] has been suspended. Whereas Schneider speaks about how the Western may only be appropriately regarded as a "pure play world," Sontag places similar value on "the difference . . . between the thing as meaning something, anything, and the thing as pure artifice."[49] The latter is equally decisive for camp, and Sontag also emphasizes the importance of time in the production of this effect through fading and decontextualization, in order to "dethrone the serious."[50] Sontag writes: "Time liberates the work of art from moral relevance, delivering it over to the Camp sensibility . . . Another effect: time contracts the sphere of banality. (Banality is, strictly speaking, always a category of the contemporary.) What was banal can, with the passage of time, become fantastic."[51]

Sontag places clearer emphasis than Schneider on instances of inner ambivalence in relation to the camp attitude, and in fact the described de-realization offers a space for various affects. Thus the "nonliteral relationship of meaning,"[52] as Hans Jürgen Wulff writes more recently, provides the basis for *irony*. Investigating the constitutive role of irony for parody, Linda Hutcheon similarly notes: "On the semantic level, irony can be defined as a marking of difference in meaning. . . . There is one signifier and two signifieds."[53] It is therefore no surprise that Sontag identifies a close relationship between camp and irony. Camp not only means "a victory of 'style' over 'content'" but also "of irony over tragedy."[54]

But irony is not the only effect grounded in nonliteral reading. The tendency toward transfiguration—such as the nostalgic idealizing of long worn-out stereotypes—is also rooted in the same effect, as the example of *Once Upon a Time in the West* demonstrates. Essentially every form of transfiguration is paradoxically inscribed with elements of distanciation and displacement.

Sontag's notion of camp is also related to transfiguration. She articulates a perspective alternating between irony and celebration. In this sense she distinguishes camp from the kind of *traditional* irony involving derision and "bitter or polemical comedy."[55] She observes: "The traditional means for going beyond straight seriousness—irony, satire—seem feeble today, inadequate to the culturally oversaturated medium in which contemporary sensibility is schooled. Camp introduces a new standard: artifice as an ideal, theatricality."[56] An enamored stance toward the "banal" shines through the aloofness of the nonliteral. More consistently than Schneider, Sontag discusses how forms experienced as stylistic excess and mannerism, fantastical exaggerations, melodramatic absurdities, or other peculiarities kindle a true sense of pleasure. Camp is simply "the proper mixture of the exaggerated, the fantastic, the passionate, and the naïve."[57]

Busby Berkeley's ornamental film choreographies are for Sontag a classical example of camp. Although camp is grounded in a nonliteral reading and always carries a tone of mild irony, this sensibility in fact ultimately boils down to a glorification and enjoyment of the given subject matter. Camp loves and glorifies its objects but at the same time flirts with their banality. Overall, it is a complex stance: "Camp discloses innocence, but also, when it can, corrupts it."[58]

In this sense, camp closes the gap between the intellectual and the popular by simultaneously creating a sense of both confidence (through distanciation and insight) and pleasure. Camp delights "in the arts of the masses" and also in their stereotypes, which this sensibility understands "to possess . . . in a rare way."[59] Sontag herself speaks of "gestures full of duplicity"[60] inherent in the camp experience, which in this sense is also deeply ironic.[61]

This form of ambivalence toward the stereotypes of the popular became a medially widespread cultural skill in the 1960s and was not limited to camp (in a narrow sense) as an interpretive mode or sensibility. There arose a wide range of aesthetic offerings with narrative and visual structures organized in a manner to suggest such a reading. The dual tone of camp was equally employed in texts, films, and images. Sontag calls this "deliberate camp."[62] Sergio Leone's both reflexive and transfiguring approach to the stereotypes of the Western, in which nostalgia occasionally turns into mild irony, can— at least in terms of this dual meaning—be regarded as a central example.

Exhibiting a very similar ambivalence in its reflection of popular phenomena, the visual-arts movement of Pop Art flourished—not incidentally—at the same time.

Pop Art was understood as an antiart movement in opposition to the prevailing trend of sublime abstraction. It provocatively embraced representation in incorporating ordinary, everyday objects from industrial society, especially the "banal" systems of representation in advertising, comics, and so on. Particularly in the use of the latter it also addressed the mechanism of "stereotypization."[63]

At first glance, the works of Pop Art appeared to present everyday objects simply in enlarged form: Coca Cola posters, Campbell's soup cans, images from comics. But it essentially operated in a very similar manner to *Once Upon a Time in the West*. Reduction, isolation, enlargement, and serial repetition (as with Warhol's photo series of Marilyn Monroe) in Pop Art represented the aesthetic principles of deautomatization, as also employed in Leone's film. The art historian Walter Biemel remarks on the function of Pop Art's technique of staging nonliteral reading: "The repetition of advertising . . . is intended to activate a reflection on advertising, to jolt the immediacy of everyday awareness. . . . In its naïve manner of expression it aims to counteract naïveté."[64]

He further states that "the revelation of everyday life as a world of stereotypes" and "seeing through this mechanism" were functions of this form of art.[65] Biemel also senses the ambiguity that permitted both pleasure *and* insight. With respect to Roy Lichtenstein's comic-book paintings, he talks about the "ambivalent"[66] effects of Pop Art. His description of this ambivalence is interesting:

> These images may be read . . . in different ways, in a naïve sense in which the representation is taken for real (and the images are then in fact simply monumental comic strips) or in the sense of looking beneath their appearance, and then they lead to critical distance, to reflection. The enjoyment of the images is then no longer immediate but comes from smiling at this former immediacy. In this smile is a slight dread of the world, in which all people must look the same, feel the same, and say the same, desire the same, and despair of the same.[67]

Both readings are in fact possible, since the visual structure of Pop Art is open-ended enough to serve as a screen onto which highly divergent approaches and dispositions can be projected. The comic-strip image, enlarged and displayed in isolation, seems to invite reflection on popular culture and its workings, and especially on the stereotype. Biemel's *critical* interpretation is, however, not the only appropriate approach. Instead, there are other voices advocating neutral appraisal and deconstruction, which directly lead to the "transfiguration of the common-place," to use the phrase of Arthur Danto.[68] Hence, another view with entirely different emphases than Biemel's emerges.

This other perspective associates the pleasure of seeing through the stereotype less with an impulse of dread or critique but more with an acknowledged fascination for and enjoyment of patterns. This is a reading ultimately equivalent to

Sontag's "rare way" of appropriating mass phenomena. From this perspective, camp, Italo-Westerns, and Pop Art are related.

Since then a similar ambiguity in the approach toward the stereotypes of the popular has been consistently emphasized with respect to a wide range of postmodern cinema. In the process, corresponding techniques have also been introduced to popular cinema. A key reason for this is that over the course of the 1960s stereotypes also became commercially interesting across the board. Two functions are significant in this context.

First, there is the function for the reflective spectator who is critically aware of the predominating mass-media stereotypes. Here the dual tone of the nonliteral—oscillating between irony and glorification of the patterns that are played with—forms a kind of bridge between the two. On the one hand, this function does not force recipients to undercut their own awareness of stereotypes but still allows them to experience an echo of the pleasurable, naïve, and direct enjoyment of the stereotype. Using this same logic, Thomas Elsaesser speaks of the "simultaneous co-presence of the desire for the myth and a cynicism about its efficacy."[69] In a now famous passage, Umberto Eco offers a particularly vivid description of the circumstances of this tendency, which he considers a central mechanism of postmodernity:

> I think of the postmodern attitude as that of a man who loves a very cultivated woman and knows he cannot say to her "I love you madly," because he knows that she knows (and that she knows that he knows) that these words have already been written by Barbara Cartland. Still, there is a solution. He can say, "As Barbara Cartland would put it, I love you madly." At this point, having avoided false innocence, having said clearly that it is no longer possible to speak innocently, he will nevertheless have said what he wanted to say to the woman: that he loves her, but he loves her in an age of lost innocence. If the woman goes along with this, she will have received a declaration of love all the same. Neither of the two speakers will feel innocent, both will have accepted the challenge of the past, of the already said, which cannot be eliminated; both will consciously and with pleasure play the game of irony. . . . But both will have succeeded, once again, in speaking of love.[70]

To apply Eco's thoughts to cinema, one could say that a film like *Once Upon a Time in the West* encouraged the number of viewers (by now no means small but truly a mass audience), who in 1968 knew about the "lost innocence" and the stereotypes of the genre to play along and both confidently and nostalgically enjoy the film's grasp of the repertoire of stereotypes. The dual tone thus enables a *recycling* of long worn-out generic forms.

The second function is interwoven with the first and of similar significance for postmodern mainstream cinema. This is a sort of sociointegrative function, for productions of this type not only make it possible to address opposing tendencies within a group of recipients but also unite in one film different audience groups with varying aesthetic dispositions—ranging from a critical to a naïve and direct mode of reception. The function is thus a form of closing the gap, as articulated in Leslie Fiedler's programmatic text of postmodernism.[71]

One might counter at this point that both the recycling of worn-out forms as well as attempts to satisfy divergent audience groups with one product have a long history in commercial cinema, and particularly in Hollywood. The classical double plot, which combines elements of a melodramatic love story with action, is considered one technique for addressing both female and male audiences. And forms of parody, for example in comedies, are among the longstanding and tried-and-true techniques of recycling. A film musical such as *Singin' in the Rain* (Stanley Donen, Gene Kelly, 1952) with its reflexive and often parodic film-within-film construction, already amounted to a successful attempt to revive forms and stereotypes—long considered overused or old fashioned—from the film musicals of the 1930s as elements of a part ironic, part nostalgic transfiguring of a reflexive, historical staging. In this sense, the film addresses the musicals of early sound cinema.

By the 1960s, however, both the need for recycling worn-out generic forms and audience integration took on new cultural significance. For one thing, not only critics but also the mass audience now came equipped with many years of evolving media experience; they possessed the media literacy that necessarily entailed a heightened sense for the conventional and also a tendency to reflect on stereotypes. For another, the new accessibility of film through television multiplied this effect exponentially. Through this new everyday medium, it was possible to constantly watch cinema films from a whole variety of periods. Again, the United States was a forerunner in this tendency.

By the second half of the 1950s, the already significant number of television companies on the American market had already purchased the rights to the older films of most studios and used them to fill their airtime.[72] But it was in the 1960s that American households became private film museums,[73] at least in the opinion of Robert Ray, who studied the connection between film and television and the changes in film production in the United States. With few exceptions, older films were swept out of the cinemas by the constant flood of new products and sank more or less into (sometimes merciful) oblivion, but since then Hollywood's past—and of cinema as a whole—has been constantly present on TV, also in Europe, if with some delay.

This new presence was not without consequences. It strengthened the latent film-historical and intertextual awareness of the audience and additionally honed its ability to distinguish stereotyping. The continuous television presence of older movies, including weak films and B-pictures that would have never stood a chance in cinemas, encouraged comparison and produced an acute sense for the stereotype. Conventional patterns became much more noticeable than before due to the deautomatizing effect of the temporal decontextualization of film production and reception, which up until then in the cinema had been the exception. The previously discussed sequential offering of many similar films was now supplemented by this temporal "stacking," which substantially contributed to the new situation.

Still another factor was that television did not hesitate to use successful narrative patterns from theatrical films in its own productions, that is, TV series. Much in the way cinema once drew on nineteenth-century literary genres, television now used film genres as a similar resource. In order to fill their massive programming schedules, American television companies in particular reproduced almost all the classical film genres: Westerns, gangster and detective films, screwball comedies, musicals, horror films, and so on. These series supplanted the classical production of B-pictures, whereby the number of productions and viewers continued to increase. From a qualitative perspective, this certainly did not mean greater difference or increased complexity in the approach to stereotypes.

As a whole, this supports the thesis that the stereotypical nature of generic forms—some already worn out from decades of use—finally entered the consciousness of a wide audience. This marked the beginning of a new phase.

This new, at very least latent, consciousness was additionally furthered by a special-interest audience, since around this time there was a movement—from the bottom up—toward film studies as an academic discipline. A flood of courses was offered on the ideological critique of the medium or on genres and their conventional forms. Reigning structuralist paradigms contributed to a particular interest in the latter. The establishment of art-house cinemas may also be viewed in this context, a trend contributing to the visibility of film history through retrospectives and other film-historical programs. Additionally, there was new interest in a critique of the culture industry as advocated by Horkheimer and Adorno.

This new situation faced two divergent audience-response patterns, which the film and television industries immediately grasped and incorporated. On the one hand, Ray elaborates (what he calls) a "Left" response of ideological critique, which attempted—in the context of complex social and cultural change—to oppose the classical mythology of the media and develop a *counterculture*. On the other hand, he identifies a conservative (or, in his words, "Right") reaction, which developed a persistently nostalgic relationship to the crisis of patterns and myths that accompanied this development and the concomitant economic crisis of Hollywood.

Although both types of responses predominate in different groups of audiences, it seems impossible to make clear distinctions. At this time, the critics still belonged to the first true film *and television* generation in terms of their frame of experience, and therefore they almost symbiotically adhered to corresponding myths and stereotypes. These had long become discursive elements of daily life, which were inseparable from individual biographies and shaped the repertoires of the personal imaginary. Referring to this generation, Ray observes: "Faced with the need to find suitable lifestyles, its members often appeared to be acting out of a grab bag of movie myth, including even those which the counterculture's own rational premises had disowned."[74] In reverse, one may assume that also the "nostalgics" did not remain unaffected by the medial logic of overuse.

In this situation, the film industry as well as the television companies responded in the mid-1960s with a conspicuously large number of films openly reflecting the stereotypes of their genres—ironizing, reflexively transfiguring, and sometimes even critically questioning them. This included a wave a genre parodies. Possibly the most famous, *Cat Ballou* (Elliot Silverstein, 1965) is packed with benign irony and plays an utterly reflexive game with the genre, in this case the Western, to an even greater extent than the film *Viva Maria!* (Louis Malle, 1965), which appeared at almost the same time in France. Stereotypes are clearly satirized, for instance, the character of the aging and tired drunken gunman (played by Lee Marvin), who gears himself up for one last fight. The female lead (Jane Fonda) reads Western novels, in which she encounters the figure of the mythic gunfighter before he appears for real. And the entire film narrative is presented as a comic ballad sung by two wandering street singers, who paradoxically have discursive authority despite being diegetic figures. It is telling that the ironic and simultaneously nostalgic film was in 1966 the first genre parody ever to win an Academy Award.[75]

Almost at the same time, ABC began the TV series *Batman*, which, in Sontag's terms, follows the rules of deliberate camp, and the James Bond film *Thunderball* (Terence Young, UK, 1965), also intentionally styled as camp, became the biggest box-office hit of 1966. But also films that *critically* deconstructed their genres and attempted to foreground their lack of realism, for example, *McCabe and Mrs. Miller* (Robert Altman, 1971) and *Little Big Man* (Arthur Penn, 1970), now stood a chance at the box office.

Looking back in the early 1980s, Ray remarks that "between 1966 and 1980, an enormous number of films depended on their audience's ability to recognize them as overt parodies, 'corrected' genre pictures, or exaggerated camp versions of Hollywood's traditional mythology."[76] And: "No other period in Hollywood history had produced so many overtly satiric movies."[77] This incisive trend demonstrates the wide scope of possibilities of recycling presented by the reflexive approach to generic stereotypes and its play with their ambivalent meanings. It also becomes clear how practical this approach was in terms of mediating between critical and more nostalgic perspectives and their respective audiences. Films *critically* deconstructing their genres are an expression of the same genre-reflexive tendency, but they were certainly never able to negotiate these two groups as well as the other types of production.

Undoubtedly these circumstances largely explain why the half-ironic, half-transfiguring play with overt stereotypes—now the epitome of postmodern cinema—today remains the predominant form of appropriating genre cinema. However, the filmic forms and techniques of deautomatization have changed in equal measure with the continuous increase in audience recognition of media stereotypes. Various factors have contributed to the multiplication and constant availability of audiovisual products: the introduction of new media, that is, initially video, the expansion and commercialization of television providers in Europe as a result of satellite and cable technologies, and finally digital technology with its multimedia applications. On the one hand, this has created a distinct awareness for signs, which is also founded on filmic stereotypes. On the other, it has produced new means of defamiliarizing stereotypes and continuous hybridization. The previously described dual tone remained characteristic of the approach to genre stereotypes in films intended for theatrical release, and it has meanwhile become the sign of that "multiple encoding"[78] considered quintessentially postmodern.

Theory has also become more radicalized in the wake of postmodern discourses. In the 1960s, Susan Sontag and Peter Schneider still claimed a special aesthetic realm for an art incorporating the conventional, a sphere set apart from reality and where traditional value schemata (including those vis-à-vis stereotype) did not apply. For postmodern theorists, the perception of the world meanwhile seems so pervasively steeped in stereotypical media simulations, signs, and conventions, and so on that the question of an underlying "real" world is no longer even posed. This further obviates the question of the correspondence of media stereotypes with the real world, and artistic creativity boils down to the ability to virtuously play with patterns, which, in the best of cases, results in a reflexive laying bare of the role that media stereotypes play.

This latter point has been a consistent source of dissent. Intellectual critics of medial perception, such as Gilles Deleuze, insist on searching for the genuinely "new image"[79] free of the stereotype. In other words, the fundamental ideas on the approach to filmic stereotypes explored and described here are not to be understood as a mere succession of individual, overcome phases, although their order closely corresponds with the evolution of medial experience. Key conceptual motifs from *all* these theories will certainly continue to inform current discourses.

PART III

FILM ANALYSIS

Critique and Transfiguration—Three Case Studies

NINE

MCCABE AND BUFFALO BILL: ON THE CRITICAL REFLECTION OF STEREOTYPES IN TWO FILMS BY ROBERT ALTMAN

Despite all the progress in techniques of representation, all the rules and specialties, all the gesticulating bustle, the bread on which the culture industry feeds humanity, remains the stone of stereotype. . . . All this consolidates the immutability of the existing circumstances.

—MAX HORKHEIMER AND THEODOR W. ADORNO, *DIALECTIC OF ENLIGHTENMENT* (1947)

Similar discourses to those conducted by theorists and writers on the stereotype were and are carried out—reflexively—in actual films. This was already elaborated in the section "Ways of Emancipation from the Stereotype" in chapter 3 and also in the detailed discussion of Leone's *Once Upon a Time in the West* in the previous chapter. In this last section of this study, two basic forms of the immediate filmic discourse on the stereotype—"critique" and transfiguring, "celebratory revelation"—will be examined more closely, together with associated techniques of narration and representation. Following the principle of *pars pro toto*, three films will be used as case studies.

The last of these examples, discussed in the next chapter (chapter 10), addresses the celebratory and overtly self-referential use of stereotypes in a *postmodern* film, *The Hudsucker Proxy* (Joel and Ethan Coen, 1994). Given that many fundamental issues have already been expanded upon in respect to Leone's Western, here the specific focus will be on the aspect of acting. The confident play with overtly displayed stereotypes will be investigated through the performance of the actress Jennifer Jason Leigh.

But first, this chapter will undertake a double analysis of two works from the 1970s by the director Robert Altman: the films *McCabe & Mrs. Miller* (1971) and *Buffalo Bill and the Indians, or Sitting Bull's History Lesson* (1976). In their *critical* explorations of the stereotype world of the Western, these two films are best categorized as *modernist* cinema.[1]

THE FAILURE OF THE INDIVIDUAL IN THE FACE OF THE STEREOTYPE: *MCCABE & MRS. MILLER*

The film opens with a male figure, a solitary rider. He is driving a few pack mules through the wilderness and approaches the small, still provisional settlement of Presbyterian Church in the American West. The rider, John McCabe, is a professional poker player. Immediately after his arrival, he makes his way to the saloon to pursue business.

The film jumps forward in time to show McCabe having taken up an even more profitable business: he brings three whores to Presbyterian Church. His initially extremely primitive bordello becomes a genuinely flourishing enterprise when he avails himself of the expert knowledge of Mrs. Miller, a self-confident and truly professional whore traveling through town, and makes her his business partner. She sets up a whorehouse that is managed as a serious business and even represents a certain cultural niveau, not only with its casino but also its bathhouse.

The modest success story is interrupted by the greediness of a powerful mining company, which is buying up all the profitable businesses in the area. When McCabe hesitates too long to accept their offer, they send hit men to kill him. The film ends with a fight between McCabe and the gunmen. Although McCabe manages to kill them, he himself is fatally wounded and dies.

In telling the story in this manner, there seems to be hardly any doubt that the film is a Western. Even if the candid depiction of prostitution, the setting of the bordello, and the death of the main character seem unusual, at least compared to *classical* Westerns, key moments in the story are marked by significant narrative stereotypes highly familiar from the genre's conventionalized imaginary. To name a few, important examples, there is the lonely horseman riding into town at the beginning of the film and heading to the saloon, the status of the McCabe character as a professional gambler, his reputation as a legendary gunfighter both feared and admired, the story of the development of the small town in the West, the band of gunmen sent by a hostile power, and the big, solitary showdown between the protagonist and the killers.

A closer examination of how all these narrative stereotypes of the genre are actually employed, however, reveals the great extent to which Altman's film departs from the conventional imaginary world of the Western by disavowing and in many ways inverting its mythology. It soon becomes apparent that the film does not adhere to the stereotype world of the Western but—*reflexively*—*conducts a critical discourse on it*.

This dimension of critical self-reflection is revealed in an examination of the leading male character of the story. Played by Warren Beatty, John McCabe is far from the embodiment of the perfect hero type who is fighting for the cultural ideals of progress and justice—a type characteristic of hero constructions in the epic Westerns of the 1920s and 1930s. Nor does McCabe represent the even older and more long-lasting generic figure of the *good bad guy*. Although assuming the role of the criminal or outlaw, the latter is typically compelled, either by a deep-seated sense of honor or basic human dignity, to defend his own reputation, the community, or the weak. And McCabe is equally incompatible with the heroes of the 1950s, who having become aged and resigned—in parallel with the genre—must face one more challenge and gear themselves up for an ultimate contest.

The fundamental difference between McCabe and all these hero stereotypes is that he has no "natural" identity. He instead proves to be a character with an inherent identity problem, who consistently puts on a role—immediately recognized by viewers—within the story world of the film. This role clearly refers to a Western stereotype. David Denby hits the mark in describing McCabe as "a man who adopts the manner of some famous or legendary character of the Old West, but who actually has the imagination and humor of a second-rate traveling salesman."[2] He surrounds himself with the aura of the Western hero, who is said to have shot a certain Bill Roundtree, although the film indicates this as doubtful from the very beginning and, later on, increasingly so. Whereas for those around him McCabe persistently cultivates this reputation and the associated type of the "faster draw," the sly and hardened professional gambler, inwardly he seems to have the desire, at least at first, to convince himself of his capabilities, to master his surroundings through his own superiority.

However, the film's narrative soon makes clear that he is not capable of living up to his pretensions. Although the assumed role and real capacities of McCabe diverge, the role he puts on does not simply remain superficial and inconsequential. The image he projects does affect, even if only partially, how he *consciously* presents himself, his self-awareness. Mythological construct and self-image become confused in McCabe ultimately to the point of having lethal consequences for him. The reason for this failure is his overestimation of himself and the delusion caused by the limited imagination—clearly an imagination from the Western genre—in his perception of himself. These character traits alone relay a critical self-reflection of Western mythology and stereotypes.

That self-dramatization is as an aspect of McCabe's character is made clear in the film from the beginning. McCabe prepares himself for his first appearance in the saloon at the start of the film as if getting ready for a show performance. Having arrived at the outskirts of Presbyterian Church and still on horseback, he dons a bowler hat, which, although inappropriate to the region and the weather, is intended to lend him an aura of distinction. Once in the saloon, he unrolls a special tablecloth for the poker game. He jovially hands out cigars, buys a bottle of whiskey for the men, and spectacularly takes his own drink with a raw egg in it.

Thus at the very start, he performs a repertoire of showing-off behaviors, which he later repeatedly employs but with decreasing success. Altman thereby defines a set of symbolic attitudes, which become visual crystallizations of the increasing breakdown of the character's overt role performance. Initially, however, we experience McCabe in situations where his attempts to impress seem to work: in playing cards with the proletarian saloon guests and bargaining for the first three whores. And the initial images of the film function in the same manner. McCabe is introduced with crane shots, conventional for such situations in the genre. Cloaked in a huge fur coat, a solitary, mysterious man rides through a setting that calls for a rugged man, through the obviously cold, rainy late fall of a mountainous scenery. A melancholic ballad by Leonard Cohen is sung nondiegetically in the background. It tells of the "sort of man" familiar in the Western and—complementing the image—conjures up both a stereotype and an allegorical interpretation:

> I know that sort of man, it's hard
> To hold the hand of anyone
> Who's reaching for the sky, just surrender
> Who's reaching for the sky, just surrender.

Up to this point, the introductory sequence shows an image of McCabe "as he would like to be seen,"[3] as Diane Jacobs notes. But already Cohen's lyrics, with their tension of imagination versus miserable reality, between "reaching for the sky" and "just surrender," suggest McCabe's problem. The film then later breaks down the character's role image and his view of himself step by step.

This deconstruction begins with the appearance of Constance Miller, played by Julie Christie. She is an unusually emancipated and self-confident woman for a Western, and all McCabe's attempts to dominate her with his customary and so far successful show-off demeanor now fall flat. Just as McCabe is trying his whiskey-and-egg number she says to his face: "Hey, you know if you wanna make out you're such a fancy dude, you might wear something besides that cheap Jockey Club cologne."[4] Nevertheless, he still gets involved with her. Probably first and foremost because it bolsters his ego to be associated with such a confident and attractive woman, but also because her plans and know-how correspond to his desire of operating a profitable business.

From the moment she appears, the masculine Western role he tries to play is systematically undermined. We see no trace of superiority and the "natural" authority over women that normally define this role. The character of Constance Miller far surpasses all classical character stereotypes and behavioral repertoires of women in Westerns. The knowledgeable character with a sense of power relationships and shifts in circumstances is Mrs. Miller, not McCabe. *Her* business ideas, based on hygienic standards and comfort, and thus also on investment, are persistently realized despite his doubts; they become a success, and he shares in the profits. *She* is capable of managing the bookkeeping and the figures, and as she proves this to him his abilities in this capacity are revealed as limited. She immediately realizes that one cannot turn down the powerful mining company's buying offer, if one wishes to survive. Overestimating himself, he believes that he can play poker with the powerful in the same way as he plays with the simple-minded clientele of the local saloon.

When McCabe begins to sense that he has pushed his luck too far with the representatives of the mining company and is now in danger, he seeks the help of a lawyer in the next sizeable town, who lectures him with the abstract ideals of his profession without really going into the specifics of McCabe's dilemma. He dispatches him with platitudes on law and order while urging him to take the mining company to court, ideas utterly impractical given the situation. And he cynically sends him off to certain death by singing the praises of free enterprise and "dying for freedom" if necessary.

McCabe clings to these phrases, although not without a degree of skepticism. Echoing lines of dialogue from classical Westerns, they fit well with his tendency to meet increasing challenges to his self-misconceptions with bullheaded stubbornness. His problems only mount in the process. In contrast, Mrs. Miller cuts through these empty phrases with a single sentence. She incorporates the principle of hard-nosed realism in opposition to the illusions of (the Western's) mythical thinking.

Even the sexual dimension of the relationship between McCabe and Mrs. Miller shows him at a disadvantage. She concedes to have sex with him from a position of superiority. Although a different kind of relationship between the two has developed, he still must pay like any other customer. That he agrees to this conveys something about his character—in contrast to the role he projects—and his relationship to her.

The illusions surrounding McCabe's public persona are finally destroyed when he tries to negotiate with the leader of the gunmen who have come to kill him. Viewers recognize the latter as an obvious hit man at first glance. He is sparingly characterized by a few external traits: primarily his symbolically oversized weapon, but also his large stature, his dark complexion and clothing with a huge fur coat similar to the one McCabe wore at the beginning, as well as his sparing dialogue. Rooted in power, his taciturn and authoritative bearing exudes the type of control that McCabe would like to imagine for himself.

The trappings of the figure immediately activate the stereotype of the hit man, without this pattern being deconstructed or provided with psychological nuances, in contrast to most other characters. Quite the opposite, the film uses the figure of the professional killer as nothing more than a purely emblematic construction, in the sense elaborated in chapter 7 ("The Stereotype as Intelligible Form"). As a naked allegory, he appears as the executor of evil. The men at his side embody different variations of the pure sidekick: they have the function of enhancing the power and threat of the hit man through their presence.

The killer has no mandate to negotiate and no interest in doing so. He brings McCabe, who now senses the mortal danger and begins to panic, to the point of openly humiliating himself out of fear. From the very beginning, McCabe is in an inferior position in the attempted negotiations. His effort to achieve a dominant, obliging stance by offering a cigar, one of his customary behaviors to impress, fails miserably. By no means the master of the situation anymore, he then destroys his own public image and, as later shown, runs into an open knife. In his attempt to demonstrate submission, he even is willing to give away his possessions, insisting to the killer, and in the presence of the saloon clientele, that the story about Bill Roundtree was nothing more than a legend. All without success.

Not only the stereotypes of the classical male hero and of the complementary female are deconstructed but also are the associated action programs typical of the Western. Altman's film equally dismantles the conventional romance schema that traditionally serves as a secondary plotline in the classic Western and almost all genre films in Hollywood (and elsewhere).

McCabe is the only one to express his emotions in the McCabe–Mrs. Miller relationship, and he does so, not incidentally, at his lowest point, at the moment of existential threat. Just before the film culminates in the final showdown he acknowledges his desire for a real relationship with her, a desire that at this particular moment in the plot seems to come also from a need for solidarity and emotional support.

In contrast to the Western stereotype of the whore with the heart of gold (or, more precisely, the saloon girl with heart, since prostitution is cloaked and symbolically insinuated in the classical Western), Mrs. Miller responds with bitter scorn for his failure. Immediately after being publicly humiliated by the killer, he complains to himself about her coldness and also about how she never allowed him any leeway to dominate, at least sometimes: "I keep tryin' and tryin' to tell ya in a lotta different ways—if just one time you could be sweet without no money around. . . . Can't never say nothing to you! If you'd just one time let me run the show, I'd—freezing' my soul, that's what you're doin', freezin' my soul!"

With "freezin' my soul," McCabe verbalizes the lack of emotion characterizing all the relationships between the main characters and also his own behavior up to the point when his image and force of agency were still intact. There is no trace here of the traditional romance, in which the woman usually assumes the emotional role of articulating an unrealized desire. In a world with no place for any feeling of harmony, the romantic concept of love, the basic formula of any romance, is as absent and indeed absurd as the myths of honor, justice, or solidarity. And if such ideals are presented, they are only clearly recognizable platitudes.

All relationships function as deliberate strategies of economic expedience or power. It is therefore fitting that sexuality is first and foremost a commodity. Once McCabe expresses this lack of human relationship for the first time, after having been ultimately stripped of his projected identity, he dies. And Mrs. Miller, whose actions are a manner of survival, fills the emotional emptiness with an opium high, as she has regularly done before. This is carefully concealed from McCabe throughout.

Finally, McCabe fights by himself for bare survival in the empty setting of the town and the landscape. On the one hand, the thrillingly dramatized showdown constitutes a sequence compatible with the genre, in its dynamically orchestrated tension and narrative function as the conclusion. On the other hand, it is far removed from the classical Western's ritualized form of the open and almost sportsmanlike confrontation on Main Street. In Altman's film, both parties are ambushed from positions of cover by shots in the back (!).

Despite moments of retardation, such as the death of the two first hit men, the narrative precludes us from believing in McCabe's success, through the hidden presence and hence potential ubiquitousness of the gunmen. Even if he were to survive, it would be meaningless in the face of the impersonal, overarching power of the mining company. This is underscored by the film's ending. Instead of a cold-blooded gambler or a fair-minded hero, both character patterns of the Western, we witness a man whose profound loneliness, fear, desperation, and vulnerability are expressed to great psychological effect.

Thus the viewer's attitude toward McCabe enters a third and final phase. Initially, his character was established as a wily, clever gambler with a legendary, even if doubtful, aura who was able to successfully present himself even in the mold of a genre stereotype. Then in the second phase, the central part of the film, the film's character construction was aimed at distant, cool observation. We watch the breakdown of McCabe's role image. Although certain moments evoke a sense of empathy, the film is predominantly inscribed with an observational gaze directed from without—as if onto a world in a bell jar—onto McCabe and the unhappy entanglements with his own self-image.

In the third phase, McCabe reaches his low point. His external role has been destroyed. Publicly and privately humiliated, hopeless and alone, he is confronted by the almost unavoidable threat of death embodied by the gunmen in front of his window, whose superiority and ruthlessness have already long been established. Now the film constructs a viewer perspective on McCabe that one could describe as a natural, almost automatic sense of empathy for a degraded man fighting for pure survival.

In other words, the film projects and then systematically dismantles a stereo-typical Western role in the figure of McCabe. Within the story world, the lack of viability and even lethal danger of the conventional imagination is revealed as *self-deception* in confrontation with reality. In the end, the individual is left stripped of all hope and all masks of assumed roles. Alone, he struggles for bare existence without a real chance. As intended by the dramaturgic concept, it is only now, at the moment of his demise, that McCabe becomes truly accessible to viewer without distanciation.

This only heightens the depressing conclusion. Like all of Altman's films from this period, *McCabe & Mrs. Miller* depicts the individual as a helpless victim of society.[5] The film thereby also exhibits a maximum critical difference to the *optimism* and belief in the power of the individual, which prevail in the classical Western. And Altman polemically draws on a genre whose mythology conveys the settlement of the West as driven by dreams and ideals. What Peter Wollen writes about John Ford's Westerns may, more or less generally, also be applied to the Westerns of the classical period as a whole: "The master antinomy in Ford's films is that between the wilderness and the garden . . . from the wilderness left in the past to the garden anticipated in the future."[6]

Altman's film turns this image into its opposite. The driving forces now appear as the exchange values and power relations that dominate all human relationships. This leads, as emphasized by the plot, to pervasive human coldness, violence, and racism. The latter is demonstrated by, among other things, the inhumane attitude of the white inhabitants of Presbyterian Church toward the Chinese miners in the town. Instead of transforming the wilderness into a garden, a miserable world is replaced by one even worse, the *world of alienation*.

However, in this regard *McCabe & Mrs. Miller* shares one characteristic with the classical Western, even if in an opposing sense: the dimension of fate. The film is a particular example of the type of cinema aesthetically predominant in the 1970s, for which Thomas Elsaesser coined the term "pathos of failure."[7]

In this context, a more symbolic setting than the bordello is hardly conceivable. It is the institution in which alienation—as a result of the commodification of human relationships—is most exemplarily evident. The film presents multiple variations on the theme of human relationships as commodity. A particularly drastic example is John McCabe's purchase of the first three whores prior to his encounter with Mrs. Miller. McCabe treats them like objects.

Not only the bordello but also the institution of marriage is treated as a form of commodified relationships. One town inhabitant, the miner Bart, orders himself a wife by mail. Ida arrives without having seen him and marries him. Searching for a provider, she has no alternative. When Bart is later beaten to death while defending his wife from being compared to a whore, the young widow is ironically forced to actually enter the bordello.

Mrs. Miller uses this occasion to explain that she is essentially doing just what she did in her marriage, earning her keep through sex. In response to Ida's objection that she was performing her conjugal duties with Bart, Mrs. Miller replies: "It wasn't your duty Ida—you did it to pay for your bed and board—and you do this to pay for your bed and board too—only you get to keep a little extra for yourself. . . . You don't have to ask nobody for nothin'—it's more honest, to my mind."

The film proves her right, on the one hand, in showing the previous history of Ida and Bart's marriage and, on the other, in portraying the situation in the whorehouse as an actual improvement. Here, for the first time, she seems cheerful and relaxed.

This turn of events could be seen as a contradiction to the symbolic logic of the bordello as a place of alienation. However, the bordello is simultaneously presented as the place where the exchange value of human relationships is at least not masked by conventional, unreal mythological phrases and self-deception. Also, the action played out in the whorehouse serves as a frontal attack on the classical Western's bourgeois decorum, which is unveiled in absentia as an unreal conventional pose.

That the few fleeting moments of human warmth and closeness conveyed by the film are set precisely in this house of sin can also be understood as an indirect polemic. It is no coincidence that the bordello reformed by Mrs. Miller is visually set apart by its warm colors and lighter tones from the rest of the overwhelmingly dark or (snowy-)cold world of the film.

As demonstrated, in many aspects *McCabe & Mrs. Miller* constructs an opposing image to the imaginary world of the Western. It is therefore not surprising that this confrontation with myth operates and crystallizes on an additional symbolic level in the film.

Already the name of the main setting has inherent symbolism: Presbyterian Church. According to logic of the story world, the town is named after the wooden church that is being built, with its towering, pointed bell tower. The symbolism carried by the church, its varied appearance at different key points in the plot, and its significance in the visual staging suggest a reading of the church as emblematic of the mythologies confronted in the film.

Shown briefly, the construction of the church is carried out by people in bitter need of improving the miserable housing in which they live and spend their time. Why are they building a church? Out of piety? Out of faith, hope, or a feeling of community? Altman consistently avoids anything that might point in this direction. Religion basically plays no role in the daily life of Presbyterian Church. Even the church's completed exterior frame remains unused as a permanent construction site.

The film's only religious act is the burial of the slain Bart. It is made clear that those attending are simply *satisfying convention*. In classical Westerns, funerals are moving scenes, acts of original faith. Philip French describes this in his study of the Western: "Good or bad, a Westerner is entitled to a Christian burial and his passing is marked. That life may be easily taken does not mean that it is cheap and of no significance. Scenes of dying and the rituals of burial on the plains or in the frontier cemeteries abound and constitute some of the most poignant sequences in the genre."[8] Altman's film also undermines this pattern, and worldly misery, the conventional, and even the grotesque are emphasized in the funeral ritual. A small party of miners and whores stand in the mud and rain. A short, conventional prayer is spoken, the saloon fiddler plays a tune, the gathered prostitutes sing "Asleep in Jesus," and Mrs. Miller gives the young widow pointed looks across the open grave to offer her an economic future as a whore.

The church itself is apparently being built, because this too is dictated by convention. As the film clearly communicates, essentially a set is being constructed, a symbol of a myth providing nothing more than an empty ritualistic formula vis-à-vis daily life. A formula and an institution closed to the needs of nonalienated humanity (as with the lawyer's platitudes or the bordello's sexual commodification). Here the church in effect appears as the ultimate symbolic locus of alienation.

The church grows with the modest prosperity of the tiny settlement. When McCabe has bargained for his first three whores as if they were cattle and subsequently rides into town with them, the film links their arrival with a cut to a long, static take of the cross being raised on the top of the bell tower in the setting sun.

Shortly thereafter, when one of the whores goes berserk and attacks a customer with a knife, the latter ends up sprawled on boards, forming the shape of a cross, in a symbolic image that will be repeated later. And when Ida's husband Bart is killed, Altman has the Christmas song "Silent Night" play in the background. Heightening the sarcasm even more, the song has a diegetic—yet symbolic—origin in the previous scene. It sounds from a mechanical music box (which can be read as a reference to the mechanics of the mythical), which plays for the whores and their clients in the bordello.

The repellent institution of myth and the deadly consequences of trusting its imaginary (a motive linked with McCabe's self-deception) are demonstratively enacted in the end, when McCabe is pursued by the hit men and hides in the church so as to espy his pursuers from the tower. Whereas the lawyer sent McCabe—mentally disarmed, so to speak—to his death with platitudes about justice, now the preacher relieves him of his actual weapon, his rifle, by saying that it does not belong in the "House of God." He subsequently forces McCabe, utterly unprotected and unarmed, out into the range of fire.

Despite the preacher's actions, neither he nor the church are spared by the killers. One of McCabe's pursuers shoots the clergyman, thereby setting the church on fire. While none of the inhabitants come to McCabe's aid, they immediately gather to save the church façade and organize attempts to put out the fire. Meanwhile McCabe, already shot, continues his solitary fight and finally sinks, unnoticed and bleeding to death, into the snow. A more radical symbolism is hardly conceivable.

All these observations in sum once again raise the question: Is *McCabe & Mrs. Miller* still a Western? Is it an "outstanding Western,"[9] as it has been called, or a film "rooted in fact"[10]—in contrast to the conventional-imaginary world of the genre—that is therefore more appropriately considered a historically realistic narrative (or its equivalent)?

At first glance, much speaks for the keyword "realism." For in its systematically organized differences to the mythological world of the genre, the film seems to wish to express: Look, this is the abject reality hidden behind by the mythical world of appearances.

This is achieved not only by the film's previously elaborated deviations from the narrative stereotypes of the genre but also through the entire visual design of the mise en scène. The films presents images that have nothing in common with the orchestrated magnificence and exoticism of the southern regions preferred as settings for classical Westerns: no panorama shots showing the sunny expanse of space, none of Monument Valley's flat-topped mountains, no play of clouds over an endless plain, no mail coach or rider romanticism, no tidy arcades of a Main Street populated by pistol-toting men in Stetsons and mild-mannered citizens in city clothing. The West has a different look in Altman. The film thus systematically breaks with conventional visual formulas as it does with role stereotypes.

This is because the film situates its sphere of action in an atypical location: a thickly wooded, rainy northwestern territory in late fall and winter. We are often shown brown-toned places full of mud and murkiness or, as in the showdown, cold scenes in the snow. These images function as "everyday" contrasts to the conventional scenery of Arizona and simultaneously form an external aura of the characters in correspondence with their emotional states. Only sometimes is the beauty of nature employed as a contrast to human-caused misery.

Aside from the showdown, hardly any action is presented in a romantic land-scape. Instead it takes place largely in interiors or (in medium shots) the limited world of the settlement. In this regard, too, the setting of a majority of the action within the bordello suggests a difference. Altogether, the buildings and spaces—and also curious means of transport, such as steam tractors, which appear here in place of the "real" iron horses of the West—in no way correspond to the models customary of the genre.

Sheehan's Saloon, for example, where McCabe first lands, is a rough, improvised space lacking all the "classical" insignia of a saloon, from the long counter in front of a mirrored shelf to the swinging doors. The room is presented in low-key images pervaded by an almost monochrome brown, which enhance a cavelike, labyrinthine impression of the space; the editing is also spatially disorienting. No cowboys, no quirky stereotypical townspeople (such as the "Doc," the coffin maker, the banker, the sheriff, the newspaper editor, and so on), and no saloon girls are to be seen. Instead, the room is populated by a very different kind of all-male society.

The group largely consists of miners, alcoholic, unkempt, and aged beyond their years. These ragged figures are shown in medium close-ups. No one here car-ries a weapon except McCabe, who has one for effect, and no one wears a Stetson. We encounter a *lumpenproletariat* milieu, which demonstratively seems to refer to historical reality instead of the imaginary world of the genre. This makes sense given that the rooms, clothing, and types were supposedly modeled on historical photographs from proletarian and subproletarian settings in the West.

However, the term "realism" has limited relevance in describing *McCabe & Mrs. Miller*. It is precisely *not* the intention of the film to explore the "real" histori-cal West and thereby tell a "realistic" story far removed from and untouched by the stereotype world of the genre. The film precludes radical notions of realism and clearly does not adhere to the prescription that Siegfried Kracauer articulated in his *Theory of Film*, to (inductively) investigate physical reality from the bottom up with the camera and trace the flow of life.

But even in another less phenomenological or ontological sense, the emphasis suggested by the idea of realism seems to provide only a limited degree of clarity in this context.

For Thomas Elsaesser, Altman was "a realist, even if of the didactic-satirical sort. Making cinema for Altman is to construct machines—social not ontological—for the exploration of reality."[11] This may be valid, but only in an extremely indirect manner, for the primary aim of this film—an aim even more pronounced in the second film analyzed here, *Buffalo Bill and the Indians*—is *not* the "exploration of reality" but is instead a *critical commentary* on the mythology of the Western and the critical deconstruction of the conventional, imaginary stereotype world of the genre, but in reference to a reality conceived as a world of alienation. The accent is placed, however, on a criticism of mythology and the stereotype system of the genre. Classifications of the film as an "anti-Western,"[12] a "revisionist Western,"[13] or, more precisely, a "genre-commentary film"[14] make reference to this.

This also means that the film basically does not function without the audience's generic knowledge, to which the film is symbiotically bound. In attempting to sketch an artistic-intellectual auteur profile of Altman, Neil Feineman mentions "Altman's unparalleled use of stereotypes"[15] as one of the director's signature traits.

At key points in the plot, *McCabe & Mrs. Miller* explicitly introduces largely intact stereotypes of the genre. Again, one recalls the hit men as allegories of evil. To an even greater extent the film implicitly and indirectly summons these patterns in absentia. In other words, the stereotype repertoire of the Western genre serves as a foil and structural context of reference. Even if large portions of the film treat stereotypes antithetically and criticize them (particularly personal stereotypes) as false or dangerous images and ideas, the approach and visuals of the film only unfold their complex meaning if perceived as *antithetical* to the stereotype world of the genre. Drawing on the historical sequence of preceding Westerns, Altman's film substantially operates with this *quality of difference*.

But also when the film clearly displays references to historical reality, which it does by no means consistently, these forms of reference are subordinate to the overarching strategy of a discourse working against the genre. The same *deconstructive games* occur with Western stereotypes implemented less in terms of critique than pure play.

There are many such deconstructive games in the film. For example, after Bart's burial, where McCabe is warned of the mining company's probable revenge, an unknown rider suddenly appears before him. He carries a pistol in a holster. Silhouetted against the sky in a shot filmed slightly from below, the rider is introduced in an almost classical manner: a visual stereotype. Together with McCabe we immediately fear the awaited arrival of a killer, but after the conventional situation builds to the point of McCabe reaching for his gun, at the last minute the situation reveals itself as a "red herring," as Hitchcock would say, and the rider turns out to be a harmless future bordello customer. There follows an immediate cut to the arrival—initially unnoticed by McCabe—of the real killers! Seen as a whole, such playful tricks are part of the film's strategy as a critical commentary on the genre.

Despite all its criticism of mythical content, *McCabe & Mrs. Miller* is by no means a radical departure from the *principal structures* of filmic narrative, which are characteristic of classical storytelling. Feineman calls it a transitional film that, in contrast to Altman's later work, still predominantly relies on traditional modes of narration.

Supporting this is the film's dense, mostly causal and linear plot structure, with the presentation of a conflict, a resolution, and highpoints of tension, with few loose ends or open-ended meanings. On a macrostructural level, the plot construction is clearly framed and contained by the arrival of McCabe at the beginning and his death at the end. The film creates an overarching tension of sorts with skillfully calculated culminating points, particularly in the final act.

On the microstructural level of episodic segments, there are hardly any elements—apart from a few surface details still to be discussed—that do not contribute to the central idea. This becomes particularly clear in the treatment of supporting characters. Ida, the lawyer, and the preacher are all *functional characters* less in terms of propelling the main storyline, as in the classical Western, but more in terms of presenting an argument for a specific worldview. In situations serving to present such an ideology, even the handed-down stereotypes of the genre are left intact, as in the case of the hit man.

But formal aspects of the film exhibit certain differences to the genre's conventional narrative mode. There are three particularly notable tendencies.

First, although the narrative is largely closed and contained, at specific moments the film loosens the strict causality of images and events. Marginal observations, which have little immediate relevance for advancing plot, character motivation, or the explication of a worldview, have greater significance than in classical cinema. They form the periphery of the actual plotline and create a particularly evocative sense of reality, because they are not directly imbedded in the causality or symbolism of the plot.

Here are two examples. When McCabe travels to a neighboring town in order to buy the three prostitutes, the camera (in losing McCabe) presents a long take of a man selling hot potatoes. This is neither a symbolic commentary on the action, nor does it have any other significance for the further plot development. Instead the camera independently conveys an impression of a relatively unrelated action and thereby achieves a kind of documentary effect. A barman in Sheehan's Saloon who only takes part in two conversations functions in a similar manner: first, in wondering aloud to a guest whether he should shave off his beard and, second, once he has shaved it off, in asking for the guest's opinion.

Second, Altman conspicuously employs music in a different way than is customary in traditional Westerns and classical genre cinema as a whole. He forgoes all the tunes conventional to the genre. The only extradiegetic film music is the song fragments sung by Leonard Cohen to the guitar, which are inserted from time to time. The lyrics comment on the story, lending it a gentle touch of irony. Their ballad-like character enhances an atmosphere in keeping with the *pathos of failure*. Apart from a few diegetic instances of music, such as the sarcastic use of "Silent Night" when Bart is killed or the sound of the saloon fiddle, the film employs no additional music. Thus, the principle of difference operates on this level too, for it is almost impossible to imagine a classical Western without the emotional effect of a score. Even Italo-Westerns relied on music, certainly noticeably altered compared to that of classical films and employed to evoke, if anything, even stronger emotional responses. In contrast, lasting for over a quarter of an hour, even the major showdown in Altman's film manages to completely forgo any musical dramatization.

Third, some of the editing differs from classical narration. Although major dialogues are broken down into conventional shot/countershot patterns, other situations clearly depart from this classical principle. By no means does the montage always create clear spatial relationships; leaps in time in longer, elliptical phases are barely marked as such (especially in the beginning, before the arrival of Mrs. Miller), and above all, the image-sound editing is sometimes unorthodox. Sound, and spoken dialogue in particular, is carried over from one image to the next, a technique well outside classical sound bridges. This in part serves as ironic commentary and in part gives the impression of apparent disorganization and randomness. A further consideration may have been an aspect of reflexivity regarding the technical devices of film, which are therefore not kept completely "invisible."[16]

Nevertheless, despite the film's aberration from the content of (Western) genre film—indeed its critical reflection thereof—and the detailed, formal discrepancies just described, *McCabe & Mrs. Miller* preserves the principle structures of "classical" narration. In later works, Altman would go decidedly further, particularly in *Nashville* (1975) and in his second film from the 1970s to deal with the mythology of the Western, *Buffalo Bill and the Indians*. This latter film noticeably intensified both the deconstruction of conventional generic narratives—of myths or stereotypes—as well as the critical discourse about them, and it now also used the underlying conventional structures of narration to serve this demolition.

THE CRITIQUE OF MYTH PRODUCTION:
BUFFALO BILL AND THE INDIANS

Like McCabe, Buffalo Bill is another character whose self-presentation as a Western figure blurs his self-perception. However, in the 1976 film this theme is heightened and articulated more explicitly than in 1971 and now sharpened by a shift in perspective. Buffalo Bill is a figure who, unlike McCabe, is not developed as a victim of the mythic imagination but as one who plays an active role in the mechanisms that produce mythic stereotypes, with—at least commercial— success. Disturbances in self-perception caused by his role not only affect him as the leading character of the narrative but society as a whole. As portrayed in this film, due to the interests of power, status, and money as well as their resulting dependencies, society appears to be adverse to and subsequently *incapable* of distinguishing between mythic imagination and reality.

Here, too, at the center of the film is a critique of the mythological system of the Western as false consciousness and, above all, of the mechanisms leading to its production and distribution. Narratives and stereotypes from the genre are overtly displayed as media creations, which essentially have nothing to do with historical reality. But in contrast to the postmodern perspective, Altman's film is unable to garner any enjoyment from these circumstances. Instead, his biting criticism outlines the relationships between myth production, the economic dynamics of mass-cultural production, and the need for an ideology glorifying Western expansion and the Indian Wars.

Unlike in *McCabe & Mrs. Miller*, this film does not spotlight a no-name gambler projecting himself as a big-time player but instead depicts a popular figure of Western mythology: the legendary Buffalo Bill, a man whom the pubic had deemed a major, although indeed largely imaginary, figure and who had a claim to authenticity in his person and actions, at least in terms of his original story.

With Buffalo Bill, Altman chose a figure modeled on a historical personality, a former army scout in the Indian Wars of the last third of the nineteenth century, who already before the turn of the century began to produce and economically capitalize on his image as a hero in a large, successful Wild West Show.

The historical Buffalo Bill, actually William Frederick Cody, propagated an image of himself as an original man of the West, a frontier's man between the world of the Indians, on the one hand, and that of the new, white settlers as well as the army, on the other. His loyalty rested with the army. However, he knew and understood the Indians better than most commanders and tried to diffuse unnecessary conflict and domesticate the Indians in a less violent manner. However, in military disputes he understood how to respond more efficiently. This much may be said of the mythic image corresponding to the basic structure of the classical Western hero, a character who is on the "right" side but who fascinates by bringing together elements of the two worlds in conflict.[17]

Buffalo Bill was an early media figure. Already in 1894 he was so popular that he was filmed for Edison's Kinetoscope.[18] Newspaper reports and stories from the Indian Wars and the period thereafter contributed to this popularity, but most significant was the Wild West Show he founded, a mixture of a circus and the new institution of the ethnographic exhibition, which was popular around 1900 in the colonial era.

His rise to a classical figure of cinema began with the first appearances of Buffalo Bill, or his show, in early film. From 1897 through the late 1910s, a regular production of short films showed images from the Wild West Show and parades of the show's troupes, or they intended to "document" his deeds, as in *The Adventures of Buffalo Bill* (1917). Later played by an actor, the figure enjoyed a subsequent career of appearances in numerous feature films up through the 1950s, including *In the Days of Buffalo Bill* (Edward Laemmle, 1922), *Buffalo Bill on the U. P. Trail* (Frank S. Mattison, 1926), or the twelve-part silent film series *Fighting with Buffalo Bill* (Ray Taylor, 1926; book by William F. Cody). This development was additionally furthered by the success of the episodes of his 1928 autobiography,[19] which was so successful that it was translated into numerous languages and overshadowed an earlier biography supposedly written by his sister.[20]

At least from this point on, the figure of Buffalo Bill belonged to the popular repertoire of the cinematic Western. This included films displaying his name in the title, such as the, also twelve-part series, this time with sound, *Battling with Buffalo Bill* (Ray Taylor, 1931), the films *Young Buffalo Bill* (Joseph Kane, 1940), *Days of Buffalo Bill* (Thomas Carr, 1946), *Buffalo Bill Rides Again* (Bernard Ray, 1947), or the fifteen-episode series *Riding with Buffalo Bill* (Spencer Gordon Bennet, 1954). There were also films that did not mention him directly or feature him prominently in the storyline but that still place him at center stage, such as Cecil B. DeMille's epic Western *The Plainsman* (1936) or *Pony Express* (Jerry Hopper, 1953), to name but two examples.

A particularly striking exemplar of the canonical presentation of the figure is William A. Wellman's *Buffalo Bill* (1936). It is structured as his biography, beginning with his heroic deeds in the West. The initial sequence is typical in how it brings together all the constitutive elements of the stereotype to which the figure adheres.

The sequence begins with images of a buffalo herd, first in a medium and then in a long shot of an expansive western landscape. A voice-over mentions the name of the not yet visible hero, as the voice describes, the champion of young and old, rich and poor, whose story the film tells. Furiously choreographed images follow of an Indian attack on a stagecoach. The Indians shoot at the coach and its four white passengers, an old sergeant in uniform, the coachman, two other men, and a young woman in urban dress. The coach turns over in a curve. With the sergeant's revolver as their only weapon, the four passengers take cover behind the overturned coach from the superior Indian force. Suddenly a close shot shows the barrel of a rifle protruding from a bush on a cliff above. The shots it fires drive away the attackers. Accompanied by rising, anthemic (extradiegetic) music, a rider, obviously the shooter, shown slightly from below, appears above on the cliff—unmistakably the entrance of the hero, in keeping with the stereotype. Of course, the old sergeant immediately recognizes the legendary rider and introduces him: Buffalo Bill.

Senator Frederici and his daughter, two of the travelers, thank him politely for their rescue.

SENATOR: We need more men like you to exterminate these savages. They must be wiped out, root and branch.

BUFFALO BILL: There are some white men that need wiping out.

SENATOR: I don't understand you, sir.

BUFFALO BILL (POINTING TO AN INDIAN ARROW): This is not a war arrow, it's a hunting arrow, and no barbs . . . I mean that those were Agency Indians crazy drunk on white man's whiskey.

SENATOR'S DAUGHTER (SARCASTICALLY): I suppose that excuses them, out here!

BUFFALO BILL: Well, the red man and whiskey don't mix, ma'am.

The sergeant then assigns the five people to the two mules and Buffalo Bill's horse. The senator's daughter insists on riding together with Bill on his horse, to which the sergeant concedes with a smile and Bill with pleasure. After Bill skillfully jumps onto the back of his horse, where the young lady has already taken her place, they ride away. This concludes both the opening sequence as well as the filmic establishment of the hero.

At this early point in the film, the brief dialogue makes things clear, even in the unlikely case that a viewer of 1944 did not yet know Bill. He is shown to be a man who acts as a cultural mediator between the world of the Indians and the world of the approaching civilization of the whites. He takes a stand against those behaving irresponsibly toward the Indians, either out of ignorance or greed of gain. However, Bill's actions simultaneously show that he clearly belongs to the world of the whites and that he will fight for them if it comes down to it—and also that in such fights he can shoot better and act in a superior and fairer manner than others. Finally, the little episode of accompanying the young lady on his horse not only unambiguously points to the initiation of the film's romance but also to Buffalo Bill as a *gallant hero*.

This outlines the precise pattern that essentially dominates all classical Westerns dealing with Buffalo Bill and that is then carried through the structure of Wellman's film. After the conflicts in the West and a twist of fate that undeservedly leads to Bill's fall from grace, at the end one sees him triumph once again: as the master of the Wild West Show. Here he is celebrated by simple audiences as well as American presidents and the crowned heads of Europe, all of whom are shown sitting in the grandstand, one after the other, in a highly accelerated montage sequence. The film ends in a sentimental apotheosis: wearing a white glamour outfit and riding through the arena on a white horse, Buffalo Bill takes leave of his audience.

Wellman's film presents the filmic or narrative world of myth and stereotypes encompassing the hero in almost pure form. Exactly where this film ends, Altman's begins: in the Wild West Show. But whereas in 1944 Bill's life and deeds in the West formed the core of the plot, and the show enters the picture only at the end in an accelerated sequence lasting no more than three minutes, Altman's *Buffalo Bill and the Indians* takes place solely within the setting of the Wild West Show.

This shift in focus corresponds to a completely different interest in the figure and its world of myth. The beginning of the film already marks this change. Altman uses an artistic device typical of many autothematic films, namely, *a surprising shift in the diegetic status* of the initial images.

As our experience with Westerns tells us, we are presented with apparent images of a U.S. Army fort in Indian territory. A military bugle sounds and a standard is raised. A text in historical lettering appears across the screen: "Robert Altman's Absolutely Unique and Heroic Enterprise of Inimitable Lustre!" Then the framing of the image shifts, and with a slowly panning long shot the sequence shot first shows a distant mountain chain and then, more toward the foreground, a little log cabin surrounded by cattle fences. In the next moment, the peaceful white settlers are attacked by a wild horde of Indians on horseback. As in Wellman's film, Altman inserts a voice-over. Just like the preceding text, the speaker directly addresses us as viewers in a historicizing tone recalling both the classical voice-over as well as announcers at funfairs and the circus: "Ladies and Gentlemen, your attention please. What you are about to experience is not a show for entertainment. It is a review of the down-to-earth events that made the American frontier." After this verbal glorification of "the anonymous settler" and the hard, dangerous existence on the frontier, the voice-over continues: "Welcome then, to real events enacted by the men and women of the American frontier, to whose courage, strength, and above all their faith this piece of our history is dedicated." Once again imposed over the film images, a medallion with the portrait of Buffalo Bill, the main title, and the film credits follow. Immediately thereafter one hears a clearly diegetic voice from off screen shouting: "Cease the action! From the beginning, one, two . . . " Meanwhile, the camera position has shifted upward and the frame of the image has widened to reveal that the previous events involving the settlers and the attack are, in contrast to first assumptions, part of a choreographed show, or rather, a show rehearsal taking place within the diegetic world of the film. In retrospect, this also changes the status of the voice-over. Although there is no palpable change in tone, the perception of the voice-over alternates between a classical voice-over, the film's narrative voice ("Robert Altman's . . . Enterprise"), and the voice of the announcer in the diegetic show, or in other words, between discourse and story-world.

This opening makes a dual reference. First, it indicates that the film does not present the world of the West, or more precisely, the world of Western narratives directly but instead as a staged show within the diegesis. The film does not relate the myth but tells of the production and exploitation of the myth in the Wild West Show it presents. The winter quarters where the troupe rehearses and also puts on shows is thus introduced, and this will remain the setting of the entire film. The Wild West Show can be read as a metaphor for other institutions dedicated to the dissemination of myth, including the Western film. The subject matter of the film has a largely *reflexive* function.

At the same time, the initial deception regarding the status of the images and the alternation of the voice-over between discourse and story announces a deeper underlying motif of the film. Having been repeatedly told and accompanied by established stereotypes, the narrative discourses and the repetitively sedimented plot worlds they present have subsumed all remnants of reality. This is one of the film's basic ideas. Even when it becomes clear that key moments of the narrative are not based on fact, the characters of the story do not seem able to accurately distinguish between mythic imagination and reality. The mythical narrative of the West and its dramatization have supplanted reality. The participants' awareness oscillates between both of these spheres, much in the way the voice-over alternates between story and discourse. The narrative confusion caused at the beginning of the film is carried forward. Through such manipulations, Altman obviously wants to reflexively draw spectators into the blurring of levels. And he seems to indicate that in this world hardly anything is what it seems.

Contrary to the ironic claims of the voice-over, Altman's film is not concerned with a reconstruction of "real events" nor of the Wild West Show. Instead, it strives to serve as an exemplary revelation of the power and dynamics as well as the fragility of myth and its constitutive stereotypes. With its initial sequences, the film immediately addresses how the existence of mythic narratives depends more on the interests of the narrator and the predispositions of the narratees than on reality, that they in fact replace reality.

A standard figure of the Buffalo Bill narrative comes into play here, the writer Ned Buntline. In Wellman's film, he plays his customary role as a journalistic reporter of Cody's heroic acts and later his friend. In Altman's film, he has meanwhile been excluded from show business and pushed to the sidelines. Buntline still hangs around the show's quarters and tells of how he *invented* the figure of Buffalo Bill and his deeds through the journalistic stories he once wrote and how he helped the utterly insignificant William Cody, a thin little fellow, establish both his name and his aura as a Western hero through his now legendary acts.

A scene follows immediately with an older man in a sergeant's uniform, as in the opening of Wellman's film. He tells children visiting the winter quarters of the show that he had once encountered the great buffalo hunter Cody in the West and that *he himself* had given Cody the nickname *Buffalo Bill*. This doubling of contradictory information indicates from the beginning that one may not believe any of the stories told in the film's diegetic world.

The film consequently places great value on depicting the discrepancy between the orchestrated mythological stereotype of Bill and his pathetic reality. But it also raises questions about the economic forces behind the production of myth. Even before Bill first appears on screen, his voice is heard from the diegetic offstage of an adjacent room. His first statements are about securing his economic interests: "Remember, anything historical is mine."

Almost simultaneously, one learns during a close shot of glasses accompanied by Buntline's commentary that Bill is an alcoholic and drinks a tankard of whiskey a day. Up to this point, Buffalo Bill himself is only visually present as a painting in his living quarters, in which he strikes a pose recalling the end of Wellman's film: waving triumphantly on a rearing white horse.

Then comes his grand entrance, a show entrance on horseback—introduced by the superlatives of a loudspeaker voice—including the same pose. The "real" Bill enters the scene as playing out a prefigured schema. There could hardly be a greater difference between the staged stereotype and what the viewer now knows about Bill's off-show persona.

Whereas this is also to be understood as a rehearsal for a number in the show, as in the opening scene, his second grand appearance ultimately blurs the line between the staged show and the everyday routine in the troupe's winter quarters. A group of Indians previously interred by the army arrive. They are headed by Sitting Bull, who is to serve as the next season's new attraction. Although no audience is present, their reception is orchestrated like a show number and simultaneously treated as a historic event. Buffalo Bill appears before Sitting Bull on horseback and with two riders holding a banner bearing his name above him. His entrance is announced by loudspeaker and accompanied by (diegetic) marching music. Such mingling of the theatrical show and the off-show world of the winter quarters, which reoccurs later in a number of ways, is a variation of the previously described alternation between two spheres of "reality." All of this recalls the diegetic logic of many a film musical.

Although the discrepancy between the image and the reality of Buffalo Bill is almost grotesquely illustrated and, indeed, overtly caricaturized, this does not matter to the show people or to Bill himself. He repeatedly proves himself incapable of living up to his reputation. He is unable to find the disappeared Sitting Bull or, in a tantrum, to shoot a bird in a cage, instead firing wildly into the air around him. But this does not bother anyone. The power of myth—and all participants' tangible interest in maintaining it—seem so immense that for them myth and reality coincide. The self-deception that McCabe suffered from is here presented as a model case of systematic, collective autosuggestion.

Only occasionally do individual characters reflect on what they are doing. For example, Nate, the manager of the Wild West Show, announces in a play on Bill's given name of Cody: "I going to codify the world." Only Ned Buntline, fired from the show, is assigned a consistent, reflexive external position, motivated by his role as an outsider. His statements not only apply to the diegetic show but also indirectly to cinema as a mythmaking machine. Thus, one of his rhetorical questions directly aims at the phenomenon of self-deception: "That's why stars spend so much time in front of the mirror. Seeing if their good looks and word delivery can overcome their judgment. . . . A star like Buffalo Bill Cody makes a judgment. It becomes a commitment. It's got to stick no matter what the risk."

A reverse angle shows us Cody in front of a mirror as he autosuggestively practices phrases of an explanation intended to justify how Sitting Bull could first give him the slip and then reappear without Bill having done anything. Instead of acknowledging the humiliation, he practices empty phrases: "I am generous and flexible." And, in fact, his failure does not affect his reputation in the troupe.

"From the beginning"—this sentence, a diegetic stage direction called out at the beginning of the film immediately following the credits, spotlights the film's focus on the phenomenon of repetition early on. The importance of repetition—the basis of stereotypization—for the functioning of the collective imagination is repeatedly emphasized in a reflexive manner. Bill clearly articulates this in a dialogue with Ned Buntline at the end of the film.

NED: You ain't changed, Bill.

BILL: I ain't supposed to. That's why people pay to see me.

NED: Well, this has been the most sobering experience I've ever had. Damn near religious awakening.

Altman's film makes clear that the Wild West Show's repeated claim of "authenticity" is grounded in nothing more than the assimilation of stereotypes through repetition.

But the principle of repetition simultaneously has a different function in the film, namely, as a principle of storytelling. Altman seems to express his rejection of the mythological world of the Western and his critical metaposition not only by deconstructing the stereotypes of the Western but also by refusing to comply with the genre's fundamental narrative structures. Here he departs from such structures to a far greater degree than in *McCabe & Mrs. Miller*. There are three significant aspects to be considered in this context.

First, classical genre films are ultimately based on a linear, causal "fabula," which recipients are able to interpolate from the altered timeframe of the "syuzhet," or plot, as David Bordwell describes.[21] In their narrative presentation of the syuzhet, these films emphasize an interest in a sequence of events, for example, by building and relieving tension in cycles coordinated with the overarching plot development of the whole film. This form of linearity is largely suspended in *Buffalo Bill and the Indians*. The viewers are denied an overarching main tension. Instead, the plot unfolds in individual episodic complexes not embedded within comprehensive causal chains. Whereas the syuzhet does not completely suspend the temporal progression of the conveyed events, the action is nevertheless not sequentially constructed so as to gradually proceed toward the resolution of one or two linked major challenges, which in the Western can take the form of the fight against a threat, for example. More important than generating tension and developing a fabula seems to be the unfolding of a certain image of the central character and the society surrounding him through the presentation of a series of situations. A certain degree of coherency is achieved in that individual situations repeat, vary, and expand on certain basic ideological motifs—such as the difference between image and reality or the blurring of different levels. Virtually symbolic of this structure, which uses the principle of intratextual repetition as a means of encircling an idea, are the repeating circular movements of the acrobats and Buffalo Bill in the arena of the Wild West Show, which can be interpreted as an allegory of the mechanism of the myth-producing apparatus.

Second, this rejection of linearity and suspense corresponds to the mosaic-like quality of the narration and its visual design. Although Buffalo Bill is the thematic focus of the narrative as the title character, the way the story is told through a number of revealing individual observations tends toward a decentralized complex of an ensemble cast, through which a portrait of a group or society is rendered.[22] On a visual level, this is reflected in the tableau-like shots and sequence shots filled with people. Often the camera does not focus on the character speaking but instead unconventionally pans away and focuses on objects shown in large close-up. It follows the movements of individuals and often also entire groups or turns away from them, whereby particularly in outdoor scenes the zoom is often used to additionally alter the framing. Altman's "special way of using camera movement in combination with zooms and actor movements,"[23] as Barry Salt describes Altman's films of the 1970s, is particularly apparent.

Third, this effect is further enhanced by Altman's use of (in comparison with classical films) unconventional editing techniques of image and sound. Whereas in *McCabe & Mrs. Miller* he only sparingly employed overlapping dialogue that was carried over into the visual transition to the next scene, he now uses this technique extensively. This not only includes retaining the sound of one scene when shifting to the next but also a number of sentences from the dialogue of a subsequent scene are laid over the previous one. Additionally, there is Altman's preference for multichannel recordings, which are mixed to allow multiple on-screen dialogues to overlap at certain moments and enable different characters to speak almost simultaneously.[24] This all produces a complicated fabric displaying a clear difference to the centralized focus of attention in classical genre films.

Not only because of these fundamental differences vis-à-vis the narrative mode of genre cinema, the popularity of Altman's film was understandably limited. Some critics faulted the film for failing to provide characters that the audience could feel an affinity to or "identify" with. But this was the price of creating aesthetic difference and radically critiquing stereotypes. Altman obviously intended just this: to suspend any form of identification and make the role of the hero itself transparent as an imaginary stereotype construct and to critically illuminate the mechanisms behind the construction of the hero.

It has already been mentioned that, from a different perspective, Gilles Deleuze criticized Altman's films from this period: in Altman's work the "apparatus" of genre cinema that produced the "action-image" "extends itself, but becomes empty and starts to grate . . . content to parody the cliché instead of giving birth to a new image."[25] Deleuze calls for nothing less than "an aesthetic and political project capable of constituting a positive enterprise."[26] In other words, a concept transcending genre stereotypes, an aesthetic utopia.

Altman's *Buffalo Bill and the Indians* does in fact provide, more explicitly than *McCabe & Mrs. Miller*, *a reflexive cinema critiquing the stereotypes of generic cinema*, particularly the Western. Even while taking this aesthetic difference as far as possible, the film naturally remains symbiotically attached to its subject matter, the stereotype world of the genre. Deleuze is right in this respect. However, it addresses the mechanisms that lead to the production and success of mythical stereotype worlds, and in doing so he goes far beyond simple parody. Both of these films, like his work in the 1970s as a whole, are part of the same project: an ideological critique of the illusions created by medial stereotypes. This is a project that also shaped theoretical discourses during this period, including those of film theory.

TEN

ENJOYING THE STEREOTYPE AND INTENSE DOUBLE-PLAY ACTING: THE PERFORMANCE OF JENNIFER JASON LEIGH IN *THE HUDSUCKER PROXY*

The nostalgia film was never a matter of some old-fashioned "representation" of historical content, but instead approached the "past" through stylistic connotation, conveying "pastness" by the glossy qualities of the image . . . connotation as the purveying of imaginary and stereotypical idealities.

—FREDRIC JAMESON, *POSTMODERNISM; OR, THE CULTURAL LOGIC OF LATE CAPITALISM* (1996)

Within the scope of classical-realist theories of film acting, much has been written about rolling back conventional patterns and acting stereotypes. These attracted particular resentment when they became all too obvious, either because as conventional acting patterns they clearly departed from corresponding everyday patterns of behavior, or because they seemed overly accentuated or vulgarized, or because they no longer seemed "truly felt" but were rather used in a masklike, symbolic, or even mechanical manner. Often all of these aspects together became a source of criticism.

Originating from the stage, realist theories of acting are not a novelty of film. Stanislavski's concept was simply one of the most influential theories of its kind. The reason that film-acting theories drew so readily on the realist tradition is because the mainstream was primarily interested in imaginations presented as verisimilitudinous, and on the part of many cineastes there was an interest in the *redemption of physical reality* (Kracauer). In contrast to the theater, the unique qualities of film did in fact offer new possibilities of intimate acting, which, based on subtle signs and nuances, seemed to forgo the criticized stereotypes.

Only a few critics of realism addressed its acceptance of conventional forms of acting. Herbert Jhering's contribution has already been discussed (in part I) as an example of a dialectical view of the acting stereotype. "If the cliché is infused with personal energies, then it ceases to be such and becomes the necessary freedom of the creative artist."[1] So reads his core statement. Here the stereotype seems to be an acceptable and constitutive factor of acting, and he is interested in how stereotypes are suspended when one is in the thrall of a creative individual and how they are renaturalized and reclaimed to enable the authentic expression of the actor.

In addition to the radical critique of the stereotype and the numerous strains of realist theory, there were also traditions of acting that did not attempt to conceal acting as such or the use of conventional forms—forms of acting not denying or hiding their artificial character or their inherent play with a given repertoire but that reveal and display these elements. These modes of acting, which, as opposed to the psychological-realist art of acting, can be described in terms of "performance," have gained significance in the more recent films generally labeled as *postmodern*. Unlike Robert Altman's films from the 1970s, this cinema not only has no problem with stereotypes but actually reflects the patterns found within a given genre or the history of the medium in a celebratory manner. And it does so with the same verve of Altman's former critique.

There are many variations of the revelation of stereotypes. A primary one is acting within acting, which still bridges realistic acting. A character is played, who is in turn playing a role, whereby in strictly realistic cinema only indications of this secondary role, that is, that of the diegetic character, are revealed. This is an interesting task for actors, since it calls for an inner split of the character. However, other variations clearly transcend the limits of the realistic tradition: grotesquely comical acting, for example, which systematically overdoes certain outrageous ticks and often displays (as in slapstick) the uncontrollable mechanics of stereotypical sequences of expressions or movements. Or stylization through accentuated, repeated poses and finally the disruption of empathy through the split between the actor and the role in the sense of Brechtian techniques of estrangement (*Verfremdung*). James Naremore has enumerated and elaborated all of these techniques.[2] What he does not discuss in depth, however, is a variation of performance that, although not fundamentally new, has proven to be particularly important in the cinema of the last decade: the play with historical reminiscences, the emphasis on intertextual recall of historical acting stereotypes. Even acting styles thus become connotative of the imaginary's past.

Watching Jennifer Jason Leigh in her roles, one soon notices that she is an actress for whom the emphasis on *acting as acting* and the emblematic use of repeating forms have special significance. Her role in *The Hudsucker Proxy* (Joel and Ethan Coen, 1994) is an example of performative recourse to historical acting patterns. Leigh and especially her appearance in this film therefore deserve closer scrutiny.

AN EMPHASIS ON PLAYING
WITH THE ACTOR'S REPERTOIRE

Jennifer Jason Leigh, born in 1962 in Hollywood, began her career as an actress in film and television productions in the early 1980s, when she was about twenty years old. Since then she has made an extensive series of notable film appearances,[3] including no small number of leading roles, especially since the 1990s. In other words, today Leigh is a recognized actress, but she is not a star in a narrower sense of the word. This has to do with the types of roles she plays, her specialization in characters not readily accommodated by popular ideals. Although often central characters in their respective films, they are never characters that invite straightforward identification.[4] Neither the "pretty woman," the "erotic dream," nor the wholesome "girl next door" intended to win the sympathies of the audience are part of her on-screen image. Although still youthful, even early on in her career she embodied characters not given to happy and uncomplicated symbolism. At the same time, the range of her roles is remarkably broad and varied. She typically performs her parts with excessive abandon, often without fearing ugliness—indeed sometimes priding in the ugly. As unique and incisive as Leigh's characters appear, one might cautiously generalize that her obvious specialty are women with some sort of defect. As viewers, we are affected by her performance but always from a perspective similar to analytical distance; her characters appear as if under glass.

These women often seem tortured and in a bad mood, depressed and aggressive. They gesticulate dismissively and curse obnoxiously, unsatisfied with their lives but hardly able to extricate themselves from their palpable dilemmas. They also display destructive traits that are almost impossible to control and sometimes directed against themselves. But one could never describe them as women who accept their lot and surrender, at least not before they are finally broken. They defiantly put up a fight and try to dominate the men around them, at least verbally and in gesture. In general, they tend to assume a position of superiority in their dealings with others, or they try, though sometimes ineffectually, to take on this pose. However, this attitude is connected with flashes of insight into their private lives, the fragility and loneliness hidden behind all the assertiveness.

Putting on an act of superiority seems particularly fitting when Leigh plays the part of the confident, emancipated intellectual: for example, the initially self-assured and celebrated computer expert Allegra Geller in *eXistenZ* (David Cronenberg, 1999) or the writer Dorothy Parker in *Mrs. Parker and the Vicious*

Circle (Alan Rudolph, 1994), who manages to achieve success in a male society—thereby revealing an ambition taken to the point of egocentric cynicism—but increasingly experiences an inner emptiness.

However, social outsiders are also part of her core repertoire: the harbor prostitute Tralala in Uli Edel's *Last Exit to Brooklyn* (West Germany/USA, 1989); Sadie, the desperate little bar singer in *Georgia* (Ulu Grosbard, 1995); the phone-sex operator Lois in Robert Altman's *Short Cuts* (1993); or the wannabe hardened gun-toting Blondie O'Hara in *Kansas City* (Robert Altman, 1996). Even coming from a socially inferior position, these female characters are marked by their will to assert themselves at all costs. This is expressed in an overtly displayed air of superiority toward the men who desire them, an attitude often verging on contempt. This gesture of dominance often seems *clearly recognizable as an assumed mask* concealing desperation or emptiness, and even the ambition to dominate is itself felt to be the result of a precarious inner state. This drive for the upper hand combined with the masking of other emotions and a sense of desperation repeatedly borders on the psychotic. Leigh took this attitude to the extreme as Hedra Carlson, who, driven by extreme jealousy, tyrannizes the woman sharing her apartment with diabolical brutality in *Single White Female* (Barbet Schroeder, 1992).

Her tendency to play characters of such psychologically extreme conditions, in a kind of self-masking that does and should remain transparent, as a variation of the role-within-the-role, seems to be part of Leigh's special acting skills. Rarely do we experience her in parts characterized by moderate moods or tones. Neutral behavior combined with reserved gestures, as in daily life, are almost completely absent in her acting. She tends to swing between sharply accentuated extremes. As the prostitute Tralala, she shifts almost seamlessly from a flood of high-pitched curses and bitter sarcasm, on the one hand, to a fragility revealing sadness and even desperation, on the other. She unifies these two states through a marked mask of feigned indifference clearly articulated as the social façade of the prostitute. Similar alternations between extremes played in overtly harsh tones is the mark of most of her major performances.

In keeping with her disposition to such accentuations, Leigh seldom speaks or acts without carrying out multiple and precisely calculated symbolic gestures. The film *Georgia* is a good example. At the low point, the unhappy Sadie, wracked by alcohol and drugs and close to breakdown, tries to buy a ticket at an airline counter for her flight home. Oscillating between helplessness and aggression, she leans across the counter and berates the airline employee; garish facial expressions (in medium close-up) accompany spastic hand gestures. Similarly drastic performances, demonstrating Leigh's ability convey a panoply of ugliness, can be seen in *Last Exit to Brooklyn* and *Single White Female*.

However, she also exhibits this tendency of strained gesture in less dramatic scenes, in which this inclination is subdued for a few moments in favor of a quieter, less forced mode of acting. For example, at the end of *Georgia* the character is marked by an atypical, obviously unusual state with moments of calm and relaxation. But more characteristic of her acting is Sadie's dialogue with her sister, the more successful country singer Georgia. While the latter, although clearly upset by the conflict with her sister, remains calm while unpacking a bag of groceries, her insecure little sister, a failed singer and verging on alcoholism, is in constant motion. She seems compulsively agitated. While talking, she leans over the kitchen counter and swings her legs; she pulls at the front of her dress, strides around the room with an assumed cool and casual air; she mumbles her words and gathers together a pile of bedsheets with demonstrative carelessness; when talking, she hits her forehead with the palm of her hand (as a recognizable exaggerated gesture of sudden, self-ironic realization); she uses the conventional gesture of the raised thumb as a sign of happy, pretended agreement and grimaces when she speaks with the corners of her mouth contorted. Her tone alternates between the display of a good mood and pretended coolness, on the one hand, and sarcasm, on the other. During the dialogue, her gestures characterize an insecure girl trying to seem strong in front of her sister, while her almost desperate mood and the tension with her sister come through clearly.

This demonstrates Leigh's affinity for playing characters who themselves are playing a role. In such moments, one of their specific traits is accentuated. One seldom has the sense that she derives their gestures from her own personal experience, let alone intuitively allowing them to erupt from within. Instead, one consistently senses a performative intelligence at work, which is based on a precise, almost analytical *observation of a repertoire of behavioral forms* associated with the given social and behavioral roles of her female characters. From this repertoire Leigh carefully selects typical individual forms, gestures, movements, physiognomic details and uses them—in intertextual repetition—in a forceful and condensed fashion. This is how she veritably constructs her characters while only partially "renaturalizing" them. Despite all their intensity, Leigh's female characters remain recognizable as artifacts clearly belonging to the world of the film, precisely because of their sharply exaggerated outlines. This results in the previously mentioned sense of observing them as if under glass. As viewers, we watch these strange beings with almost analytical interest, yet in certain moments of the performance they are also able to move us.

The latent recognizability of her roles as artistic products, as forced constructs of forms deriving from the careful observation of a repertoire of gestures and facial expressions, this fundamental, unique quality of her acting corresponds to an affinity to characters who themselves are putting on a role in film diegesis. For in such cases the actress (as an additional factor) also has to convey the nonimmediate quality of the gestures. Such recognizability is the intended result of an intelligent and confident form of acting. At least in terms of some of her roles this also predisposes Leigh toward an involvement in the type of (postmodern) cinema that displays its artificiality and, like Leone's Western, makes no secret of celebrating a repertoire of *filmic* stereotypes.

Much in this sense the *Sight and Sound* critic Lizzie Francke remarks that Leigh's prostitute in Uli Edel's *Last Exit to Brooklyn* is "a study in a particular style of acting": "Tralala seems to be played strutting along the waterfront imagining she is Jane Mansfield."[5] This brings us to an additional facet of Leigh's abilities, historical-intertextual role playing. As competently as she observes social behaviors of women in daily life as a basis for developing acting schemata, she is similarly capable of accurately analyzing, intensifying, and symbolically using acting styles from other periods, with their unique characteristics, tics, and historical stereotypes.

SECONDHAND CONSTRUCTIONS

This latter ability may have been decisive in the Coen Brothers' casting of Leigh in the role of the newspaper reporter Amy Archer in their film *The Hudsucker Proxy*. Here she could give full play to her taut, highly accentuated acting style, which does not conceal but emphasizes acting as acting. Here she could perform her roles within a role, thereby condensing an analysis of specific acting styles and stereotypes from other periods of film history into a performance replete with allusions.

The concept of *The Hudsucker Proxy* provided the appropriate backdrop. On the surface, the film is presented as a kind of screwball comedy. It combines elements of extreme caricature with slapstick and benignly ironizes familiar story stereotypes: of social rise, fall, and recovery, of love, crisis, and the happy ending. On another level, the film provides a knowledgeable audience with a dense, multilayered, historical-intertextual fabric, which unfolds almost exclusively in references to classical American cinema. We experience a film no longer really based in "extrafilmic" reality; it instead proves to be an intertextual product par excellence, for which the imaginary world of classical Hollywood serves as the actual point of reference. The most important models for the core plotline are Frank Capra's films of the late 1930s and early 1940s, which merge comedy and social fairytale: *Mr. Deeds Goes to Town* (1936), *Mr. Smith Goes to Washington* (1939), and *Meet John Doe* (1941). As in these three films, which share a family resemblance, in

The Hudsucker Proxy a young man (Tim Robbins), initially portrayed as a simple-ton, comes from a rural town to New York, where he experiences an incredible social rise. In the process he is, unbeknownst to him, subject to the manipulations of a group of powerful men headed by a dastardly capitalist. In true Capraesque fashion, the capitalist uses the naïve new arrival as a kind of straw man behind whose back he is able to go about business as he pleases and consolidate his power. And he lets the newcomer fall by trying to destroy his public reputation once he is no longer useful and even begins to disrupt the capitalist's play for power by making his own deci-sions. Among Capra's regular cast of characters is the story-hungry female reporter who finagles the hero's trust, either in order to cooperate with the manipulation or to expose him as a useful idiot, as in *Mr. Deeds Goes to Town* and now in *The Hudsucker Proxy*. However, the reporter, Leigh's Amy Archer, falls in love with the hero—as usual in Capra—as he does with her. Over the course of the hero's fall he unmasks her dual role, just like his cinematic predecessors, and rejects her. Finally, the story of professional intrigue takes a happy and particularly fairytale-like turn for the young hero, and the romance is resolved with a happy ending.

The classical construction of *The Hudsucker Proxy* simultaneously uses key nar-rative scenes and typical figures from previous films and accentuates and distills their repetitive distinctive features, so that a scene in part seems to be distilled from multiple variants of similar scenes. In other words, this is a classical way of con-touring the stereotype beneath the surface of the similar. The multiple references range from costume and make-up (for example, the appearance of Mr. Hudsucker unmistakably recalls that of the capitalist Edward Arnolds in *Meet John Doe*) to decoration, the composition of the images, and individual visual concepts. And Capra is by no means the only source of reference. The Coens relocate the rise-and-fall story in a skyscraper, in which rise and fall can be directly staged in a spa-tial dimension. For example, there is the elevator ride—recalling Lang's *Metropo-lis* (Germany, 1925/1926)— from the depths of the building's nether regions, the mailroom, up to the immense executive offices at the top; this has numerous prec-edents, for example, Griffith's *Intolerance* (1916), King Vidor's *The Fountainhead* (1949), or, again, Lang's *Metropolis*. Also, the circle of board members constitutes a true stereotype, which reappears in an *endless number* of American films from the 1930s through 1950s, as a place where the plot points are set and insight is pro-vided into the motives of the powerful. This group of board members particularly resembles that of *The Big Clock* (John Farrow, 1948). Social downfall is visualized as an actual fall to the depths. Apart from the skyscraper and the attempted sui-cide from its top included in *Meet John Doe* (which *The Hudsucker Proxy* alludes to even down to the inner montage of the shots accompanying the distraught hero on his way to the skyscraper), the film is a fusion of almost the entire genre of

FIGURE 11 The distraught hero on his way to leap off the skyscraper: *Meet John Doe* (1941) (left); *The Hudsucker Proxy* (1994) (right).

classical skyscraper films, from Harold Lloyd's *Safety Last!* (1923) to King Vidor's *The Crowd* (1928), John Farrow's *The Big Clock* (1948), Robert Wise's *Executive Suite* (1954), and Edward Dmytryk's *Mirage* (1965).[6] The closest reference is to the comedy *The Horn Blows at Midnight* (Raoul Walsh, 1945), from which the plummets from the skyscraper are recreated even down to the specific framing of individual shots. Grotesquely hanging, like Tim Robbins, from a ledge of the top floor, the star comedian Jack Benny falls just as the great clock strikes midnight.

Thus a patchwork is created—but also a partial synthesis, a layering of similar motifs, which in synthetic form usually no longer clearly recall *any single* film. Rather, a network of overt stereotypes from classical Hollywood genres emerges, and it enables the film to appear, in Genette's sense, as a hypertext of indirect transformation and imitation.[7] The playfully ironic approach to stereotypes evokes the character of pastiche,[8] but much more than a mere pastiche of Capra. Instead, what emerges is an homage to classical Hollywood cinema in general. This is also indicated by the strange timelessness of the film, whose plot is purportedly set in 1959, but the 1950s are merged with the cinema age of the 1930s and 1940s, not only in the modeling of the story but also in the decorations and sets, which summon a familiar yet alien imaginary world. This is a paradigmatic example of what Fredric Jameson describes as "the waning of our historicity" in nostalgic retrocinema with its "stereotypical past."[9] For Jameson, this "distance of a glossy mirage" is typical of postmodernity, as is the suggestion that the narrative is "set in some eternal thirties, beyond real historical time."[10]

Already the opening images of the film leave no doubt that the entire plot unfolds in this world of cinematic imagination. Deep blue images take us on a flight over New York at night. These pictures immediately betray that this is not the real city but an imaginary New York, a fairy-tale world. The entire film was shot in the studio with carefully and expensively constructed Art Deco sets. This nocturnal shot of New York, meticulously and painstakingly constructed as a gathering of classical, stepped skyscrapers that do not appear in this condensed form in actuality,[11] does not conceal that this is an imaginary world. Both through the narrator's voice accompanying the credits and the décor the viewer is introduced to a world characterized by that atmosphere somewhere between realism and the imaginary so typical of the sets of 1930s and 1940s cinema.

However, the comedy is not simply nostalgic effect. It joins the sentimental attitude with benign irony and an element of analyzing and deconstructing its precedents. In order to achieve this, the film multiplies, condenses, and heightens its set pieces and stereotypes, including those of acting, often to the point of the grotesque. It thus strips away the melodramatic and sentimental substance so prevalent in Capra's films. At the same time, the social ideals for which his heroes strove are eliminated. They are replaced by efforts made on behalf of absurd inventions, such as the hula hoop. Furthermore, all the characters appear as caricatures who are completely absorbed by their two-dimensionality. Film reviews tended to mention their proximity to comic-book heroes, which are perceived without emotion because they embody pure stereotypes.[12] This is particularly apparent with the stock characters, which in turn refer to the stock comical characters of the classical screwball comedy but are here exaggerated to the utterly grotesque and therefore incapable of uttering much more than a punchline or a single scream.

Resonating with moments of pathos, Capra's films had a sentimental-comical appeal to U.S. audiences and were ultimately intended as serious. They were conceived to support New Deal politics and defend American society's ideal of individual rights against the excessive mafioso corruption of capitalism, which blossomed in the era of the Great Depression. This attitude of mobilizing the audience with the sincere, direct appeal of the stereotype is overwhelmingly alien to the creators of *The Hudsucker Proxy*, the disillusioned offspring of the Reagan era. From their distanced historical perspective, they analytically extract unintentionally comical aspects of Capra's story constructions and deconstruct the prevailing mechanisms of Hollywood's fairy tales by openly displaying and exaggerating them and letting them tip over into *the grotesque.*

This is once again made clear at the end of the film. Inhabiting the great clock tower of the Hudsucker Building and equipped with visionary powers, Moses, the African American warden of the clock initially serves as a classical extradiegetic frame narrator in the voiceover accompanying the opening credits.[13] Over the course of the film, his status changes to that of a diegetic character, who repeatedly assumes the function of the extradiegetic narrator and is, for example, able to address film viewers directly. At the end of the film he then, as a diegetic figure, paradoxically takes the story into his own hands.

François Truffaut once expressed his admiration for Frank Capra: "He was a navigator who knew how to steer his characters into the deepest dimensions of desperate human situations . . . before he reestablished a balance and brought off the miracle that let us leave the theater with a renewed confidence in life."[14] Truffaut associated this dramatic effect with "the secrets of the *commedia dell'arte*,"[15] based more on convention than illusion. Whereas in Capra the dramatic deux ex machina held a hand over the fallen hero and ultimately helped him back on his feet while always remaining thinly shrouded in the coherent world of the narrative, in the Coens' film this mechanism is not only clearly displayed but also personified. Moses, the keeper of the clock, is able to stop time by inserting a broomstick into the gears of the clock and thus halt the hero just before he is about to hit the ground. The jump in time so produced not only allows the hero to flop harmlessly onto the street, but it also serves as an entry for an angel (another Capra motif from *It's a Wonderful Life*, 1946, and also found in Walsh's *The Horn Blows at Midnight*), who ensures the happy ending. The diegetic figure of Moses turns around to us in the process and asks whether we could have come up with a better solution? The stereotypes of Hollywood fairy tales could hardly be revealed and deconstructed more conspicuously.

This also applies to the newspaper reporter Amy Archer, both in terms of her narrative development and Jennifer Jason Leigh's acting. Here, in a comedy role, she fully capitalizes on her proclivity for pointed performance and even takes it to extremes against the backdrop of the film's comical strategy. Here her technique of adapting historical acting styles is much more pronounced than usual.

The figure of the female reporter is an important character type in the American cinema of the 1930s and had appeared in the Capra films *Mr. Deeds Goes to Town* and *Meet John Doe*, respectively with Jean Arthur and Barbara Stanwyck as the reporter. In addition to such films only partially set in a newspaper milieu, the figure of the female reporter appeared in a whole series of explicit newspaper films, a popular genre of the 1930s. Whereas the newspaper setting represented extreme modernity in its filmic iconography and the clear display of cynicism among the reporters readily corresponded with the disillusioned mood of the audience in the Depression era—as did the concomitant cinematic popularity of the gangster— the female reporter reflected ambivalence. On the one hand, departing from the traditional representations of women's roles, the character stereotype was exhibited as an attractive symbol of modernity (and emancipation). On the other, it was also clearly readable as a sign of crisis. Usually, the woman reporter initially seemed tougher and more cynical than her male colleagues, only to then return to a greater emphasis of more traditional female values, either through marriage or a conscious, moral rejection of the brutal practices of the profession.

The most significant departure from this pattern of the turnaround, which Capra also employed, appears in Howard Hawks's *His Girl Friday* (1940). Played by Rosalind Russell, his female reporter Hildy even forgets her decision to marry someone outside the field and leave newspaper work while in the midst of an exciting story. She displays the filmic characteristics of the female reporter from this period, and she shares most traits with female reporters from other films, but with heightened emphasis. This includes incorporating numerous behaviors and gestures that had previously been connoted as male, such as casual smoking, hectically taking off and putting on clothing, or the handling of hats in the heat of a story.

Hildy is not only equal but superior to her male competitors; she is at least equally quick-witted and capable of confident, cheeky, and blunt exchanges with men. Like her female colleagues in the two Capra films, she is characterized by her sly tricks and ability to make quick decisions. This is externally expressed by a marked tendency to deliver fast dialogue, which additionally accelerates the breakneck tempo of the screwball comedy. She is spatially framed by the typical décor of newspaper films, the usual editorial offices with their telegraphs, typewriters, and telephones, the "principal instrument[s] of this world,"[16] as Cavell says. Russell and

FIGURE 12 Gesture of superiority: Katherine Hepburn (left) in *Bringing Up Baby* (1938) and Jennifer Jason Leigh (right).

the actresses in the other films use these instruments frequently and hectically, not least in order to lend their characters additional dynamic and professionalism.

The Hudsucker Proxy picks up on this type. In terms of plot, this occurs with a Capraesque variation of the moral reversal caused by a romantic relationship. However, already the manner in which the scenes are staged foregrounds the Coens' fundamental approach. Individual scenes refer to, usually multiple, precedents. These are then compiled, almost like extracts, and the comical refraction they sometimes entailed is now enhanced. For those familiar with classical cinema, the stereotype seems even more pronounced than before. For those who are not, there is nevertheless a sense of reduction and exaggeration, just as in a comic.

Exactly this approach is reflected in Leigh's performance of the character. Using behaviors similar to those of the female reporters in the model films, she combines a series of acting patterns and attitudes employed by actresses of the era. In characterizing Amy, Leigh thus engages in the typical exchanges and verbal dueling of the newspaper office as well as the customary actions of the individual female reporter. Not only the previously mentioned actresses who played reporters,

Arthur, Stanwyck, and above all Russell, are incorporated into this process, but so are other screwball-comedy actresses from the 1930s who projected the image of the confident, quick-witted woman. This includes Katherine Hepburn, for example, whose triumphal gesture of the raised arm belongs to Amy's standard repertoire.[17]

True to her forced acting style, Leigh clearly compiles the tics and acting stereotypes of her precedents and gives them additional emphasis. For example, Rosalind Russell's Hildy underscores her character of the hard-boiled reporter through a set of behaviors and tics, which semiotically represent the world and dynamics of the newspaper as well as confident dealings with men. In addition to the fast tempo of acting and talking already mentioned, this includes constantly handling phones, high-speed typing, provocative smoking, and, most of all, hectic dual actions: typing while speaking with someone else or talking on two telephones at once. In addition, in condensing her character Russell did not omit employing a degree of irony—intrinsic to comedy—in the portrayal of the typical behavioral patterns of female film reporters.

Jennifer Jason Leigh now extensively draws on this repertoire and presents it in the form of an extract, comparable to the overarching strategy of the Coens' film. Amy is not only able to do two things at once, but she condenses multiple symbolic behaviors almost to the point of simultaneity. She types her article in a newspaper office shown with a depth of field similar to that of *Citizen Kane* (Orson Welles, 1941) and uniting all the insignias of 1930s newspaper films. She can talk on the telephone while typing and talks just as fast if not faster than Rosalind Russell. She glibly counters her male sidekick, is able to take his cigarette from him, smoke, and also provide a fitting solution to a crossword-puzzle editor in the background, who seems to be a blend of all the editorial attendants of the genre. If Russell's biographer already described Hildy as "super-charged" and equipped "with almost giddy eccentricity" and "breakneck verbal slapstick,"[18] then Leigh is able to tighten the screws a full rotation to exaggerate this to the point of the grotesque.

Nonetheless, she still develops a coherent character. As Amy, she can fully display her affinity for role playing. She not only remains a celebratory performance of loud, symbolically implemented secondhand stereotypes, and thus palpably artificial—to an even greater degree than Russell's Hildy—but much about her remains aloof and reflexive. Different role models dominate in different scenes. Toward the end of the film the attributes of the hard-nosed reporter give way to a more melodramatic repertoire—as dictated by the story—which is, however, demonstratively performed with similar detachment. Already in the scene in which Amy meets the main male character, Norville Barnes, she has much more

FIGURE 13 Smoking as provocation: Katherine Hepburn (left) in *Bringing Up Baby* (1938) and Jennifer Jason Leigh (right).

FIGURE 14 Hectic activity at the typewriter: Rosalind Russell (left) in *His Girl Friday* (1940) and Jennifer Jason Leigh (right).

FIGURE 15 Fainting as pretense: Jean Arthur (left) in *Mr. Deeds Goes to Town* (1936) and Jennifer Jason Leigh (right).

in common with the model character of Jean Arthur from Capra's *Mr. Deeds Goes to Town* than Rosalind Russell's Hildy.

This episode is also interesting, because in comparison to the parallel scene in Capra's film it becomes clear to what extent the strategy here is aimed at the display of acting, the sketch-like fun of the role within a role. In both cases, the reporter is trying to arouse the protective instincts of the hero by pretending to faint and thus create an opportunity to meet him. Jean Arthur plays this in such a manner that her immediate acting gives almost no hint of her fainting as pretended; it is almost acted like a "real" faint, even if somewhat fitfully. The viewer understands she is putting on an act through the context—and particularly by her announcing the trick beforehand to the men accompanying her in a taxi, which preserves the diegetic coherence.

However, this very element is omitted in the parallel scene of *The Hudsucker Proxy*, similar to the black clock warden's interference in the narrative. Leigh's feigned act of fainting is expressed clearly as play within play, for example, through controlling glances recalling the demonstrative explicitness of silent slapstick cinema or by poking herself in the eyes to cause tears. Here too there are two observers, a pair of taxi drivers (who from their appearance could have stepped out of a 1930s or 1940s film). They, however, are assigned a commentary departing from the diegetic logic of the film, and their task is to intradiegetically remark on the action as a (familiar) story perceived against the backdrop of intertextual experience, elevate the scene to a paradoxically reflexive level, and finally create a break in coherence. This all serves the film's strategy of exposing the mechanisms of the comedy genre to make *them* the object of laughter.

In sum, one may say that Leigh's comical performance in *The Hudsucker Proxy* exemplifies a high point of her specialty in pronounced, highly accentuated acting, in which she compounds and then enhances an analytically selected comedy repertoire of gestures and traits. The basis for this repertoire is not rooted in an observation of real, everyday behaviors but in the comic interpretation of recurring idiosyncrasies and stereotypes used by comedians in Hollywood in the 1930s and 1940s. The manner in which Leigh performs the character thus corresponds precisely with the aesthetic principle of retrocomedy. It serves as an example of the reflexive, celebratory approach to acting stereotypes and provides entry into the almost fully self-referential world of this film.

EPILOGUE

While the point of a great film is now, more than ever, to be a one-of-a-kind achievement, the commercial cinema has settled for a policy of bloated, derivative filmmaking, a brazen combinatory or re-combinatory art, in the hope of reproducing past successes. Every film that hopes to reach the largest possible audience is designed as some kind of remake. Cinema, once heralded as *the* art of the twentieth century, seems now, as the century closes numerically, to be a decadent art.

—SUSAN SONTAG, "A CENTURY OF CINEMA" (1995)

The neglect of the stereotype encouraged by euphoric concepts of film as art during the initial years of film theory (from Münsterberg to Balázs), the subsequent disappointment of the late 1920s associated with a fundamental critique of popular film's stereotypes, French filmology's estimation of the filmic stereotype as the basis for the new "intelligibility" of cinema two decades later, and finally the reflexive transfiguration of stereotypes in postmodern thought: this "chronology" already accentuated by the organization of this book's chapters is not to be understood as a rigid, successive progression of paradigms. There are numerous transitions, simultaneities, and reversions. However, the chosen order does seem to reflect the fundamental historical trend of theoretical reflection on the stereotype in film.

This trend also corresponds to the logic underlying the approach to conventional patterns in—advanced—cinema itself. The consternation about and criticism of the stereotype, for example, provided an important impulse to Italian neorealism, which was committed to forgoing stereotypes and conventional patterns of the imaginary to directly convey everyday reality. The major productions of classical Hollywood cinema from the 1930s to the 1950s closely corresponded—in terms of their strategy of interplay between stereotype, innovation, variation, and individual style—with the emergence of the *politique des auteurs* in the 1950s. Around the same time, as a new medium of film reception, television ushered in an expanded awareness of the cultural power of stereotypes. The ideological critique of genre films as stereotype constructs subsequently dominated much of the emerging academic film studies. Within this context, the reflexive treatment of fixed patterns gained significance. This also included the type of critical reflection described here as characteristic of Altman's works and constituting the cinematic equivalent to theorists' ideological critique of genre film.

Meanwhile, during the same period numerous films made the shift toward a reflexive but simultaneously celebratory and glorifying—and often nostalgic— treatment of the patterns. *Once Upon a Time in the West* by Sergio Leone was discussed as an early example and *The Hudsucker Proxy* (in particular the reflexive acting of Jennifer Jason Leigh) as a later instance that also exhibits a more pronounced use of hybrid genre patterns. Such tendencies have largely gained the upper hand in contemporary cinema. Distinct cinematic visual and narrative patterns have long been transferred to other media. Both music clips as well as advertising employ elliptic filmic stereotypes as their basic semiotic material, used in a symbolic (and usually reflexive) manner.

The current influence of the postmodernist self-referential approach to stereotypes is even revealed in Robert Altman's films from the 1990s. *The Player* (1992), *Prêt-à-Porter* (1994), or *Kansas City* (1996) no longer exhibit the director's former sharp polemic against the stereotypes of commercial cinema. Incorporated patterns are treated with a mixture of fascination and nostalgia as well as ridicule and irony. This game is played out in an infinite loop, from which there is no escape to an external reality, as *The Player* seems to conclude.

Whereas the progression from the variegated play with stereotypes, on the one hand, to their reflexive critique, on the other, has led to a carnivalesque, transfigurative, and self-referential approach to the patterns, this must be seen as following the inherent logic of continuous stereotypization, which leads to an increasingly comprehensive conventionalization, accompanied by derealization. The logic of the intellectual response could be roughly outlined as follows: Intense criticism initially predominated, but the more obvious the power of the criticized stereotypes became as a constitutive condition of mass-cultural production, the greater the pragmatic acceptance of the reality of the patterns. Dialectical concepts and, later, transfiguration and hybridization now became the prevailing ways of confidently dealing with stereotypes.

However, all of this is not a linear or monocausal process running its course once and for all. Many of the described points of conflict between the stereotype and artistic consciousness are still latently present or replicate themselves in altered form.

It is no coincidence that a theorist such as Gilles Deleuze contemplated—in contrast to the prevailing aesthetic of the zeitgeist—the "crisis of the action-image" and the search for a genuinely "new image." At first glance, the credo of the Dogme 95 group seems just as "outmoded," even if in a different way. Drawing on the auteur discourses of the 1950s and 1960s, in their programmatic pamphlet of 1995 they called for a radical break with mainstream film. Lars von Trier, Thomas Vinterberg, and others objected to a cinema that creates conventional imaginations ("illusions") to generate emotional effects and thereby draws on stereotypes proven to arouse such emotions: "Is that what '100 years' have brought us? Illusions via which emotions can be communicated? . . . By the individual artist's free choice of trickery? Predictability (dramaturgy) has become the golden calf around which we dance."[1] The manifesto is based on a number of aesthetic arguments already articulated in their essence by Hermann Broch. The reigning cinema was to give way to films not oriented toward the repertoire of conventionalized imagination. Some statements recall those of Roberto Rossellini: "Genre movies are not acceptable," and "My supreme goal is to force the truth out of my characters and settings."[2] However, these positions are now associated with the visual aesthetic of improvisation, especially the video look of the handheld camera as a new marker of difference from convention and new sign of "realism." Interestingly, however, the manifesto was presented in a rather postmodern gesture of self-irony, which conveyed an understanding and acknowledgment of the *topological* nature of the groups' ideas within the history of such manifestos. The self-proclamation of an avant-garde manifesto as "dogma" is the work of ironists and those with a good sense for marketing.

Recalling the Dogme concept here merely serves as an indication that the reflexive transfiguration of the stereotype under the banner of postmodernism did *not* represent the logical culmination of the history elaborated in *Film and Stereotype*. Many of the concepts and paradigms as well as the many aesthetic means of mastering stereotypes articulated throughout the discourse on the subject will be diversified by the impact of new media developments and as such will reappear in conjunction with new discourses.

The hope remains that the overview and investigation of past theoretical and filmic discourses presented here will provide fertile ground for the analysis of future trends, sharpen insights, and help cultivate discerning assessments.

NOTES

INTRODUCTION

1. For the sources and further details, see chapter 6.
2. Fülöp-Miller, "The Motion Picture in America: A History in the Making" [German 1931], in *The American Theatre and the Motion Picture in America: A History in the Making*, ed. John Andersen and René Fülöp-Miller (New York: The Dial Press, 1938), 111.
3. Ibid., 117.
4. Umberto Eco, "Innovation and Repetition: Between Modern and Post-Modern Aesthetics," *Daedalus* 114, no. 4 (Fall 1985): 166.
5. Roland Barthes, *The Pleasure of the Text* [French 1973], trans. Richard Miller (New York: Hill and Wang, 1975), 40.
6. John Thornton Caldwell, *Televisuality: Style, Crisis, and Authority in American Television* (New Brunswick, N.J.: Rutgers University Press, 1994).

1. THE STEREOTYPE IN PSYCHOLOGY AND THE HUMANITIES

1. Walter Lippmann, *Public Opinion* (1922; repr., New York: Macmillan, 1961).
2. This phrase is already used as the title of the introduction.
3. Lippmann, *Public Opinion*, 95.
4. Daniel Katz and Kenneth W. Braly, "Racial Stereotypes of One Hundred College Students," *Journal of Abnormal and Social Psychology* 28 (1933): 280–290; Daniel Katz and Kenneth W. Braly, "Racial Prejudice and Racial Stereotypes," *Journal of Abnormal and Social Psychology* 30 (1935): 175–193. Concerning an important precursor in this respect, see Stuart Arthur Rice, "Stereotypes: A Source of Error in Judging Human Character," *Journal of Personality Research* 5 (1926/1927): 267–276.
5. A detailed critical overview of this line of research up to the mid-1960s is provided by Wolfgang Manz, *Das Stereotyp. Zur Operationalisierung eines sozialwissenschaftlichen*

Begriffs (Meisenheim: Anton Hain, 1968). For later developments, see Bernhard Six, "Stereotype und Vorurteile im Kontext sozialpsychologischer Forschung," in *Erstarrtes Denken. Studien zu Klischee, Stereotyp und Vorurteil in englischsprachiger Literatur*, ed. Günther Blaicher (Tubingen: Narr, 1987), 41–54.

6. Katz and Braly, "Racial Prejudice and Racial Stereotypes," 181.

7. Alexander Mitscherlich, "Die Vorurteilskrankheit," *Psyche* 16 (1962): 241–245.

8. S. I. Hayakawa, "Recognizing Stereotypes as Substitute for Thought," *ETC.: A Review of General Semantics* 7 (1950): 208–210.

9. Adam Schaff, "Sprache und Stereotyp," in *Sprechen—Denken—Praxis*, ed. Gerd Simon and Erich Straßner (Weinheim: Beltz, 1979), 164.

10. The influence of American psychology in postwar Germany had a bearing on this shift. Its most prominent advocate was Peter R. Hofstätter, *Das Denken in Stereotypen* (Gottingen: Vandenhoeck & Ruprecht, 1960). However, there are earlier indications of a developing pragmatic position: Peter R. Hofstätter, *Die Psychologie der öffentlichen Meinung* (Vienna: Braumüller, 1949); and Kripal Singh Sodhi and Rudolf Bergius, *Nationale Vorurteile. Eine sozialpsychologische Untersuchung an 881 Personen* (Berlin: Duncker & Humblot, 1953). For the corresponding developments in the United States, see Manz, *Das Stereotyp*, 8–9.

11. Lippmann, *Public Opinion*, 80.

12. Ibid., 81.

13. Ibid., 88.

14. Ibid.

15. Ibid., 119.

16. Ibid. Lippmann believed that our surroundings provide a sufficient number of "uniformities" for stereotype-based perceptions to function (see 89–90).

17. Ibid., 84.

18. Ibid., 125.

19. Ibid., esp. 119–126.

20. Ibid., 124.

21. Ibid., 81; my emphasis.

22. Ibid., 119.

23. Ibid., 95.

24. Ibid., 96.

25. Ibid., p. 95.

26. Ibid., 3, 104.

27. See, for example, Francisco J. Varela, *Kognitionswissenschaft-Kognitionstechnik. Eine Skizze aktueller Perspektiven* (Frankfurt am Main: Suhrkamp, 1990), esp. 110. The German edition is the translation of an unpublished English manuscript titled *Cognitive Science: A Cartography of Current Ideas*.

28. Lippmann, *Public Opinion*, 90.

29. Ibid., 90–91.

30. Hofstätter, *Das Denken in Stereotypen*, 7. Hofstätter brings the idea of interconnectedness into play: "Strictly speaking, a stereotype is a complex of prejudices, which often appear in concert, rely on each other and thus form a gestalt-like whole" (8).

31. Ibid., 7.

32. Ibid., 32.

33. Ibid., 13 (insertion by J. S.).

34. Ibid, 34. Elsewhere (17) Hofstätter writes: "Inhuman heterostereotypes are borderline cases; one should always refrain from entertaining them, because 'holding on to' them poses a serious challenge to one's own humanity."

35. H. Tajfel, "Cognitive Aspects of Prejudice," *Journal of Social Issues* 25 (1969): 79–97; and H. Tajfel, "Soziales Kategorisieren," in *Forschungsberichte der Sozialpsychologie*, ed. S. Moscovici (Frankfurt: Fischer Athenäum, 1975), 1:345–388.

36. Waldemar Lilli, *Grundlagen der Stereotypisierung* (Gottingen: Hogrefe, 1982).

37. Ibid., 13.

38. Ibid.

39. Daniel Bar-Tal, Carl F. Graumann, Arie W. Kruglanski, and Wolfgang Stroebe, eds., *Stereotyping and Prejudice: Changing Conceptions* (New York: Springer, 1989).

40. Walter G. Stephan, "A Cognitive Approach to Stereotyping," in *Stereotyping and Prejudice: Changing Conceptions*, ed. Daniel Bar-Tal et al. (New York: Springer, 1989), 37.

41. Ibid.

42. For a critique of the cognitivistic computer metaphor, see Varela, *Kognitionswissenschaft*, 37–53.

43. See for example, Helge Gerndt, ed., *Stereotypenvorstellungen im Alltagsleben. Beiträge zum Themenkreis Fremdbilder, Selbstbilder, Identität. Festschrift für Georg R. Schronbek zum 65. Geburtstag* (Munich: Vereinigung für Völkerkunde, 1988).

44. Walter Lippmann writes in *Public Opinion*: "Thus there can be little doubt that the moving picture is steadily building up imagery which is then evoked by the words people read in their newspapers. In the whole experience of the race there has been no aid to visualization comparable to the cinema. . . . Your hazy notion, let us say, of the Ku Klux Klan, thanks to Mr. Griffith, takes vivid shape when you see *The Birth of a Nation*. . . . I doubt whether anyone who has seen the film and does not know more about the Ku Klux Klan than Mr. Griffith will ever hear the name again without seeing those white horsemen" (91–92).

45. In constructivistic terminology, this kind of analytically almost impossible to isolate reciprocity between mental and medial constructs is aptly described as "structural coupling." On the term "coupling," see the work of H. R. Maturana, "Biologie der Sozialität," in *Der Diskurs des radikalen Konstruktivismus*, ed. Siegfried J. Schmidt (Frankfurt am Main: Suhrkamp, 1992), 287. The term "medial coupling" is also common. See Peter M. Spangenberg, "TV, Hören und Sehen," in *Materialität der Kommunikation*, ed. Hans Ulrich Gumbrecht and K. Ludwig Pfeiffer (Frankfurt am Main: Suhrkamp, 1988), 778–792.

46. Franz W. Dröge, *Publizistik und Vorurteil* (Münster: Regensburg, 1967). In particular, see part 2: "Stereotypen im publizistischen Prozess," 214–225.

47. Ibid., 121.

48. Peter Pleyer, *Nationale und soziale Stereotypen im gegenwärtigen deutschen Spielfilm. Eine aussageanalytische Leitstudie* (Münster: Institut für Publizistik, 1968).

49. Steve Neale, "The Same Old Story: Stereotypes and Difference," in *The Screen Education Reader: Cinema, Television, Culture*, ed. Manuel Alvarado, Edward Buscombe, and Richard Collins (1979/1980; repr., New York: Columbia University Press, 1993), 41–47.

50. Irmela Schneider, "Zur Theorie des Stereotyps," *Beiträge zur Film- und Fernsehwissenschaft*, 43 (1992):129–147.

51. Ibid., 43:140.

52. Ibid.

53. Ibid.

54. Ibid., 143.

55. Ibid., 142.

56. Ibid.

57. W. J. T. Mitchell, *What Do Pictures Want: The Lives and Loves of Images* (Chicago: University of Chicago Press, 2005), 298.

58. Ibid., 29.

59. Ibid., 296.

60. Ibid.

61. Ibid., 298.

62. Ibid.

63. Ibid., 296.

64. Blaicher, ed., *Erstarrtes Denken*.

65. Ibid., 9.

66. James Elliot, Jürgen Pelzer, and Carol Poore, eds., *Stereotyp und Vorurteil in der Literatur. Untersuchungen zu Autoren des 20. Jahrhunderts* (Gottingen: Vandenhoeck und Ruprecht, 1978).

67. Ibid., 7.

68. Ibid. My emphasis.

69. Ibid., 11.

70. Uta Quasthoff, "The Uses of Stereotype in Everyday Argument," *Journal of Pragmatics* 2 (1978): 6. See also Uta Quasthoff, *Soziales Urteil und Kommunikation. Eine sprachwissenschaftliche Analyse des Stereotypes* (Frankfurt am Main: Athenäum Fischer, 1973), 28.

71. Angelika Wenzel, *Stereotype in gesprochener Sprache. Form Vorkommen und Funktion in Dialogen* (Munich: Max Hueber, 1978), 30.

72. Primarily objecting to Quasthoff's concept of judgment, Wenzel attempts to render her definition more precisely: "A stereotype is the verbal expression of a belief which is directed towards social groups or single persons as members of these groups. The stereotype has the logical form of a general statement, which ascribes or denies certain properties to a set of persons in an unwarrantably simplifying way, with an emotionally evaluative tendency." Ibid., 28.

73. Ibid., 30. My emphasis.

74. Ibid.

75. Adam Schaff, for example, considers the "stereotype" a fact of social psychology, but it is "like the concept, always associated with a word." Adam Schaff, "Sprache und Stereotyp," 162. And "it is, in fact—particularly in relation to social problems—a matter of the word content, which most often conveys simplified and false opinions; these, in

turn, are not based on one's own experiences but on a belief [*sic*] in the authority of the public opinion of a given milieu. This is why such opinions are so persistent and hard to overcome" (163).

76. Florian Coulmas, *Routine im Gespräch. Zur pragmatischen Fundierung der Idiomatik* (Wiesbaden: Athenaion, 1981), 3.

77. Ibid., 55.

78. Ibid., 10.

79. Ibid., 66.

80. Ibid., 15.

81. Ibid., 13.

82. Ibid.

83. Ibid., 68.

84. See ibid, 10, 68–69.

85. Ibid., 14.

86. For example, Harald Scheel similarly defines the stereotype: "Linguistic stereotypes are lexeme combinations, which—due to the linguistic-communicative standards and expectations of the communicators in a communication situation—represent common standardizations of both form and content; and because of their ability to trigger mental subroutines such stereotypes entail elements of mental economy. As fixed collocations they represent a specific form of repeated speech, and as elements of vocabulary are part of the language system." Harald Scheel, *Untersuchungen zum sprachlichen Stereotyp* (thesis, Leipzig, 1983), 57.

87. Michael Riffaterre, *Essais de stylistique structurale* (Paris: Flammarion, 1971).

88. Gérard Genette, *Palimpsests: Literature in the Second Degree* [French 1982], trans. Channa Newman and Claude Doubinsky (Lincoln: University of Nebraska Press, 1997), esp. 14–15, 78–79. However, Genette only uses the term in passing and without discussing it explicitly.

89. Roland Barthes, *Elements of Semiology* [French 1964] (New York: Hill and Wang, 1973). Here Barthes specifically mentions "stereotyped syntagms" (62). However, the concept of the stereotype has key significance for him within a substantially broader understanding of the term, as some of his other writings articulate (as will be discussed further on).

90. See Riffaterre, *Essais de stylistique structurale*, 163. "Il importe de bien souligner que la stéréotypie à elle seule ne fait pas le cliché: il faut encore que la séquence verbale figée par l'usage présente un fait de style, qu'il s'agisse d'une métaphore comme *fourmilière humaine*, d'une antithèse comme *meurtre juridique*, d'une hyperbole comme *mortelles inquiétudes*, etc. Toutes les catégories stylistiques son susceptibles d'entrer dans des clichés."

91. Ibid. "Son effet est donc, si j'ose dire, en conserve."

92. Roland Barthes, *The Pleasure of the Text* [French 1975] (New York: Hill and Wang, 1975), 43.

93. Riffaterre, *Essais de stylistique structurale*, 171.

94. Ibid., 163.

95. Ibid., 171.

96. Genette, *Palimpsests*, 79.

97. Ibid., 15.

98. Ibid., 79.

99. Yuri M. Lotman, *The Structure of the Artistic Text* [Russian 1970], trans. Gail Lenhoff and Ronald Vroon (Ann Arbor: University of Michigan, 1977), 290.

100. Ibid., 286.

101. Ibid., 290.

102. John G. Cawelti, "The Concept of Formula in the Study of Popular Literature," *Journal of Popular Culture* 3, no. 3 (1969): 381–390.

103. Umberto Eco, "The Myth of Superman," in *The Role of the Reader: Explorations in the Semiotics of Texts* (Bloomington: University of Indiana Press, 1979), 117.

104. Coulmas, *Routine im Gespräch*, 3.

105. Lotman, *The Structure of the Artistic Text*, 290.

106. Ibid., 75.

107. Ibid., 288.

108. Ibid., 290.

109. Ibid., 291.

110. Ruth Amossy, *Les idées reçues. Sémiologie du stéréotype* (Paris: Nathan, 1991).

111. Ruth Amossy, "Stereotypes and Representation in Fiction," *Poetics Today* 5, no. 4 [1984]: 691.

112. Ibid., 690.

113. Ibid.

114. Ibid., 692–693.

115. Ibid., 694.

116. Ibid., 693.

117. Ibid.

118. Ibid., 694–695.

119. Ibid., 700.

120. Ibid., 699.

121. Amossy, *Les idées reçues*. In this later text, she clearly places emphasis on other ideas and views the criteria of such assessments themselves as products of history.

122. Arnold Hauser, *The Social History of Art* (1951; repr., New York: Routledge, 1999), 1:56.

123. Arnold Hauser, *The Sociology of Art* [German 1974], trans. Kenneth J. Northcott (Chicago: University of Chicago Press, 1982), 29–31.

124. Ibid., 30.

125. Ibid.

126. Ibid., 30.

127. Ibid., 21.

128. Hauser, *The Social History of Art*, 56.

129. Ibid., 54.

130. Ibid., 53.

131. Ernst H. Gombrich, *Art and Illusion: A Study in the Psychology of Pictorial Representation* (1960; repr., London: Phaidon, 1977), especially the chapter "Truth and Stereotype," 55–78.

132. Ibid., 76.

133. Ibid., 53.

134. Ibid., 148.

135. See ibid., 19–20.

136. See ibid., 61.

137. Ibid., 76.

138. Ibid., 61.

139. Ibid., 124.

140. Ibid., 61.

141. Ibid., 76.

142. For example, in relation to the stereotype, Dröge talks *expressis verbis* about "composite traits" (*Merkmalsvergesellschaftung*). See Dröge, *Publizistik und Vorurteil*, 211.

143. *The Oxford English Dictionary*, 2nd ed., s.vv. "stereo-" and "type."

144. Ludwig Wittgenstein, *Philosophical Investigations* [German 1953], trans. G. E. M. Anscombe, P. M. S. Hacker, and Joachim Schulte (Chichester, West Sussex: Wiley Blackwell, 2009), §66–67, p. 36.

145. I am drawing on the model of a classification of facets, which was introduced in film studies by Hans Jürgen Wulff (who employed it in genre analysis) in opposition to hierarchical classification. See Hans Jürgen Wulff, "Drei Bemerkungen zur Motiv- und Genreanalyse am Beispiel des Gefängnisfilms," in *Sechstes Film- und Fernsehwissenschaftliches Kolloquium/Berlin 1993*, eds. Jörg Frieß, Stephen Lowry, and Hans Jürgen Wulff (Berlin: Gesellschaft für Theorie und Geschichte audiovisueller Kommunikation, 1994), 149–154.

146. Amossy, "Stereotypes and Representation in Fiction," 685.

147. Pierre Bourdieu, *The Logic of Practice* [French 1980] (Stanford, Calif.: Stanford University Press, 1990), 87.

148. Francisco J. Varela, *Kognitionswissenschaft*, 88ff. Varela, however, talks about "patterns" rather than schemata.

149. See Siegfried Schmidt and Siegfried Weischenberg, "Mediengattungen, Berichterstattungsmuster, Darstellungsformen," in *Die Wirklichkeit der Medien: eine Einführung in die Kommunikationswissenschaft*, ed. Klaus Merten, Siegfried J. Schmidt, and Siegfried Weischenberg (Opladen: Westdeutscher Verlag, 1994), 214–215.

150. Niklas Luhmann, *The Reality of the Mass Media* [German 1995], trans. Kathleen Cross (Cambridge: Polity Press, 2000), 109.

151. This is described in greater detail in Schmidt and Weischenberg, "Mediengattungen," 213.

152. On the term "emergence," see Varela, *Kognitionswissenschaft*, 60–67, 70–76. Somewhat further on (93–94) Varela explains such *overarching co-operation* by using the example of language: "One must know the language as a whole in order to understand the multiple meanings of an individual word, and this understanding in turn influences the meaning of all other words. The categorization of any one aspect of our natural environment does *not* permit sharp delineations of any kind."

153. See T. E. Perkins, "Rethinking Stereotypes," in *Ideology and Cultural Production*, ed. Michèle Barrett, Philip Corrigan, Annette Kuhn, and Janet Wolff (London: Croom Helm, 1979), 135–159. Perkins gives an example on 139: "to refer 'correctly' to someone

as a 'dumb blonde,' and to understand what is meant by that, implies a great deal more than hair colour and intelligence. It refers immediately to her sex, which refers to her status in society, her relationship to men, her inability to behave or think rationally, and so on. In short, it implies knowledge of a complex social structure."

154. See Eleanor Rosch, "Principles of Categorization," in *Cognition and Categorization*, ed. Eleanor Rosch and Barbara B. Lloyd (Hillsdale, N.J.: L. Erlbaum, 1978). Lakoff, however, discusses it in more detail. See George Lakoff, *Women, Fire, and Dangerous Things: What Categories Reveal about the Mind* (Chicago: University of Chicago Press, 1987), 48–49.

155. This the title of article by Ivan Pavlov, "Dinamicheskaia stereotipiia vysshego otdela golovnogo mozga [The Dynamic Stereotype of the Higher Section of the Brain]," in I. P. Pavlov, *Polnoe sobranie sochineniy*, 2nd ed., enlarged, vol. 3, pt. 2 (Moscow: Izdatel'stvo Akademii Nauk SSSR, 1933), 240–244. This text is not included in the English collections of his writings. A particularly incisive definition of his theory is presented in "Uslovnyi Refleks" [The Conditioned Reflex], in *Bol'shaia Sovetskaia Enziklopediia* 56 (Moscow, 1936), 322–337.

156. Pavlov, "Uslovniy Refleks," 330.

157. Pavlov, "Dinamicheskaia stereotipiia," 244.

158. Ibid., 243–244.

159. This is the chosen subtitle of Peter Wuss, *Filmanalyse und Psychologie. Strukturen des Films im Wahrnehmungsprozess* (Berlin: Edition Sigma, 1993).

160. Ibid., 62.

161. Ibid.

162. Ibid., 60–61.

163. Umberto Eco, "The Role of the Reader," in *The Role of the Reader: Explorations in the Semiotics of Texts* (Bloomington: University of Indiana Press, 1979), 3–43.

164. Peter Wuss, *Cinematic Narration and Its Psychological Impact: Functions of Cognition, Emotion, and Play* (Newcastle upon Tyne: Cambridge Scholars Publishing, 2009), 40.

165. Ibid., 60.

166. Barthes, *The Pleasure of the Text*, 40.

167. Coulmas, *Routine im Gespräch*, 16.

168. Cf. Stephen Heath, *Questions of Cinema* (1981; repr., Bloomington: University of Indiana Press, 1991), 16.

169. Barthes, *Elements of Semiology*, 41.

170. Ibid.

171. Luhmann, *The Reality of the Mass Media*, 110.

172. Rüdiger Kunow, *Das Klischee. Reproduzierte Wirklichkeiten in der englischen und amerikanischen Literatur* (Munich: Fink, 1994), 110.

173. Wolfgang Iser, *The Fictive and the Imaginary: Charting Literary Anthropology* [German 1991] (Baltimore, Md.: The Johns Hopkins University Press, 1993), 2.

174. Ibid., xiii.

175. See, for example, Eco, "The Myth of Superman."

176. Textual schemata ultimately are always also mental constructs, even if they specially refer to texts and are, in turn, actualized in texts, which are subject to a unique dynamic (detached from the individual) in the intertextual sphere.

177. Henri Bergson, *Creative Evolution* [French 1907], trans. Arthur Mitchell (New York: Henry Holt, 1911), 162.

178. Ibid., 287.

179. Kunow has published the previously mentioned comprehensive study on the terminology of the cliché in literary analysis. See Kunow, *Das Klischee*. Worthy of note is that Kunow presents a broad and nuanced interpretation of the term "cliché," similar to the treatment and semantics of "stereotype" in this volume.

2. SOME ASPECTS AND LEVELS OF STEREOTYPIZATION IN FILM

1. Irmela Schneider, "Zur Theorie des Stereotypes," *Beiträge zur Film- und Fernsehwissenschaft* 43 (1992): 129–147.

2. Steve Neale, "The Same Old Story: Stereotypes and Difference" [1979/80], in *The Screen Education Reader: Cinema, Television. Culture*, ed. Manuel Alvarado, Edward Buscombe, and Richard Collins (New York: Columbia University Press, 1993), 41–47.

3. See Richard Dyer, "Stereotyping," in *Gays in Film* (London: BFI, 1977), 27–39. Also see Richard Dyer, *The Matter of Images: Essays on Representation* (London: Routledge, 1993), esp. 11–18 ("The Role of Stereotypes").

4. Neale, "The Same Old Story," 41.

5. Dyer, *The Matter of Images*, 13.

6. This was the title of a dossier compiled for teaching purposes. See Richard Dyer, *The Dumb Blonde Stereotype: Documentation for EAS Class-Room Materials* (London: BFI, 1979).

7. Umberto Eco, "Die praktische Anwendung der literarischen Person," in *Apokalyptiker und Integrierte. Zur kritischen Kritik der Massenkultur* (Frankfurt am Main: Fischer, 1986), 169. This essay is not included in the partial English translation (*Apocalypse Postponed*, 1994) of Eco's *Apocalitticie e integrati* (1964).

8. Ibid., 171.

9. Ibid., 175.

10. Ibid., 173.

11. Ibid., 177.

12. Manfred Pfister, *Das Drama. Theorie und Analyse* (Munich: Fink, 1977), 234.

13. See Bernhard Asmuth, *Einführung in die Dramenanalyse* (Stuttgart: Metzler, 1980), 96–98.

14. E. M. Forster, *Aspects of the Novel* [1927] (San Diego, Calif.: Harcourt Brace, 1985), 67.

15. Ibid., 69.

16. Ibid., 78.

17. Dyer, *The Matter of Images*, 13.

18. Eco, "Die praktische Anwendung," 178–179.

19. See Robert Müller, "Von der Kunst der Verführung: der Vamp," in *Diesseits der 'dämonischen Leinwand.' Neue Perspektiven auf das späte Weimarer Kino*, ed. Thomas Koebner (Munich: edition text+kritik, 2003), 259–280.

20. See Asmuth, *Einführung in die Dramenanalyse*, 88.

21. This corresponds to the etymological relationship between the words. Like "stereotype," type also derives from printing terminology. The "type" was originally the image on the coin die and then later the actual print it created. See Heinrich Lausberg, *Handbook of Literary Rhetoric: A Foundation for Literary Study*, ed. David E. Orton and R. Dean Anderson, trans. Matthew T. Bliss, Annemiek Jansen, and David E. Orton (Leiden: Brill, 1998), §901.

22. Stanley Cavell, *The World Viewed: Reflections on the Ontology of Film* (Cambridge, Mass.: Harvard University Press, 1979), 33.

23. Ibid.

24. Ibid.

25. Ibid.

26. This may be due to the context of his argument, which criticizes one of Panofsky's theses. The latter had argued that with the introduction of sound the naive, clear-cut iconography of the types already *introduced* and visually easily recognizable now lost significance, because the public no longer needed the explanatory element inherent to them. Cavell objected to this argument: "Films have changed, but that is not because we don't need such explanations any longer; it is because we can't accept them" (ibid.). This should mean not that types disappear, but only the stereotypes, the *intertextually* established figures.

27. Paul Loukides and Linda F. Fuller, *Beyond the Stars (1): Stock Characters in American Popular Film* (Bowling Green, Ohio: Bowling Green University Popular Press, 1990).

28. The same applies to every kind of fictional narration, not just the cinematic.

29. Siegfried Kracauer, "National Types as Hollywood Presents Them," *Public Opinion Quarterly* 13, no. 1 (1949): 53–72.

30. Howard Good, *The Drunken Journalist: The Biography of a Film Stereotype* (Lanham, Md.: Scarecrow Press, 2000).

31. Yuri M. Lotman, *Semiotics of Cinema* [Russian 1973], trans. Mark Suino (Ann Arbor: University of Michigan Press, 1976), 22.

32. This does not mean, however, that one should disclaim any relationship that a figure might have to conventional ideas directly based on reality.

33. Ernst H. Gombrich, "Norm and Form: The Stylistic Categories of Art History and Their Origins in Renaissance Ideals" [lecture 1963], in *Norm and Form: Studies in the Art of the Renaissance* (London: Phaidon Press, 1966), 96.

34. Ibid.

35. Ibid., 98.

36. See Florian Coulmas, *Routine im Gespräch. Zur pragmatischen Fundierung der Idiomatik* (Wiesbaden: Athenaion, 1981).

37. See Richard Dyer, *Stars* (London: BFI, 1979).

38. See Richard Dyer, *Heavenly Bodies: Film Stars and Society* (London: Macmillan, 1987), 2.

39. Asmuth, *Einführung in die Dramenanalyse*, 99.

40. See Margrit Tröhler and Henry M. Taylor, "De quelques facettes du personnage humain dans le film de fiction," *Iris* 24 (1997): 48.

41. Viktor Shklovsky, "Tarzan" [in Russian], *Russkij sovremennik* 4 (1924): 253.

42. Joachim Paech, *Literatur und Film* (Stuttgart: Metzler, 1988), 48.

43. Yuri Lotman, "Proiskhozhdenie siuzheta v tipologicheskom osveshchenii [The Development of the Plot from a Typological Perspective]," in *Stat'i po tipologii kul'tury* (Tartu, 1973), 10.

44. Vladimir Propp, *Morphology of the Folktale* [Russian 1928], trans. Laurence Scott (American Folklore Society Publications, 2003).

45. Joseph Campbell, *The Hero with a Thousand Faces* [1949], Bollingen Series 17 (Princeton, N.J.: Princeton University Press, 1973).

46. Ibid., 21.

47. Ibid., 35.

48. Ibid., 12.

49. Ibid., 13.

50. Ibid., 19.

51. Ibid., 11.

52. Ibid., 18–19.

53. Ibid., 19.

54. Ibid., 38.

55. Christopher Vogler, *The Writer's Journey: Mythic Structure for Writers*, 3rd ed. (Studio City, Calif.: Michael Wiese Productions, 2007).

56. This is the title of a subchapter. Ibid., 3.

57. Campbell, *The Hero*, 13.

58. Ibid., viii.

59. Britta Hartmann discussed this several years ago in regard to American gangster films. Britta Hartmann, "Topographische Ordnung und narrative Struktur im klassischen Gangsterfilm," *Montage AV* 8, no. 1 (1999): 111–133.

60. See François Truffaut, *Hitchcock* [French 1966], with the collaboration of Helen G. Scott (New York: Simon and Schuster, 1985), 79–80.

61. Yuri Lotman, "Beseda o kinematografii [A Conversation on Film]" [in Russian], *Kino* 1 (1986).

62. Lubomír Doležel, *Heterocosmica: Fiction and Possible Worlds* (Baltimore, Md.: The Johns Hopkins University Press, 1998), 18.

63. Ibid., x. Elaborating further, he, however, places value on emphasizing the specific character of fictional worlds in relation to the possible worlds of logic and philosophy and in articulating features "that are special for the fictional worlds of literature, that is, those features that cannot be derived from the possible worlds model" (16).

64. Ibid., 16.

65. Ibid.

66. Umberto Eco, *Lector in fabula. Die Mitarbeit der Interpretation in erzählenden Texten* (Munich: dtv, 1990), 157. This is a translation of the German text, which is a reworked version of "Lector in Fabula: Pragmatic Strategy in a Metanarrative," in *The Role of the Reader: Explorations of Semiotic Texts* (Bloomington: University of Indiana Press, 1979).

67. Knut Hickethier, *Die Fernsehserie und das Serielle des Fernsehens*. Lüneburger Beiträge zur Kulturwissenschaft 2 (Lüneburg: University of Lüneburg, 1991), 44.

68. Ibid., 45.

69. This is certainly related to the etymology of "myth," or "mythos," whose relevance in antiquity is described by Wellek and Warren: "Its antonym and counterpoint is logos. The 'myth' is narrative, story, as against dialectical discourse, exposition; it is also the irrational or intuitive as against the systematically philosophical: it is the tragedy of Aeschylus against the dialectic of Socrates. . . . In the seventeenth and eighteenth centuries, the Age of Enlightenment, the term had commonly a pejorative connotation: a myth was a fiction—scientifically or historically untrue. But already since the *Scienza Nuova* of Vico, the emphasis has shifted to what, since the German Romanticists, Coleridge, Emerson, and Nietzsche, has become gradually dominant—the conception of 'myth' as, like poetry, a kind of truth or an equivalent of truth, not a competitor to historic or scientific truth but a supplement. Historically, myth follows and is correlative to ritual." René Wellek and Austin Warren, *The Theory of Literature* (New York: Harcourt, Brace, and Company, 1949), 169.

70. Will Wright, *Sixguns and Society: A Structural Study of the Western* (Berkeley: University of California Press, 1975).

71. Ibid., 22.

72. See ibid., 20.

73. Ibid., 48–49.

74. John G. Cawelti, "The Concept of Formula in the Study of Popular Literature," in *Journal of Popular Culture* 3, no. 3 (1969): 390.

75. Barbara Flückiger, *Sound Design. Die virtuelle Klangwelt des Filmes* (Marburg: Schüren, 2002), 182. See also Barbara Flückiger, "Sound Effects. Strategies for Sound Effects in Film," in *Sound and Music in Film and Visual Media: An Overview*, ed. Graeme Harper, Ruth Doughty, and Jochen Eisentraut (London: Continuum, 2009), 151–179, esp. 160.

76. Flückiger, *Sound Design*, 181.

77. Corinna Dästner, "Sprechen über Filmmusik. Der Überschuss von Bild und Musik," in *Sound: Zur Technologie und Ästhetik des Akustischen in den Medien*, ed. Harro Segeberg and Frank Schätzlein (Marburg: Schüren, 2005), 89.

78. Herbert Jhering, "Schauspielerische Klischees," *Blätter des Deutschen Theaters* 2, no. 30 (1912/1913): 487–488.

79. Ibid., 487.

80. Erwin Panofsky, "Style and Medium in the Motion Pictures" [1947], in *Three Essays on Style* (Cambridge, Mass.: The MIT Press, 1995), 39.

81. Herbert Jhering, "Der Schauspieler im Film" [1920], in *Von Reinhardt bis Brecht. Vier Jahrzehnte Theater und Film*, ed. Edith Krull (Berlin: Henschel, 1958), 1:382.

82. See Heide Schlüpmann, *The Uncanny Gaze: The Drama of Early German Cinema* [German 1990], trans. Inga Pollmann (Urbana: University of Illinois Press, 2010). See esp. the chapters "Excursus: Henny Porten, or, The Realism of Melodrama" and "Contradictions of Social Drama."

83. Jhering, "Schauspielerische Klischees," 487.

84. See Ruth Amossy, "On Commonplace Knowledge and Innovation," *SubStance* 62/63, special issue, "Thought and Motivation" (1991): 146–147.

85. Carl Michel, *Die Gebärdensprache dargestellt für Schauspieler sowie Maler und Bildhauer*, part 1: *Die körperliche Beredsamkeit: Gebärden–Seelenzustände–Stimme. Rollenstudium–Spielen* (Cologne: DuMont-Schauberg, 1886), 96–97.

86. Wilhelm Scheffer, "Mimische Studien mit Reißzeug und Kamera," *Der Welt-Spiegel. Halb-Wochenschrift des Berliner Tagesblatts* 10 (February 1, 1914): 2.

87. Ibid.

88. Jhering, "Schauspielerische Klischees," 488.

89. See Knut Hickethier, "Das Zucken der Mundwinkel. Schauspielen in den Medien," *TheaterZeitSchrift* 1, no. 2 (1982): 15–31; "Schauspielen in Film und Fernsehen," in *Kinoschriften. Jahrbuch der Gesellschaft für Filmtheorie* (Vienna: Verband der Wissenschaftlichen Gesellschaften Österreichs, 1990), 2:45–68; and "Poetik des Kleinen," in *Schauspielkunst im Film*, ed. Thomas Koebner (St. Augustin: Gardez!, 1998), 37–48.

90. Knut Hickethier, *Film- und Fernsehanalyse* (Stuttgart: Metzler, 1993), 163.

91. See Kristin Thompson, Yuri Tsivian, and Ekaterina Khokhlova, "The Rediscovery of a Kuleshov Experiment: A Dossier," *Film History* 8, no. 3 (1996): 357–364. See Hans Beller, *Handbuch der Filmmontage. Praxis und Prinzipien des Filmschnitts* (Munich: TR-Verlagsunion, 1993), 157–159.

92. Roberta Pearson, *Eloquent Gestures: The Transformation of Performance Style in the Griffith Biograph Films* (Berkeley: University of California Press, 1992), 38–51.

93. Joseph August Lux, "Das Kinodrama" [1914], in *Prolog vor dem Film*, ed. Jörg Schweinitz (Leipzig: Reclam, 1992), 320.

94. Joseph August Lux, "Menschendarsteller im Film. Porträts. I. Asta Nielsen," *Bild und Film* 3, no. 7 (1913/1914): 165.

95. Ibid.

96. Hickethier, *Film- und Fernsehanalyse*, 163.

97. Herbert Jhering, *Werner Krauss. Ein Schauspieler und das neunzehnte Jahrhundert*, ed. Sabine Zolchow and Rudolf Mast (Berlin: Vorwerk 8, 1997), 43.

98. Ibid.

99. Karl Prümm, "Klischee und Individualität. Zur Problematik des Chargenspiels im deutschen Film," in *Der Körper im Bild: Schauspielen—Darstellen—Erscheinen*, ed. Heinz B. Heller, Karl Prümm, and Birgit Peulings (Marburg: Schüren, 1999), 99.

100. Ibid., 101.

101. Ibid.

102. Jhering, "Schauspielerische Klischees," 487.

103. Albert Klöckner, "Das Massenproblem in der Kunst" [1928], in *Medientheorie 1888–1933. Texte und Kommentare*, ed. Albert Kümmel and Petra Löffler (Frankfurt am Main: Suhrkamp, 2002), 304. See also 302.

104. Heike Kühn, "Zwischen Überfluß und Mangel. Die 37. Internationalen Kurzfilmtage in Oberhausen," *Frankfurter Rundschau* 104 (May 6, 1991): 21.

105. Vladimir Nilsen, *The Cinema as a Graphic Art* [Russian 1936] (New York: Hill & Wang, 1957), 177.

106. Ibid., 179.

107. Ibid., 176.

108. Ibid., 177.

109. Ibid., 179.

110. Jean-Loup Bourget, *Le mélodrame hollywoodien* (Paris: Stock, 1985). English quotation from Robert Lang, *American Film Melodrama: Griffith, Vidor, Minelli* (Princeton, N.J.: Princeton University Press, 1989), 50.

111. Heinrich Koch and Heinrich Braune, *Von deutscher Filmkunst. Gehalt und Gestalt* (Berlin: Scherping, 1943).

112. An exhaustive study of this visual stereotype and its variants has been undertaken by Christine Noll Brinckmann. See Christine N. Brinckmann, "Das Gesicht hinter der Scheibe" [1996], in *Die anthropomorphe Kamera und andere Schriften zur filmischen Narration*, ed. Mariann Lewinsky and Alexandra Schneider (Zurich: Chronos, 1997), 200–213. This key image will be examined again at the beginning of chapter 8.

113. Yury Tynyanov, "On Literary Evolution" [Russian 1927], in *Readings in Russian Poetics*, ed. Ladislav Matejka and Krystyna Pomorska (Champaign-Urbana: Dalkey Archive, 2002), 70.

114. Yury Tynyanov, "The Literary Fact" [Russian 1924], in *Modern Genre Theory*, ed. David Duff, trans. Ann Shukman (Harlow, Essex: Longman, 2000), 32.

115. Ibid., 46

116. Tynyanov, "On Literary Evolution," 69.

117. Tynyanov, "The Literary Fact," 35.

118. Ibid., 34.

119. Ibid., 35.

120. Northrop Frye, *Anatomy of Criticism* (Princeton, N.J.: Princeton University Press, 1957).

121. See Cawelti, "The Concept of Formula."

122. Christian Metz, *Language and Cinema* [French 1971], trans. Donna Jean Umiker-Sebeok (The Hague: Mouton, 1974), 130.

123. Teun A. van Dijk, *Tekstwetenschap. Een interdisciplinaire inleiding* (Utrecht: Het Spectrum, 1978).

124. Stuart Kaminsky, *American Film Genres*, 2nd rev. ed. (Chicago: Nelson Hall, 1985), 7.

125. Ibid., 9.

126. Peter Wollen writes about the "master antinomy" between "the wilderness left in the past" and "the garden anticipated in the future." Edward Buscombe similarly describes "stories about the opposition between man and nature and about the establishment of civilization." See Peter Wollen, *Signs and Meaning in the Cinema* [1968] (London: BFI, 1998), 66; and Edward Buscombe, "The Idea of Genre in the American Cinema," in *Film Genre Reader*, ed. Barry Keith Grant (Austin: University of Texas Press, 1986), 16.

127. Buscombe, "The Idea of Genre," 14.

128. Ibid., 14–15.

129. Wright, *Sixguns and Society*.

130. Buscombe, "The Idea of Genre," 13.

131. For an articulation of the concept of "emergent networks," see the section "First Facet: Schema, Reductionism, and Stability" in chapter 1.

132. Stephen Heath, *Questions of Cinema* (Bloomington: University of Indiana Press, 1981), 16.

133. Rick Altman, "Reusable Packaging: Generic Products and the Recycling Process," in *Refiguring American Film Genres: History and Theory*, ed. Nick Browne (Berkeley: University of California Press, 1998), 9.

134. Tzvetan Todorov, *The Fantastic: A Structural Approach to a Literary Genre* [French 1970], trans. Richard Howard (Ithaca, N.Y.: Cornell University Press, 1975), 13–14. Also Tzvetan Todorov, *Genres in Discourse* (Cambridge: Cambridge University Press, 1990), 17. In both of these texts, Todorov expresses his belief that it is possible to analytically establish a correspondence between "theoretical" genre constructions, which are based on commonly shared characteristics, and a historical awareness of genre. In *Genres in Discourse*, 17, he writes: "The study of genres, which has as its starting point the historical evidence of the existence of genres, must have as its ultimate objective precisely the establishment of these [common] properties." And: "I am ultimately more optimistic than authors of two recent studies. . . . Lejeune and Ben-Amos are prepared to see an unbridgeable gap between the abstract and the concrete, between genres as they have existed historically and the categorical analysis to which they can be subjected today."

135. Ludwig Wittgenstein, *Philosophical Investigations* [German 1953], trans. G. E. M. Anscombe, P. M. S. Hacker, and Joachim Schulte (Chichester, West Sussex: Wiley-Blackwell, 2009), §77, p. 40e.

136. Tynyanov, "The Literary Fact," 34.

137. Steve Neale, "Melo Talk: On Meaning and Use of the Term 'Melodrama' in the American Trade Press," *Velvet Light Trap* 32 (1993): 66–89.

138. Thomas Elsaesser, "Tales of Sound and Fury: Observations on the Family Melodrama" [1972], in *Film Theory and Criticism*, eds. Gerald Mast, Marshall Cohen, and Leo Braudy (Oxford: Oxford University Press, 1992), 512–535.

139. Ibid., 532–524.

140. Neale, "Melo Talk," 69.

141. Quoted from Steve Neale, *Genre and Hollywood* (London: Routledge, 2000), 186.

142. See Lang, *American Film Melodrama*.

143. Tom Gunning, "'Those That Are Drawn with a Fine Camel Haired Brush': The Origins of Film Genres," *Iris* 20 (1995): 55.

144. Christine Gledhill, "Rethinking Genre," in *Reinventing Film Studies*, ed. Christine Gledhill and Linda Williams (London: Arnold, 2000), 242.

145. For an instructive overview of his film-genre theory, see Rick Altman, *Film/Genre* (London: BFI, 1999).

146. Rick Altman, "A Semantic/Syntactic Approach to Film Genre" [1984], in *Film Genre Reader*, ed. Barry Keith Grant (Austin: University of Texas Press, 1986), 26–40.

147. Rick Altman, *The American Film Musical* (Bloomington: University of Indiana Press, 1987).

148. I already discussed this in greater detail in Jörg Schweinitz, "'Genre' und lebendiges Genrebewusstsein," *Montage AV* 3, no. 2 (1994): 99–118.

149. Wittgenstein, *Philosophical Investigations*, 36e.

150. George Lakoff, *Women, Fire, and Dangerous Things: What Categories Reveal About the Mind* (Chicago: University of Chicago Press, 1987).

151. Ibid., 5.

152. Ibid., 8.

153. Ibid., 6.

154. Ibid., 84.

155. David Bordwell, *Making Meaning: Inference and Rhetoric in the Interpretation of Cinema* (Cambridge, Mass.: Harvard University Press, 1989), 148.

156. Lev S. Vygotsky, "Thinking and Speech," in *The Collected Works of L. S. Vygotsky* [Russian 1934], ed. Robert W. Rieber and Aaron S. Carton, trans. Norris Minick (New York: Plenum Press, 1987), 1:136.

157. Ibid., 1:138.

158. Ibid., 1:140.

159. Irmela Schneider, "Von der Vielsprachigkeit zur 'Kunst der Hybridisation.' Diskurse des Hybriden," in *Hybridkultur: Medien, Netze, Künste*, ed. Irmela Schneider and Christian W. Thomsen (Cologne: Wienand, 1997), 13–66.

160. Mikhail Bakhtin, *The Dialogic Imagination: Four Essays* [Russian 1975], trans. Michael Holquist and Caryl Emerson (Austin: University of Texas Press, 1981), 358.

161. Ibid., 359.

162. "Hybrid" is understood similarly when the term "hybrid culture" surfaces in debates. See Irmela Schneider, "Von der Vielsprachigkeit," 57; and Elisabeth Bronfen, Benjamin Marius, and Therese Steffen, *Hybride Kulturen. Beiträge zur anglo-amerikanischen Multikulturalismusdebatte* (Tubingen: Stauffenburg, 1997).

163. Schneider, "Von der Vielsprachigkeit," 57.

164. Ihab Hassan, "Postmoderne heute," in *Wege aus der Moderne. Schlüsseltexte der Postmoderne-Diskussion*, ed. Wolfgang Welsch (Weinheim: VCH Acta humaniora, 1988), 52.

165. Ibid., 53.

166. Frank Gruber, "The Western," in *TV and Screen Writing*, ed. Lola G. Yoakem (Berkeley: University of California Press, 1958).

167. Russell's photograph "East and West Shaking Hands" is printed in Michel Frizot, ed., *Neue Geschichte der Fotografie* (Cologne: Könemann, 1998), 216.

168. Roland Barthes, *Mythologies* [French 1957], trans. Annette Lavers (New York: Hill and Wang, 1972).

169. In this case, a kiss with the "wrong" partner, who is ultimately eliminated in the next sequence.

170. Tynyanov, "The Literary Fact," 34–35.

171. See Tynyanov, "On Literary Evolution," 69–70.

172. In Germany, Ines Steiner, Marcus Erbe, and Andreas Gernemann have analyzed the hybrid narrative structure and referentiality of this film, largely in regard to sound design. See Claudia Liebrand and Ines Steiner, eds., *Hollywood Hybrid. Genre und Gender im zeitgenössischen Mainstream-Film* (Marburg: Schüren, 2004), esp. 297–316.

3. THE INTELLECTUAL VIEWPOINT VERSUS THE STEREOTYPE IN MASS CULTURE

1. Dieter Prokop, *Faszination und Langeweile. Die populären Medien* (Stuttgart: Enke, 1979), 77.

2. Wolfgang Iser, *The Fictive and the Imaginary: Charting Literary Anthropology* [German 1991] (Baltimore, Md.: The Johns Hopkins University Press, 1993), 3.

3. Peter Bächlin, *Der Film als Ware* [1947] (Frankfurt am Main: Athenäum Fischer, 1975), 162.

4. Ibid., 164.

5. Ibid., 163.

6. Vinzenz Hediger, *Verführung zum Film. Der amerikanische Kinotrailer seit 1912*, Zürcher Filmstudien 5 (Marburg: Schüren, 2001), 209. See also 52.

7. Bächlin, *Der Film als Ware*, 164.

8. Ibid, 171 (my emphasis).

9. David Bordwell, Janet Staiger, and Kristin Thompson, *The Classical Hollywood Cinema: Film Style and Mode of Production to 1960* (New York: Columbia University Press, 1985). Staiger's section is part 2, "The Hollywood Mode of Production to 1930," 85–154.

10. Ibid., 92.

11. Bächlin, *Film als Ware*, 185.

12. Ibid., 186.

13. Bordwell, Staiger, and Thompson, *The Classical Hollywood Cinema*, 97.

14. Viktor Shklovsky, "Art as Technique" [Russian 1916], in *Russian Formalist Criticism: Four Essays*, trans. Lee T. Lemon and Marion J. Reis (Lincoln: University of Nebraska Press, 1965), 3–24.

15. Richard Avenarius, *Philosophie als Denken der Welt gemäß dem Prinzip des kleinsten Kraftmaßes. Prolegomena zu einer Kritik der reinen Erfahrung* (Berlin: J. Guttentag, 1903).

16. Ibid., 17.

17. Shklovsky, "Art as Technique," 13.

18. Ibid., 12.

19. Ibid., 13.

20. Ibid., 22.

21. Ibid., 18.

22. Ibid., 13.

23. Walter Benjamin, "The Work of Art in the Age of Its Technical Reproducibility: Second Version" [French 1936], in *The Work of Art in the Age of Its Technical Reproducibility and Other Writings on Media*, trans. Edmund Jephcott et al., ed. Michael W. Jennings, Brigid Doherty, and Thomas Y. Levin (Cambridge, Mass.: Harvard University Press, 2008), 37.

24. Viktor Shklovsky, "Plot in Cinematography" [Russian 1923], in *Literature and Cinematography* (Champaign, Ill.: Dalkey Archive, 2008), 42.

25. Viktor Shklovsky, "Tarzan" [in Russian], *Russkii sovremennik* 4 (1924): 253–254.

3. THE INTELLECTUAL VIEWPOINT VERSUS THE STEREOTYPE

26. Ibid, 253.

27. Max Weber, "Science as Vocation" [German 1919], in *From Max Weber: Essays in Sociology*, ed. and trans. Hans H. Gerth and C. Wright Mills (London: Routledge, 1991), 139.

28. Siegfried Kracauer, "The Mass Ornament" [German 1927], in *The Mass Ornament: Weimar Essays*, ed. and trans. Thomas Y. Levin (Cambridge, Mass.: Harvard University Press, 1995), 80.

29. Siegfried Kracauer, "The Little Shop-Girls Go to the Movies" [German 1927], in *The Mass Ornament: Weimar Essays* (Cambridge, Mass.: Harvard University Press, 1995), 291–306.

30. Kracauer, "The Mass Ornament," p. 80

31. Siegfried Kracauer, "Ein feiner Kerl. Analyse eines Ufa-Films" [German 1931], in *Von Caligari zu Hitler* (Frankfurt am Main: Suhrkamp, 1984), 507.

32. Max Horkheimer and Theodor W. Adorno, *Dialectic of Enlightenment: Philosophical Fragments* [German 1947], trans. Edmund Jephcott (Stanford, Calif.: Stanford University Press, 2002).

33. See Umberto Eco, "The Myth of Superman," in *The Role of the Reader* (Bloomington: University of Indiana Press, 1979).

34. In this context, "myth" is an emphasis on phantasmagoria and is understood not as the eternal repetition of the same, that is, not as an ahistoric or suprahistoric structure.

35. Edmund Husserl, *Phantasy, Image Consciousness, and Memory* [German 1980, papers published posthumously], in *Husserliana: Edmund Husserl, Collected Works*, trans. John B. Brough (Dordrecht: Springer, 2006), 23:642.

36. Pierre Bourdieu, *Distinction: A Social Critique of the Judgment of Taste*, trans. Richard Nice (London: Routledge & Kegan Paul, 1984), 270.

37. Helmut Lethen, *Neue Sachlichkeit 1924–1932. Studien zur Literatur des "weißen Sozialismus"* (Stuttgart: Metzler, 1970), 420.

38. Hermann Broch, "Evil in the Value System of Art" [German 1933], In *Geist and Zeitgeist: The Spirit in an Unspiritual Age—Six Essays*, trans. John Hargraves (New York: Counterpoint, 2002), 37.

39. Ibid., 16.

40. Ibid., 17.

41. Ibid.

42. Ibid., 18.

43. Jochen Schulte-Sasse, *Die Kritik der Trivialliteratur seit der Aufklärung. Studien zur Geschichte des modernen Kitschbegriffs* (Munich: Fink, 1971), 26.

44. Broch, "Evil in the Value System of Art," 37.

45. Ibid., 34.

46. Ibid., 33–34.

47. Ruth Amossy, *Les idées reçues. Sémiologie du stéréotype* (Paris: Nathan, 1991), 77.

48. Peter Zima, *Moderne—Postmoderne: Gesellschaft, Philosophie, Literatur* (Tubingen: Francke, 1997), 272.

49. Himself rooted in this mode of thought, Zima, for example, is irritated by the stance of the postmodernist Leslie Fiedler primarily because he does not seem "to be bothered by . . . standard stereotypes." He also objects to Jim Collins's position: "The idea does not

occur to Collins that this aesthetic and cultural plurality could be a superficial plurality orchestrated by the cultural industry, which eternally varies the countless ideological and commercial stereotypes."

50. Adorno and Horkheimer, *Dialectic of Enlightenment*, 119.

51. Theodor W. Adorno, "The Schema of Mass Culture" [German 1942, in manuscript], in *The Culture Industry: Selected Essays on Mass Culture*, ed. J. M. Bernstein (New York: Routledge, 2001), 91.

52. Miriam Hansen, "Ein Massenmedium konstruiert sein Publikum: King Vidor's The Crowd," *Die Neue Gesellschaft. Frankfurter Hefte* 40, no. 9 (1993): 843.

53. Siegfried Kracauer, *Theory of Film: The Redemption of Physical Reality* [1960], with an introduction by Miriam Bratu Hansen (Oxford: Oxford University Press, 1997), 309.

54. Shklovsky, "Art as Technique," 18.

55. See Kracauer, *Theory of Film*, 287–300.

56. Ibid., 46.

57. Ibid.

58. Ibid., 48.

59. My choice of words is intended to indicate a parallel to Roland Barthes's aesthetics of photography. See Roland Barthes, *Camera Lucida: Reflections on Photography* [French 1980], trans. Richard Howard (London: Jonathan Cape, 1982).

60. Gilles Deleuze, *Cinema 2: The Time Image* [French 1985], trans. Hugh Tomlinson and Robert Galeta (London: Continuum, 2005), 20.

61. Roberto Rossellini, "A Discussion of Neorealism. An Interview with Mario Verdone" [Italian 1952], in *My Method: Writings and Interviews*, ed. Adriano Aprà (New York: Marsilio, 1995), 36.

62. Ibid, 35.

63. Ibid., 36.

64. Roberto Rossellini, "L'idée néo-réaliste," in *Roberto Rossellini*, ed. Mario Verdone (Paris: Édition Seghers, 1963), 28.

65. Ibid.

66. Yuri Lotman, *Semiotics of Cinema* [Russian 1973], trans. Mark Suino (Ann Arbor: University of Michigan Press/Michigan Slavic Contributions, 1976), 20–21.

67. Stanley Cavell pointed out that despite schematic conceptions about European cinema in America, even classical European directors (he mentions Renoir and Vigo, among others) do extensively use character types in their narratives. This by no means diminishes their artistic achievement, since the latter is not based on the creation of (individual) characters rather than types. See Stanley Cavell, "More of the World Viewed," *Georgia Review* 28 (1995): 582.

68. Gilles Deleuze, *Cinema 1: The Movement Image* [French 1983], trans. Hugh Tomlinson and Barbara Habberjam (London: Continuum, 2005), 215.

69. Herbert Jhering, "Schauspielerische Klischees" *Blätter des Deutschen Theaters* 2, no. 30 (1912/1913): 488.

70. See André Bazin, "Extract from André Bazin, 'La politique des auteurs'" [French 1957], in *Theories of Authorship*, ed. John Caughie (London: Routledge, 1981), 44–46.

71. Joachim Paech, "Gesellschaftskritin und Provokation—Nouvelle Vague: Sie küssten und sie schlugen ihn," in *Fischer Filmgeschichte*, ed. Werner Faulstich und Helmut Korte (Frankfurt am Main: Fischer, 1990), 377.

72. See François Truffaut, "A Certain Tendency in the French Cinema" [French 1954], in *Movies and Methods*, ed. Bill Nichols (Berkeley: University of California Press, 1976), 1:224–237.

73. Bazin, "Extract from André Bazin," 45–46 (my emphasis).

74. Ibid., 45.

75. Ibid., 46.

76. Ibid.

77. Andrew Sarris, "Notes on the Auteur Theory in 1962," in *Film Theory and Criticism*, ed. Gerald Mast, Marshall Cohen, and Leo Braudy (Oxford: Oxford University Press, 1992), 585–588.

78. Shklovsky, "Art as Technique," 12.

79. Ibid., 13.

80. Kristin Thompson, *Breaking the Glass Armor: Neoformalist Film Analysis* (Princeton, N.J.: Princeton University Press, 1988), 11.

81. Ibid.

82. Ibid., 12.

83. Yury Tynyanov, "On Literary Evolution" [Russian 1927], in *Readings in Russian Poetics: Formalist and Structuralist Views*, ed. Ladislav Matejka and Krystyna Pomorska (Champaign, Ill.: Dalkey Archive, 2002), 69.

84. Yury Tynyanov, "The Literary Fact" [Russian 1924], in *Modern Genre Theory*, ed. David Duff, trans. Ann Shukman (Harlow, Essex: Longman, 2000), 34.

85. Pauline Kael, "Some Speculations on the Appeal of the Auteur Theory" [1963], in Pauline Kael, *I Lost It at the Movies* (Boston: Little, Brown, and Co., 1965), 315, 311, 319.

86. Mast, Cohen, and Braudy, *Film Theory and Criticism*, 580. This quotation appears in the introduction to chapter 6, "The Film Artist."

87. See Siegfried J. Schmidt, *Der Diskurs des radikalen Konstruktivismus* (Frankfurt am Main: Suhrkamp, 1992).

88. Fredric Jameson, *Postmodernism; or, The Cultural Logic of Late Capitalism* (London: Verso, 1996), 12.

89. Jean Baudrillard, *Symbolic Exchange and Death* [French 1976] (London: Sage, 2002), 2.

90. Jameson, *Postmodernism*, 15.

91. Vilém Flusser, "Typen und Charaktere," in *Die Revolution der Bilder. Der Flusser-Reader zu Kommunikation, Medien und Design* (Berlin: Bollmann, 1995), 194.

92. Ibid., 195–196.

93. See the analysis in part 3 of this book.

94. On the term "self-referentiality," or *Selbstreferentialität* in German, see Kay Kirchmann, "Zwischen Selbstreflexivität und Selbstreferentialität. Überlegungen zur Ästhetik des Selbstbezüglichen als filmischer Modernität," *Film und Kritik* 2 (1994): 23–28. The phenomenon of openly self-referential stereotype worlds will be discussed in more detail in chapter 8.

95. Jameson, *Postmodernism*, 9–10.

96. Viktor Shklovsky, "Chaplin" [Russian 1923], in *Literature and Cinematography*, trans. Irina Masinovsky (Champaign, Ill.: Dalkey Archive, 2008), 67.

97. Drawing on Paul Ricoeur, Jane Feuer sees the "myth of entertainment," as connected with the interplay of demystification and remythicization, at work in reflexive classical film musicals. This idea can be expanded to include the self-reflexive treatment of the genre's stereotypes. See Jane Feuer, "The Self-Reflexive Musical and the Myth of Entertainment," in *Film Genre Reader*, ed. Barry Keith Grant (Austin: University of Texas Press, 1986), 331.

4. PRELUDE: WALTHER RATHENAU'S CULTURAL CRITICISM, HUGO MÜNSTERBERG'S EUPHORIC CONCEPT OF FILM AS ART, AND THE NEGLECT OF THE STEREOTYPE

1. Arnold Höllriegel, *Das Hollywood Bilderbuch* (Leipzig: E. P. Tal, 1927), 9 (my emphasis).

2. Egon Erwin Kisch, *(beehrt sich darzubieten) Paradies Amerika* [1929] (Berlin: Aufbau, 1994), 109.

3. This is described by Deniz Göktürk, *Künstler, Cowboys, Ingenieure: Kultur und mediengeschichtliche Studien zu deutschen Amerika-Texten 1912–1920* (Munich: Fink, 1998).

4. Sigfried Giedion, *Mechanization Takes Command* (Oxford: Oxford University Press, 1948), 115.

5. Ibid., 116.

6. Walter Rathenau, *Zur Kritik der Zeit* (Berlin: Fischer, 1912).

7. Ibid., 81.

8. See Norbert Elias, *The Civilizing Process: Sociogenetic and Psychogenetic Investigations* [German 1939] (Oxford: Blackwell, 2000). See in particular vol. 1, part 1, pp. 5–30 ("Sociogenesis of the Antithesis Between *Kultur* and *Zivilisation* in German Usage").

9. Rathenau, *Zur Kritik der Zeit*, 16.

10. Walther Rathenau, *Zur Mechanik des Geistes* (Berlin: S. Fischer, 1913). The cinema is relegated to the category of a "soulless place" (43).

11. Ibid., 58.

12. Ibid., 62.

13. Ibid., 63.

14. Ibid., 75.

15. Ibid., 76–77.

16. Ibid., 86.

17. Ibid., 89.

18. bid., 94.

19. Walter Benjamin, "The Work of Art in the Age of Its Technical Reproducibility: Second Version" [French 1936], in *The Work of Art in the Age of Its Technical Reproducibility and Other Writings on Media*, trans. Edmund Jephcott et al., ed. Michael W. Jennings, Brigid Doherty, and Thomas Y. Levin (Cambridge, Mass.: Harvard University Press, 2008), 39–41.

20. Ibid., 89.

21. Ibid., 94.

22. Ibid.

23. Ibid., 106.

24. Ibid., 116.

25. Ibid., 118.

26. Ibid.

27. Drawing on Habermas's terminology, Heinz B. Heller studied the German intellectual discourse on cinema during the era of silent film from this vantage point. See Heinz B. Heller, *Literarische Intelligenz und Film. Zu Veränderungen der ästhetischen Theorie und Praxis unter dem Eindruck des Films 1910–1930 in Deutsch*land (Tubingen: Niemeyer, 1985).

28. Walther Rathenau, "Vom Werte und Unwerte des Kinos" [answer to a survey by the Frankfurter Zeitung, 1912] in *Kino-Debatte*, ed. Anton Kaes (Munich: dtv, 1978), 66.

29. Ibid.

30. Rathenau, *Zur Kritik der Zeit*, 94–95.

31. See Jörg Schweinitz, ed. *Prolog vor dem Film: Nachdenken über ein neues Medium 1909–1914* (Leipzig: Reclam, 1992). The original German texts of Franz Pfemfert, "Kino als Erzieher," [1911] and Egon Friedell [1913] are reprinted in *Prolog vor dem Film*, part 3, pp. 145–222.

32. Alfred Kerr, "Kino" [1912/1913], in *Kino-Debatte*, 76.

33. Eileen Bowser, *The Transformation of Cinema: 1907–1915*, vol. 2, *History of the American Cinema* (New York: Scribner, 1990), esp. 167–190.

34. David Bordwell, Janet Staiger, and Kristin Thompson, *The Classical Hollywood Cinema: Film Style and Mode of Production to 1960* (New York: Columbia University Press, 1985), 85–153.

35. Ibid., 121.

36. Bowser, *Transformation of Cinema*, 54.

37. Bordwell, Staiger, and Thompson, *Classical Hollywood Cinema*, 54.

38. Cited in ibid., 121. The quotation originally stems from *Motography* (July 1911).

39. Ibid., 124. Staiger describes corresponding activities in the Triangle-Fine-Arts-Studio in 1916.

40. Hugo Münsterberg, *The Photoplay: A Psychological Study* [1916], in *Hugo Münsterberg on Film*, ed. Allan Langdale (New York: Routledge, 2002).

41. See Jörg Schweinitz, "The Aesthetic Idealist as Efficiency Engineer: Hugo Münsterberg's Theories of Perception, Psychotechnics and Cinema," in *Film 1900: Technology, Perception, Culture*, ed. Annemone Ligensa and Klaus Kreimeier (Eastleigh: Libbey, 2009), 77–86.

42. Hugo Münsterberg, *Grundzüge der Psychotechnik* (Leipzig: J. A. Barth, 1914), 435.

43. Ibid.

44. Ibid.

45. Ibid.

46. Ibid.

47. Ibid., 424.

48. Ibid., 423.

49. Ibid.

50. Ibid., 650.

51. Münsterberg, *Photoplay*, 55.

52. The passage reads: "Advertising and the culture industry are merging technically no less than economically. In both, the same thing appears in countless places, and the mechanical repetition of the same culture product is already that of the same propaganda slogan. In both, under the same dictate of effectiveness, technique is becoming psychotechnique." Max Horkheimer and Theodor W. Adorno, *Dialectic of Enlightenment*, trans. Edmund Jephcott (Stanford, Calif.: Stanford University Press, 2002), 133.

53. Hugo Münsterberg, *The Eternal Values* [German 1908] (Boston: Houghton Mifflin, 1909), 204–253.

54. Jörg Schweinitz, "Psychotechnik, idealistische Ästhetik und der Film als mental strukturierter Wahrnehmungsraum: Die Filmtheorie von H. Münsterberg" [foreword], in Hugo Münsterberg, *Das Lichtspiel. Eine pschologische Studie (1916) und andere Schriften zum Film*, (Vienna: Synema, 1996), 9–26.

55. Münsterberg, *Photoplay*, 160.

56. John Dewey, "*The Eternal Values*. By Hugo Münsterberg" [review], *The Philosophical Review* 19 (1910): 190.

5. BÉLA BALÁZS'S NEW VISUAL CULTURE, THE TRADITION OF LINGUISTIC SKEPTICISM, AND ROBERT MUSIL'S NOTION OF THE "FORMULAIC"

1. The term "high culture" is here not intended as a value judgment but indicates the self-image of a specific cultural discourse.

2. Béla Balázs, "Visible Man or the Culture of Film" [German 1924], in *Béla Balázs: Early Film Theory*, ed. Erica Carter, trans. Rodney Livingstone (New York: Berghahn Books, 2010), 1–90.

3. Rudolf Harms, *Philosophie des Films. Seine ästhetischen und metaphysischen Grundlagen* (Leipzig: Meiner, 1926).

4. Gertud Koch, "The Physiognomy of Things," *New German Critique*, no. 40 (Winter 1987): 167–177.

5. Hanno Loewy, *Béla Balázs—Märchen, Ritual und Film* (Berlin: Vorwerk 8, 2003).

6. Joseph Zsuffa, *Béla Balázs. The Man and the Artist* (Berkeley: University of California Press, 1987).

7. See Joachim Paech, "Disposition der Einfühlung. Anmerkungen zum Einfluss der Einfühlungs-Ästhetik des 19. Jahrhunderts auf die Theorie des Kinofilms," in *Der Film in der Geschichte* (GFF-Schriften 6), ed. Knut Hickethier, Eggo Müller, and Rainer Rother (Berlin: Sigma, 1997), 106–121. In addition to discussing more general concepts, Paech specifically deals with the influence of Ernst Iros on film theory.

8. Theodor Lipps, *Grundlegung der Ästhetik* [1903] (Leipzig: Voss, 1923), 1:112.

9. See Knut Hickethier, "Der Schauspieler als Produzent. Überlegungen zur Theorie des medialen Schauspielens," in *Der Körper im Bild. Schauspielen—Darstellen—Erscheinen*

(Gff-Schriften 7), ed. Heinz B. Heller, Karl Prümm, and Brigitte Peulings (Marburg: Schüren, 1999), 9–30, esp. 12–14; and Frank Kessler, "Lesbare Körper," *KINtop* 7 (1998): 15–28.

10. See Klaus Kreimeier, ed. *Metaphysik des Dekors. Raum, Architektur und Licht im klassischen deutschen Stummfilm* (Marburg: Schüren, 1994); and Hermann Kappelhoff, *Der möblierte Mensch: G. W. Pabst und die Utopie der Sachlichkeit—ein poetologischer Versuch zum Weimarer Autorenkino* (Berlin: Vorwerk 8, 1995).

11. Max Bruns, "Kino und Buchhandel" [1913], in *Prolog vor dem Film*, ed. Jörg Schweinitz (Leipzig: Reclam, 1992), 275. The text is a response to a survey on cinema and the publishing industry.

12. Franz Pfemfert, "Kino als Erzieher" [1911], in *Prolog vor dem Film*, 165–169.

13. Konrad Lange, "Die Zukunft des Kinos," [1914], in *Prolog vor dem Film*, 114.

14. Friedrich Kittler, *Discourse Networks 1800/1900* [German 1985], trans. Michael Metteer with Chris Cullens (Stanford, Calif.: Stanford University Press, 1990), 229.

15. See Thomas Koebner, "Der Film als neue Kunst—Reaktionen der literarischen Intelligenz. Zur Theorie des Stummfilms (1911–24)," in *Literaturwissenschaft—Medienwissenschaft*, ed. Helmut Kreuzer (Heidelberg: Quelle & Meyer, 1977), 1–31; and Heinz B. Heller, *Literarische Intelligenz und Film. Zur Veränderung der ästhetischen Theorie und Praxis unter dem Eindruck des Films 1910–1930 in Deutschland* (Tubingen: Niemeyer, 1985).

16. Hugo von Hofmannsthal, *The Lord Chandos Letter* [German 1902], trans. Russell Stockman (Marlboro, Vt.: Marlboro Press, 1986).

17. Ibid., 23.

18. Ibid., 19.

19. The German *Begriff* unifies the meanings of "term," "concept," and "idea" in English. In this chapter, these words will be used interchangeably to refer to *Begriff*.

20. Hugo von Hofmannsthal, "Eine Monographie," 266.

21. Hofmannsthal, *Lord Chandos*, 22.

22. Walter Rathenau, *Zur Kritik der Zeit* (Berlin: S. Fischer, 1912), 146–147.

23. Hofmannsthal, "Eine Monographie. Friedrich Mittenwurzer, von Eugen Guglia" [1895], *Gesammelte Werke in Einzelausgaben, Prosa I* (Frankfurt am Main: S. Fucher, 1950), 265.

24. Ibid., 266.

25. Ibid.

26. Hofmannsthal, *Lord Chandos*, 21.

27. Walter Benjamin, "The Work of Art in the Age of Its Technical Reproducibility: Second Version" [French 1936], in *The Work of Art in the Age of Its Technical Reproducibility and Other Writings on Media*, trans. Edmund Jephcott et al., ed. Michael W. Jennings, Brigid Doherty, and Thomas Y. Levin (Cambridge, Mass.: Harvard University Press, 2008), 24.

28. In a letter to Leopold Freiherr von Adrian zu Werburg from January 16, 1903, Hofmannsthal remarks on the arguments he has Chandos articulate: "the content should by all means be a matter of interest to me and those close to me." Cited in Karl Pestalozzi, *Sprachskepsis und Sprachmagie im Werk des jungen Hofmannsthal* (Zurich: Atlantis, 1958), 117.

29. Mauthner and Hofmannsthal corresponded in October and November 1902, in which they mutually confirmed their agreement on a language critical position in regard to *The Lord Chandos Letter* and *Beiträge zu einer Kritik der Sprache*. Both letters can be found in Hugo von Hofmannsthal, *Sämtliche Werke*, ed. Rudolf Hirsch (Frankfurt am Main: Fischer, 1991), 31:286–287.

30. Fritz Mauthner, *Beiträge zu einer Kritik der Sprache*, vol. 1, *Zur Sprache und zur Psychologie* [1901/1902] (Frankfurt am Main: Ullstein, 1982), 115.

31. Ibid., 114.

32. Ibid., 421.

33. Ibid., 695.

34. See Kristina Mandalka, *August Stramm und kosmischer Mystizismus im frühen zwanzigsten Jahrhundert* (Herberg: Bautz, 1992).

35. Already Rathenau was disgusted by the popularity of such words as "synthesis" in colloquial language. They appeared to him semantically hollow and indicative of the mechanization of the world, which was the theme of his cultural criticism: "Never has one used the word 'synthesis' so frequently as today; but what are syntheses? Similarities, analogies, images, symbols, contexts; the more exotic, the better-known, the more presumptuous, the more trivial, always presented, explained, defended, and proven according to the same recipe." Rathenau, *Zur Kritik der Zeit*, 147. This kind of language critique still prevails. Seventy-five years after Rathenau, Uwe Pörksen dedicated an entire book to similar concepts, which he calls "plastic words" and associates with "recent changes of vernacular language." Uwe Pörksen, *Plastic Words: The Tyranny of a Modular Language* [German 1988], trans. Jutta Mason and David Cayley (Philadelphia: The Pennsylvania State University Press, 1995), xvii. Interestingly, in a second survey Pörksen addresses similar phenomena in the sphere of visual media as "visiotypes": "I use the word 'visiotype' in parallel with 'stereotype' and what I mean by this is . . . this type of quickly standardized visualization." Uwe Pörksen, *Weltmarkt der Bilder. Eine Philosophie der Visiotype* (Stuttgart: Klett-Cotta, 1997), 27.

36. That metaphors ultimately become inconspicuous as metaphors and turn into words no longer considered metaphoric is a much-studied phenomenon in linguistics. Karl Bühler, for one, pointed out that "much that was originally metaphorical gradually stops being felt to be such in the course of the history of the language." Karl Bühler, *Theory of Language—The Representational Function of Language* [German 1934], trans. Donald Fraser Goodwin (Amsterdam: John Benjamins B.V., 1990), 393.

37. Mauthner, *Kritik der Sprache*, 131.

38. Thus, according to Fritz Mauthner: "Every single word has been impregnated by its own history, every single word intrinsically comprises an endless development from metaphor to metaphor. If someone using a word were aware of but a small part of this metaphorical development of language, he would not manage a single utterance for the very copiousness of its history; but he is not aware of this, and so he uses every single word only according to its current value, as token." Ibid., 115.

39. Ibid., 131–132 (My emphasis).

40. Roland Barthes, *Roland Barthes* [French 1975], trans. Richard Howard (New York: Hill and Wang, 1977), 89.

41. Hofmannsthal, "Eine Monographie," 265.

42. Hofmannsthal, "The Substitute for Dreams" [German 1921], in *German Essays on Film*, ed. Richard W. McCormick and Alison Guenther-Pal, trans. Lance W. Garmer (New York: Continuum, 2004), 54.

43. Egon Friedell, "Prolog vor dem Film" [1913], in *Prolog vor dem Film*, ed. Jörg Schweinitz (Leipzig: Reclam, 1992), 205.

44. Ibid., 205–206.

45. Alfred Baeumler, "Die Wirkungen der Lichtbildbühne. Versuch einer Apologie des Kinematographentheaters" [1912], in *Prolog vor dem Film*, 192.

46. As Balázs elaborates in *Visible Man*: "In close-ups every wrinkle becomes a crucial element of character and every twitch of a muscle testifies to a pathos that signals great inner events" (37). Later he coins the term "microphysiognomy" to describe this phenomenon. See Béla Balázs, "The Spirit of Film" in *Béla Balázs: Early Film Theory* (see note 2), 103.

47. It is therefore no coincidence that precisely Balázs, with his affinity to Marxism, would use the word "race" to describe cultural differences in repertoires of expressive movement. However, Balázs's arguments were seldom coherent: at another juncture he raises the possibility of changing culturally based modes of expression through the international impact of film, which he remarkably considers a positive process of "normalization." See Balázs, "Visible Man," 14–15.

48. Lipps, *Grundlegung der Ästhetik*, 1:108.

49. Maurice Merleau-Ponty, "The Film and the New Psychology" [Lecture, French 1945], in *Sense and Non-Sense*, trans. H. Dreyfus and P. Dreyfus (Evanston, Ill.: Northwestern University Press, 1964), 48–59.

50. Ibid. Merleau-Ponty rejects *all* semiotic mediation of expressive movement (as signifier) and meaning (signified), arguing that they "should not be considered two externally related items . . . the body incarnates a manner of behavior." Instead of assuming that successive conventionalization produces (via automatization) a *fiction* of the natural, Merleau-Ponty too retreats to a vague notion of the naturalness of expressive movement, of organic unity, which renders the distinction between the signified and signifier meaningless. Although he did admit (somewhat inconsistently with his thinking) that "we recognize a certain common structure in each person's voice, face, gestures, and bearing" and that this plays a role in the perception of another person's expressive movement, for him this structure has nothing in common with the conventional, on the one hand, and it does not concern recognition but a metaphysical transference, on the other: "The new psychology has, generally speaking, revealed man to us not as an understanding which constructs the world but as a being thrown into the world and attached to it by a natural bond. As a result it re-educates us in how to see this world which we touch at every point of our being" (53–54).

51. Lipps, *Grundlegung der Ästhetik*, 108.

52. Carl Hauptmann, "Film und Theater" [1919], in *Kinodebatte. Texte zum Verhältnis der Literatur und Film*, ed. Anton Kaes (Munich: dtv, 1978), 125.

53. On the affinity in German film theory of the period for the mythical notion associated with the prefix *Ur-* ("primal," "primeval," "original," or "ancient"), see Loewy, *Béla Balázs*, 300–302.

54. Hauptmann, "Film und Theater," 127.

55. Balázs, "Visible Man," 11.

56. Ibid., 13.

57. Ibid., 9.

58. Béla Balázs, "Sensationsfilme" [review 1924], *Der sichtbare Mensch. Kritiken und Aufsätze 1922–1926. Schriften zum Film*, ed. Helmut H. Diederichs and Wolfgang Gersch (Berlin: Henschel, 1982), 1:266.

59. Balázs, "Visible Man," 9.

60. Ibid., 10.

61. Georg Simmel, "The Aesthetic Significance of the Face" [German 1901], in *Essays on Sociology, Philosophy, and Aesthetics*, ed. K. H. Wolff (New York: Harper & Row, 1959), 276–281.

62. Ibid., 83.

63. Baeumler, "Wirkungen der Lichtbildbühne," 190–191.

64. Robert Musil, "Toward a New Aesthetic: Observations on a Dramaturgy of Film" [German 1925], in *Precision and Soul: Essays and Addresses*, ed. and trans Burton Pike and David S. Luft (Chicago: University of Chicago Press, 1995), 193. See also Arno Rusegger, " 'Denn jede Kunst bedeutet ein eigenes Verhältnis des Menschen zur Welt, eine eigene Dimension der Seele'—Béla Balázs' Filmtheorie als Paradigma für eine meta-fiktionale Poetik bei Robert Musil," in *Kinoschriften* (Vienna: Verband der Wissenschaftlichen Gesellschaften Österreichs, 1990), 2:131–144.

65. Musil, "Toward a New Aesthetic," 198.

66. Ibid.

67. See Frank Kessler, "Photogénie und Physiognomie," in *Kinoschriften* (Vienna: Synema, 1996), 4:125–136.

68. Benjamin, *The Work of Art*, 37.

69. On Bazin, see Margrit Tröhler, "Film–Bewegung und die ansteckende Kraft von Analogien: Zu André Bazins Konzeption des Zuschauers," *Montage AV* 18, no. 1 (2009): 49–74.

70. Balázs, "The Spirit of Film," 128.

71. Friedrich Nietzsche, *Gesammelte Werke*, vol. 14, *Aus der Zarathustra- un Umwerthungszeit 1882–1884* (Munich: Musarion, 1925), 22.

72. Balázs, "Visible Man," 46–51.

73. Ibid., 53: "Landscape is a physiognomy, a face that all at once, at a particular spot, gazes out at us, as if emerging from the chaotic lines of a picture puzzle." Joachim Paech has pointed out the close relationship between these ideas and Rilke's concept of the thing (*Ding*). See Joachim Paech, "Rodin, Rilke—und der kinematographische Raum," in *Kinoschriften* (Vienna: Verband der Wissenschaftlichen Gesellschaften Österreichs, 1990), 2:150.

74. Balázs, "Visible Man," 41.

75. Both Gertrud Koch and Sabine Hake discuss the advantages of Balázs's typical essay style of the period, which, on the one hand, produced theoretical inconsistencies and incoherencies but, on the other, conveyed actual observations and the spirit of contemporary cinema with great transparency. See Gertud Koch, "Béla Balázs: The Pysiognomy

of Things," 174; and Sabine Hake, *The Cinema's Third Machine: Writing on Film in Germany, 1907–1933* (Lincoln: University of Nebraska Press, 1993), 246.

76. Lotte H. Eisner, *The Haunted Screen: Expressionism in the German Cinema and the Influence of Max Reinhardt* [French 1952] (Berkeley: University of California Press, 2008), 11.

77. Balázs, "Visible Man," 51.

78. Musil, "Toward a New Aesthetic," 198.

79. Mikhail Iampolski, "Neozhidannoe rodstvo: Rozhdenie kinoteorii dukha fiziognomiki [The Birth of Film Theory out of the Spirit of Physiognomy]," *Iskusstvo kino* 12 (1986): 94–104. "Die Geburt der Filmtheorie aus dem Geist der Physiognomik" *Beiträge zur Film- und Fernsehwissenschaft* 27, no. 2 (1986): 79–98.

80. In her study on August Stramm, Kristina Mandalka has exhaustively elaborated the correlation between linguistic skepticism and a mystical notion of the cosmos. As she states: "The *invocation of cosmic reality was a favorite theme* in the period of *Lebensmystik* (life mysticism) and *Lebenspathos* (life pathos), the period of the monistic notion of utter unity. Mombert and Däubler are the main representatives of a cosmically oriented poetry, which validated the age-old idea of the *one pervading all* as the *innermost principle of the world*, which put forth the gnostic equation *light = Weltinstinkt* (world instinct) = *soul = love*." Mandalka, *August Stramm*, 14.

81. Iampolski has also studied this tradition of cinematic utopia. See Mikhail Iampolski, "Die Utopie vom kosmischen Schauspiel und der Kinematograph," *Beiträge zur Film- und Fernsehwissenschaft* 29, no. 34 (1988): 177–191.

82. Hauptmann, "Film und Theater," 126.

83. Ibid.

84. Paul Scheerbarth, *Die große Revolution* [1902] (Leipzig and Weimar: Kiepenhauer, 1983).

85. Harms, *Philosophie des Films*, 185 (my emphasis). From the written assessment of Harms's doctoral thesis *Untersuchungen zur Aesthetik des Spielfilms* (Studies on the Aesthetics of Film) by Johannes Volkert (dated June 19, 1922, and preserved in the archives of the University of Leipzig), such passages apparently provoked the following judgment: "What the writer ultimately presents as a metaphysics of film I can only deem fantastic ideas." The handwritten dissertation submitted in May 1922—of which apparently later revised typed copies were made for the library of the UFA-Lehrschau film institute (today preserved in the HFF Library Babelsberg), among others—served as the basis for an expanded text published in 1926 in book form. The common opinion that Harms's book is merely an unoriginal repetition of a number of theses from Balázs's *Visible Man* (1924) does not do the text full justice in light of the dates when it was written.

86. Siegfried Kracauer, "Bücher vom Film," in *Frankfurter Zeitung* 71, no. 505, *Literaturblatt* 60, no. 28 (July 10, 1927): 5.

87. Balázs, "Visible Man," 38.

88. Ibid., 84. This idea was thoroughly characteristic of the physiognomic discourse in film theory. As Heinz B. Heller observes: "For literary intellectuals it was . . . their own sense social alienation, manifested in language, that was prefigured by the myth of gesture in silent film." Heinz B. Heller, *Literarische Intelligenz und Film. Zu Veränderung der ästhetischen Theorie und Praxis unter dem Eindruck des Filmes 1910–1930 in Deutschland* (Tubingen: Niemeyer, 1985), 179.

89. Balázs, "Visible Man," 84.

90. Kracauer, "Bücher vom Film," 5. At first glance, it may seem paradoxical that Kracauer, who mistrusted all abstraction and argued so phenomenologically in his later *Theory of Film*, to a certain extent evinced a different style of thinking in this polemic dating from 1927. Most astonishing is his attack on the interpretation of film as a medium of new visibility and his plea theory. In this context, Kracauer exhibited a way of thinking that displayed a clear preference for analytical knowledge and an understanding of the inter-relationships *behind* the appearances of reality. In contrast, the later Kracauer would glorify the surface.

91. Musil, "Toward a New Aesthetic," 199.

92. Ibid., 201.

93. Ibid., 202.

94. Ibid., 200.

95. Already during his studies and work on his doctoral thesis with Carl Stumpf in Berlin, Musil came in close contact with Gestalt theory. On the influence of Gestalt theory on Musil, see Matthias Bauer, "Der Film als Vorbild literarischer Ästhetik: Balázs, Musil und die Folgen," in *Grauzonen: Positionen zwischen Literatur und Film, 1910–1960*, ed. Stefan Keppler-Tasaki and Fabienne Liptay (Munich: Edition Text und Kritik, 2010), 41–79.

96. Musil, "Toward a New Aesthetic," 201.

97. Ibid. (My emphasis).

98. Ibid., 198. (My emphasis).

99. See Hartmut Winkler, *Der filmische Raum und der Zuschauer. 'Apparatus'—Semantik— 'Ideologie'* (Heidelberg: Winter, 1982). See chap. 3, esp. 164–173.

100. Umberto Eco, *Einführung in die Semiotik*, ed. Jürgen Trabant (Munich: Fink, 1972), 202–203. See also the subchapter "Ist das ikonische Zeichen konventionell?" (200–214). This German book is a reworked and expanded translation of *La struttura assente* (1968). The English volume, *A Theory of Semiotics* (Bloomington: University of Indiana Press, 1976), is essentially a new work written directly in English—which was later trans-lated into Italian as *Trattato di semiotica generale*. See the introduction to *A Theory of Semiotics*, vii–viii.

101. Ibid., 254.

102. Musil, "Toward a New Aesthetic," 203.

103. Ibid., 201.

104. Ibid., 202.

105. Ibid.

106. Ibid.

107. Here I am referring to Petra Löffler's term *sekundäre Inszenierung*. See Petra Löffler, "Eine sichtbare Sprache. Sprechende Münder im stummen Film," *Montage AV* 13, no. 2 (2004): 54–74. Löffler uses it to differentiate between primary, or everyday, facial expressions and the medial transformation thereof that comes with secondary staging. "Thus the question presents itself as to how one can here [in silent film] regard the human figure as simultaneously 'natural' *and* 'artificial,' as a primary phenomenon *and* a secondary effect of medial transformations. Obviously film forces us to tolerate the

discrepancy between a familiar and therefore unquestioned appearance and the staged version thereof" (73). The notion of the acting stereotype may help to further illuminate some of the aspects of the conundrum described here.

108. Musil, "Toward a New Aesthetic," 203.

109. Ibid.

110. Ibid.

111. Ibid.

112. Ibid.

113. Balázs, "Visible Man," 4. On this Sabine Hake comments: "Here the most advanced technology of mass entertainment makes possible the (imaginary) return to a preindustrial culture and an idealized definition of folklore." Sabine Hake, *The Cinema's Third Machine* (Lincoln: University of Nebraska Press, 1993), 228.

114. Balázs, "Visible Man," 30.

115. See Rusegger, "Béla Balázs' Filmtheorie," 56.

116. Musil, "Toward a New Aesthetic," 206.

117. Albert Klöckner, "Das Massenproblem in der Kunst. Über Wesen und Wert der Vielfältigung (Film und Funk)" [1928], in *Medientheorie 1888–1933. Texte und Kommentare*, ed. Albert Kümmel and Petra Löffler (Frankfurt am Main: Suhrkamp, 2002), 303.

118. Ibid., 302.

119. Ibid., 305–306.

6. THE READYMADE PRODUCTS OF THE FANTASY MACHINE: RUDOLF ARNHEIM, RENÉ FÜLÖP-MILLER, AND THE DISCOURSE ON THE "STANDARDIZATION" OF FILM

1. The German term *Konfektion* is associated with the industrial production of ready-made/ready-to-wear garments.

2. See David Bordwell, Janet Staiger, and Kristin Thompson, *The Classical Hollywood Cinema: Film Style and Mode of Production to 1960* (New York: Columbia University Press, 1985), 85–153.

3. Henry Ford, *My Life and Work* [1922], in collaboration with Samuel Crowther (New York: Arno Press, 1973). Published in Germany as *Mein Leben und Werk* (Leipzig: List, 1923).

4. Helmut Lethen, *Neue Sachlichkeit 1924–1932. Studien zur Literatur des "Weißen Sozialismus"* (Stuttgart: Metzler, 1970), 29.

5. See Harro Segeberg, *Literarische Technik-Bilder. Studien zum Verhältnis von Technik- und Literaturgeschichte im 19. und frühen 20. Jahrhundert* (Tubingen: Niemeyer, 1987), 198ff.

6. Sigfried Giedion, *Mechanization Takes Command: A Contribution to Anonymous History* (Oxford: Oxford University Press, 1948), 121.

7. Lethen, *Neue Sachlichkeit*, 58.

8. One of the most prominent representatives of this line of thought was Antonio Gramsci, who placed his hopes in Fordism. See Antonio Gramsci, *Prison Notebooks*, vol. 3, trans. Joseph A. Buttigieg (New York: Columbia University Press, 2007), § 52.

9. Adolf Behne, "Kunstausstellung Berlin," *Das Neue Berlin. Monatshefte für Probleme der Grossstadt* 1 (1929): 150.

10. Ibid.

11. Ibid., 152. The ambivalence of Behne's argument is revealed by a sentence that he adds to this passage: "Apart from the moving assembly line is a world unto itself, the still laboratory of researchers and critics" (ibid.).

12. The series of images beneath Behne's text (ibid.) originally stems from the satirical newspaper *Punch* (September 1, 1926).

13. Kurt Karl Eberlein, "Januskopf und Maske" [1928], in *Medientheorie 1888–1933. Texte und Kommentare*, ed. Albert Kümmel and Petra Löffler (Frankfurt am Main: Suhrkamp, 2002), 285–298.

14. Ibid., 20. Eberlein here alludes to the widespread media stereotype of the "girl."

15. See Jörg Schweinitz, ed., *Prolog vor dem Film: Nachdenken über ein neues Medium 1909–1914* (Leipzig: Reclam, 1992), 223–230.

16. Stefan Zweig, "The Monotonization of the World" [1925], in *The Weimar Republic Sourcebook*, ed. Anton Kaes, Martin Jay, and Edward Dimendberg (Berkeley: University of California Press, 1994), 397–400.

17. Stefan Zweig, "Die Monotonisierung der Welt" [1925], in *Weimarer Republik. Manifeste und Dokumente zur deutschen Literatur 1918–1933*, ed. Anton Kaes (Stuttgart: Metzler, 1983), 272. The German original is cited here, since the published English translation (see note 16) is abbreviated.

18. Stefan Zweig, "The Motonization of the World," 397.

19. Ibid., 398.

20. Charles S. Maier, "Between Taylorism and Technocracy: European Ideologies and the Vision of Industrial Productivity in the 1920s," *Journal of Contemporary History* 5, no. 2 (1970): 54.

21. Charlotte Lütkens, "Europäer und Amerikaner über Amerika," *Archiv für Sozialwissenschaft und Sozialpolitik* 62 (1929), 2:625.

22. Adolf Halfeld, *Amerika und Amerikanismus. Kritische Betrachtungen eines Deutschen und Europäers* (Jena: Diederichs, 1928), 97.

23. Peter Wollen, *Raiding the Icebox: Reflections on Twentieth-Century Culture* (London: Verso, 1993), 44.

24. See Wilhelm Pocher, *Die Rezeption der englischen und amerikanischen Literatur in Deutschland in den Jahren 1918–1933* (thesis, University of Jena, 1972).

25. Erhard Schütz, "Fließband—Schlachthof—Hollywood. Literarische Phantasien über die Maschine USA," in *Willkommen und Abschied der Maschinen*, ed. Erhard Schütz and Norbert Wehr (Essen: Klartext, 1988), 125.

26. Ibid., 122. See also Erhard Schütz, *Kritik der literarischen Reportage* (Munich: Fink, 1977), 17–116; and Peter J. Brenner, *Der Reisebericht in der deutschen Literatur* (Tubingen: Max Niemeyer, 1990), 609–628.

27. See Schütz, *Fließband*, 74–75.

28. Halfeld, *Amerika*, 104.

29. See Kurt Pinthus, ed. *Das Kinobuch* [1913/1914] (Zurich: Arche, 1963). Here he published individual scenarios under the name Arnold Höllriegel (a pseudonym) and under

his real name, Richard A. Bermann, respectively. In January 1913, Höllriegel's novel *Die Films der Prinzessin Fantoche* (The Films of Princess Fantoche) was serialized in *Der Roland von Berlin*. A new edition of the novel was published in 2003, ed. Michael Grisko (Berlin: Aviva, 2003). See also Jörg Schweinitz, "Von Automobilen, Flugmaschinen und einer versteckten Kamera. Technikfaszination und Medienreflexivität in Richard A. Bermanns Kinoprosa," in *Mediengeschichte des Filmes*, vol. 2, *Die Modellierung des Kinofilms*, ed. Corinna Müller and Harro Segeberg (Munich: Fink, 1998), 221–241.

30. Arnold Höllriegel [Richard A. Bermann], *Hollywood Bilderbuch* (Leipzig: E. P. Tal, 1927), 15.

31. Ibid., 9.

32. Bernhard Goldschmidt, *Von New York bis Frisco. Ein deutsches Tagebuch* (Berlin: Reimer, 1925), 56–57.

33. Egon Erwin Kisch, *(beehrt sich darzubieten) Paradies Amerika* [1929] (Berlin: Aufbau, 1994), 108. The passage reads as follows: "In every mid-sized city in America either a collegian picture or a Western picture is shown before the main feature. The collegian picture always follows the same plot: the awkward student, ridiculed by his colleagues and spurned by the popular crowd, enters a competition or game at the last minute, secures the victory for his team, and wins fame and the girl for himself. However, the Western pictures are more elaborate, not all having one and the same plot, but instead there are at least two different kinds of plots, ha-ha-ha!"

34. Ibid., 113.

35. See Kristin Thompson, "Early Alternatives to the Hollywood Mode of Production: Implications for Europe's Avant-gardes," *Film History* 5, no. 4 (1993): esp. 392–396.

36. See Thomas Elsaesser, "Kunst und Krise: Die Ufa in den 20er Jahren," in *Das Ufa-Buch*, ed. Hans-Michael Bock and Michael Töteberg (Frankfurt am Main: Zweitausendeins, 1992), 96–105.

37. Ibid., 98.

38. Thomas J. Saunders, *Hollywood in Berlin. American Cinema and Weimar Germany* (Berkeley: University of California Press, 1994), 117.

39. See ibid., 54. Whereas in 1923 there were still ninety-four domestic productions in contrast to 149 imports from the United States, by 1927 only three German short films made it onto the market, which was flooded with 394 U.S. short films.

40. Peter Bächlin, *Der Film als Ware* [1947] (Frankfurt am Main: Athenäum Fischer, 1975), 174.

41. Saunders, *Hollywood in Berlin*, 121.

42. Ibid., 118.

43. Siegfried Kracauer, "Film 1928" [German 1928], in *The Mass Ornament: Weimar Essays*, ed. Thomas Y. Levin (Cambridge, Mass.: Harvard University Press, 1995), 308.

44. Klaus Kreimeier, *The Ufa Story: A History of Germany's Greatest Film Company, 1918–1945* [German 1992], trans. Robert and Rita Kimber (New York: Hill and Wang, 1996). See the chapter "The Balance After Liquidation: The Cathedral in Crisis," 121–131.

45. Elsaesser, "Kunst und Krise," 104. See also Anonymous, "Die Organisation der Ufa-Produktion," *Lichtbildbühne* 20, no. 290 (December 5, 1927).

46. Thompson, "Early Alternatives," 395.

47. Rudolf Leonhard, "Zur Soziologie des Films," in *Der Film von morgen*, ed. Hugo Zehder (Berlin and Dresden: Kaemmerer, 1923), 101.

48. Ibid.

49. Ibid.

50. Ibid., 103.

51. See *Das Tagebuch* (Berlin, 1928), first six months. In addition to Kurt Pinthus (574–580), other contributors included Willy Haas (713–714), Béla Balázs (759–760), and the Hollywood producer of German descent, Carl Laemmle (969–970).

52. Herbert Leisegang, "Sprechfilm—Rundfunk—Bildfunk—Filmfunk—Zukunftstheater," *Freie Volksbildung* 4 (1929): 15–16.

53. See Willy Haas, "Die Film-Krisis," *Das Tagebuch* 17 (1928): 714.

54. Ibid., 715.

55. Ibid.

56. Kracauer, "Film 1928," 308.

57. Ibid., 312–313.

58. Siegfried Kracauer, "The Mass Ornament" [German 1927], in *The Mass Ornament* (see note 43), 80.

59. Ibid.

60. Ibid, 81.

61. Ibid, 78.

62. Ibid, 80.

63. Ibid.

64. The contexts and details of this concept have been elaborated more fully by Inka Mülder, *Siegfried Kracauer—Grenzgänger zwischen Theorie und Literatur. Seine frühen Schriften 1913—1933* (Stuttgart: Metzler, 1985), esp. 56–57.

65. Kracauer, "Film 1928," 308.

66. Ibid., 313.

67. Siegfried Kracauer, "The Little Shop-Girls Go to the Movies" [German 1927], in *The Mass Ornament* (see note 43), 294.

68. Siegfried Kracauer, "Neue Filmliteratur" [1932], in *Kleine Schriften zum Film*, vol. 6.3, ed. Inka Mülder-Bach (Frankfurt am Main: Suhrkamp, 2004), 15–19. The three books were also reviewed together by Carl Dreyfuß in *Zeitschrift für Sozialforschung* 1 (1932) 1/2, 227–228.

69. Already discussed in the introduction, the parody of the genre-film stereotypes in Alexander Granowski's film *Die Koffer des Herren O.F.*, which appeared at the same time (1931), offers further evidence of this.

70. Ilya Ehrenburg, *Die Traumfabrik. Chronik des Films* (Berlin: Malik, 1931). A note in the first edition states: "written from February to April, 1931 and published in November of the same year."

71. René Fülöp-Miller, *Die Phantasiemaschine. Eine Saga der Gewinnsucht* (Berlin: Zsolnay, 1931). This book is an expanded version of an essay by Fülöp-Miller from the same year: "Das amerikanische Kino," in Joseph Gregor and René Fülöp-Miller, *Das amerikanische Theater und Kino. Zwei kulturgeschichtliche Abhandlungen* (Zurich: Amalthea, 1931).

In the article "Neue Filmliteratur" (see note 68), Kracauer, otherwise commendatory, criticized *Die Phantasiemaschine* for bringing "in quotes from all possible directions, which do more to fill pages than offer illumination." This may be due to the expansion of the original essay into a book.

72. Rudolf Arnheim, *Film als Kunst* [1932] (Munich: Hanser, 1974), 185–205. Arnheim's *Film as Art* (first published in 1957 by the University of California Press) is not a complete translation of *Film als Kunst* (originally published in 1932) but instead includes selections from the original German and four additional essays. The chapters mentioned above were omitted in the U.S. publication. For this reason, citations are made exclusively from the German text.

73. René Fülöp-Miller, "The Motion Picture in America. A History in the Making," in John Anderson and René Fülöp-Miller, *The American Theatre and the Motion Picture in America. A History in the Making* (New York: Dial Press, 1938), 104–189. This English edition of Fülöp-Miller's original essay was published the year he emigrated to the United States (see note 71). Quotations in the following are taken from the English edition.

74. Ehrenburg, *Traumfabrik*, 142.

75. Ibid., 169.

76. Ibid., 310.

77. Kracauer, "Neue Filmliteratur," 16.

78. Fülöp-Miller, "Motion Picture in America," 111.

79. Kracauer, "Neue Filmliteratur," 17.

80. Fülöp-Miller, "Motion Picture in America," 117.

81. Ibid., 134.

82. Ibid., 148.

83. Ibid., 147.

84. Ibid., 153.

85. Ibid., 158.

86. Ibid., 156.

87. Ibid., 146.

88. Ibid.

89. Ibid., 149.

90. Ibid.

91. Ibid., 148–149.

92. Kracauer, "Neue Filmliteratur," 17.

93. Arnheim, *Film als Kunst*, 186.

94. Ibid., 193.

95. Ibid., 189.

96. Luis Buñuel, for example, played with this kind of chart: "In my frequent moments of idleness, I devoted myself to a bizarre document—a synoptic table of the American cinema. There were several moveable columns set up on a large piece of pasteboard; the first for 'ambience' (Parisian, western, gangster, war, tropical, comic, medieval, etc.), the second for 'epochs,' the third for 'main characters,' and so on. Altogether, there were

four or five categories, each with a tab for easy maneuverability. What I wanted to do was show that the American cinema was composed along such precise and standardized lines that, thanks to my system, anyone could predict the basic plot of a film simply by lining up a given setting with a particular era, ambience, and character." Luis Buñuel, *My Last Sigh* [French 1982], trans. Abigail Israel (Minneapolis: University of Minnesota Press, 2003), 131–132.

97. As early as 1923, Shklovsky polemically referred to a "machine that produced plots": "Imagine a row of films wound on special spools. One of the reels contains people's professions, the second one—countries of the world, the third one—various ages, the fourth one—human acts (for example, kissing, climbing a pipe, knocking someone down, jumping into the water, shooting). A person takes hold of the cranks leading to these reels and spins them. Then he peers through a special slot and reads the resulting gibberish. The machine is rather strange, but apparently it gives American brains the jolt they require." Victor Shklovsky, "Plot in Cinematography" [Russian 1923], in *Literature and Cinematography*, trans. Irina Masinovsky (Champaign, Ill.: Dalkey Archive Press, 2008), 42.

98. Arnheim, *Film als Kunst*, 186.

99. Ibid., 190.

100. Vladimir Nilsen, *The Cinema as a Graphic Art* [Russian 1936] (New York: Hill & Wang, 1957), 177.

101. Bächlin, *Film als Ware*, 171.

102. Arnheim, *Film als Kunst*, 193.

103. Ibid., 191. My emphasis.

104. Arnheim's obtained his doctorate in 1928 with the thesis *Experimentell-psychologische Untersuchungen zum Ausdrucksproblem* (Experimental-Psychological Investigations on the Problem of Expression) at the University of Berlin, where he had studied art history, musicology, and psychology with Max Wertheimer, Wolfgang Köhler, and Kurt Lewin.

105. See Gertrud Koch, "Rudolf Arnheim: The Materialist of Aesthetic Illusion—Gestalt Theory and Reviewer's Practice," *New German Critique* 51 (Fall 1990): 164–178. Regarding Gestalt psychologists in general and Arnheim in particular she specifically emphasizes: "their compatibility with modern thinking which they joined, perhaps sometimes on trivial grounds, later on, crowded by stronger, logic based assumptions of 'system,' 'structure,' or 'form.'" (178).

106. This was described in greater detail in chapter 1.

107. Rudolf Arnheim, "Il cifrario del successo," *Cinema* (Rome) 38 (January 25, 1938): 44.

108. Arnheim, *Film als Kunst*, 219–220.

109. Ibid., 220. My emphasis.

110. Ibid.

111. Arnheim, *Film als Kunst*, 11.

112. Rudolf Arnheim, "Die Kunst im Volke," *Weltbühne* 24, no. 3 (1928): 100.

113. Ibid.

114. Kracauer, "Neue Filmliteratur," 18.

115. Arnheim, *Film als Kunst*, 12.

116. Rudolf Arnheim, "In Praise of Character Actors" [German 1931], in *Film Essays and Criticism*, trans. Brenda Benthien, (Madison: University of Wisconsin Press, 1997), 52–54. The translation of the German title "Lob der Charge" is a bit misleading.

117. Kurt Pinthus, "Die Film-Krisis," *Das Tagebuch* 14: 579.

118. Rudolf Arnheim, "For the First Time" [German 1931], in *Film Essays and Criticism*, trans. Brenda Benthien, (Madison: University of Wisconsin Press, 1997), 15.

119. Rudolf Arnheim, "Die Zukunft des Tonfilms" [circa 1934], in Rudolf Arnheim, *Die Seele in der Silberschicht*, ed. Helmut H. Diederichs (Frankfurt am Main: Suhrkamp, 2004), 239.

120. The title of a text written in 1938 (and first published in Italian) on sound film explicitly refers to Lessing. See Rudolf Arnheim, "A New Laocoön: Artistic Composites and the Talking Film," in *Film as Art* (Berkeley: University of California Press, 1957), 199.

121. Arnheim, *Film als Kunst*, 187. The original title of the mentioned film is *Les nouveaux messieurs* (France 1929).

122. Gottfried Böhm, "Die Krise der Repräsentation. Die Kunstgeschichte und die moderne Kunst," in *Kategorien und Methoden der deutschen Kunstgeschichte 1900–1930*, ed. Lorenz Dittman (Stuttgart: Steiner, 1985), 113.

123. Fülöp-Miller, "Motion Picture in America," 158.

124. Ibid., 184. This viewpoint is expressed more forcefully in Fülöp-Miller's *Die Phantasiemaschine* (see note 71), cf. esp. 121–139.

125. Fülöp-Miller, "Motion Picture in America," 171.

126. Ibid., 187.

127. Béla Balázs, "Die Film-Krisis" [1928], in Béla Balázs, *Schriften zum Film*, vol. 2, *Der Geist des Filmes*, ed. Helmut H. Diederichs and Wolfgang Gersch (Berlin: Henschel, 1984), 232.

128. Ibid.

129. Fülöp-Miller, "Motion Picture in America," 163.

130. Bertolt Brecht, "The Threepenny Lawsuit" [German 1931], in *Bertolt Brecht on Film and Radio*, ed. and trans. Marc Silbermann (London: Methuen, 2000), 165. (My emphasis).

131. Ibid., 162.

132. Theodor W. Adorno and Hanns Eisler, *Composing for the Films* [1947] (New York: Continuum, 2005), 16–17.

133. Hugo von Hofmannsthal, "The Substitute for Dreams" [German 1921], trans. Lance W. Garmer, in *German Essays on Film*, ed. Richard W. McCormick and Alison Guenther-Pal (New York: Continuum, 2004), 52–56.

134. The corresponding passage in Fülöp-Miller (Fülöp-Miller, "Motion Picture in America," 80–81) reads like a summary of sections 4, 5, and 6 from Münsterberg's *The Photoplay*. Even the sequence of arguments is the same. Given that Fülöp-Miller's text was written after studies undertaken in the United States, it is possible that he was familiar with Münsterberg's work.

135. Jean-Louis Baudry, "The Apparatus: Metapsychological Approaches to the Impression of Reality in the Cinema" [French 1975], in *Narrative, Apparatus, Ideology: A Film Theory Reader*, ed. Philip Rosen (New York: Columbia University Press, 1986), 286–318.

136. Fülöp-Miller, "Motion Picture in America," 150.

137. Ibid., 117.

138. Ibid., 188.

139. Theodor W. Adorno, "The Schema of Mass Culture" [German 1942], in *The Culture Industry: Selected Essays on Mass Culture*, ed. J. M. Bernstein (New York: Routledge, 2003), 92.

140. I describe this more extensively in Jörg Schweinitz, "Der selige Kintopp (1913/14): Eine Fundsache zum Verhältnis vom literarischem Expressionismus und Kino," in *Film, Fernsehen, Video und die Künste. Strategien der Intermedialität*, ed. Joachim Paech (Stuttgart, Weimar: Metzler, 1994), 72–88.

141. Georg Lukács, "Thoughts Toward an Aesthetics of Cinema" [German 1913, 2nd version], in *German Essays on Film*, ed. Richard W. McCormick and Alison Guenther-Pal (New York: Continuum, 2004), 15.

142. Arnheim, *Film als Kunst*, 193.

143. Ibid., 195.

144. Ibid.

145. Ibid., 194.

146. Ibid.

147. Ibid., 13.

148. Theodor W. Adorno, "Scientific Experiences of a European Scholar in America" [1968], in *Critical Models: Interventions and Catchwords*, ed. and trans. Henry W. Pickford (New York: Columbia University Press, 1998), 216.

149. The result was the study: Rudolf Arnheim, "The World of the Daytime Serial," in *Radio Research, 1942–43,* ed. Paul F. Lazarsfeld and Frank N. Stanton (New York: Arno Press, 1979), 34–85.

150. Theodor W. Adorno, "On the Fetish-Character in Music and the Regression of Listening" [German 1938], in *The Essential Frankfurt School Reader*, ed. Andrew Arato and Eike Gebhardt (New York: Continuum, 1982), 274.

151. In addition to the already mentioned texts, see in particular the study that Adorno wrote for the radio project. Theodor W. Adorno, "On Popular Music," with the assistance of George Simpson, in *Studies in Philosophy and Social Science* (New York: Institute of Social Research, 1941), 9:17–48.

152. Max Horkheimer and Theodor W. Adorno, *Dialectic of Enlightenment: Philosophical Fragments* [German 1947], ed. Gunzelin Schmid Noerr, trans. Edmund Jephcott (Stanford, Calif.: Stanford University Press, 2002), 119.

153. Ibid., 65.

154. Ibid., 98.

155. Adorno, "The Schema of Mass Culture," 66.

156. Ibid., 67.

157. Horkheimer and Adorno, *Dialectic of Enlightenment*, 108.

158. Ibid., 106.

159. Ibid., 132.

160. Ibid., 125.

161. Ibid.

162. Arnheim, "The World of the Daytime Serial," 34.

163. Rudolf Arnheim, "Il cinema e la folla," *Cinema* 25 (October 30, 1949): 219.

164. Ibid., 220.

165. Ibid.

166. Rudolf Arnheim, "Erich von Stroheim" [German 1934], in *Film Essays and Criticism*, trans. Brenda Benthien (Madison: University of Wisconsin Press, 1997), 223.

167. Rudolf Arnheim, "Il cinema e la folla," 219.

168. Ibid.

169. Ibid.

170. Ibid.

171. Ibid.

172. Ibid.

173. See Thomas Y. Levin, "Iconology at the Movies: Panofsky's Film Theory," in *Meaning in the Visual Arts: Views from the Outside*, ed. Irving Lavin (Princeton, N.J.: Institute for Advanced Study, 1995). At the beginning of his text, Levin provides a detailed overview of the development and publication history of Panofsky's film essay.

174. Erwin Panofsky, "Style and Medium in the Motion Pictures" [1947], in *Three Essays on Style* (Cambridge, Mass.: The MIT Press, 1995).

175. Ibid., 95.

176. Ibid.

177. Ibid., 112.

178. Ibid.

179. Ibid.

180. Ibid.

181. Ibid., 113.

182. Ibid.

183. Ibid.

184. Ibid.

185. Walter Hasenclever, "Der Kintopp als Erzieher. Eine Apologie" [1913], in *Prolog vor dem Film* (see note 15), 221.

186. Panofsky, "Style and Medium," 96.

187. Ibid.

188. Panofsky, "Style and Medium," 94.

189. Levin, "Iconology at the Movies," 324.

190. Ibid., 321–322.

191. Ibid., 325.

192. Panofsky, "Style and Medium," 94.

193. Ibid., 100.

194. Ibid.

195. Ibid., 96.

196. Ibid., 123.

197. See Regine Prange, "Stil und Medium. Panofsky 'On Movies,'" in *Erwin Panofsky. Beiträge des Symposiums Hamburg 1992*, ed. Bruno Reudenbach (Berlin: Akademie Verlag, 1994), 171–190.

198. Arnheim, *Film als Kunst*, 11.

199. Panofsky, "Style and Medium," 123.

7. THE STEREOTYPE AS INTELLIGIBLE FORM:
COHEN-SÉAT, MORIN, AND SEMIOLOGY

1. The last significant contributor to classical (prescriptive) film theory is considered to be Siegfried Kracauer, *Theory of Film: The Redemption of Physical Reality* [1960] (Oxford: Oxford University Press, 1997).

2. Gilbert Cohen-Séat, *Essai sur les principes d'une philosophie du cinéma* (Paris: Presses universitaires de France, 1946). Simultaneously with the publication of this essay, the Association Française pour la Recherche Filmologique was founded in Paris in 1946. Cohen-Séat's essay is a founding text of filmology.

3. On the movement of filmology and Cohen-Séat's role therein see Edward Lowry, *The Filmology Movement and Film Study in France* (Ann Arbor, Mich.: UMI Research Press, 1985). On the influence of filmology on German film scholarship, see Joachim Paech, "Die Anfänge der Filmwissenschaft in Westdeutschland nach 1945," in *Zwischen Gestern und Morgen* (Frankfurt am Main: Deutsches Filmmuseum, 1989), 266–281.

4. Edgar Morin, *Le cinéma ou l'homme imaginaire* (Paris: Minuit, 1956). The English edition, *The Cinema, or The Imaginary Man*, trans. Lorraine Mortimer (Minneapolis: University of Minnesota Press, 2005), will be quoted henceforth.

5. Morin, *The Cinema*, 176.

6. Ibid., 180.

7. Ibid., 181.

8. Rudolf Arnheim, *Film als Kunst* [1932] (Munich: Hanser, 1974), 220.

9. The quotation reads: "Film art . . . aspires to be an object worthy of your meditations: it calls for a chapter in those great traditions where everything is talked about, except film." Introductory motto to Morin, *The Cinema*.

10. Béla Balázs, "Visible Man" [German 1924], in *Béla Balázs: Early Film Theory*, ed. Erica Carter, trans. Rodney Livingstone (New York: Berghahn: 2010), 13.

11. Ibid.

12. Ibid., 14.

13. Morin, *The Cinema*, 198. (My emphasis.)

14. Cohen-Séat, *Essai sur les principes*, 119.

15. On the history of the metaphor of "film language," see Karl-Dietmar Möller-Naß, *Filmsprache. Eine kritische Theoriegeschichte* (Munster: MAks, 1986).

16. Raymond Spottiswoode, *A Grammar of the Film: An Analysis of the Film Technique* (London: Faber and Faber, 1935).

17. Boris Eikhenbaum, "Problems of Cine-Stylistics" [Russian 1927], trans. Richard Sherwood, in *The Poetics of Cinema*, ed. Richard Taylor (Oxford: RPT Publications, 1982), 5–31.

18. Ibid., 23.

19. Ibid., 12. Incidentally, this idea would resurface decades later in a very similar fashion in Branigan's narratology, in which "verbal (re)description" is a central activity in the reception of narrative films. See Edward Branigan, *Narrative Comprehension and Film* (London: Routledge, 1992), 111, see also 112.

20. On the Kuleshov experiment, see Kristin Thompson, Yuri Tsivian, and Ekaterina Khokhlova, "The Rediscovery of a Kuleshov Experiment: A Dossier," *Film History* 8, no. 3 (1996): 357–364; and Hans Beller, ed., *Handbuch der Filmmontage* (Munich, TR-Verlagsunion, 1993), 157–159.

21. Eikhenbaum, "Problems of Cine-Stylistics," 29.

22. Sergei Eisenstein, "Béla Forgets the Scissors" [Russian 1926], in *The Film Factory: Russian and Soviet Cinema in Documents 1896–1939*, ed. and trans. R. Taylor (London: Routledge & Kegan Paul, 1988), 147.

23. Wolfgang Beilenhoff, "Filmtheorie und -praxis der russischen Formalisten," in *Poetik des Films. Deutsche Erstausgabe der filmtheoretischen Texte der russischen Formalisten*, ed. Wolfgang Beilenhoff (Munich: Fink, 1974), 139.

24. Cohen-Séat, *Essai sur les principes*, 124.

25. Ibid., 119.

26. Ibid., 120.

27. Ibid.

28. Ibid., 123.

29. Ibid., 144.

30. Orson Welles, quoted in Alexandre Astruc, "The Birth of a New Avant-garde: La Caméra-Stylo" [French 1948], in *Film and Literature: An Introduction and Reader*, ed. Timothy Corrigan (New Jersey: Prentice-Hall, 1999), 158–162.

31. Ibid., 159–161.

32. Cohen-Séat, *Essai sur les principes*, 121.

33. Ibid.

34. Boris Eikhenbaum, "Problems of Cine-Stylistics," 28.

35. Eikhenbaum did occasionally state that "we are already used to a whole series of typical clichés of cine-langage" (ibid., 30), but he was thinking about "the basic devices of montage" and not genre stereotypes (18). He also mentions in passing that "even the very slightest innovation in this sphere strikes us with no less force than the appearance of a new word in language itself" (30). His actual theoretical interest in connection with the language metaphor did not, however, concern the semantic and pragmatic potential of such stereotypization as produced by intertextual repetition.

36. Ibid., 28.

37. Ibid, 31.

38. In this context, Balázs writes in *The Spirit of Film*, "When a statue falls from its pedestal in Eisenstein's *October*, this is intended to signify the fall of Czarism. When the broken fragments are reassembled, this is supposed to signify the restoration of bourgeois power. These are signs that have a meaning, just as the cross, the section sign, or Chinese ideograms have a meaning. But images should not *signify* ideas; they should *give shape* to and *provoke* thoughts that then arise in us as inferences, rather than being already formulated in the image as symbols or ideograms. For in the latter case the montage ceases to be productive. It degenerates into the reproduction of puzzle pictures. Images of the filmic material acquire the status of ready-made symbols that are, as it were, imported from elsewhere." Béla Balázs, "The Spirit of Film" in *Béla Balázs:*

Early Film Theory (see note 10), 128. In reference to this idea, Getrud Koch discusses a conflict between Balázs and Eisenstein, which was never fully elaborated. See Gertrud Koch, "Béla Balázs: The Physiognomy of Things," *New German Critique* 40 (1987): 175–176.

39. "Les formes du langage conventionnel," the title of the chapter cited here. Cohen-Séat, *Essai sur les principes*, 120.

40. "Le discours filmique" is even the title of chapter 9. Cohen-Séat, *Essai sur les principes*, 134.

41. Ibid., 138.

42. Ibid., 123. (My emphasis.)

43. Ibid.

44. Ibid., 123–124.

45. Ibid., 124.

46. Morin, *The Cinema*, 174.

47. Ibid.

48. Arnheim, *Film als Kunst*, 190.

49. Morin, *The Cinema*, 173.

50. Ibid.

51. Cohen-Séat, *Essai sur les principes*, 139.

52. Morin, *The Cinema*, 172.

53. Ibid., 173–74.

54. Ibid., 180.

55. Ibid., 174.

56. Ibid.

57. Ibid.

58. Erwin Panofsky, "Style and Medium in the Motion Pictures" [1947], in *Three Essays on Style* (Cambridge, Mass.: The MIT Press, 1995), 112.

59. Morin, *The Cinema*, 194.

60. Edgar Reitz, Alexander Kluge, Wilfried Reinke, "Wort im Film," *Sprache im technischen Zeitalter* 13, special issue: *Die Rolle des Wortes im Film* (1965): 1018.

61. Ibid., 1019.

62. Ibid.

63. Ibid., 1021.

64. Ibid., 1019.

65. Ibid.

66. Ibid.

67. *Neuer deutscher Film* (New German Cinema) is a term used to describe West Germany's "other cinema" represented by young directors working outside of established commercial cinema who sought to radically renew German film in the 1960s. Influenced by Nouvelle Vague, they attempted to set their work apart, in terms of style and content, from the commercial genre films of the Adenauer era of the 1950s, which was perceived as restorative. A main concern in the era leading up to the 1968 movement was the filmic articulation of critical and nonconformist thinking, and the Oberhausen Manifesto of

1962 is considered a programmatic document of this position. Directors who emerged from this decade of upheaval, also known as the era of *Junger Deutscher Film* (Young German Cinema), include Alexander Kluge, Edgar Reitz, Volker Schlöndorff, Wim Wenders, Werner Herzog, Werner Schroeter, and Rainer Werner Fassbinder.

68. Ibid., 1012.

69. Cohen-Séat, *Essai sur les principes*, 123.

70. See Peter Wollen, *Signs and Meaning in the Cinema*, expanded edition [1968] (London, BFI, 1998), 103–105.

71. Roland Barthes, *Mythologies* [French 1957], trans. Annette Lavers (New York: Hill and Wang, 1972), 114.

72. Ibid., 118.

73. Ibid., 124–125.

74. Ibid., 56.

75. Ibid., 125.

76. Morin, *The Cinema*, 201.

77. Ibid., 181.

78. Ibid., 115.

79. Ibid., 112

80. Ibid.

81. Ibid., 154.

82. Ibid., 167.

83. Cohen-Séat, *Essai sur les principes*, 21.

84. Ibid., 23.

85. See Rick Altman, *The American Film Musical* (Bloomington: University of Indiana Press, 1987), 93–94.

86. Joachim Paech describes the unique quality of filmology as being dedicated to an "interdisciplinary basic research (as we would say today) into cinema and thereby managed to almost never talk about individual films." Joachim Paech, "Von der Filmologie zur Mediologie? Film und Fernsehtheorie zu Beginn der 60er Jahre in Frankreich," in *Körper—Ästhetik—Spiel. Zur filmischen écriture der Nouvelle Vague*, ed. Scarlett Winter and Susanne Schlünder (Munich: Fink, 2004), 31.

87. Cohen-Séat, *Essai sur les principes*, 31.

88. Ibid., 20.

89. Ibid., 19.

90. Ibid.

91. Ibid., 35 and 36.

92. Ibid., 34.

93. Yuri Lotman, *The Structure of the Artistic Text* [Russian 1970], trans. Gail Lenhoff and Ronald Vroon (Ann Arbor: University of Michigan Press, 1977), 289.

94. Yuri Lotman, *Semiotics of Cinema* [Russian 1973], trans. Mark Suino (Ann Arbor: University of Michigan Press, 1976), 22.

95. Karl Bühler, *Theory of Language—The Representational Function of Language* [German 1934], trans. Donald Fraser Goodwin (Amsterdam: Benjamins B.V., 1990), 161.

96. Morin, *The Cinema*, 175.

97. Cohen-Séat, *Essai sur principes*, 138.

98. Christian Metz, "Sur un profil d'Etienne Souriau," in *L'art instaurateur: Revue d'Esthétique* 3/4, p. 144.

99. Lowry, *The Filmology Movement*, 169.

100. Frank Kessler, "Etienne Souriau und das Vokabular der filmologischen Schule," *Montage AV* 6, no. 2 (1997): 135.

101. See Etienne Souriau, "La structure de l'univers filmique et le vocabulaire de la filmologie," *Revue Internationale de Filmologie* 7–8 (1951): 231–240.

102. Umberto Eco, *Einführung in die Semiotik* (Munich: Fink, 1972), 225. Here I have chosen to cite the German text for reasons already explained (see chapter 5, note 100).

103. Christian Metz, *Langage et cinéma* (Paris: Larousse, 1971). The English edition will be quoted in the following: Christian Metz, *Language and Cinema*, trans. Donna Jean Umiker-Sebeok (The Hague: Mouton, 1974).

104. Metz, *Language and Cinema*, 130. See also chaps. IV.1 and V.3.

105. Winkler takes a similar view; see Hartmut Winkler, *Der filmische Raum und der Zuschauer. 'Apparatus'—Semantik—'Ideology'* (Heidelberg: Winter, 1982). "Morin . . . outlines a mechanism of *conventionalization*, which impacts the level of filmic techniques of representation and the subject matter of a film in an completely parallel fashion. . . . Morin thus also described a mechanism of the *genesis* of signs, which is solely grounded in factual repetition" (139). However, Winkler probably underestimates the incisiveness of Morin's thought in stating: "Various indications in Morin's text and, most of all, the relative isolation of the quoted passages suggest that Morin himself did not fully become aware of the significance of this idea" (ibid). That the fundamental concept of the formation of signs in cinema through repetition/conventionalization was indeed so emphatically articulated in the work of Cohen-Séat indicates that the filmologists had a far-reaching understanding of their work's implications.

106. Pier Paolo Pasolini, "The Cinema of Poetry" [Italian 1965], in *Heretical Empiricism*, ed. Louise K. Barnett, trans. Ben Lawton and Louise K. Barnett (Bloomington: University of Indiana Press, 1988), 167–186.

107. Ibid., 170. The passage reads: "It is true that a kind of dictionary of film, that is, a convention, has established itself during the past fifty years of film. This convention is odd for the following reason: it is stylistic before it is grammatical. Let us take the image of the wheels of a train which turn among puffs of steam: it is not a syntagma, it is a stylema. . . . [The filmmaker] must be satisfied, insofar as rules are concerned, with a certain number of expressive devices which lack in articulation, and which, born as stylemas, have become syntagmas. On the positive side of the ledger, the filmmaker, instead of having to refine a centuries-old stylistic tradition, works with one whose history is counted in decades. In practical terms this means that there is no convention to upset by excessive outrage."

108. Ibid.

109. Ibid., 171.

110. Christian Metz, *Film Language: A Semiotics of the Cinema* [French 1968], trans. Michael Taylor (Chicago: University of Chicago Press, 1990). The chapter "The Modern Cinema and Narrativity" is based on the 1966 essay "Le cinéma moderne et la narrativité."

111. Ibid., 214.

112. Ibid., 222.

113. Ibid., 214.

114. Metz, *Language and Cinema*, 41–42.

115. Pier Paolo Pasolini, "The Nonverbal as Another Verbality" [from a letter interview with S. Arecco, Italy 1971], in *Heretical Empiricism* (see note 105), 261.

116. Metz, *Film Language*, 223.

117. Ibid., 222.

118. Ibid., 223.

119. Christian Metz, "La grande syntagmatique du film narratif," *Communications* (Paris) (1966), 120–124. An expanded version of this text was incorporated into chapter 5 in *Film Language*, "Problems of Denotation in the Fiction Film," 108–148.

120. An instructive overview of Metz's theoretical work and its phases may be found in Dominique Blüher, "Sensibilisierung für die Konstruktion der Filme," *Filmbulletin* 2 (1990): 47–55. See also Dominique Blüher and Margrit Tröhler, "'Ich habe nie gedacht, dass die Semiologie die Massen begeistern würde,' Ein Gespräch mit Christian Metz," in *Filmbulletin* no. 2: 51–55.

121. Metz, *Film Language*, 222.

122. Ibid. In this context, Metz also wrote: "The image of the wheels of the train . . . is a cliché, a stereotype. And it can be so only because it is a singular fact. Grammar has never dictated the content of thought that each sentence should have; it merely regulates the general organization of the sentences. *A grammatical fact can be neither a cliché nor a novelty*, unless it is so at the moment of its first historical occurrence; it exists beyond the level where the antithesis cliché/novelty even begins to have a meaning—that is to say, it remains confined to the stage of the initial idiom and not to that of the secondary language of art. The present of the indicative, as used by Robbe-Grillet, is still a vulgar present of the indicative, entirely 'banal,' and yet no one accuses it of being a cliché. And no one accuses Malherbe of triteness for using the objective predicate, or Victor Hugo for using the relative clause, or Baudelaire for the conjunction of two adjectives. The image of the wheels of the train is in no way the filmic equivalent to these examples; rather it would correspond to Malherbe's metaphorical comparison of a young girl to a rose, which is a *singular* construction (formal and semantic) and must accordingly be judged according to the categories of originality and triteness. As long as one considers such examples, one will have the elements not of a 'stylistic grammar' of the cinema, but of a *pure rhetoric* that has nothing grammatical" (ibid.).

123. Christian Metz must be largely exempted from this statement. Dominique Blüher aptly remarks that in Metz's work "concepts from the theory of language [are] not simply applied to film (as one certainly does find in film *grammars*), but in contrast precisely the dissimilarities [are] laid out in addition to any possible correspondences among the

given 'languages': the sign system of *film* is juxtaposed with the sign system of natural language." Blüher, "Sensibilisierung," 48.

124. Fritz Mauthner, *Beiträge zu einer Kritik der Sprache*, vol. 1, *Zur Sprache und zur Psychologie* [1901/1902] (Frankfurt am Main: Ullstein, 1982), 51.

125. Cohen-Séat, *Essai sur principes*, 79.

126. Roland Barthes, *S/Z: An Essay* [French 1970], trans. Richard Miller (New York: Hill and Wang, 1974), 20.

127. Cohen-Séat, *Essai sur principes*, 123.

128. Metz, *Film Language*, 145.

129. Roger Odin later argued in favor of semiopragmatics. See Roger Odin, "For a Semio-Pragmatics of Film," in *The Film Spectator: From Sign to Mind*, ed. Warren Buckland (Amsterdam: Amsterdam University Press, 1995), 213–226.

130. Morin, *The Cinema*, 112.

131. Ibid., 97.

132. Ibid., 112.

133. Algirdas Julien Greimas, "L'actualité du saussurisme (à l'occasion du 40e anniversaire de la publication du Cours de linguistique générale)" *Le Français Moderne* (Paris) 24, no. 3: 191–203.

134. Anne Hénault, *Histoire de la sémiotique* (Paris: PUF, 1997), 36.

8. IRONY AND TRANSFIGURATION: THE POSTMODERN VIEW OF THE STEREOTYPE

1. On the melodramatic visual stereotype of the woman behind the window, see the section "Acting, Image, and a Brief Consideration of Sound" in chapter 2.

2. See Christian Metz, *L'énonciation impersonnelle, ou le site du film* (Paris: Méridiens Klincksieck, 1991).

3. In German, and to some extent in the English, the terms "self-reflexivity" (in German: *Selbstreflexivität*) or autoreflexivity are commonly used. However, film theorists such as Christian Metz or Robert Stam, who have investigated this topic more closely, instead use the term "reflexivity" to refer to the same set of facts and circumstances. Ibid. See, in addition, Robert Stam, *Reflexivity in Film and Literature* (New York: Columbia University Press, 1992). Hans J. Wulff agrees in so far with Metz and Stam that the "auto" in "autoreflexivity" is redundant. See Hans J. Wulff, *Darstellen und Mitteilen* (Tubingen: Narr, 1999), 62–76. Similar arguments have been made regarding the "self" in "self-reflexivity." Here I subscribe to Metz's argument.

4. Britta Hartmann describes how the beginning of a film provides an initiatory program: "*In its initial phase, every film organizes and constructs its own learning and experiential program.* If one comprehends film reception in this sense, as a textually-driven process of learning and experience, then the beginning is the place where the specific conditions of this process are rehearsed." Britta Hartmann, *Aller Anfang. Zur Initialphase des Spielfilms* (Marburg: Schüren, 2009), 101.

5. On the basis of quantitative analyses, Salt confirmed that "the young European makers of 'art films' used even longer takes . . . the use of long takes is . . . associated with high artistic ambition." Barry Salt, *Film Style and Technology: History and Analysis* (London: Starword, 1992), 266.

6. Roland Barthes, *Mythologies* [French 1957] (New York: Hill and Wang, 1972), 143.

7. Horst Königstein, "Es war einmal ein Westen: Stereotyp und Bewusstsein," in *Visuelle Kommunikation: Beiträge zur Kritik der Bewusstseinsindustrie*, ed. Hermann K. Ehmer (Cologne: DuMont Schauberg, 1971), 318.

8. Wim Wenders, "From Dream to Nightmare: The Terrifying Western *Once Upon a Time in the West*" [German film review 1969] in *Emotion Pictures: Reflections on the Cinema*, trans. Sean Whiteside (London: Faber and Faber, 1991), 24.

9. Here the term "allusion" is intended to indicate this form of reference. "Quotation," on the other hand, is reserved only for the direct transfer of material from another film. In this I am following Metz, who also associates "quotation" (*citation*) with the use of entire segments from other films, which are intended to be recognized as such. See Metz, *L'énonciation*, 95–96. Metz thus ascribes to the philological logic according to which the "quotation" refers to an acknowledged *literal* appropriation, whereas "allusion" indicates a less explicit and *less literal* appropriation, that is, a statement "whose full meaning presupposes the perception of a relationship between it and another text, to which it necessarily refers by some inflections that would otherwise remain unintelligible." Gérard Genette, *Palimpsests: Literature in the Second Degree* [French 1982], trans. Channa Newman and Claude Doubinsky (Lincoln: University of Nebraska Press, 1997), 2.

10. Quoted in Christopher Frayling, *Spaghetti Westerns: Cowboys and Europeans from Karl May to Sergio Leone* (London: Routledge & Kegan Paul, 1981), 195.

11. Ibid.

12. The term "intertextual" is here understood in Genette's sense "as a relationship of copresence between two texts or among several texts . . . as the actual presence of one text within another," especially in the form of quotation, plagiarism, or allusion. Genette, *Palimpsests*, 1–2. It should be noted that intertextuality is also realized in relationship to entire series of texts, whereby the relationship is established by recourse to stereotypes.

13. Bertolt Brecht, "The Threepenny Lawsuit," in *Brecht on Film and Radio*, ed. and trans. Marc Silberman (London: Methuen, 2000), 165.

14. See Metz, *L'énonciation*, 110–111. Metz otherwise does not discuss intertextuality as a basis for enunciative disclosure. But he does indicate at least one—in his opinion usually indirect—connection, without elaborating further: " 'Behind' and not 'within' film there can also be invisible, physically absent films which are still in a way very present. These concern a different manner of playing with memory that is not directly connected with enunciation, because they do not double it, and the film remains free of any external elements. . . . We have thus arrived at the well-known problem of transtextuality, in particular that of the hyper- and architext, as defined with exceptional clarity by Gérard Genette."

15. Aby Warburg uses this term to denote poses and forms that have become conventional for the expression of emotions in the visual arts. He traces these forms through different genres in his famous *Mnemosyne* image atlas of 1929. In view of the concept of the stereotype, the *Pathosformel* appears as a specification thereof.

16. Here "pastiche" is used in the second sense articulated by Dyer, namely "pastiche as imitation." See Richard Dyer, *Pastiche* (London: Routledge, 2007), 21–51.

17. Wenders, "From Dream to Nightmare," 24. The published English translation reads: "This one is the limit. This one is a killer." However, this does not convey the full sense of the German, which has therefore been translated differently here.

18. See Frayling, *Spaghetti Westerns*, 40, 215.

19. Bernhard von Dadelsen, "Höhe- und Wendepunkte klassischer Genres: *Spiel mir das Lied vom Tod* (*C'era una volta il West*, 1968)," in *Fischer Filmgeschichte*, ed. Werner Faulstich and Helmut Korte (Frankfurt am Main: Fischer, 1992), 4:161.

20. Ibid.

21. Ibid., 4:163.

22. Quoted in ibid., 4:159.

23. Königstein, "Es war einmal ein Westen," 320.

24. Frayling, *Spaghetti Westerns*, 194.

25. Silvie Pierre, "Il était une fois dans l'Ouest," *Cahiers du cinéma* 218 (March 1970): 53–54.

26. Kay Kirchmann, "Zwischen Selbstreflexivität und Selbstreferentialität. Überlegungen zur Ästhetik des Selbstbezüglichen als filmischer Modernität," *Film und Kritik* 2: 23–37.

27. Ibid., 28. (My emphasis.)

28. Königstein, "Es war einmal ein Westen," 330.

29. Ibid., 312.

30. Ibid.

31. Ibid., 331.

32. I use "postmodernity/postmodern" not as a conceptual term in accordance with postmodernity's own understanding but rather in the sense of a borrowed label. It has become customary as a designation for a type of cinema that is described here in terms of its conspicuously reflexive, self-referential, and often hybrid *treatment of stereotypes*. The term is therefore not taken literally, and I do not intend to enter into discussing philosophical and cultural theories of (questionable) binary concepts such as postmodern versus modern.

33. Frederic Jameson, *Postmodernism, or, The Cultural Logic of Late Capitalism* (London: Verso, 1996), 19.

34. Metz, *L'énonciation*, 103.

35. Ibid.

36. Leslie Fiedler, "Cross the Border—Close the Gap" [1969], in *A Fiedler Reader*, ed. Leslie Fiedler (Briarcliff Manor, N.Y.: Stein & Day, 1977), 270–294.

37. Peter Schneider, "Vom Nutzen des Klischees. Betrachtungen zum Wildwestfilm," *Sprache im technischen Zeitalter* 13, special issue: *Die Rolle des Worts im Film* (1965): 1105.

38. Ibid., 1092.

39. Ibid., 1105.

40. Ibid., 1093

41. Ibid., 1104. (My emphasis.)

42. See the section in the previous chapter, "Stereotypes Form Codes: Filmology and Semiology."

43. Schneider, "Vom Nutzen des Klischees," 1103.

44. Ibid., 1105.

45. Theodor W. Adorno and Hanns Eisler, *Composing for the Films* [1947] (New York: Continuum, 2005), 16. See also chap. 3 of this book.

46. Susan Sontag, "Notes on Camp," in *Against Interpretation and Other Essays* (London: Eyre & Spottiswoode, 1967), 275–292.

47. Ibid., 276.

48. Ibid., 286.

49. Ibid., 281.

50. "The whole point of Camp is to dethrone the serious." Ibid., 288.

51. Ibid., 285. Ellipsis in original.

52. Wulff, *Darstellen und Mitteilen*, 262.

53. Linda Hutcheon, *A Theory of Parody: The Teaching of Twentieth-Century Art Forms* (Urbana: University of Illinois Press, 2000), 54. See also by Hutcheon, *Irony's Edge: The Theory and Politics of Irony* (London: Routledge, 1995), 57–88.

54. Sontag, "Notes on Camp," 287.

55. Ibid., 288.

56. Ibid.

57. Ibid., 283.

58. Ibid.

59. Ibid., 289.

60. Ibid., 281.

61. Wayne Booth distinguishes between stable and unstable irony. The latter, whose semantics and value system cannot be clearly resolved, is closely related to ambiguity. See Wayne Booth, *A Rhetoric of Irony* (Chicago: University of Chicago Press, 1974), esp. chap. 1, "The Ways of Stable Irony" (1–31) and chap. 3, "Is it Ironic?" (47–86).

62. Sontag, "Notes on Camp," 282. She distinguishes between deliberate camp and naive camp, that is, productions read as camp in contradiction to their original intention.

63. Walter Biemel, "Das Problem der Wiederholung in der Kunst der Gegenwart," in *Sprache und Begriff. Festschrift für Bruno Liebrucks*, ed. Heinz Röttgers, Brigitte Scheer, and Josef Simon (Meisenheim am Glan: Anton Hain, 1974), 290.

64. Walter Biemel, "Pop-Art und Lebenswelt," in *Ästhetik*, ed. Wolfgang Heckmann (Darmstadt: Wissenschaftliche Buchgesellschaft, 1979), 160.

65. Ibid., 172.

66. Biemel, "Problem der Wiederholung," 289.

67. Biemel, "Pop-Art und Lebenswelt," 172–173.

68. See Arthur C. Danto, *The Transfiguration of the Commonplace: A Philosophy of Art* (Cambridge, Mass.: Harvard University Press, 1981).

69. Thomas Elsaesser, "Specularity and Engulfment: Francis Ford Coppola and *Bram Stoker's Dracula,*" in *Contemporary Hollywood Cinema,* ed. Steve Neale and Murray Smith (London: Routledge, 1998), 193.

70. Umberto Eco, "Postmodernism, Irony, the Enjoyable," in *Reflections on* The Name of the Rose, trans. William Weaver (London: Secker and Warburg, 1985), 67–68.

71. See Fiedler, "Cross the Border."

72. "In 1955 and 1956, all the major Hollywood studios (except MGM) had sold the bulk of their pre-1948 films to distributors who promptly rechanneled them to local stations. In the early 1960s, the major networks followed." Robert Ray, *A Certain Tendency of the Hollywood Cinema, 1930–1980* (Princeton, N.J.: Princeton University Press, 1985), 263–264.

73. See ibid., 264.

74. Ibid., 256.

75. The Oscar for Best Actor was awarded to Lee Marvin in the leading role.

76. Ray, "Certain Tendency," 257.

77. Ibid., 260.

78. Norbert Bolz, *Chaos und Simulation* (Munich: Fink, 1992), 102.

79. Gilles Deleuze, *Cinema 1: The Movement-Image* [French 1983] (London: Continuum, 2005), 215.

9. MCCABE AND BUFFALO BILL: ON THE CRITICAL REFLECTION OF STEREOTYPES IN TWO FILMS BY ROBERT ALTMAN

1. Within postclassical cinema I distinguish—loosely and in a heuristic sense—between modernist and postmodern(ist) tendencies in the treatment of stereotypes from classical cinema. Whereas modernist films tend to destroy or criticize classical cinematic stereotypes and myths, postmodern films instead tend toward a mildly ironic but celebratory and, indeed, even glorifying approach to such elements (as demonstrated with respect to Leone's film in chapter 8). A reflexive approach to stereotypes characterizes both tendencies. The distinction between the two does not follow a sequential progression from modernist to postmodern film, since both tendencies appear almost simultaneously with the emergence of postclassical cinema. Also, this differentiation has little to do with the established categorization of "modernity" versus "postmodernity," which also encompasses classical cinema.

2. David Denby, ed., *Film 71/72* (New York: Simon & Schuster, 1972), 127.

3. Diane Jacobs, *Hollywood Renaissance* (New York: A. S. Barnes, 1977), 77.

4. This and the following film dialogues stem from film transcriptions.

5. See Neil Feineman, *Persistence of Vision: The Films of Robert Altman* (New York: Arno Press, 1978). Feineman draws a similar conclusion about Altman's films between 1969 and 1975: "Perhaps most constant in the nine films are Altman's beliefs about society. From the beginnings of modern America, he tell us in *McCabe,* the individual has been a helpless, if willing, victim of civilization" (189).

6. Peter Wollen, *Signs and Meaning in the Cinema* [1968], exp. ed. (London: BFI, 1998), 66.

7. Thomas Elsaesser, "Notes on the Unmotivated Hero—the Pathos of Failure: American Films in the '70s," *Monogram* 6 (1975): 13.

8. Philip French, *Westerns* (Oxford: Oxford University Press, 1977), 124.

9. See Hans Günther Pflaum and Hans Helmut Prinzler, eds., *Robert Altman* (Munich: Hanser, 1981), 93.

10. Ibid., 94.

11. Thomas Elsaesser, "*Nashville*: Putting on the Show," *Persistence of Vision* 1 (1984): 39.

12. Robert T. Self, *Robert Altman's Subliminal Reality* (Minneapolis: University of Minnesota Press, 2002), 91.

13. Robert B. Ray, *A Certain Tendency of the Hollywood Cinema, 1930–1980* (Princeton, N.J.: Princeton University Press, 1985), 258.

14. Norman Kagan, *American Skeptic: Robert Altman's Genre-Commentary Films* (Ann Arbor, Mich.: Pierian Press, 1982). Kagan's excellent analysis of Altman's films from the 1970s has served as an important source of inspiration for this study.

15. Feineman, *Persistence of Vision*, 195.

16. This is difficult to determine from today's perspective, since the status of the unconventional has been gradually exhausted, as has the effect of reflexivity.

17. This corresponds to the structural model that Wright developed for the Western hero. See Will Wright, *Sixguns and Society: A Structural Study of the Western* (Berkeley: University of California Press, 1975).

18. See Charles Musser, *The Emergence of Cinema: The American Screen to 1907*, vol. 1, *History of the American Cinema* (New York: Scribner, 1990), 78.

19. William Frederick Cody, *An Autobiography of Buffalo Bill* (New York: Cosmopolitan, 1928).

20. Helen Cody Wetmore, *Last of the Great Scouts; The Life Story of Col. William F. Cody ("Buffalo Bill") as Told by His Sister Helen Cody Wetmore* (Duluth, Minn.: Duluth Press Printing Co., 1899).

21. David Bordwell, *Narration in the Fiction Film* (London: Methuen, 1985), 49–53.

22. The theory and history of decentered character constellations in multiple-protagonist films has been exhaustively studied by Margrit Tröhler in her postdoctoral thesis. See Margrit Tröhler, *Offene Welten ohne Helden. Plurale Figurenkonstellationen im Film* (Marburg: Schüren, 2007). For a comprehensive overview in English, see Margrit Tröhler, "Multiple Protagonist Films: A Transcultural Everyday Practice," in *Characters in Fictional Worlds: Interdisciplinary Perspectives*, ed. Jens Eder, Fotis Jannidis, and Ralph Schneider (Berlin: De Gruyter, 2010), 459–477.

23. Barry Salt, *Film Style and Technology: History and Analysis* [1983] (London: Starword, 1992), 281.

24. See ibid., 281–282.

25. Gilles Deleuze, *Cinema 1: The Movement Image* [French 1983], trans. Hugh Tomlinson and Barbara Habberjam (London: Continuum, 2005), 215.

26. Ibid.

10. ENJOYING THE STEREOTYPE AND INTENSE DOUBLE-PLAY ACTING: THE PERFORMANCE OF JENNIFER JASON LEIGH IN *THE HUDSUCKER PROXY*

1. Herbert Jhering, "Schauspielerische Klischees," *Blätter des Deutschen Theaters* (Berlin) 2, no. 30 (1912/1913): 488.

2. James Naremore, *Acting in the Cinema* (Berkeley: University of California Press, 1988).

3. Her filmography as an actress in the Internet Movie Database (as of July 2010) lists over seventy major roles in films for the theatre and television since 1973, her television debut. Since 1980, she has appeared on average in at least two productions a year.

4. A typical viewer response to one of Leigh's characters, Sadie in *Georgia* (Ulu Grosbard, 1995), from the "user comments" section of the Internet Movie Database reads: "Jennifer Jason Leigh is an incredible actress . . . making you feel what the character feels. She accomplishes that to an intense degree as Sadie Flood in *Georgia*. The problem is that I don't want to feel what Sadie felt. She scared and disgusted me . . . it felt like more an assignment than entertainment." From a theoretical perspective, such characters tellingly confirm how important it is to distinguish, in Murray Smith's terms, between "alignment" and "allegiance" with respect to spectatorial participation, that is, between the attention given to a character (alignment) and recipients' positive or negative evaluations of a character (allegiance). See Murray Smith, *Engaging Characters: Fiction, Emotion, and the Cinema* (Oxford: Clarendon Press, 1995).

5. Lizzie Francke, "All About Leigh," *Sight and Sound* 5, no. 2 (February, 1995): 8.

6. In addition to the skyscraper references and the fall from its heights, with which the film begins, *The Hudsucker Proxy* also borrows from the slogan of Dmytryk's film "The future is here" with its motto "The future is now."

7. See Gérard Genette, *Palimpsests: Literature in the Second Degree* [French 1982], trans. Channa Newman and Claude Doubinsky (Lincoln: University of Nebraska Press, 1997), 5–10. "Imitation, too, is no doubt a transformation, but one that involves a more complex process: it requires . . . a previously constituted model of generic competence . . . drawn from that singular performance . . . one that is capable of generating an indefinite number of mimetic performances. This model, then, introduces between the imitated text and the imitative one a supplementary stage and a mediation that are not to be found in the simple or direct type of transformation" (6).

8. Ibid., 24–28.

9. Fredric Jameson, *Postmodernism; or, The Cultural Logic of Late Capitalism* (London: Verso, 1996), 21.

10. Ibid.

11. On the architecture of the film see W. C. Odien, "The Rise and Fall of Norville Barnes," *Cinefex* 58 (June, 1994): 66–81.

12. For a survey of German reviews, see Daniel Kothenschulte, "The Hudsucker Proxy," in *Joel and Ethan Coen*, ed. Peter Körte and Georg Seeßlen (Berlin: Bertz, 1998), 141–164.

13. This is a reference to the terminology of Genette, who introduced the binary terms "extradiegetic" and "intradiegetic" as well as "heterodiegetic" and "homodiegetic." Extra-/intradiegetic refers to the location of the narrator with respect to the diegesis, the fictional narrative space (first- or second-level narrator). In the same sense, Sarah Kozloff speaks about framing or embedded narrators. Genette's second pair of terms distinguishes whether or not the narrator appears as a character in his or her own story. See Gérard Genette, *Narrative Discourse: An Essay in Method* [French 1972], trans. Jane E. Lewin (Ithaca, N.Y.: Cornell University Press, 1983), 227–237, 243–247; and Sara Kozloff, *Invisible Storytellers: Voice-Over Narration in American Fiction Film* (Berkeley: University of California Press, 1988), 42–43.

14. François Truffaut, "Frank Capra, The Healer" [French 1974], in *The Films in My Life*, trans. Leonard Mayhew (London: Allen Lane, 1980), 69.

15. Ibid.

16. Stanley Cavell, *Pursuits of Happiness: The Hollywood Comedy of Remarriage* (Cambridge, Mass.: Harvard University Press, 1981), 172.

17. See Katherine Hepburn in the prison scene of *Bringing Up Baby* (Howard Hawks, 1938).

18. Nicholas Yanni, *Rosalind Russell* (New York: Pyramid, 1975), 56.

EPILOGUE

1. Lars von Trier and Thomas Vinterberg, "Dogme 95: The Vow of Chastity" [1995], in *Technology and Culture: The Film Reader*, ed. Andrew Utterson (London: Routledge, 2005), 87–88.

2. Ibid., 88.

BIBLIOGRAPHY

Adorno, Theodor W., with the assistance of George Simpson. "On Popular Music." In *Studies in Philosophy and Social Science*, 9:17–48. New York: Institute of Social Research, 1941.

——. "On the Fetish-Character in Music and the Regression of Listening." In *The Essential Frankfurt School Reader*, edited by Andrew Arato and Eike Gebhardt, 270–299. New York: Continuum International Publishing Group, 1982. Originally published as "Über den Fetischcharakter in der Musik und die Regression des Hörens." *Zeitschrift für Sozialforschung* 7 (1938): 321–357.

——. "The Schema of Mass Culture" [German 1942, in manuscript]. In *The Culture Industry: Selected Essays on Mass Culture*, edited by J. M. Bernstein, 61–97. New York: Routledge, 2001. Originally published as "Das Schema der Massenkultur." In *Gesammelte Schriften*, edited by Rolf Tiedemann, 3: 299–335. Frankfurt am Main: Suhrkamp, 1981.

——. "Scientific Experiences of a European Scholar in America" [1968]. In *Critical Models: Interventions and Catchwords*, edited and translated by Henry W. Pickford, 215–244. New York: Columbia University Press, 1998.

Adorno, Theodor W., and Hanns Eisler. *Composing for the Films* [1947]. New York: Continuum International Publishing Group, 2005.

Altman, Rick. *The American Film Musical*. Bloomington: University of Indiana Press, 1987.

——. *Film/Genre*. London: BFI, 1999.

——. "Reusable Packaging: Generic Products and the Recycling Process." In *Refiguring American Film Genres: History and Theory*, edited by Nick Browne, 1–41. Berkeley: University of California Press, 1998.

——. "A Semantic/Syntactic Approach to Film Genre." In *Film Genre Reader*, edited by Barry Keith Grant, 26–40. Austin: University of Texas Press, 1986.

Amossy, Ruth. "Autobiographies of Movie Stars: Presentation of Self and Its Strategies." *Poetics Today* 7, no. 4 (1986): 673–703.

——. "The Cliché in the Reading Process." *SubStance* 11, no. 2 (1982): 34–45.

——. *Les Idées reçues. Sémiologie du stéréotype*. Paris: Nathan, 1991.

——. "On Commonplace Knowledge and Innovation." *SubStance* 62/63, special issue: *Thought and Novation* (1991): 145–156.

——. "Stereotypes and Representation in Fiction." *Poetics Today* 5, no. 4 (1984): 689–700.

——. "Des Topoï aux stéréotypes. Le doxique entre logos et pathos." In *Zeitschrift für französische Sprache und Literatur*, supplement 32: *Topoï, discours, arguments*, edited by Ekkehard Eggs. Stuttgart: Steiner, 2002.

——. "Types ou stéréotypes? Les physiologies et la littérature industrielle." *Romantisme* 64, no. 2 (1989): 113–123.

Amossy, Ruth, and Anne Herschberg-Pierrot. *Stéréotypes et clichés. Langue, discours, societé*. Paris: Nathan, 1997.

Amossy, Ruth, and Elisheva Rosen. *Le discours du cliché*. Paris: CDU—Société d'édition d'enseignement supérieur, 1982.

Arnheim, Rudolf. "Il cifrario del successo." *Cinema* 38 (January 25, 1938): 44.

——. "Il cinema e la folla." *Cinema* 25 (October 30, 1949): 219–220.

——. "Erich von Stroheim" [1958, German manuscript 1934]. In *Film Essays and Criticism*, translated by Brenda Benthien, 223–227. Madison: University of Wisconsin Press, 1997.

——. *Film als Kunst* [1932]. Munich: Hanser, 1974.

——. *Film as Art*. Berkeley: University of California Press, 1957.

——. *Film Essays and Criticism*, translated by Brenda Benthien. Madison: University of Wisconsin Press, 1997.

——. "For the First Time." In *Film Essays and Criticism*, translated by Brenda Benthien, 13–15. Madison: University of Wisconsin Press, 1997. Originally published as "Zum ersten Mal." *Berliner Tageblatt* 504 (October 25, 1931).

——. "In Praise of Character Actors." In *Film Essays and Criticism*, translated by Brenda Benthien, 52–54. Madison: University of Wisconsin Press, 1997. Originally published as "Lob der Charge." *Filmtechnik/Filmkunst* 20 (October 3, 1931): 2–3.

——. "Die Kunst im Volke." *Die Weltbühne* 24, no. 3 (1928): 97–100.

——. "A New Laocoön: Artistic Composites and the Talking Film." In *Film as Art*, 199–230. Berkeley: University of California Press, 1957. Originally published as "Nuovo Laocoonte." *Bianco e Nero* 8 (August 31, 1938): 3–33.

——. "The World of the Daytime Serial" [1943]. In *Radio Research 1942–1943*, edited by Paul F. Lazarsfeld and Frank N. Stanton, 34–85. New York: Arno Press, 1979.

——. "Die Zukunft des Tonfilms" [manuscript ca. 1934]. In *Die Seele in der Silberschicht. Medientheoretische Texte. Photographie—Fim—Rundfunk*, edited by Helmut H. Diederichs, 232–247. Frankfurt am Main: Suhrkamp, 2004.

Asmuth, Berhard. *Einführung in die Dramenanalyse*. Stuttgart: Metzler, 1980.

Astruc, Alexandre. "The Birth of a New Avant-garde: La Caméra-Stylo." In *Film and Literature: An Introduction and Reader*, written and compiled by Timothy Corrigan. Upper Saddle River, N.J.: Prentice-Hall, 1999. Originally published as "Naissance d'une nouvelle avant-garde: La caméra stylo." *L'écran français* 30, no. 144 (March 1948).

Avenarius, Richard. *Philosophie als Denken der Welt gemäß dem Prinzip des kleinsten Kraftmaßes. Prolegomena zu einer Kritik der reinen Erfahrung*. Berlin: J. Guttentag, 1903.

Bächlin, Peter. *Der Film als Ware* [1947]. Frankfurt am Main: Athenäum Fischer, 1975.

Baeumler, Alfred. "Die Wirkungen der Lichtbildbühne. Versuch einer Apologie des Kinematographentheaters" [1912]. In *Prolog vor dem Film: Nachdenken über ein neues Medium 1909–1914*, edited by Jörg Schweinitz, 186–194. Leipzig: Reclam, 1992.

Bakhtin, Mikhail M. *The Dialogic Imagination: Four Essays*. Translated by Michael Holquist and Caryl Emerson. Austin: University of Texas Press, 1981.

Balázs, Béla. "Die Film-Krisis" [1928]. In *Der Geist des Films. Artikel und Aufsätze 1925–1931. Schriften zum Film*. Vol. 2. Edited by Helmut H. Diederichs and Wolfgang Gersch, 2:231–233. Berlin: Henschel, 1984.

——. "Sensationsfilme" [1924]. In Balázs, *Der sichtbare Mensch. Kritiken und Aufsätze 1922–1926. Schriften zum Film*. Edited by Helmut H. Diederichs and Wolfgang Gersch, 1:266–267. Berlin: Henschel, 1982.

——. "The Spirit of Film." In *Béla Balázs: Early Film Thoery*, edited by Erica Carter, translated by Rodney Livingstone, 91–230. New York: Berghahn Books, 2010. Originally published as *Der Geist des Films*. Halle: Wilhelm Knapp, 1930.

——. "Visible Man or the Culture of Freedom." In *Béla Balázs: Early Film Thoery*, edited by Erica Carter, translated by Rodney Livingstone, 1–90. New York: Berghahn Books, 2010. Originally published as *Der sichtbare Mensch oder Die Kultur des Films*. Vienna: Deutsch-Österreichischer Verlag, 1924.

Bar-Tal, Daniel, Carl Graumann, Arie Kruglanski, and Wolfgang Stroebe, eds. *Stereotyping and Prejudice: Changing Conceptions*. New York: Springer, 1989.

Barthes, Roland. *Camera Lucida: Reflections on Photography*. Translated by Richard Howard. London: Jonathan Cape, 1982. Originally published as *La chambre claire: Notes sur la photographie*. Paris: Gallimard, Seuil, and Cahiers du cinema, 1980.

——. *Elements of Semiology*. Translated by Annette Lavers and Colin Smith. New York: Hill and Wang, 1973. Originally published as "Eléments de sémiologie." *Communications* 4 (1964): 91–135.

——. *Mythologies*. Translated by Annette Lavers. New York: Hill and Wang, 1972. Originally published as *Mythologies*. Paris: Éditions du Seuil, 1957.

——. *The Pleasure of the Text*. Translated by Richard Miller. New York: Hill and Wang, 1975. Originally published as *Le plaisir du texte*. Paris: Éditions du Seuil, 1973.

——. *Roland Barthes*. Translated by Richard Howard. New York: Hill and Wang, 1977. Originally published as *Roland Barthes par Roland Barthes*. Paris: Éditions du Seuil, 1975.

——. *S/Z: An Essay*. Translated by Richard Miller. New York: Hill and Wang, 1974. Originally published as *S/Z*. Paris: Éditions du Seuil, 1970.

——. "Upon Leaving the Movie Theater." In *The Cinematographic Apparatus*, edited by Theresa Hak Kyung Cha, 1–4. New York: Tanam Press, 1980. Originally published as "En sortant du cinéma." *Communications* 23 (1975): 104–107.

Baudrillard, Jean. *Symbolic Exchange and Death*. Translated by Iain Hamilton Grant. London: Sage, 2002. Originally published as *L'échange symbolique et la mort*. Paris: Gallimard, 1976.

Baudry, Jean-Louis. "The Apparatus: Metapsychological Approaches to the Impression of Reality in the Cinema." In *Narrative, Apparatus, Ideology: A Film Theory Reader*, edited by Philip Rosen, 286–318. New York: Columbia University Press, 1986. Originally published as "Le dispositif: Approches métapsychologique de l'impression de réalité." *Communications*, no. 23 (1975): 56–72.

Bauer, Matthias. "Der Film als Vorbild literarischer Ästhetik: Balázs, Musil und die Folgen." In *Grauzonen: Positionen zwischen Literatur und Film 1910–1960*, edited by Stefan Keppler-Tasaki and Fabienne Liptay. Munich: edition text+kritik, 2010.

Bazin, André. "Extract from André Bazin : 'La politique des auteurs.'" In *Theories of Authorship*, edited by John Caughie, 45–46. London: Routledge, 1981. Originally published as "De la politique des auteurs." *Cahiers du Cinéma* 79 (1957): 2–11.

——. *What Is Cinema?* Translated by Hugh Gray. Berkeley: University of California Press, 2005. Originally published as *Qu'est-ce que le cinéma?* Paris: Les éditions du CERF, 1958–1962.

Behne, Adolf. "Kunstausstellung Berlin." *Das neue Berlin. Monatshefte für Probleme der Grossstadt* 1 (1929): 150–152.

Beilenhoff, Wolfgang. "Filmtheorie und -praxis der russischen Formalisten." In *Poetik des Films: Deutsche Erstausgabe der filmtheoretischen Texte der russischen Formalisten*, edited by Wolfgang Beilenhoff, 139–147. Munich: Fink, 1974.

——, ed. *Poetika Kino. Theorie und Praxis des Films im russischen Formalismus.* Frankfurt am Main: Suhrkamp, 2005.

Beller, Hans, ed. *Handbuch der Filmmontage. Praxis und Prinzipien des Filmschnitts.* Munich: TR-Verlagsunion, 1993.

Benjamin, Walter. "The Work of Art in the Age of Its Technical Reproducibility: Second Version." In *The Work of Art in the Age of Its Technical Reproducibility and Other Writings on Media*, translated by Edmund Jephcott, Rodney Livingstone, Howard Eiland, et al., 19–55. Cambridge, Mass.: Harvard University Press, 2008. Originally published as "L'oeuvre d'art à l'époque de sa reproduction mécanisée." *Zeitschrift für Sozialforschung* 5 (1936): 40–68.

Bergson, Henri. *Creative Evolution.* Translated by Arthur Mitchell. New York: Henry Holt, 1911. Originally published as *L'évolution créatrice.* Paris: Alcan, 1907.

Biemel, Walter. "Pop-Art und Lebenswelt." In *Ästhetik*, edited by Wolfgang Heckmann, 148–189. Darmstadt: Wissenschaftliche Buchgesellschaft, 1979.

——. "Das Problem der Wiederholung in der Kunst der Gegenwart." In *Sprache und Begriff. Festschrift für Bruno Liebrucks*, edited by Heinz Röttgers, Brigitte Scheer, and Josef Simon, 269–329. Meisenheim am Glan: Anton Hain, 1974.

Blaicher, Günther, ed. *Erstarrtes Denken. Studien zu Klischees, Stereotyp und Vorurteil in englischsprachiger Literatur.* Tubingen: Narr, 1987.

Blüher, Dominique. "Sensibilisierung für die Konstruktion der Filme." *Filmbulletin* 2 (1990): 47–55.

Böhm, Gottfried. "Die Krise der Repräsentation. Die Kunstgeschichte und die moderne Kunst." In *Kategorien und Methoden der deutschen Kunstgeschichte 1900–1930*, edited by Lorenz Dittmann, 113–128. Stuttgart: Steiner, 1985.

Bolz, Norbert. *Chaos und Simulation.* Munich: Fink, 1992.

Booth, Wayne. *A Rhetoric of Irony.* Chicago: University of Chicago Press, 1974.

Bordwell, David. *Making Meaning: Inference and Rhetoric in the Interpretation of Cinema.* Cambridge, Mass.: Harvard University Press, 1989.

——. *Narration in the Fiction Film.* London: Methuen, 1985.

Bordwell, David, Janet Staiger, and Kristin Thompson. *The Classical Hollywood Cinema: Film Style and Mode of Production to 1960*. New York: Columbia University Press, 1985.

Bourdieu, Pierre. *Distinction: A Social Critique of the Judgment of Taste*. Translated by Richard Nice. London: Routledge & Kegan Paul, 1984. Originally published as *La distinction: critique sociale du jugement*. Paris: Les Éditions de Minuit, 1979.

———. *The Logic of Practice*. Stanford, Calif.: Stanford University Press, 1990. Originally published as *Le sens pratique*. Paris: Les Éditions de Minuit, 1980.

Bourget, Jean-Loup. *Le mélodrame hollywoodien*. Paris: Stock, 1985.

Bowser, Eileen. *The Transformation of Cinema: 1907–1915*. Vol. 2 of *History of the American Cinema*. New York: Scribner, 1990.

Branigan, Edward. *Narrative Comprehension and Film*. London: Routledge, 1992.

Brecht, Bertolt. "The Threepenny Lawsuit" [German 1931]. In *Bertolt Brecht on Film and Radio*. Edited and translated by Marc Silberman. London: Methuen, 2000. Originally published as "Der Dreigroschenprozess. Ein soziologisches Experiment." In *Versuche 3*. Berlin: Kiepenheuer, 1931.

Brenner, Peter J. *Der Reisebericht in der deutschen Literatur*. Tubingen: Niemeyer, 1990.

Brinckmann, Christine N. "Das Gesicht hinter der Scheibe." In *Die anthropomorphe Kamera und andere Schriften zur filmischen Narration*, edited by Mariann Lewinsky and Alexandra Schneider, 200–213. Zürcher Filmstudien 3. Zurich: Chronos, 1997.

Broch, Hermann. "Evil in the Value System of Art." In *Geist and Zeitgeist: The Spirit in an Unspiritual Age—Six Essays*, translated by John Hargraves, 30–40. New York: Counterpoint, 2002. Originally published as "Das Böse im Wertsystem der Kunst." *Neue Rundschau* 44, no. 2 (1933): 157–191.

Bronfen, Elisabeth. "Recycling von Gewalt und Gesetzlosigkeit." In *New Hollywood 1967–1976: Trouble in Wonderland*, edited by Hans Helmut Prinzler and Gabriele Jatho, 15–32. Berlin: Bertz, 2004.

Bronfen, Elisabeth, Marius Benjamin, and Therese Steffen. *Hybride Kulturen. Beiträge zur anglo-amerikanischen Multikulturalismusdebatte*. Tubingen: Stauffenburg, 1997.

Bruns, Max. "Kino und Buchhandel" [1913]. In *Prolog vor dem Film: Nachdenken über ein neues Medium 1909–1914*, edited by Jörg Schweinitz, 272–277. Leipzig: Reclam, 1992.

Bühler, Karl. *Theory of Language—The Representational Function of Language*. Translated by Donald Fraser Goodwin. Amsterdam: John Benjamins B.V., 1990. Originally published as *Sprachtheorie: Die Darstellungsfunktion der Sprache*. Jena: Gustav Fischer Verlag, 1934.

Buñuel, Luis. *My Last Sigh*. Translated by Abigail Israel. Minneapolis: University of Minnesota Press, 2003. Originally published as *Mon dernier soupir*. Paris: Éditions Robert Laffont, 1982.

Buscombe, Edward. "The Idea of Genre in the American Cinema." In *Film Genre Reader*, edited by Barry Keith Grant, 11–25. Austin: University of Texas Press, 1986.

Caldwell, John Thornton. *Televisuality: Style, Crisis, and Authority in American Television*. New Brunswick, N.J.: Rutgers University Press, 1994.

Campbell, Joseph. *The Hero with a Thousand Faces* [1949]. Bollingen Series 17. Princeton, N.J.: Princeton University Press, 1973.

Cavell, Stanley. "More of the World Viewed." *Georgia Review* 28 (1995): 571–631.

——. *Pursuits of Happiness: The Hollywood Comedy of Remarriage*. Cambridge, Mass.: Harvard University Press, 1981.

——. *The World Viewed: Reflections on the Ontology of Film*. Cambridge, Mass.: Harvard University Press, 1979.

Cawelti, John G. "The Concept of Formula in the Study of Popular Literature." *Journal of Popular Culture* 3, no. 3 (1969): 381–390.

Clair, René. *Reflections on the Cinema*. Translated by Vera Traill. London: W. Kimber, 1953. Originally published as *Réflexion faite*. Paris: Gallimard, 1951.

Cody, William Frederick. *An Autobiography of Buffalo Bill*. New York: Cosmopolitan, 1928.

Cody Wetmore, Helen. *Last of the Great Scouts; the Life Story of Col. William F. Cody ("Buffalo Bill") as Told by His Sister Helen Cody Wetmore*. Duluth, Minn.: Duluth Press Printing Co., 1899.

Cohen-Séat, Gilbert. *Essai sur les principes d'une philosophie du cinéma*. Paris: Presses universitaires de France, 1946.

Coulmas, Florian. *Routine im Gespräch. Zur pragmatischen Fundierung der Idiomatik*. Wiesbaden: Athenaion, 1981.

Dadelsen, Bernhard von. "Höhe- und Wendepunkte klassischer Genres: *Spiel mir das Lied vom Tod* (*C'era una volta il West*, 1968)." In *Fischer Filmgeschichte*, edited by Werner Faulstich and Helmut Korte, 4:154–166. Frankfurt am Main: Fischer, 1992.

Dall'Asta, Monica. "Maciste—ein Stereotyp westlicher Männlichkeit." *KINtop. Jahrbuch zur Erforschung des frühen Films*, vol. 7, special issue: *Stummes Spiel, sprechende Gesten* (1998): 85–98.

Danto, Arthur C. *The Transfiguration of the Commonplace: A Philosophy of Art*. Cambridge, Mass.: Harvard University Press, 1981.

Dästner, Corinna. "Sprechen über Filmmusik. Der Überschuss von Bild und Musik." In *Sound. Zur Technologie und Ästhetik des Akustischen in den Medien* (GFM-Schriften 12), edited by Harro Segeberg and Frank Schätzlein, 83–95. Marburg: Schüren, 2005.

Deleuze, Gilles. *Cinema 1: The Movement Image*. Translated by Hugh Tomlinson and Barbara Habberjam. London: Continuum, 2005. Originally published as *Cinéma 1: L'image-mouvement*. Paris: Les Éditions de Minuit, 1983.

——. *Cinema 2: The Time Image*. Translated by Hugh Tomlinson and Robert Galeta. London: Continuum, 2005. Originally published as *Cinéma 2: L'image-temps*. Paris: Les Éditions de Minuit, 1985.

Denby, David, ed. *Film 71/72*. New York: Simon & Schuster, 1972.

Dewey, John. "*The Eternal Values*. By Hugo Münsterberg [review]." *The Philosophical Review* 19 (March 1910): 188–192.

Diederichs, Helmut H., ed. *Geschichte der Filmtheorie. Kunsttheoretische Texte von Meliès bis Arnheim*. Frankfurt am Main: Suhrkamp, 2004.

Doležel, Lubomír. *Heterocosmica: Fiction and Possible Worlds*. Baltimore, Md.: The Johns Hopkins University Press, 1998.

Dröge, Franz W. *Publizistik und Vorurteil*. Münster: Regensberg, 1967.

Dyer, Richard. *The Dumb Blonde Stereotype: Documentation for EAS Classroom Materials*. London: BFI, 1979.

——. *Heavenly Bodies: Film Stars and Society*. London: Macmillan, 1987.

——. *The Matter of Images: Essays on Representation*. London: Routledge, 1993.

——. *Pastiche*. London: Routledge, 2007.

——. *Stars*. London: BFI, 1979.

——. "Stereotyping." In *Gays in Film*, 27–39. London: BFI, 1977.

Eberlein, Kurt Karl. "Januskopf und Maske" [1928]. In *Medientheorie 1888–1933. Texte und Kommentare*, edited by Albert Kümmel and Petra Löffler. Frankfurt am Main: Suhrkamp, 2002.

Ebert, Roger. *The Little Book of Hollywood Clichés: A Compendium of Movie Clichés, Stereotypes, Obligatory Scenes, Hackneyed Formulas, Shopworn Conventions, and Outdated Archetypes*. London: Virgin, 1995.

Eco, Umberto. *Apocalypse Postponed*, edited and translated by Robert Lumley, 17–35. Bloomington: University of Indiana Press, 1994.

——. *Apokalyptiker und Integrierte. Zur kritischen Kritik der Massenkultur*. Frankfurt am Main: S. Fischer, 1986. Originally published as *Apocalittici e integrati: comunicazioni di massa e teorie della cultura di massa*. Milan: Bompiani, 1964 and [revised edition] 1977.

——. *Einführung in die Semiotik*. Edited by Jürgen Trabant. Munich: Fink, 1972. Originally published as *La struttura assente. Introduzione alla ricerca semiologica*. Milan: Bompiani, 1968.

——. "Innovation and Repetition: Between Modern and Post-Modern Aesthetics." *Daedalus* 114, no. 4 (Fall 1985): 161–184.

——. *Lector in fabula: Die Mitarbeit der Interpretation in erzählenden Texten* [1979]. Munich: dtv, 1990.

——. "The Myth of Superman." In *The Role of the Reader: Explorations in the Semiotics of Texts*, edited by Thomas Sebeok, 107–124. Bloomington: University of Indiana Press, 1979.

——. "Postmodernism, Irony, the Enjoyable." In *Reflections on* The Name of the Rose, translated by William Weaver, 65–72. London: Secker and Warburg, 1985.

——. "Die praktische Anwendung der literarischen Person." In *Apokalyptiker und Integrierte. Zur kritischen Kritik der Massenkultur*, 161–126. Frankfurt am Main: Fischer, 1986.

——. *The Role of the Reader: Explorations in the Semiotics of Texts*. Edited by Thomas Sebeok. Bloomington: University of Indiana Press, 1979.

Ehrenburg, Ilya. *Die Traumfabrik. Chronik des Films*. Berlin: Malik, 1931. Originally published as *Fabrika snov: chronika našego vremeni*. Berlin: Petropolis, 1931.

Eikhenbaum, Boris. *Problems of Cine-Stylistics*. Translated by Richard Sherwood. In *The Poetics of Cinema*, edited by Richard Taylor, 5–31. Oxford: RPT Publications, 1982. Originally published as "Problemy kino-stilistiki." In *Poétika kino*, edited by Boris Eikhenbaum, 13–52. Moscow/Leningrad: Kinopechat, 1927.

Eisenstein, Sergei M: "Béla Forgets the Scissors." In *The Film Factory: Russian and Soviet Cinema in Documents, 1896–1939*, edited and translated by Richard Taylor, 149–149. London: Routledge and Kegan Paul, 1988. Originally published as "Bela zabyvaet nozhnitsy." *Kino* (August 16, 1926).

Eisner, Lotte H. *The Haunted Screen: Expressionism in the German Cinema and the Influence of Max Reinhardt*. Translated by Roger Greaves. Berkeley: University of California Press, 2008. Originally published as *L'écran démoniaque: Les influences de Max Reinhardt et de l'expressionnisme*. Paris: A. Bonne, 1952.

Elias, Norbert. *The Civilizing Process. Sociogenetic and Psychogenetic Investigations.* Oxford: Blackwell, 2000. Originally published as *Über den Prozess der Zivilisation: soziogenetische und psychogenetische Untersuchungen.* Basel: Verlag Haus zum Falken, 1939.

Elliot, James, Jürgen Pelzer, and Carol Poore, eds. *Stereotyp und Vorurteil in der Literatur. Untersuchungen zu Autoren des 20. Jahrhunderts.* Göttingen: Vandenhoeck und Ruprecht, 1978.

Elsaesser, Thomas. "Kunst und Krise. Die UFA in den 20er Jahren." In *Das UFA-Buch*, edited by Hans-Michael Bock and Michael Töteberg, 96–105. Frankfurt am Main: Zweitausendeins, 1992.

——. "*Nashville*: Putting on the Show." *Persistence of Vision* 1 (1984): 35–43.

——. "Notes on the Unmotivated Hero—The Pathos of Failure: American Films in the '70s." *Monogram* 6 (1975): 13–19.

——. "Specularity and Engulfment: Francis Ford Coppola and *Bram Stoker's Dracula*." In *Contemporary Hollywood Cinema*, edited by Steve Neale and Murray Smith, 191–208. London: Routledge, 1998.

——. "Tales of Sound and Fury: Observations on the Family Melodrama." In *Film Theory and Criticism: Introductory Readings*, edited by Gerald Mast, Marshall Cohen, and Leo Braudy, 512–535. Oxford: Oxford University Press, 1992.

Engell, Lorenz. *Sinn und Industrie. Einführung in die Filmgeschichte.* Frankfurt am Main: Campus, 1992.

Feineman, Neil. *Persistence of Vision: The Films of Robert Altman.* New York: Arno Press, 1978.

Feuer, Jane. "The Self-Reflexive Musical and the Myth of Entertainment." In *Film Genre Reader*, edited by Barry Keith Grant, 329–343. Austin: University of Texas Press, 1986.

Fiedler, Leslie. "Cross the Border—Close the Gap" [1969]. In *A Fiedler Reader*, edited by Leslie Fiedler, 270–294. Briarcliff Manor, N.Y.: Stein & Day, 1977.

Flückiger, Barbara. *Sound Design. Die virtuelle Klangwelt des Films.* Marburg: Schüren, 2002.

——. "Sound Effects. Strategies for Sound Effects in Film." In *Sound and Music in Film and Visual Media: An Overview*, edited by Graeme Harper, Ruth Doughty, and Jochen Eisentraut, 151–179. London: Continuum, 2009.

Flusser, Vilém. *Die Revolution der Bilder. Der Flusser-Reader zu Kommunikation, Medien und Design.* Berlin: Bollmann, 1995.

Ford, Henry, in collaboration with Samuel Crowther. *My Life and Work* [1922]. New York: Arno Press, 1973.

Forster, E. M. *Aspects of the Novel* [1927]. San Diego, Calif.: Harcourt Brace, 1985.

Francke, Lizzie. "All About Leigh." *Sight and Sound* 5, no. 2 (1995): 8.

Frayling, Christopher. *Spaghetti Westerns: Cowboys and Europeans from Karl May to Sergio Leone.* London: Routledge and Paul, 1981.

French, Philip. *Westerns.* Oxford: Oxford University Press, 1977.

Friedell, Egon. "Prolog vor dem Film" [1913]. In *Prolog vor dem Film: Nachdenken über ein neues Medium 1909–1914*, edited by Jörg Schweinitz, 201–208. Leipzig: Reclam, 1992.

Frieß, Jörg, Britta Hartmann, and Eggo Müller, eds. *Nicht allein das Laufbild auf der Leinwand . . . Strukturen des Films als Erlebnispotentiale: Festschrift für Peter Wuss zum 60. Geburtstag.* BFF 60. Berlin: Vistas, 2001.

Frizot, Michel, ed. *A New History of Photography.* London: Konemann, 1998.

Frye, Northrop. *Anatomy of Criticism*. Princeton, N.J.: Princeton University Press, 1957.

Fülöp-Miller, René. "The Motion Picture in America. A History in the Making." In *The American Theatre and the Motion Picture in America: A History in the Making*, edited by John Andersen and René Fülöp-Miller, 104–189. New York: The Dial Press, 1938. Originally published as "Das amerikanische Kino." In *Das amerikanische Theater und Kino. Zwei kulturgeschichtliche Abhandlungen*, edited by Joseph Gregor and René Fülöp-Miller, 57–96. Zurich, Leipzig, and Vienna: Amalthea, 1931.

——. *Die Phantasiemaschine. Eine Saga der Gewinnsucht*. Berlin: Paul Zsolnay, 1931.

Genette, Gérard. *Narrative Discourse: An Essay on Method*. Translated by Jane E. Lewin. Ithaca, N.Y.: Cornell University Press, 1983. Originally published as *Discours du récit*. Paris: Éditions du Seuil, 1972.

——. *Palimpsests: Literature in the Second Degree*. Translated by Channa Newman and Claude Doubinsky. Lincoln: University of Nebraska Press, 1997. Originally published as *Palimpsestes: La littérature au second degré*. Paris: Éditions du Seuil, 1982.

Gerndt, Helge, ed.. *Stereotypvorstellungen im Alltagsleben. Beiträge zum Themenkreis Fremdbilder, Selbstbilder, Identität. Festschrift für Georg R. Schronbek zum 65. Geburtstag*. Munich: Vereinigung für Völkerkunde, 1988.

Giedion, Sigfried. *Mechanization Takes Command: A Contribution to Anonymous History*. Oxford: Oxford University Press, 1948.

Gledhill, Christine. "Rethinking Genre." In *Reinventing Film Studies*, edited by Christine Gledhill and Linda Williams, 221–243. London: Arnold, 2000.

Göktürk, Deniz. *Künstler, Cowboys, Ingenieure: Kultur- und mediengeschichtliche Studien zu deutschen Amerika-Texten 1912–20*. Munich: Fink, 1998.

Goldschmidt, Berhard. *Von New York bis Frisco. Ein deutsches Tagebuch*. Berlin: D. Reimer, 1925.

Gombrich, Ernst H. *Art and Illusion. A Study in the Psychology of Pictorial Representation* [1960]. London: Phaidon Press, 1977.

——. *Norm and Form: Studies in the Art of the Renaissance*. London: Phaidon Press, 1966.

Good, Howard. *The Drunken Journalist: The Biography of a Film Stereotype*. Lanham, Md.: Scarecrow Press, 2000.

Gramsci, Antonio. *Prison Notebooks*. Translated by Joseph A. Buttigieg. New York: Columbia University Press, 2007. Originally published as Gramsci, Antonio. *Quaderni del carcere*. Torino: Einaudi, 1948–1951.

Grant, Barry Keith, ed. *Film Genre Reader*. Austin: University of Texas Press, 1986.

Greimas, Algirdas Julien. "L'actualité du saussurisme (à l'occasion du 40e anniversaire de la publication du Cours de linguistique générale)." *Le Français Moderne* 24, no. 3 (1956): 191–203.

Gruber, Frank. "The Western." In *TV and Screen Writing*, edited by Lola G. Yoakem. Berkeley: University of California Press, 1958.

Gunning, Tom. "'Those That Are Drawn with a Fine Camel Haired Brush': The Origins of Film Genres." *Iris* 20 (1995): 49–61.

Haas, Willy. "Die Film-Krisis." *Das Tagebuch* 17 (1928): 713–714.

Hake, Sabine. *The Cinema's Third Machine: Writing on Film in Germany, 1907–1933*. Lincoln: University of Nebraska Press, 1993.

Halfeld, Adolf. *Amerika und Amerikanismus: Kritische Betrachtungen eines Deutschen und Europäers.* Jena: Diederichs, 1928.

Hansen, Miriam. "Ein Massenmedium konstruiert sein Publikum: King Vidor's *The Crowd.*" *Die neue Gesellschaft. Frankfurter Hefte* 40, no. 9 (1993): 834–843.

Harms, Rudolf. *Philosophie des Films. Seine ästhetischen und metaphysischen Grundlagen* [expanded edition in book form of his *Untersuchungen*]. Leipzig: Meiner, 1926.

——. *Untersuchungen zur Aesthetik des Spielfilms. Inaugural-Dissertation zur Erlangung der Doktorwürde der hohen philosophischen Fakultät der Universität Leipzig* [handwritten manuscript]. Diss., University of Leipzig, 1922.

Hartmann, Britta. *Aller Anfang. Zur Initialphase des Spielfilms.* Marburg: Schüren, 2009.

——. "Topographische Ordnung und narrative Struktur im klassischen Gangsterfilm." *Montage AV* 8, no. 1 (1999): 111–133.

Hasenclever, Walter. "Der Kintopp als Erzieher" [1913]. In *Prolog vor dem Film: Nachdenken über ein neues Medium 1909–1914,* edited by Jörg Schweinitz, 219–222. Leipzig: Reclam, 1992.

Hassan, Ihab. "Postmoderne heute." In *Wege aus der Moderne. Schlüsseltexte der Postmoderne-Diskussion,* edited by Wolfgang Welsch, 47–56. Weinheim: VCH Acta humaniora, 1988.

Hauptmann, Carl. "Film und Theater" [1919]. In *Kino-Debatte,* edited by Anton Kaes, 123–130. Munich: dtv, 1978.

Hauser, Arnold. *The Social History of Art* [1951]. In collaboration with Stanley Godman. London: Routledge & Kegan Paul, 1999.

——. *The Sociology of Art.* Translated by Kenneth J. Northcott. Chicago: University of Chicago Press, 1982. Originally published as *Soziologie der Kunst.* Munich: C. H. Beck, 1974.

Hayakawa, S. I. "Recognizing Stereotypes as a Substitute for Thought." *ETC.: A Review of General Semantics* 7 (1950): 208–210.

Heath, Stephen. *Questions of Cinema.* Bloomington: University of Indiana Press, 1981.

Hediger, Vinzenz. *Verführung zum Film. Der amerikanische Kinotrailer seit 1912.* Zürcher Filmstudien 5. Marburg: Schüren, 2001.

Heller, Heinz B. *Literarische Intelligenz und Film. Zu Veränderungen der ästhetischen Theorie und Praxis unter dem Eindruck des Films 1910–1930 in Deutschland.* Tubingen: Niemeyer, 1985.

Heller, Heinz B., Karl Prümm, and Birgit Peulings, eds. *Der Körper im Bild: Schauspielen–Darstellen–Erscheinen.* GFF-Schriften 7. Marburg: Schüren, 1999.

Hénault, Anne. *Histoire de la sémiotique.* Paris: PUF, 1997.

Hickethier, Knut. *Die Fernsehserie und das Serielle des Fernsehens.* Lüneburger Beiträge zur Kulturwissenschaft 2. Lüneburg: University of Lüneburg, 1991.

——. *Film- und Fernsehanalyse.* Stuttgart: Metzler, 1993.

——. "Poetik des Kleinen." In *Schauspielkunst im Film,* edited by Thomas Koebner, 37–48. St. Augustin: Gardez!, 1998.

——. "Der Schauspieler als Produzent. Überlegungen zur Theorie des medialen Schauspielers." In *Der Körper im Bild. Schauspielen—Darstellen—Erscheinen,* edited by Heinz B. Heller, Karl Prümm, and Birgit Peulings, 9–30. Marburg: Schüren.

——. "Schauspielen in Film und Fernsehen." In *Kinoschriften: Jahrbuch der Gesellschaft für Filmtheorie,* 2:45–68. Vienna: Verband der Wissenschaftlichen Gesellschaften Österreichs, 1990.

——. "Das Zucken der Mundwinkel. Schauspielen in den Medien." *TheaterZeitSchrift* 1, no. 2 (1982): 15–31.

Higson, Andrew, and Richard Maltby. *'Film Europe' and 'Film America': Cinema, Commerce and Cultural Exchange 1920–1939.* Exeter: University of Exeter Press, 1999.

Hofmannsthal, Hugo von. *The Lord Chandos Letter.* Translated by Russell Stockman. Marlboro, Vt.: Marlboro Press, 1986. Originally published as "Ein Brief." *Der Tag* (October 18, 1902).

——. "Eine Monographie. Friedrich Mittenwurzer, von Eugen Guglia" [1895]. In *Gesammelte Werke in Einzelausgaben, Prosa I,* 265–270. Frankfurt am Main: S. Fischer, 1950.

——. "The Substitute for Dreams." In *German Essays on Film,* edited by Richard W. McCormick and Alison Guenther-Pal, translated by Lance W. Garmer. New York: Continuum, 2004. Originally published as "Der Ersatz für die Träume." *Prager Presse* [Easter supplement] (March 27, 1921).

Hofstätter, Peter R. *Das Denken in Stereotypen.* Göttingen: Vandenhoek & Ruprecht, 1960.

——. *Die Psychologie der öffentlichen Meinung.* Vienna: Braumüller, 1949.

Höllriegel, Arnold [Pseudonym for Richard A. Bermann]. *Das Hollywood-Bilderbuch.* Leipzig: E. P. Tal, 1927.

——. *Die Films der Prinzessin Fantoche* [1913], edited by Michael Grisko. Berlin: Aviva, 2003.

Horkheimer, Max, and Theodor W. Adorno. *Dialectic of Enlightenment.* Translated by Edmund Jephcott. Stanford, Calif.: Stanford University Press, 2002. Originally published as *Dialektik der Aufklärung. Philosophische Fragmente.* Amsterdam: Querido, 1947.

Horwarth, Alexander, Thomas Elsaesser, and Noel King. *The Last Great American Picture Show: New Hollywood Cinema in the 1970s.* Amsterdam: Amsterdam University Press, 2004.

Husserl, Edmund. *Phantasy, Image Consciousness, and Memory* [German 1898–1925, papers published posthumously]. In *Husserliana—Edmund Husserl, Collected Works,* vol. 23. Translated by John B. Brough. Dordrecht: Springer, 2006. Originally published as *Phantasie, Bildbewußtsein, Erinnerung. Zur Phänomenologie der anschaulichen Vergegenwärtigungen. Texte aus dem Nachlass (1898–1925), Husserliana 23.* Edited by Eduard Marbach. The Hague, Boston, London: Niijhoff, 1980.

Hutcheon, Linda. *Irony's Edge. The Theory and Politics of Irony.* London: Routledge, 1995.

——. *A Theory of Parody: The Teaching of Twentieth-Century Art Forms.* Urbana: University of Illinois Press, 2000.

Iampolski, Mikhail. "Neozhidannoe rodstvo: Rozhdenie kinoteorii dukha fiziognomiki [The Birth of Film Theory out of the Spirit of Physiognomy]" [Russian]. *Iskusstvo kino* 12 (1986): 93–104. Also published in German as "Die Geburt der Filmtheorie aus dem Geist der Physiognomik." *Beiträge zur Film- und Fernsehwissenschaft* 27, no. 2 (1986): 79–98.

——. "Die Utopie vom kosmischen Schauspiel und der Kinematograph." *Beiträge zur Film- und Fernsehwissenschaft* 29, no. 34 (1988): 177–191.

Iser, Wolfgang. *The Fictive and the Imaginary: Charting Literary Anthropology.* Baltimore, Md.: The Johns Hopkins University Press, 1993. Originally published as *Das Fiktive und das Imaginäre: Perspektiven literarischer Anthropologie.* Frankfurt am Main: Suhrkamp, 1991.

Jacobs, Diane. *Hollywood Renaissance.* New York: A. S. Barnes, 1977.

Jameson, Fredric. *The Political Unconscious.* London: Methuen, 1981.

———. *Postmodernism; or, The Cultural Logic of Late Capitalism.* London: Verso, 1996.

Jhering, Herbert. "Der Schauspieler im Film" [1920]. In *Von Reinhardt bis Brecht. Vier Jahrzehnte Theater und Film,* edited by Edith Krull, 1:378–414. Berlin: Henschel, 1958.

———. "Schauspielerische Klischees." *Blätter des Deutschen Theaters* 2, no. 30 (1912/1913): 487–488.

———. *Werner Krauss. Ein Schauspieler und das neunzehnte Jahrhundert* [first publication of an article written in 1943/1945], edited by Sabine Zolchow and Rudolf Mast. Berlin: Vorwerk 8, 1997.

Kael, Pauline, "Some Speculations on the Appeal of the Auteur Theory" [1963]. In *I Lost It at the Movies,* 310–319. Boston and Toronto: Little, Brown, and Co., 1965.

Kaes, Anton, ed. *Kino-Debatte.* Munich: dtv, 1978.

———, ed. *Weimarer Republik. Manifeste und Dokumente zur deutschen Literatur, 1918–1933.* Stuttgart: Metzler, 1983.

Kaes, Anton, Martin Jay, and Edward Dimendberg, eds. *The Weimar Republic Sourcebook.* Berkeley: University of California Press, 1994.

Kagan, Norman. *American Skeptic: Robert Altman's Genre-Commentary Films.* Ann Arbor, Mich.: Pierian Press, 1982.

Kaminsky, Stuart M. *American Film Genres.* 2nd (revised) ed. Chicago: Nelson Hall, 1985.

Kappelhoff, Hermann. *Der möblierte Mensch: G. W. Pabst und die Utopie der Sachlichkeit—ein poetologischer Versuch zum Weimarer Autorenkino.* Berlin: Vorwerk 8, 1995.

Katz, Daniel, and Kenneth W. Braly. "Racial Stereotypes of One Hundred College Students." *Journal of Abnormal and Social Psychology* 28 (1933): 280–290.

———. "Racial Prejudice and Racial Stereotypes." *Journal of Abnormal and Social Psychology* 30 (1935): 175–193.

Kerr, Alfred. "Kino" [1912/1913]. In *Kino-Debatte,* edited by Anton Kaes, 75–77. Munich: dtv, 1978.

Kessler, Frank. "Etienne Souriau und das Vokabular der filmologischen Schule." *Montage AV* 6, no. 2 (1997): 132–139.

———. "Lesbare Körper." *KINtop. Jahrbuch zur Erforschung des frühen Films,* vol. 7, special issue: *Stummes Spiel, sprechende Gesten* (1998): 15–28.

———. "Photogénie und Physiognomie." In *Kinoschriften: Jahrbuch der Gesellschaft für Filmtheorie,* 4:125–136. Vienna: Synema, 1996.

Kirchmann, Kay. "Zwischen Selbstreflexivität und Selbstreferentialität. Überlegungen zur Ästhetik des Selbstbezüglichen als filmischer Modernität." *Film und Kritik* 2 (1994): 23–37.

Kisch, Egon Erwin. *(beehrt sich darzubieten) Paradies Amerika* [1929]. Berlin: Aufbau, 1994.

Kittler, Friedrich. *Discourse Networks, 1800/1900.* Translated by Michael Metteer with Chris Cullens. Stanford, Calif.: Stanford University Press, 1990. Originally published as *Aufschreibesysteme 1800/1900.* Munich: Fink, 1985.

Klöckner, Albert. "Das Massenproblem in der Kunst. Über Wesen und Wert der Vervielfältigung (Film und Funk)" [1928]. In *Medientheorie 1888–1933. Texte und Kommentare,* edited by Albert Kümmel and Petra Löffler, 299–311. Frankfurt am Main: Suhrkamp, 2002.

Koch, Gertrud. "Béla Balázs: The Physiognomy of Things." *New German Critique* 40 (1987): 167–178. Originally published as "Die Physiognomie der Dinge. Zur frühen Filmtheorie von Béla Balázs." *Frauen und Film* 40 (1986): 73–82.

——. "Rudolf Arnheim: The Materialist of Aesthetic Illusion—Gestalt Theory and Reviewer's Practice." *New German Critique* 51 (1990): 164–178.

Koch, Heinrich, and Heinrich Braune. *Von deutscher Filmkunst. Gehalt und Gestalt.* Berlin: Scherping, 1943.

Koebner, Thomas. "Der Film als neue Kunst—Reaktionen der literarischen Intelligenz. Zur Theorie des Stummfilms (1911–24)". In *Literaturwissenschaft—Medienwissenschaft*, edited by Helmut Kreuzer. Heidelberg: Quelle & Meyer, 1977.

——. ed. *"Diesseits der dämonischen Leinwand." Neue Perspektiven auf das späte Weimarer Kino.* Munich: edition text + kritik, 2003.

Königstein, Horst. "Es war einmal ein Westen: Stereotyp und Bewußtsein." In *Visuelle Kommunikation: Beiträge zur Kritik der Bewußtseinsindustrie*, edited by Hermann K. Ehmer, 299–333. Cologne: DuMont Schauberg, 1971.

Kothenschulte, Daniel. "The Hudsucker Proxy." In *Joel and Ethan Coen*, edited by Peter Körte and Georg Seeßlen, 141–164. Berlin: Bertz, 1998.

Kozloff, Sarah. *Invisible Storytellers. Voice-Over Narration in American Fiction Film.* Berkeley: University of California Press, 1988.

Kracauer, Siegfried. "Bücher vom Film." *Frankfurter Zeitung* 71, no. 505 (July 10, 1927); *Literaturblatt* 60, no. 28: 5.

——. "Film 1928." In *The Mass Ornament: Weimar Essays*, translated, edited, and with an introduction by Thomas Y. Levin, 307–322. Cambridge, Mass.: Harvard University Press, 1995. Originally published as "Der heutige Film und sein Publikum." *Frankfurter Zeitung* (November 30 and December 1, 1928).

——. "The Little Shop-Girls Go to the Movies." In *The Mass Ornament: Weimar Essays*, translated, edited, and with an introduction by Thomas Y. Levin, 291–306. Cambridge, Mass.: Harvard University Press, 1995. Originally published as "Die kleinen Ladenmädchen gehen ins Kino." *Frankfurter Zeitung* (March 11–19, 1927).

——. "The Mass Ornament." In *The Mass Ornament: Weimar Essays*, translated, edited, and with an introduction by Thomas Y. Levin, 75–88. Cambridge, Mass.: Harvard University Press, 1995. Originally published as "Das Ornament der Masse." *Frankfurter Zeitung* (June 9, 1927).

——. *The Mass Ornament: Weimar Essays.* Translated, edited, and with an introduction by Thomas Y. Levin. Cambridge, Mass.: Harvard University Press, 1995. Originally published as *Das Ornament der Masse.* Frankfurt am Main: Suhrkamp, 1963.

——. "National Types as Hollywood Presents Them." *Public Opinion Quarterly* 13, no. 1 (1949): 53–72.

——. "Neue Filmliteratur." *Frankfurter Zeitung* 76, no. 26 (January 10, 1932).

——. *Theory of Film: The Redemption of Physical Reality* [1960]. Oxford: Oxford University Press, 1997.

——. "Ein feiner Kerl. Analyse eines Ufa-Films" [1931]. In *Von Caligari zu Hitler*, 505–507. Frankfurt am Main: Suhrkamp, 1984.

Kreimeier, Klaus, ed. *Metaphysik des Dekors. Raum, Architektur und Licht im klassischen deutschen Stummfilm.* Marburg: Schüren, 1994.

——. *The Ufa Story: A History of Germany's Greatest Film Company, 1918–1945.* Translated by Robert and Rita Kimber. New York: Hill and Wang, 1996. Originally published as *Die UFA-Story. Geschichte eines Filmkonzerns.* Munich: Heyne, 1992.

Kühn, Heike. "Zwischen Überfluß und Mangel. Die 37. Internationalen Kurzfilmtage in Oberhausen." *Frankfurter Rundschau* 104 (May 6, 1991): 21.

Kümmel, Albert, and Petra Löffler, eds. *Medientheorie 1888–1933. Texte und Kommentare.* Frankfurt am Main: Suhrkamp, 2002.

Kunow, Rüdiger. *Das Klischee. Reproduzierte Wirklichkeiten in der englischen und amerikanischen Literatur.* Munich: Fink, 1994.

Lakoff, George. *Women, Fire, and Dangerous Things: What Categories Reveal About the Mind.* Chicago: University of Chicago Press, 1987.

Lang, Robert. *American Film Melodrama: Griffith, Vidor, Minelli.* Princeton, N.J.: Princeton University Press, 1989.

Lange, Konrad. "Die Zukunft des Kinos" [1914]. In *Prolog vor dem Film: Nachdenken über ein neues Medium 1909–1914,* edited by Jörg Schweinitz, 109–120. Leipzig: Reclam, 1992.

Lausberg, Heinrich. *Handbook of Literary Rhetoric: A Foundation for Literary Study.* Translated by Matthew T. Bliss, Annemiek Jansen, and David E. Orton. Edited by David E. Orton and R. Dean Anderson. Leiden: E. J. Brill, 1998. Originally published as *Handbuch der literarischen Rhetorik. Eine Grundlegung der Literaturwissenschaft.* Munich: Huber, 1973.

Leisegang, Herbert. "Sprechfilm—Rundfunk—Bildfunk—Filmfunk—Zukunftstheater." *Freie Volksbildung* 4 (1929): 11–19.

Leonhard, Rudolf. "Zur Soziologie des Films." In *Der Film von morgen,* edited by Hugo Zehder, 101–116. Berlin: Kaemmerer, 1923.

Lethen, Helmut. *Neue Sachlichkeit, 1924–1932. Studien zur Literatur des 'weißen Sozialismus'.* Metzler: Stuttgart, 1970.

Levin, Thomas Y. "Iconology at the Movies: Panofsky's Film Theory." In *Meaning in the Visual Arts: Views from Outside,* edited by Irving Laving. Princeton, N.J.: Institute for Advanced Study, 1995.

Liebrand, Claudia, and Ines Steiner, eds. *Hollywood Hybrid. Genre und Gender im zeitgenössischen Mainstream-Film.* Marburg: Schüren, 2004.

Lilli, Waldemar. *Grundlagen der Stereotypisierung.* Gottingen: Hogrefe, 1982.

Lippmann, Walter. *Public Opinion* [1922]. New York: Macmillan, 1961.

Lipps, Theodor. *Grundlegung der Ästhetik* [1903]. Leipzig: Voss, 1923.

Loewy, Hanno. *Béla Balázs—Märchen, Ritual und Film.* Berlin: Vorwerk 8, 2003.

Löffler, Petra. "Eine sichtbare Sprache. Sprechende Münder im stummen Film." *Montage AV* 13, no. 2 (2004): 54–74.

Lotman, Yuri. "Beseda o kinematografii [A Conversation on Film]" [Russian], *Kino* 1 (1986).

——. "Proiskhozhdenie siuzheta v tipologicheskom osveshchenii [The Development of the Plot from a Typological Perspective]." In *Stat'i po tipologii kul'tury,* 9–42. Tartu, 1973.

——. *Semiotics of Cinema.* Translated by Mark Suino. Ann Arbor: University of Michigan Press, 1976. Originally published as *Semiotika kino i problemy kinoestetiki.* Tallin: Eesti Raamat Edit, 1973.

——. *The Structure of the Artistic Text.* Translated by Gail Lenhoff and Ronald Vroon. Ann Arbor: University of Michigan Press, 1977. Originally published as *Struktura khudozhest-vennogo teksta.* Moskva: Izdatel'stvo Iskusstvo, 1970.

Loukides, Paul, and Linda F. Fuller. *Beyond the Stars (1): Stock Characters in American Popular Film.* Bowling Green, Ohio: Bowling Green University Popular Press, 1990.

Lowry, Edward. *The Filmology Movement and Film Study in France.* Ann Arbor, Mich.: UMI Research Press, 1985.

Luhmann, Niklas. *The Reality of the Mass Media.* Translated by Kathleen Cross. Cambridge: Polity Press, 2000. Originally published as *Die Realität der Massenmedien.* Opladen: Westdeutscher Verlag, 1995.

Lukács, Georg: "Thoughts Toward an Aesthetics of Cinema." In *German Essays on Film,* edited by Richard W. McCormick and Alison Guenther-Pal, translated by Lance W. Garmer, 11–16. New York: Continuum, 2004. Originally published as "Gedanken zu einer Aesthetik des Kino" [second version]. *Frankfurter Zeitung* 251 (September 10, 1913): 1–2.

Lütkens, Charlotte. "Europäer und Amerikaner über Amerika." In *Archiv für Sozialwissenschaft und Sozialpolitik,* vol. 2, 1929.

Lux, Joseph August. "Das Kinodrama" [1914]. In *Prolog vor dem Film: Nachdenken über ein neues Medium 1909–1914,* edited by Jörg Schweinitz, 319–326. Leipzig: Reclam, 1992.

——. "Menschendarsteller im Film. Portraits. I. Asta Nielsen." *Bild und Film* 3, no. 7 (1914): 164–167.

Maier, Charles S. "Between Taylorism and Technocracy: European Ideologies and the Vision of Industrial Productivity in the 1920s." *Journal of Contemporary History* 5, no. 2 (1970): 27–61.

Mandalka, Christina. *August Stramm und kosmischer Mystizismus im frühen zwanzigsten Jahrhundert.* Herzberg: Bautz, 1992.

Manz, Wolfgang. *Das Stereotyp. Zur Operationalisierung eines sozialwissenschaftlichen Begriffs.* Meisenheim am Glan: Anton Hain, 1968.

Mast, Gerald, Marshall Cohen, and Leo Braudy, eds. *Film Theory and Criticism: Introductory Readings.* Oxford: Oxford University Press, 1992.

Maturana, Humberto R. "Biologie der Sozialität." In *Der Diskurs des radikalen Konstruktivismus,* edited by Siegfried J. Schmidt, 287–302. Frankfurt am Main: Suhrkamp, 1992.

Mauthner, Fritz. *Beiträge zu einer Kritik der Sprache,* vol. 1, *Zur Sprache und zur Psychologie* [1901/1902]. Frankfurt am Main: Ullstein, 1982.

Merleau-Ponty, Maurice. "The Film and the New Psychology." In *Sense and Non-Sense.* Translated by H. Dreyfus and P. Dreyfus, 48–59. Evanston, Ill.: Northwestern University Press, 1964. Originally published as "Le cinéma et la nouvelle psychologie." In *Les temps modernes* 3, no. 26 (1947), 930–943.

Metz, Christian. *L'énonciation impersonnelle, ou le site du film.* Paris: Méridiens Klincksieck, 1991.

——. *Film Language: A Semiotics of the Cinema.* Translated by Michael Taylor. Chicago: University of Chicago Press, 1990. Originally published as *Essais sur la signification au cinéma,* vol. 1. Paris: Méridiens Klincksieck, 1968.

——. "La grande syntagmatique du film narratif." *Communications* 8 (1966): 120–124.

——. *Language and Cinema.* Translated by Donna Jean Umiker-Sebeok. The Hague: Mouton, 1974. Originally published as *Langage et cinéma.* Paris: Larousse, 1971.

——. "Sur un profil d'Etienne Souriau." *L'art instaurateur: Revue d'esthétique* 3/4 (1980): 143–158.

Michel, Carl. *Die Gebärdensprache dargestellt für Schauspieler sowie Maler und Bildhauer.* Part 1: *Die körperliche Beredsamkeit: Gebärden—Seelenzustände—Stimme. Rollenstudium—Spielen.* Cologne: Verlag der DuMont-Schauberg'schen Buchhandlung, 1886.

Mitchell, W. J. T. *What do Pictures Want: The Lives and Loves of Images.* Chicago: University of Chicago Press, 2005.

Mitscherlich, Alexander. "Die Vorurteilskrankheit." *Psyche* 16 (1962): 241–245.

Moine, Raphaëlle. "Stéréotypes et clichés." In *Cinéma et littérature,* edited by Francis Vanoye (*RITM* 19), 159–170. Paris/Nanterre: Centre de recherches interdisciplinaires sur les textes modernes de l'Université Paris X, 1999.

——. "Von Tisch zu Bett: Analyse eines filmischen Klischees." *Montage AV* 10, no. 2 (2001): 5–14.

Möller-Naß, Karl-Dietmar. *Filmsprache. Eine kritische Theoriegeschichte.* Münster: MAkS, 1986.

Morin, Edgar. *The Cinema, or The Imaginary Man.* Translated by Lorraine Mortimer. Minneapolis: University of Minnesota Press, 2005. Originally published as *Le cinéma ou l'homme imaginaire.* Paris: Les Éditions de Minuit, 1956.

Mülder, Inka. *Siegfried Kracauer—Grenzgänger zwischen Theorie und Literatur. Seine frühen Schriften 1913–1933.* Stuttgart: Metzler, 1985.

Müller, Robert. "Von der Kunst der Verführung: der Vamp." In *Diesseits der 'dämonischen Leinwand.' Neue Perspektiven auf das späte Weimarer Kino,* edited by Thomas Koebner, 259–280. Munich: edition text+kritik, 2003.

Münsterberg, Hugo. *The Eternal Values.* Boston: Houghton Mifflin, 1909. Originally published as *Philosophie der Werte. Grundzüge einer Weltanschauung.* Leipzig: J. A. Barth, 1908.

——. *Grundzüge der Psychotechnik.* Leipzig: J. A. Barth, 1914.

——. *Das Lichtspiel. Eine psychologische Studie (1916) und andere Schriften zum Film.* Edited by Jörg Schweinitz. Vienna: Synema, 1996.

——. "The Photoplay. A Psychological Study" [1916]. In *Hugo Münsterberg on Film: The Photoplay. A Psychological Study and Other Writings,* edited by Allan Langdale, 45–164. New York: Routledge, 2002.

Musil, Robert. "Toward a New Aesthetic: Observations on a Dramaturgy of Film." In *Robert Musil: Precision and Soul: Essays and Articles,* edited and translated by Burton Pike and David S. Luft, 193–207. Chicago: University of Chicago Press, 1995. Originally published as "Ansätze zu neuer Ästhetik. Bemerkungen über eine Dramaturgie des Films." *Der Neue Merkur* (March 1925).

Musser, Charles. *The Emergence of Cinema: The American Screen to 1907.* History of the American Cinema 1. New York: Scribner, 1990.

Naremore, James. *Acting in the Cinema.* Berkeley: University of California Press, 1988.

Neale, Steve. *Genre and Hollywood.* London: Routledge, 2000.

——. "Melo Talk: On the Meaning and Use of the Term 'Melodrama' in the American Trade Press." *Velvet Light Trap* 32 (1993): 66–89.

——. "The Same Old Story: Stereotypes and Difference" [1979/1980]. In *The Screen Education Reader: Cinema, Television, Culture*, edited by Manuel Alvarado, Edward Buscombe, and Richard Collins, 41–47. New York: Columbia University Press, 1993.

Nietzsche, Friedrich. *Aus der Zarathustra- und Umwerthungszeit 1882–1888*. In *Gesammelte Werke*, vol. 14. Munich: Musarion, 1925.

Nilsen, Vladimir. *The Cinema as a Graphic Art*. New York: Hill & Wang, 1957. Originally published as *Izobrazitel'noe postroenie fil'ma*. Moscow: Kinofotoizdat, 1936.

Odien, W. C. "The Rise and Fall of Norville Barnes." *Cinefex* 58 (June 1994): 66–81.

Odin, Roger. "For a Semio-Pragmatics of Film." In *The Film Spectator. From Sign to Mind*, edited by Warren Buckland, 213–226. Amsterdam: Amsterdam University Press, 1995.

"Die Organisation der Ufa-Produktion [The Organization of Ufa's Production]." *Lichtbild-bühne* 20, no. 290 (December 5, 1927).

Paech, Joachim. "Die Anfänge der Filmwissenschaft in Westdeutschland nach 1945." In *Zwischen Gestern und Morgen. Westdeutscher Nachkriegsfilm 1946–1962*, 266–281. Frankfurt am Main: Deutsches Filmmuseum, 1989.

——. "Disposition der Einfühlung. Anmerkungen zum Einfluß der Einfühlungs-Ästhetik des 19. Jahrhunderts auf die Theorie des Kinofilms." In *Der Film in der Geschichte*, edited by Knut Hickethier, Eggo Müller and Rainer Rother, 106–121. GFF-Schriften 6. Berlin: Sigma, 1997.

——. "Gesellschaftskritik und Provokation—Nouvelle Vague: Sie küssten und sie schlugen ihn." In *Fischer Filmgeschichte*, edited by Werner Faulstich and Helmut Korte, 3:362–385. Frankfurt am Main: Fischer, 1990.

——. *Literatur und Film*. Stuttgart: Metzler, 1988.

——. "Rodin, Rilke—und der kinematographische Raum." In *Kinoschriften: Jahrbuch der Gesellschaft für Filmtheorie*, 2:145–161. Vienna: Verband der Wissenschaftlichen Gesellschaften Österreichs, 1990.

——. "Von der Filmologie zur Mediologie? Film und Fernsehtheorie zu Beginn der 60er Jahre in Frankreich." In *Körper—Ästhetik—Spiel. Zur filmischen Écriture der Nouvelle Vague*, edited by Scarlett Winter and Susanne Schlünder, 31–46. Munich: Fink, 2004.

Panofsky, Erwin. "Style and Medium in the Motion Pictures" [1947]. In *Three Essays on Style*, 91–126. Cambridge, Mass.: The MIT Press, 1995.

Pasolini, Pier Paolo. "The Cinema of Poetry." In *Heretical Empiricism*, edited by Louise K. Barnett, translated by Ben Lawton and Louise K. Barnett, 167–186. Bloomington: University of Indiana Press, 1988. Originally published as "Il cinema di poesia." *Filmcritica* 156/157 (April–May 1965): 275–285.

——. "The Nonverbal as Another Verbality." In *Heretical Empiricism*, edited by Louise K. Barnett, translated by Ben Lawton and Louise K. Barnett, 261–263. Bloomington: University of Indiana Press, 1988. Originally published as a part of "Ancora il linguaggio della realtà" [a letter interview with S. Arecco]. *Filmcritica* 214 (March 1971): 125–130.

Pavlov, Ivan P. "The Conditioned Reflex." In Ivan Pavlov, *Psychopathology and Psychiatry*, ed. George Windholz, 378–386. New Brunswick, N.J.: Transaction, 1994.

——. "Dinamicheskaia stereotipiia vysshego otdela golovnogo mozga" [The Dynamic Stereotype of the Higher Section of the Brain]. In I. P. Pavlov, *Polnoe sobranie sochineniy*, 2nd ed., enlarged, vol. 3, pt. 2, 240–244. Moscow: Izdatel'stvo Akademii Nauk SSSR, 1933.

——. "Uslovnyi Refleks" [The Conditioned Reflex]. In *Bol'shaia Sovetskaia Enziklopediia* 56 (Moscow, 1936), 322–337.

Pearson, Roberta. *Eloquent Gestures: The Transformation of Performance Style in the Griffith Biograph Films*. Berkeley: University of California Press, 1992.

Perkins, T. E. "Rethinking Stereotypes." In *Ideology and Cultural Production*, edited by Michèle Barett et al., 135–159. London: Croom Helm, 1979.

Pestalozzi, Karl. *Sprachskepsis und Sprachmagie im Werk des jungen Hofmannsthal*. Zurich: Atlantis, 1958.

Pfemfert, Franz. "Kino als Erzieher" [1911]. In *Prolog vor dem Film: Nachdenken über ein neues Medium 1909–1914*, edited by Jörg Schweinitz, 165–169. Leipzig: Reclam, 1992.

Pfister, Manfred. *The Theory and Analysis of Drama*. Translated by John Halliday. Cambridge: Cambridge University Press, 1991. Originally published as *Das Drama: Theorie und Analyse*. Munich: Fink, 1977.

Pflaum, Hans Günther, and Hans Helmut Prinzler, eds. *Robert Altman*. Reihe Film 25. Munich: Hanser, 1981.

Pierre, Sylvie. "Il était une fois dans l'Ouest." *Cahiers du Cinéma* 218 (March 1970): 53–54.

Pinthus, Kurt, ed. *Das Kinobuch* [1913/1914]. Zurich: Arche, 1963.

——. "Die Film-Krisis." *Das Tagebuch* 14 (1928): 574–580.

Pleyer, Peter. *Nationale und soziale Stereotypen im gegenwärtigen deutschen Spielfilm. Eine aussageanalytische Leitstudie*. Münster: Institut für Publizistik, 1968.

Pocher, Wilhelm. *Die Rezeption der englischen und amerikanischen Literatur in Deutschland in den Jahren 1918–1933*. Diss., University of Jena, 1972.

Pörksen, Uwe. *Plastic Words: The Tyranny of a Modular Language*. Translated by Jutta Mason and David Cayley. Philadelphia: University of Pennsylvania Press, 1995. Originally published as *Plastikwörter. Die Sprache einer internationalen Diktatur*. Stuttgart: Klett-Cotta, 1988.

——. *Weltmarkt der Bilder. Eine Philosophie der Visiotype*. Stuttgart: Klett-Cotta, 1997.

Prange, Regine. "Stil und Medium. Panofsky 'On Movies.'" In *Erwin Panofsky. Beiträge des Symposiums Hamburg 1992*, edited by Bruno Reudenbach, 171–190. Berlin: Akademie Verlag, 1994.

Prokop, Dieter. *Faszination und Langeweile. Die populären Medien*. Stuttgart: Enke, 1979.

Propp, Vladimir. *Morphology of the Folktale*. Translated by Laurence Scott. American Folklore Society Publications, 2003. Originally published as *Morfologija skazki*. Leningrad: Akademija, 1928.

Prümm, Karl. "Epiphanie als Form. Rudolf Arnheims Film als Kunst im Kontext der Zwanziger Jahre." In *Film als Kunst*, by Rudolf Arnheim, 275–312. Frankfurt am Main: Suhrkamp, 2002.

——. "Erneuertes Lob der Charge." *Filmwärts*, August 23 (1992): 5–9.

——. "Klischee und Individualität. Zur Problematik des Chargenspiels im deutschen Film." In *Der Körper im Bild: Schauspielen–Darstellen–Erscheinen*, edited by Heinz B. Heller, Karl Prümm, and Birgit Peulings, 93–109. GFF-Schriften 7. Marburg: Schüren, 1999.

Quasthoff, Uta. *Soziales Vorurteil und Kommunikation. Eine sprachwissenschaftliche Analyse des Stereotyps*. Frankfurt am Main: Athenäum-Fischer, 1973.

——. "The Uses of Stereotype in Everyday Argument." *Journal of Pragmatics* 2 (1978): 1–48.

Rathenau, Walther. "Vom Werte und Unwerte des Kinos" [Answer to a survey by the *Frankfurter Zeitung*, 1912]. In *Kino-Debatte*, edited by Anton Kaes. Munich: dtv, 1978.

——. *Zur Kritik der Zeit*. Berlin: S. Fischer, 1912.

——. *Zur Mechanik des Geistes*. Berlin: S. Fischer, 1913.

Ray, Robert B. *A Certain Tendency of the Hollywood Cinema, 1930–1980*. Princeton, N.J.: Princeton University Press, 1985.

Reitz, Edgar, Alexander Kluge, and Wilfried Reinke. "Wort im Film." *Sprache im technischen Zeitalter* (Berlin) 13, special issue: *Die Rolle des Worts im Film* (1965): 1015–1030.

Rice, Stuart Arthur. "Stereotypes: A Source of Error in Judging Human Character." *Journal of Personality Research* 5 (1926/1927): 267–276.

Riffaterre, Michael. *Essais de stylistique structurale*. Paris: Flammarion, 1971.

Rosch, Eleanor. "Principles of Categorization." In *Cognition and Categorization*, edited by Eleanor Rosch and Barbara B. Lloyd. Hillsdale, N.J.: Erlbaum, 1978.

Rossellini, Roberto. "A Discussion of Neorealism. An Interview with Mario Verdone." In *My Method: Writings and Interviews*, edited by Adriano Aprà, 33–43. New York: Marsilio, 1995. Originally published as "Colloquio sul neorealismo." *Bianco e Nero*, no. 2 (February 1952): 12.

——. "L'idée néo-réaliste." In *Roberto Rossellini*, edited by Mario Verdone. Paris: Édition Seghers, 1963.

Rusegger, Arno. "'Denn jede Kunst bedeutet ein eigenes Verhältnis des Menschen zur Welt, eine eigene Dimension der Seele.'—Béla Balázs' Filmtheorie als Paradigma für eine meta-fiktionale Poetik bei Robert Musil." In *Kinoschriften: Jahrbuch der Gesellschaft für Filmtheorie*, 2:131–144. Vienna: Verband der Wissenschaftlichen Gesellschaften Österreichs, 1990.

Salt, Barry. *Film Style and Technology: History and Analysis*. London: Starword, 1992.

Sarris, Andrew. "Notes on the Auteur Theory in 1962." In *Film Theory and Criticism: Introductory Readings*, edited by Gerald Mast, Marshall Cohen, and Leo Braudy, 585–588. Oxford: Oxford University Press, 1992.

Saunders, Thomas J. *Hollywood in Berlin: American Cinema and Weimar Germany*. Berkeley: University of California Press, 1994.

Schaff, Adam. "Sprache und Stereotyp." In *Sprechen—Denken—Praxis. Zur Diskussion neuer Antworten auf eine alte Frage in Praxis, Wissenschaft und Philosophie*, edited by Gerd Simon and Erich Straßner. Weinheim and Basel: Beltz, 1979.

Scheel, Harald. *Untersuchungen zum sprachlichen Stereotyp unter besonderer Berücksichtigung konfrontativer Gesichtspunkte, dargestellt an ausgewählten Textsorten des Deutschen und Französischen*. Diss., Karl-Marx-Universität Leipzig, 1983.

Scheerbarth, Paul. *Die große Revolution* [1902]. Leipzig: Kiepenheuer, 1983.

Scheffer, Wilhelm. "Mimische Studien mit Reißzeug und Kamera." *Der Welt-Spiegel. Halb-Wochenschrift des Berliner Tageblatts* 10 (February 1, 1914).

Schlüpmann, Heide. *The Uncanny Gaze: The Drama of Early German Cinema*. Translated by Inga Pollmann. Urbana: University of Illinois Press, 2010. Originally published as *Unheimlichkeit des Blicks: Das Drama des frühen deutschen Kinos*. Basel and Frankfurt am Main: Stroemfeldt Roter Stern, 1990.

Schmidt, Siegfried J., ed. *Der Diskurs des radikalen Konstruktivismus*. Frankfurt am Main: Suhrkamp, 1992.

Schmidt, Siegfried J., and Siegfried Weischenberg. "Mediengattungen, Berichterstattungs-muster, Darstellungsformen." In *Die Wirklichkeit der Medien: eine Einführung in die Kommunikationswissenschaft*, edited by Klaus Merten, Siegfried J. Schmidt, and Siegfried Weischenberg. Opladen: Westdeutscher Verlag, 1994.

Schneider, Irmela. "Von der Vielsprachigkeit zur 'Kunst der Hybridisation.' Diskurse des Hybriden." In *Hybridkultur: Medien, Netze, Künste*, edited by Irmela Schneider and Christian W. Thomsen, 13–66. Cologne: Wienand, 1997.

——. "Zur Theorie des Stereotyps." *Beiträge zur Film- und Fernsehwissenschaft* 43 (1992): 129–147.

Schneider, Peter. "Vom Nutzen des Klischees. Betrachtungen zum Wildwestfilm." *Sprache im technischen Zeitalter* (Berlin) 13, special issue, *Die Rolle des Worts im Film* (1965): 1091–1197.

Schulte-Sasse, Jochen. *Die Kritik an der Trivialliteratur seit der Aufklärung. Studien zur Geschichte des modernen Kitschbegriffs*. Munich: Fink, 1971.

Schütz, Erhard. "Fließband—Schlachthof—Hollywood. Literarische Phantasien über die Maschine USA." In *Willkommen und Abschied der Maschinen*, edited by Erhard Schütz and Norbert Wehr, 122–143. Essen: Klartext, 1988.

——. *Kritik der literarischen Reportage*. Munich: Fink, 1977.

Schweinitz, Jörg. "The Aesthetic Idealist as Efficiency Engineer: Hugo Münsterberg's Theories of Perception, Psychotechnics and Cinema." In *Film 1900: Technology, Perception, Culture*, edited by Annemone Ligensa and Klaus Kreimeier, 77–86. Eastleigh: Libbey, 2009.

——. "'Genre' und lebendiges Genrebewußtsein." *Montage AV* 3, no. 2 (1994): 99–118.

——. "Der hypnotisierende Blick. Etablierung und Anverwandlung eines konventionellen Bildes." In *Bildtheorie des Films*, edited by Thomas Koebner and Thomas Meder, 426–443. Munich: edition text + kritik, 2006.

——, ed. *Prolog vor dem Film: Nachdenken über ein neues Medium 1909–1914*. Leipzig: Reclam, 1992.

——. "Psychotechnik, idealistische Ästhetik und der Film als mental strukturierter Wahrnehmungsraum: Die Filmtheorie von Hugo Münsterberg." Preface to Hugo Münsterberg, *Das Lichtspiel. Eine psychologische Studie (1916) und andere Schriften zum Film*, by Hugo Münsterberg, 9–26. Vienna: Synema, 1996.

——. "Der selige Kintopp (1913/14). Eine Fundsache zum Verhältnis von literarischem Expressionismus und Kino." In *Film, Fernsehen, Video und die Künste. Strategien der Intermedialität*, edited by Joachim Paech, 72–88. Stuttgart, Weimar: Metzler, 1994.

——. "Der 'Stein der Stereotypie.' Der Diskurs zur Standardisierung des Erzählens in der klassischen deutschen Filmtheorie." In *Die erzählerische Dimension*, edited by Eberhard Lämmert, 261–290. Berlin: Akademie Verlag, 1999.

——. "Das Stereotyp als kulturelle Sprachform. Theoriegeschichtliche Entdeckungen bei Gilbert Cohen-Séat und Edgar Morin." In *Nicht allein das Laufbild auf der Leinwand . . . Strukturen des Films als Erlebnispotentiale: Festschrift für Peter Wuss zum 60. Geburtstag*, edited by Jörg Frieß, Britta Hartmann, and Eggo Müller, 177–196. Berlin: Vistas, 2001.

——. "Von Automobilen, Flugmaschinen und einer versteckten Kamera. Technikfaszination und Medienreflexivität in Richard A. Bermanns Kinoprosa." In *Mediengeschichte des*

Films, vol. 2: *Die Modellierung des Kinofilms*, edited by Corinna Müller and Harro Segeberg, 221–241. Munich: Fink, 1998.

——. "Von Filmgenres, Hybridformen und goldenen Nägeln." In *Psychologie und Film—nach der kognitiven Phase?*, edited by Jan Sellmer and Hans J. Wulff, 79–92. GFM-Schriften 10. Marburg: Schüren, 2002.

——. "Wenn hinter das Klischee persönliche Energien fahren: Jennifer Jason Leigh." In *Ladies, Vamps, Companions: Schauspielerinnen im Kino*, edited by Susanne Marschall, 202–219. St. Augustin: Gardez!, 2000.

——. " 'Wie im Kino!' Die autothematische Welle im frühen Tonfilm. Figurationen des Selbstreflexiven." In *Diesseits der "dämonischen Leinwand": Neue Perspektiven auf das spate Weimarer Kino*, edited by Thomas Koebner, 373–392. Munich: edition text+kritik, 2003.

Segeberg, Harro. *Literarische Technik-Bilder. Studien zum Verhältnis von Technik- und Literaturgeschichte im 19. und frühen 20. Jahrhundert.* Tubingen: Niemeyer, 1987.

Self, Robert T. *Robert Altman's Subliminal Reality*. Minneapolis: University of Minnesota Press, 2002.

Shklovsky, Viktor. "Art as Technique." In *Russian Formalist Criticism: Four Essays*, translated by Lee T. Lemon and Marion J. Reis, 3–24. Lincoln: University of Nebraska Press, 1965. Originally published as "Iskusstvo kak priem." In *Sborniki po teorii poėtcheskogo iazyka*, 3–14. Petrograd: Sokolinskii, 1916.

——. "Chaplin." In *Literature and Cinematography*, translated by Irina Masinovsky, 64–67. Champaign, Ill.: Dalkey Archive Press, 2008. Originally published as *Chaplin: Sbornik statei*. Berlin: Izdatel'stvo. Zhurnala Kino, 1923.

——. "Plot in Cinematography." In *Literature and Cinematography*, translated by Irina Masinovsky, 41–63. Champaign, Ill.: Dalkey Archive Press, 2008. Originally published as "Siuzhet v kinematografii." In *Literatura i kinematograf*, 31–33. Berlin: Russkoe Universal'noe Izdatel'stvo, 1923.

——. "Tarzan." *Russkii sovremennik* 3 (1924): 253–254.

Simmel, Georg. "The Aesthetic Significance of the Face." In *Essays on Sociology, Philosophy and Aesthetics.*, edited by K. H. Wolff, translated by Lore Ferguson, 276–281. New York: Harper & Row, 1959. Originally published as "Die ästhetische Bedeutung des Gesichts." *Der Lotse. Hamburgische Wochenschrift für deutsche Kultur* 1.2, no. 35 (June 1, 1901): 280–284.

Six, Berhard. "Stereotype und Vorurteile im Kontext sozialpsychologischer Forschung." In *Erstarrtes Denken. Studien zu Klischees, Stereotyp und Vorurteil in englischsprachiger Literatur*, edited by Günther Blaicher, 41–54. Tubingen: Narr, 1987.

Smith, Murray. *Engaging Characters: Fiction, Emotion, and the Cinema*. Oxford: Clarendon Press, 1995.

Sodhi, Kripal Singh, and Rudolf Bergius. *Nationale Vorurteile. Eine sozialpsychologische Untersuchung an 881 Personen.* Berlin: Duncker und Humblot, 1953.

Sontag, Susan. "Notes on Camp." In *Against Interpretation and Other Essays*, 275–292. London: Eyre & Spottiswoode, 1967.

——. "A Century of Cinema." In *Where the Stress Falls*, 117–122. New York: Farrar, Straus & Giroux, 2001. Originally published in *Frankfurter Rundschau*, 1995.

Souriau, Etienne. "La structure de l'univers filmique et le vocabulaire de la filmologie." *Revue internationale de filmologie* 7–8 (1951): 231–240.

Spangenberg, Peter M. "TV, Hören und Sehen." In *Materialität der Kommunikation*, edited by Hans Ulrich Gumbrecht and K. Ludwig Pfeiffer, 776–798. Frankfurt am Main: Suhrkamp, 1988.

Spottiswoode, Raymond. *A Grammar of the Film: An Analysis of the Film Technique.* London: Faber and Faber, 1935.

Stam, Robert. *Reflexivity in Film and Literature: From Don Quixote to Jean-Luc Godard.* New York: Columbia University Press, 1992.

Stephan, Walter G. "A Cognitive Approach to Stereotyping." In *Stereotyping and Prejudice: Changing Conceptions*, edited by Daniel Bar-Tal, Carl Graumann, Arie Kruglanski, and Wolfgang Stroebe, 37–58. New York: Springer, 1989.

Tajfel, Henri. "Cognitive Aspects of Prejudice." *Journal of Social Issues* 25 (1969): 79–97.

——. "Soziales Kategorisieren." In *Forschungsberichte der Sozialpsychologie*, vol. 1, edited by S[erge] Moscovici. Frankfurt am Main: Fischer Athenäum, 1975.

Taylor, Henry, and Margrit Tröhler. "Ein paar Facetten der menschlichen Figur im Spielfilm." In *Der Körper im Bild. Schauspielen—Darstellen—Erscheinen*, edited by Heinz B. Heller, Karl Prümm, and Birgit Peulings, 137–151. Marburg: Schüren.

Thompson, Kristin. *Breaking the Glass Armor: Neoformalist Film Analysis.* Princeton, N.J.: Princeton University Press, 1988.

——. "Early Alternatives to the Hollywood Mode of Production: Implications for Europe's Avant-Gardes." *Film History* 5, no. 4 (1993): 386–404.

Thompson, Kristin, Yuri Tsivian, and Ekaterina Khokhlova, "The Rediscovery of a Kuleshov Experiment: A Dossier." *Film History* 8, no. 3 (1996): 357–364.

Todorov, Tzvetan. *The Fantastic: A Structural Approach to a Literary Genre.* Translated by Richard Howard. Ithaca, N.Y.: Cornell University Press, 1975. Originally published as *Introduction à la littérature fantastique.* Paris: Éditions du Seuil, 1970.

——. *Genres in Discourse.* Cambridge: Cambridge University Press, 1990. Originally published as *Les genres du discours.* Paris: Éditions du Seuil, 1978.

Tröhler, Margrit. "Film—Bewegung und die ansteckende Kraft von Analogien: Zu André Bazins Konzeption des Zuschauers." *Montage AV* 18, no. 1 (2009): 49–74.

——. "Multiple Protagonist Films: A Transcultural Everyday Practice." In *Characters in Fictional Worlds: Interdisciplinary Perspectives*, edited by Jens Eder, Fotis Jannidis, and Ralph Schneider, 459–477. Berlin: De Gruyter, 2010.

——. *Offene Welten ohne Helden. Plurale Figurenkonstellationen im Film.* Zürcher Filmstudien. Marburg: Schüren, 2007.

Tröhler, Margrit and Henry M. Taylor, "De quelques facettes du personnage humain dans le film de fiction." *Iris* 24 (1997): 33–57.

Truffaut, François. "A Certain Tendency in the French Cinema." In *Movies and Methods*, edited by Bill Nichols, 1:224–237. Berkeley: University of California Press, 1976. Originally published as "Une certaine tendance du cinéma français." *Cahiers du Cinéma* 31 (1954): 15–28.

——. "Frank Capra, The Healer." In *The Films in My Life*, translated by Leonard Mayhew. London: Allen Lane, 1980. Originally published as "Frank Capra, le guérisseur." In *Les Films de ma vie*, 94–95. Paris: Flammarion, 1975.

——. *Hitchcock*. With the collaboration of Helen G. Scott. New York: Simon and Schuster, 1985. Originally published as *Le cinéma selon Hitchcock*. Paris: Laffont, 1966.

Tynyanov, Yury. "The Literary Fact." In *Modern Genre Theory*, edited by David Duff, translated by Ann Shukman. 29–49. Harlow, Essex: Longman, 2000. Originally published as "Literaturnyj fakt." *LEF* 2 (1924): 101–116.

——. "On Literary Evolution." In *Readings in Russian Poetics: Formalist and Structuralist Views*, edited by Ladislav Matejka and Krystyna Pomorska, 66–78. Champaign, Ill.: Dalkey Archive Press, 2002. Originally published as "O literaturnoj evoljucii." *Na literaturnom postu* 10 (1927): 42–48.

van Dijk, Teun A. *Tekstwetenschap. Een interdisciplinaire inleiding*. Utrecht: Het Spectrum, 1978.

Varela, Francisco J. *Connaître: Les sciences cognitives. Tendances et perspectives*. Paris: Éditions du Seuil, 1988.

——. *Kognitionswissenschaft—Kognitionstechnik*. Frankfurt am Main: Suhrkamp, 1990.

Vogler, Christopher. *The Writer's Journey: Mythic Structure for Writers*. 3rd ed. Studio City, Calif.: Michael Wiese Productions, 2007.

von Trier, Lars, and Thomas Vinterberg, "Dogme 95: The Vow of Chastity" [1995]. In *Technology and Culture: The Film Reader*, edited by Andrew Utterson, 87–88. London: Routledge, 2005.

Vygotsky, Lev S. "Thinking and Speech." In *The Collected Works of L. S. Vygotsky*, vol. 1, *Problems of General Psychology*, edited by Robert W. Rieber and Aaron S. Carton, translated by Norris Minick. New York: Plenum Press, 1987. Originally published as Vygotsky, L.S. *Myšlenie i reč'*. Moscow: Accademia di Scienze Pedagogiche dell' URSS, 1934.

Weber, Max. "Science as Vocation." In *From Max Weber: Essays in Sociology*, edited and translated by Hans H. Gerth and C. Wright Mills, 129–156. London: Routledge, 1991. Originally published as *Wissenschaft als Beruf*. Munich and Leipzig: Duncker und Humblot, 1919.

Wellek, René, and Austin Warren. *Theory of Literature*. New York: Harcourt, Brace and Company, 1949.

Welsch, Wolfgang, ed. *Wege aus der Moderne. Schlüsseltexte der Postmoderne-Diskussion*. Weinheim: VCH Acta humaniora, 1988.

Wenders, Wim. "From Dream to Nightmare: The Terrifying Western 'Once Upon a Time in the West.'" In *Emotion Pictures: Reflections on the Cinema*, translated by Sean Whiteside, 24–25. London: Faber & Faber, 1991. Originally published as "Vom Traum zum Trauma: Der fürchterliche Western *Spiel mir das Lied vom Tod*." *Filmkritik* 13, no. 11 (1969).

Wenzel, Angelika. *Stereotype in gesprochener Sprache. Form, Vorkommen und Funktion in Dialogen*. Munich: Hueber, 1978.

Winkler, Hartmut. *Der filmische Raum und der Zuschauer. 'Apparatus'—Semantik—'Ideology'*. Heidelberg: Carl Winter, 1992.

Wittgenstein, Ludwig. *Philosophical Investigations*. Translated by G. E. M. Anscombe, P. M. S. Hacker, and Joachim Schulte. Chichester, West Sussex: Wiley-Blackwell, 2009. Originally published as *Philosophische Untersuchungen*. Oxford: Blackwell, 1953.

Wollen, Peter. *Raiding the Icebox: Reflections on Twentieth-Century Culture*. London: Verso, 1993.

——. *Signs and Meaning in the Cinema* [1968]. Expanded ed. London: BFI, 1998.

Wright, Will. *Sixguns and Society: A Structural Study of the Western*. Berkeley: University of California Press, 1975.

Wulff, Hans J. *Darstellen und Mitteilen. Elemente der Pragmasemiotik des Films*. Tubingen: Narr, 1999.

——. "Drei Bemerkungen zur Motiv- und Genreanalyse am Beispiel des Gefängnisfilms." In *Sechstes Film- und Fernsehwissenschaftliches Kolloquium/Berlin 1993*, edited by Jörg Frieß, Stephen Lowry, and Hans Jürgen Wulff, 149–154. Berlin: Gesellschaft für Theorie und Geschichte audiovisueller Kommunikation, 1994.

Wuss, Peter. *Cinematic Narration and Its Psychological Impact: Functions of Cognition, Emotion, and Play*. Newcastle upon Tyne: Cambridge Scholars Publishing, 2009.

——. *Filmanalyse und Psychologie. Strukturen des Films im Wahrnehmungsprozess*. Berlin: Edition Sigma, 1993.

——. *Kunstwert des Films und Massencharakter des Mediums. Konspekte zur Geschichte der Theorie des Spielfilms*. Berlin: Henschel, 1990.

Yanni, Nicholas. *Rosalind Russell*. New York: Pyramid, 1975.

Zima, Peter. *Moderne—Postmoderne: Gesellschaft, Philosophie, Literatur*. Tubingen: Francke, 1997.

Zsuffa, Joseph. *Béla Balázs: The Man and the Artist*. Berkeley: University of California Press, 1987.

Zweig, Stefan. "The Monotonization of the World." In *The Weimar Republic Sourcebook*, edited by Anton Kaes, Martin Jay, and Edward Dimendberg, 397–400. Berkeley: University of California Press, 1994. Originally published as "Die Monotonisierung der Welt." *Berliner Börsen-Courier* (February 1, 1925).

FILMOGRAPHY

Adventures of Buffalo Bill, The. 1917

All That Heaven Allows. Douglas Sirk, 1954.

Angst essen Seele auf [*Ali: Fear Eats the Soul*]. Rainer Werner Fassbinder. West Germany, 1973.

Batman. TV series. Various directors, 1966–1968.

Battling with Buffalo Bill. Ray Taylor, 1931.

Big Clock, The. John Farrow, 1948.

Birth of a Nation, The. David W. Griffith, 1915.

Bringing Up Baby. Howard Hawks, 1938.

Broken Blossoms. David W. Griffith, 1919.

Bronenosets Potyomkin [*Battleship Potemkin*]. Sergei M. Eisenstein, USSR, 1925.

Buffalo Bill. William A. Wellman, 1944.

Buffalo Bill and the Indians, or Sitting Bull's History Lesson. Robert Altman, 1976.

Buffalo Bill on the U. P. Trail. Frank S. Mattison, 1926.

Buffalo Bill Rides Again. Bernard B. Ray, 1947.

C'era una volta il West [*Once Upon a Time in the West*]. Sergio Leone, Italy/USA, 1968.

Cat Ballou. Elliot Silverstein, 1965.

Citizen Kane. Orson Welles, 1941.

Cotton Club, The. Francis Ford Coppola, 1984.

Crowd, The. King Vidor, 1928.

Das Lied vom Leben [*The Song of Life*]. Alexander Granowski, Germany, 1931.

Das Mädchen von Fanö [*The Girl from Fano*]. Hans Schweikart, Germany, 1940.

Das Stahltier [*The Steel Animal*]. Willy Zielke, Germany, 1935.

Days of Buffalo Bill. Thomas Carr, 1946.

Die Koffer des Herrn O.F. [*The Suitcases of Mr. O. F.*] Alexander Granowski, Germany, 1931.

Dodge City. Michael Curtiz, 1939.

Dr. Strangelove, or: How I Learned to Stop Worrying and Love the Bomb. Stanley Kubrick, UK, 1964.

Executive Suite. Robert Wise, 1954.

eXistenZ. David Cronenberg, Canada/UK, 1999.

Fifth Element, The. Luc Besson, France/USA, 1997.

Fighting with Buffalo Bill. Ray Taylor, 1926.

Fountainhead, The. King Vidor, 1949.

Georgia. Ulu Grosbard, 1995.

Germania anno zero [*Germany Year Zero*]. Roberto Rossellini, Italy/Germany, 1947.

Hammett. Wim Wenders, 1982.

High Noon. Fred Zinnemann, 1952.

His Girl Friday. Howard Hawks, 1940.

Home Stories. Matthias Müller. Germany, 1990.

Horn Blows at Midnight, The. Raoul Walsh, 1945.

Hudsucker Proxy, The. Joel and Ethan Coen, 1994.

I Love Lucy. TV series. Various directors, 1951–1957.

In the Days of Buffalo Bill. Edward Laemmle, 1922.

Intolerance. David W. Griffith, 1916.

Iron Horse, The. John Ford, 1924.

It's a Wonderful Life. Frank Capra, 1946.

Kansas City. Robert Altman, 1996.

La bête humaine [*The Human Beast*]. Jean Renoir, France, 1938.

La roue [*The Wheel*]. Abel Gance, France, 1923.

Last Exit to Brooklyn. Uli Edel, West Germany, 1989.

Little Big Man. Arthur Penn, 1970.

Man Who Knew Too Much, The. Alfred Hitchcock, 1956.

McCabe & Mrs. Miller. Robert Altman, 1971.

Meet John Doe. Frank Capra, 1941.

Metropolis. Fritz Lang, Germany, 1925/1926.

Miller's Crossing. Joel and Ethan Coen, 1990.

Mirage. Edward Dmytryk, 1964.

Misfits, The. John Huston, 1961.

Mother and the Law, The. David W. Griffith, 1919.

Moulin Rouge. Baz Luhrmann, USA/Australia, 2002.

Mr. Deeds Goes to Town. Frank Capra, 1936.

Mr. Smith Goes to Washington. Frank Capra, 1939.

Mrs. Parker and the Vicious Circle. Alan Rudolph, 1994.

Nashville. Robert Altman, 1975.

Natural Born Killers. Oliver Stone, 1994.

Ninotchka. Ernst Lubitsch, 1939.

Oktyabr' [*Ten Days That Shook the World/October*]. Sergei M. Eisenstein, USSR, 1927.

Once Upon a Time in America. Sergio Leone, 1984.

Once Upon a Time in the West. See *C'era una volta il West.*

One, Two, Three. Billy Wilder, 1961.

Pacific 231. Jean Mitry, France, 1949.

Plainsman, The. Cecil B. DeMille, 1936.

Player, The. Robert Altman, 1992.

Pony Express. Jerry Hopper, 1953.

Prêt-à-Porter [*Ready to Wear*]. Robert Altman, 1994.

Pulp Fiction. Quentin Tarantino, 1994.

Riding with Buffalo Bill. Spencer Bennett, 1954.

Safety Last. Fred Newmeyer and Sam Taylor, 1923.

Seven Brides for Seven Brothers. Stanley Donen, 1954.

Short Cuts. Robert Altman, 1993.

Singin' in the Rain. Stanley Donen and Gene Kelly, 1952.

Single White Female. Barbet Schroeder, 1992.

Spione [*Spies*]. Fritz Lang, Germany, 1928.

Stardust Memories. Woody Allen, 1980.

Sting, The. George Roy Hill, 1973.

Thunderball. Terence Young, UK, 1965.

Union Pacific. Cecil B. DeMille, 1939.

Viva Maria! Louis Malle, France, 1965.

Weihnachtsgedanken [*Christmas Thoughts*]. Anonymous, Germany, 1911.

Wild at Heart. David Lynch, 1990.

Wild Wild West. Barry Sonnenfeld, 1999.

Young Buffalo Bill. Joseph Kane, 1940.

INDEX

abstraction, linguistic skepticism and, 137

acting: within acting, 263; conventionalization and, 68; in Expressionism, 70; film's standardization of, 74; imitation and, 331n7; Jhering critiquing, 68; Jhering on clichés in, 63–64, 68, 73; Kuleshov effect and, 70; Leigh's style of, 263, 266, 273–74, *275*, 276, 331n4; manuals on gestures for, 64, *65–66*, 67, *69*; naturalism in, 68, 70; off-screen image and, 52; realism and, 262–63; in silent film, 70–71; Stanislavski's theory on, 70; stock actors, 72–73; underacting and, 70

acting stereotypes: facial expressions showing, *65–66*, *69*, *71*; in modern film, 68, 73; reduction and, 67–68; theatrical origins of, 64; in Westerns, 72

Adorno, Theodor W., 105, 109–10, 175–76, 237

aesthetics: Arnheim on American cinema and, 178; cliché and, 17; distortion/loss and, 38; economics disrupting,

154–55; of empathy, 135, 142; gestures in film as, 134; of identity, 19–20, 22, 40, 201, 203; Lotman on expectation and, 19–20; of opposition, 19–21, 40; of reception, 20

affective coloration, 5

Ali: Fear Eats the Soul (*Angst essen Seele auf*), 43–44

All That Heaven Allows, symbolic mechanisms in, 210, 223

allusion, 217, 267, 326n9

Altman, Rick, 84; on genre, 86

Altman, Robert, xvii; *Buffalo Bill and the Indians*, 112, 237, 252–61; *Kansas City*, 265, 278; *McCabe & Mrs. Miller*, 112, 237–51; *Nashville*, 251; *The Player*, 278; realism and, 249; *Short Cuts*, 265; sound use of, 260; victimhood in work of, 244

American cinema: Arnheim on aesthetics of, 178; art and, 123; female reporters in, 272–76; German cinema's creative freedom compared to early, 160–61; Germany importing, 161; mechanization of production influencing, 159; of 1960s, 232–33;

television and response of, 232

American Film Genres (Kaminsky), 81

Americanism: criticism of, 158; German cinema and impact of, 161–62; Germany and impact of, 155–59

Amossy, Ruth, 64, 108; on distortion/loss, 21; on repetition, 21; on stereotype, 21, 108; on stereotyped reading, 20–21, 31, 33

archetypes: Campbell on, 54–56; in Leone's work, 216; stereotypes compared to, 55–56; Vogler on, 55

Arnheim, Rudolf, 113, 164–68, 187, 192, 314n71, 315n105; on American cinema aesthetics, 178; on art and mechanization, 180; on "deficits" of film image, 172; on film as art, 170–73, 179–80; on film as "readymade," 176; Gestalt psychology and, 168–69; music studies and, 177; Panofsky compared to, 182–83; on radio soap operas, 179; on visual expression in art history, 173

FILM AND CULTURE / A SERIES OF COLUMBIA UNIVERSITY PRESS

Edited by John Belton